THE COURTS AND SOCIAL POLICY

Donald L. Horowitz

THE COURTS AND SOCIAL POLICY

The Brookings Institution
Washington, D.C.

Library of Congress Cataloging in Publication Data:

Horowitz, Donald L
    The courts and social policy.

    Includes bibliographical references and index.
    1. Judicial process—United States.   2. Socio-
logical jurisprudence.   I. Title.
KF8700.H57   347'.73'1   76-48944
ISBN 0-8157-3734-3
ISBN 0-8157-3733-5 pbk.

9 8 7 6 5 4 3 2

For Marshall, Karen, and Bruce

THE BROOKINGS INSTITUTION is an independent organization devoted to nonpartisan research, education, and publication in economics, government, foreign policy, and the social sciences generally. Its principal purposes are to aid in the development of sound public policies and to promote public understanding of issues of national importance.

The Institution was founded on December 8, 1927, to merge the activities of the Institute for Government Research, founded in 1916, the Institute of Economics, founded in 1922, and the Robert Brookings Graduate School of Economics and Government, founded in 1924.

The Board of Trustees is responsible for the general administration of the Institution, while the immediate direction of the policies, program, and staff is vested in the President, assisted by an advisory committee of the officers and staff. The bylaws of the Institution state: "It is the function of the Trustees to make possible the conduct of scientific research, and publication, under the most favorable conditions, and to safeguard the independence of the research staff in the pursuit of their studies and in the publication of the results of such studies. It is not a part of their function to determine, control, or influence the conduct of particular investigations or the conclusions reached."

The President bears final responsibility for the decision to publish a manuscript as a Brookings book. In reaching his judgment on the competence, accuracy, and objectivity of each study, the President is advised by the director of the appropriate research program and weighs the views of a panel of expert outside readers who report to him in confidence on the quality of the work. Publication of a work signifies that it is deemed a competent treatment worthy of public consideration but does not imply endorsement of conclusions or recommendations.

The Institution maintains its position of neutrality on issues of public policy in order to safeguard the intellectual freedom of the staff. Hence interpretations or conclusions in Brookings publications should be understood to be solely those of the authors and should not be attributed to the Institution, to its trustees, officers, or other staff members, or to the organizations that support its research.

Foreword

The courts have always enjoyed a special place in the American system of government. The Constitution makes the judiciary an equal and coordinate branch of government, and from the earliest days of the Republic the courts have possessed powers denied to their counterparts in other countries. Foreign observers have often noted the signal role the courts play in the American polity and in American thinking about politics. A wide range of disputes is referred to the courts, and judicial procedures are adopted as a model for decisionmaking in organizations as different as universities and factories.

Over the last decade or two, American society has increasingly looked to the courts for resolution of some of its most difficult problems. Courts have been asked, for example, to devise rules for integrating schools and neighborhoods, controlling the police, protecting the environment, and improving the lot of the poor. Complex as they are, these new challenges have taxed the traditional methods of the courts.

In this book, Donald L. Horowitz, a lawyer and political scientist, inquires whether the process of adjudication is appropriate to these challenges. He highlights the issue of judicial capacity and enumerates aspects of the judicial process that affect the efforts of courts to shape social policy, illustrating these with four case studies. The analysis raises many questions about the ability of courts to find and apply data relevant to decisions, to frame flexible solutions, and to forecast and control the effects of their decisions. Many of these difficulties seem to derive from the nature of adjudication, but Horowitz notes that the policymaking capacity and performance of the other branches of government also remain problematical. The final chapter contains suggestions of limited steps that might be taken to improve the policymaking ability of the courts.

The author benefited from the highly competent and diligent research assistance of Daniel J. Fiorino. Michael R. Leavitt provided guidance on the computer operations for chapter 4, and Christine C. de Fontenay did the programming. The author is also grateful to Allen I. Polsby for helpful comments on chapter 3; to Radmila Nikolić for typing the entire manuscript; to H. Arthur MacCord for updating and checking citations; to Johanna Zacharias for editing the manuscript; and to Florence Robinson for preparing the index.

The views expressed in this study are solely those of the author and should not be attributed to the trustees, officers, or other staff members of the Brookings Institution.

GILBERT Y. STEINER
Acting President

August 1976
Washington, D.C.

Contents

CHAPTER ONE

Social Policy and Judicial Capacity

"I care not," says Mr. Dooley, "who makes th' laws iv a nation if I can get out an injunction."[1] With his accustomed acuity, the redoubtable Dooley lays bare in an epigram one of the prominent themes of American political history: the penchant for confiding to judges a large share of the lawmaking function.

The common law of England was judge-made law, law forged in the course of contested cases. The statute was a rather late and occasional interloper. In medieval England, legislation was often regarded as simply confirming what was already established as customary law.[2] For a considerable time, statutes met with hostility at the hands of lawyers and judges. As Solicitor General of England, William Murray, later Lord Mansfield, argued that "a statute can seldom take in all cases, therefore the common law that works itself pure by rules drawn from the fountain of justice is for this reason superior to an Act of Parliament."[3]

As Chief Justice of the King's Bench, Mansfield proved to be one of the most creative spirits of the common law, shaping, modifying, and adapting it to the changing conditions of the eighteenth century. For Mansfield, an act of Parliament was not infrequently regarded as an unwelcome excrescence on the venerated body of the common law, as well as an inferior instrument of reform. Mansfield accordingly became a target of the foremost social inventor of the following generation, Jeremy Bentham. Bentham had fixed his sights on intricate schemes of

1. Quoted by Joseph W. Bishop, Jr., "Lawyers at the Bar," *Commentary,* vol. 58 (August 1974), p. 53.
2. Charles H. McIlwain, *The High Court of Parliament* (Yale University Press, 1910), pp. 42, 46.
3. *Omychund* v. *Barker,* 1 Atk. 21, 33, 26 Eng. Rep. 15, 22–23 (Ch. 1744).

1

legislative reform, and he heaped scorn on what he saw as Mansfield's excesses on the bench:

> Should there be a judge who, enlightened by genius, stimulated by honest zeal to the work of reformation, sick of the caprice, the delays, the prejudices, the ignorance, the malice, the fickleness, the suspicious ingratitude of popular assemblies, should seek with his sole hand to expunge the effusions of traditionary imbecility, and write down in their room the dictates of pure and native justice, let him but reflect that partial amendment is bought at the expense of universal certainty; that partial good thus purchased is universal evil; and that amendment from the judgment seat is confusion.[4]

Judges, said Bentham, make law after the fact, "just as a man makes laws for his dog. When your dog does anything you want to break him of, you wait till he does it, and then beat him for it."[5]

Issue was thus joined between the concreteness of judge-made law and the generality of legislature-made law—or, to stress the critical side, between law that comes too late and law that comes too early. It was, in England, an unequal battle, the outcome perhaps foreordained by the Glorious Revolution, which settled the issue of parliamentary supremacy. With kings in check, who could doubt that judges would follow Parliament rather than lead? Small wonder that the dominant jurisprudential school in England has been the brand of legal positivism that, following John Austin, defines law as the "command of the Sovereign," the Sovereign being the Queen in Parliament.[6]

In the United States, the outcome remains in doubt. A written Constitution, in need of judicial interpretation; a separation of powers that made each branch in theory the equal of the others; a profound distrust of popular legislative majorities; a strong current of natural rights; and a transplanted common-law tradition partly antedating the embodiment of natural right in Parliament: these were among the elements that sustained the creative lawmaking authority of judges.[7]

---

4. *Comment on the Commentaries* (Clarendon Press, 1928), p. 214, quoted in William Holdsworth, *Some Makers of English Law* (Cambridge University Press, 1938), p. 173.

5. Quoted in Robert H. Jackson, *The Struggle for Judicial Supremacy* (Knopf, 1941), pp. 306–07.

6. John Austin, *The Province of Jurisprudence Determined* (Weidenfeld and Nicolson, 1954; orig. pub. 1832). See, for example, Austin's explanation at the end of Lecture I of why judge-made law is law at all. Ibid., pp. 30–33.

7. See Edward S. Corwin, *The "Higher Law" Background of American Constitutional Law* (Cornell University Press, 1955); Roscoe Pound, *The Formative Era of American Law* (Little, Brown, 1938), chaps. 2–3. "Legislation," says Lawrence M. Friedman, "whatever its subject, was a threat to their [judges'] primordial

As Parliament's place was becoming more firmly fixed in the early nineteenth century, in the United States "a contest between courts and legislatures began . . . which is comparable to the contests between courts and crown in seventeenth-century England. . . ."[8] Long after the Mansfieldian tradition had been relegated in England to a distinctly subordinate creativity, it could be echoed, untamed, in America—for example, by Roscoe Pound:

Judicial finding of law has a real advantage in competition with legislation in that it works with concrete cases and generalizes only after a long course of trial and error in the effort to work out a practicable principle. Legislation, when more than declaratory, when it does more than restate authoritatively what judicial experience has indicated, involves the difficulties and the perils of prophecy.[9]

As the House of Lords was denying its authority to overrule its own prior decisions,[10] the United States Supreme Court was declaring that its constitutional decisions were always open to reexamination. And when legal positivism found expression in America, it was transmuted. For Holmes and Gray, unlike Austin and Bentham, law was not what the *legislature* ordered but what the *courts* decided in concrete cases.[11]

The difference in the scope of judicial power in England and the United States should not be exaggerated. It is primarily a difference of emphasis. There have been periods of great judicial boldness and creativity in England and periods of great passivity in America. But still the difference remains. What it has meant, in the main, is that American courts have been more open to new challenges, more willing to take on new tasks. This has encouraged others to push problems their way— so much so that no courts anywhere have greater responsibility for making public policy than the courts of the United States.

---

function, molding and declaring the law. Statutes were brute intrusions, local in scope, often shortsighted in principle or effect. They interfered in a legal world that belonged, by right, to the judges. Particularly after 1870, judges may have seen themselves more and more as guardians of a precious and threatened tradition." *A History of American Law* (Simon and Schuster, 1973), p. 316.

8. Pound, *The Formative Era of American Law*, p. 51.

9. Ibid., p. 45.

10. A doctrine abandoned only a decade ago. See the House of Lords, "Practice Statement," 110 *Solicitors' Journal* 584 (1966).

11. Oliver Wendell Holmes, "The Path of the Law," *Harvard Law Review*, vol. 10 (1897), pp. 457–78, at p. 461; John Chipman Gray, *The Nature and Sources of the Law* (2d ed.; Macmillan, 1927).

The Expansion of Judicial Responsibility

The last two decades have been a period of considerable expansion of judicial responsibility in the United States. Although the kinds of cases judges have long handled still occupy most of their time, the scope of judicial business has broadened. The result has been involvement of courts in decisions that would earlier have been thought unfit for adjudication. Judicial activity has extended to welfare administration, prison administration, and mental hospital administration, to education policy and employment policy, to road building and bridge building, to automotive safety standards, and to natural resource management.

In just the past few years, courts have struck down laws requiring a period of in-state residence as a condition of eligibility for welfare.[12] They have invalidated presumptions of child support arising from the presence in the home of a "substitute father."[13] Federal district courts have laid down elaborate standards for food handling, hospital operations, recreation facilities, inmate employment and education, sanitation, and laundry, painting, lighting, plumbing, and renovation in some prisons; they have ordered other prisons closed.[14] Courts have established equally comprehensive programs of care and treatment for the mentally ill confined in hospitals.[15] They have ordered the equalization of school expenditures on teachers' salaries,[16] established hearing procedures for public school discipline cases,[17] decided that bilingual education must be provided for Mexican-American children,[18] and suspended the use by school boards of the National Teacher Examination and of comparable tests for school supervisors.[19] They have eliminated

12. *Shapiro v. Thompson,* 394 U.S. 618 (1969).

13. *King v. Smith,* 392 U.S. 309 (1968); *Lewis v. Martin,* 397 U.S. 552 (1970).

14. *Hamilton v. Schiro,* 338 F. Supp. 1016 (E.D. La. 1970), *further relief ordered sub nom. Hamilton v. Landrieu,* 351 F. Supp. 549 (1972); *Hamilton v. Love,* 328 F. Supp. 1182 (E.D. Ark. 1971), *contempt granted,* 358 F. Supp. 338 (1973), *contempt citations revoked,* 361 F. Supp. 1235 (1973); *Hodge v. Dodd,* 1 Prison L. Rptr. 263 (N.D. Ga. 1972).

15. *Wyatt v. Stickney,* 325 F. Supp. 781 (M.D. Ala. 1971), 334 F. Supp. 1341 (1971), 344 F. Supp. 373 (1972), 344 F. Supp. 387 (1972), *affirmed in part sub nom. Wyatt v. Aderholt,* 503 F.2d 1305 (5th Cir. 1974).

16. *Hobson v. Hansen,* 327 F. Supp. 844 (D.D.C. 1971).

17. *Goss v. Lopez,* 419 U.S. 565 (1975).

18. *Serna v. Portales Municipal Schools,* 499 F.2d 1147 (10th Cir. 1974).

19. *Chance v. Board of Examiners,* 330 F. Supp. 203 (S.D.N.Y. 1971), *affirmed,* 458 F.2d 1167 (2d Cir. 1972), *affirmed as modified,* 496 F.2d 820 (2d Cir. 1974).

a high school diploma as a requirement for a fireman's job.[20] They have enjoined the construction of roads and bridges on environmental grounds[21] and suspended performance requirements for automobile tires and air bags.[22] They have told the Farmers Home Administration to restore a disaster loan program,[23] the Forest Service to stop the clear-cutting of timber,[24] and the Corps of Engineers to maintain the nation's non-navigable waterways.[25] They have been, to put it mildly, very busy, laboring in unfamiliar territory.

What the judges have been doing is new in a special sense. Although no single feature of most of this litigation constitutes an abrupt departure, the aggregate of features distinguishes it sharply from the traditional exercise of the judicial function.

First of all, many wholly new areas of adjudication have been opened up. There was, for all practical purposes, no previous judge-made law of housing or welfare rights, for example. To some extent, the new areas of activity respond to invitations from Congress or, to a much lesser extent, from state legislatures. Sometimes these take the form of judicial review provisions written into new legislation. Sometimes they take the form of new legislation so broad, so vague, so indeterminate, as to pass the problem to the courts. They then have to deal with the inevitable litigation to determine the "intent of Congress," which, in such statutes, is of course nonexistent.

If some such developments result from legislative or even bureaucratic activity (interpretation of regulations, for example), then it is natural to see the expansion of judicial activity as a mere concomitant of the growth of the welfare state. As governmental activity in general expands, so will judicial activity.

But that is not all that is involved. Much judicial activity has occurred

20. *Carter* v. *Gallagher,* 3 Lab. Rel. Rep. F.E.P. Cas. 692 (D. Minn.), *reversed in part,* 452 F.2d 315 (8th Cir. 1971), *cert. denied,* 406 U.S. 950 (1972).

21. *Scherr* v. *Volpe,* 466 F.2d 1027 (7th Cir. 1972) (highway); *D.C. Federation of Civic Associations* v. *Volpe,* 459 F.2d 1231 (D.C. Cir. 1971, 1972), *cert. denied,* 405 U.S. 1030 (1972) (bridge).

22. *H & H Tire Co.* v. *United States Department of Transportation,* 471 F. 2d 350 (7th Cir. 1972); *Chrysler Corp.* v. *Department of Transportation,* 472 F.2d 659 (6th Cir. 1972).

23. *Berends* v. *Butz,* 357 F. Supp. 143 (D. Minn. 1973).

24. *West Virginia Division of Isaac Walton League* v. *Butz,* 367 F. Supp. 422 (N.D. W. Va. 1973), *affirmed,* 522 F.2d 945 (4th Cir. 1975).

25. *Natural Resources Defense Council* v. *Calloway,* Civ. No. 74-1242 (D.D.C. 1974).

quite independent of Congress and the bureaucracy, and sometimes quite contrary to their announced policies. The very idea is sometimes to handle a problem unsatisfactorily resolved by another branch of government. In areas far from traditional development by case law, indeed in areas often covered densely by statutes and regulations, the courts have now seized the initiative in lawmaking. In such areas, the conventional formulation of the judicial role has it that courts are to "legislate" only interstitially.[26] With the important exception of judicial decisions holding legislative or executive action unconstitutional, this convenional formulation of what used to be the judicial role is probably not far from what judges did in fact do. It is no longer an adequate formulation.

What the courts demand in such cases, by way of remedy, also tends to be different. Even building programs have been ordered by courts,[27] and the character of some judicial decrees has made them, de facto, exercises of the appropriation power. A district court order rendered in Alabama had the effect of raising the state's annual expenditure on mental institutions from $14 million before suit was filed in 1971 to $58 million in 1973, a year after the decree was rendered.[28] Decisions expanding welfare eligibility or ordering special education for disturbed, retarded, or hyperactive pupils[29] have had similar budgetary effects. "For example, it is estimated that federal court decisions striking down various state restrictions on welfare payments, like residency requirements, made an additional 100,000 people eligible for assistance."[30] It is no longer even approximately accurate to say that courts exercise only a veto. What is asked and what is awarded is often the doing of something, not just the stopping of something.

To be sure, courts have always had some say in the way public funds were spent. How else could they award damages against the government? But even in the aggregate, decisions ordering a municipality to pay for an injury sustained by someone who trips over a loose manhole cover are not generally important enough to influence the setting of

26. See, e.g., Benjamin N. Cardozo, *The Nature of the Judicial Process* (Yale University Press, 1921), p. 129.

27. See *Garrett* v. *City of Hamtramck*, 503 F.2d 1236 (6th Cir. 1974).

28. *Wall Street Journal*, December 18, 1973.

29. See *Mills* v. *Board of Educ.*, 348 F. Supp. 866 (D.D.C. 1972).

30. Stuart Scheingold, *The Politics of Rights: Lawyers, Public Policy, and Political Change* (Yale University Press, 1974), p. 126.

public priorities. The recent decisions that require spendin
compliance with a newly articulated policy are something e

It is also true that both affirmative and negative relief (
something and orders to stop doing something) have a lon
English equity jurisprudence. The hoary remedies of manaamus and
specific performance both require affirmative action—but action of a
very circumscribed, precise sort, the limits of which are known in advance of the decree. Mandamus traditionally lies to compel performance
of an official duty of a clear and usually trivial sort; generally, compliance is measured by performance of one or two simple acts. Specific
performance lies to compel compliance with certain kinds of contractual
obligation, the exact nature of the obligation spelled out in the contract.
But specific performance is not traditionally awarded to compel performance of a contract for personal services, one significant reason being
that the courts would then find themselves deep in the management of a
continuing relationship, perhaps a whole business enterprise.

Again, therefore, compelling the performance of certain affirmative
acts is nothing new in principle, but it is new in degree. The decree of
a federal district judge ordering mental hospitals to adhere to some
eighty-four minimum standards of care and treatment represents an
extreme in specificity,[31] but it is representative of the trend toward demanding performance that cannot be measured in one or two simple
acts but in a whole course of conduct, performance that tends to be
open-ended in time and even in the identity of the parties to whom the
performance will be owed. Remedies like these are reminiscent of the
kinds of programs adopted by legislatures and executives. If they are
to be translated into action, remedies of this kind often require the same
kinds of supervision as other government programs do.

This leads to still another difference in degree between adjudication
as it once was and as it now is. Litigation is now more explicitly problem-
solving than grievance-answering. The individual litigant, though still
necessary, has tended to fade a bit into the background. Courts sometimes take off from the individual cases before them to the more general
problem the cases call up, and indeed they may assume—dubiously—
that the litigants before them typify the problem.

Once again, of course, it is all too easy to fabricate an idealized judi-

31. *Wyatt* v. *Stickney,* n. 15, above.

cial past that consigned judges merely to resolving individual disputes.[32] It has not been that way. In articulating the law of negligence from one case to the next, judges have tried to lay down a standard of care calculated to reduce the incidence of personal injury and property damage without unduly raising the expense of doing so. Many other common-law rules could be described in similar terms, as much efforts to frame behavioral standards as to apply them. Some of the most formidable difficulties faced by common-law judges have arisen in cases that present the judges with an inescapable choice between doing justice in the individual case and doing justice in general.[33]

For all that, however, the individual and his case remained indispensable. Courts paid particular attention to the interplay between the facts of the individual case and the facts of the class of cases they projected from it.[34] Without the particular case, the task of framing standards was devoid of meaning. It is inconceivable, for example, that even a great, innovative common-law court like the New York Court of Appeals early in this century would have countenanced deciding a case that had become moot. That some issues might forever escape judicial scrutiny because of the doctrine that a moot case is not a case at all would have struck even bold judges of a few decades ago as entirely natural.

Today it is repellant to many judges. For the view has gained ground that the judicial power is, by and large, coterminous with the governmental power. One test of this is the withering of the mootness doctrine in the federal courts. The old prohibition on the decision of moot cases is now so riddled with exceptions that it is almost a matter of discretion whether to hear a moot case.[35] The argument for deciding a case that

32. Moreover, it is no new thing for lawyers and organizations to go hunting for a plaintiff with a "grievance" in order to raise a general issue. (See the excerpts from the transcript in the Holding Company Act litigation, *Burco v. Whitworth*, 81 F.2d 721 [4th Cir. 1936], *cert. denied*, 297 U.S. 724 [1936], reprinted and discussed in Paul A. Freund, *The Supreme Court: Its Business, Purposes, and Performance* [Meridian Books, 1961], pp. 159–63.) But it has become a much more common practice.

33. See, e.g., the treatment of this problem in Richard A. Wasserstrom, *The Judicial Decision: Toward a Theory of Legal Justification* (Stanford University Press, 1961). See also Paul A. Freund, "Mr. Justice Brandeis: A Centennial Memoir," *Harvard Law Review*, vol. 70 (March 1957), pp. 769–92, at pp. 786–87.

34. See particularly Karl Llewellyn, *The Common Law Tradition: Deciding Appeals* (Little, Brown, 1960).

35. See Richard G. Singer, "Justiciability and Recent Supreme Court Cases," *Alabama Law Review*, vol. 21 (Spring 1969), pp. 229–86, at pp. 258–68.

has become moot is often the distinctly recent one that there is a public interest in the judicial resolution of important issues. In contrast, the earlier view was that there was a public interest in avoiding litigation. By the same token, dismissal for mootness has become a practice reserved for invocation when it is unimportant, inconvenient, or impolitic to decide the issues a case raises.[36]

What this shift signifies is the increasing subordination of the individual case in judicial policymaking, as well as the expansion of judicial responsibility more nearly to overlap the responsibilities of other governmental institutions. The individual case and its peculiar facts have on occasion become mere vehicles for an exposition of more general policy problems. Consequently, somewhat less care can be devoted, by lawyers and judges alike, to the appropriateness of particular plaintiffs and to the details of their grievances.

At the same time, the courts have tended to move from the byways onto the highways of policymaking. Alexander M. Bickel has captured, albeit with hyperbole, the thrust of the new judicial ventures into social policy. "All too many federal judges," he has written, "have been induced to view themselves as holding roving commissions as problem solvers, and as charged with a duty to act when majoritarian institutions do not."[37] The hyperbole is itself significant: many federal judges regard themselves as holding no such commission, yet even they have embarked on "problem-solving" ventures. This is the surest sign that the tendency is not idiosyncratic but systemic: it transcends, in some measure, individual judicial preference and calls for systematic explanation.

The Sources of Judicial Role Expansion

As I have already suggested, the remote sources of the broad sweep of judicial power in America lie deep in English and American political history. The immediate origins of recent shifts in judicial emphasis are another matter. These are several, and they have tended to build on each other.

36. See, e.g., *De Funis* v. *Odegaard*, 416 U.S. 312 (1974).

37. *The Supreme Court and the Idea of Progress* (Harper and Row, 1970), p. 134. For examples, see J. Skelly Wright, "Beyond Discretionary Justice," *Yale Law Journal*, vol. 81 (January 1972), pp. 575–97; *Environmental Defense Fund* v. *Ruckelshaus*, 439 F.2d 584, 597–98 (D.C. Cir. 1971).

Most obvious has been the influence of the school desegregation cases.[38] These decisions created a magnetic field around the courts, attracting litigation in areas where judicial intervention had earlier seemed implausible. The more general judicial activism of the Warren Court signaled its willingness to test the conventional boundaries of judicial action. As this happened, significant social groups thwarted in achieving their goals in other forums turned to adjudication as a more promising course. Some organizations saw the opportunity to use litigation as a weapon in political struggles carried on elsewhere. The National Welfare Rights Organization, for example, is said to have turned to lawsuits to help create a state and local welfare crisis that might bring about a federal guaranteed income.[39] The image of courts willing to "take the heat" was attractive, too, to legislators who were not. Such social programs as the poverty program had legal assistance components, which Congress obligingly provided, perhaps partly because they placed the onus for resolving social problems on the courts. Soon there were also privately funded lawyers functioning in the environmental, mental health, welfare rights, civil rights, and similar fields. They tended to prefer the judicial road to reform over the legislative.[40] They raised issues never before tested in litigation, and the courts frequently responded by expanding the boundaries of judicial activity.

Major doctrinal developments both followed and contributed to the increase in number and the change in character of the issues being litigated. The loosening of requirements of jurisdiction, standing, and ripeness (to name just three) helped spread judge-made law out, moving it from the tangential questions to the great principles. If these doctrinal decisions mean anything, it is that the adjudicative format is less and less an inhibition on judicial action and that the lawsuit can increasingly be thought of an option more or less interchangeable with options in other forums, except that it has advantages the other forums lack (about which I shall say more at the beginning of the next chapter). Hence the time-honored tradition that those who lose in the legislature or the bureaucracy may turn to the courts has lost none of its appeal. Only the

38. *Brown* v. *Board of Education,* 347 U.S. 483 (1954); *Bolling* v. *Sharpe,* 347 U.S. 497 (1954).

39. Joel F. Handler, "Social Reform Groups and the Legal System: Enforcement Problems" (University of Wisconsin–Madison, Institute for Research on Poverty, Discussion Paper 209-74, June 1974; processed), pp. 16–18.

40. Harry Brill, "The Uses and Abuses of Legal Assistance," *The Public Interest,* no. 31 (Spring 1973), pp. 38–55, at p. 45.

identity of those who turn from one forum to another has undergone some change. Deprived social groups have joined the advantaged in the march to the courthouse.[41]

Some major obstacles of a practical sort have also been cleared away. It still takes years to conclude most litigation, but some courts have shown a willingness to expedite hearing schedules to speed up the disposition of injunction cases. It still costs large sums of money to bring suit, and reductions in foundation funding of public-interest law firms are contracting their efforts. But decisions awarding attorneys' fees may have eased the hardship and proliferated the cases. In one decision, an attorney's fee was awarded even though the plaintiff's lawyer had agreed to represent him without charge.[42] The court said the award would encourage lawyers to represent public-interest clients without fees in the hope that a fee will be awarded—and no doubt it would have that effect. In 1975, the Supreme Court restricted the award of attorneys' fees in federal cases unless authorized by Congress.[43] But many statutes do allow attorneys' fees, and proposed legislation in some areas may be more generous in allowing expert witness fees as well.[44]

It is still true, too, that legislative remedies—when they are forthcoming—may be more systematic and inclusive than judicial remedies. Yet, more often than not, the judicial remedy has a directness, a concreteness, and a lack of equivocation notably absent in schemes that emerge from the political process. More and more, the courts have turned to decrees that afford comprehensive relief, often of a far-reaching sort. Support in the Anglo-American equity tradition for a decree as broad as the occasion warrants is unmistakable. The problem of school

41. But where the wealthy invariably want the courts to strike down action the other branches have taken, the disadvantaged often ask the courts to take action the other branches have decided not to take. The character of the demand for action is therefore different.

42. *Brandenburger* v. *Thompson*, 494 F. 2d 885 (9th Cir. 1974).

43. *Alyeska Pipeline Service Co.* v. *Wilderness Society*, 421 U.S. 240 (1975).

44. For a list of statutes permitting the award of attorneys' fees, see ibid. at 260–62 nn. 33–35. *Alyeska* seems certain to generate attempts in Congress to write fee provisions into legislation. For a recent example, see the Consumer Food Bill, which passed the Senate in 1976. It would allow awards of costs, attorneys' fees, and expert witness fees to any party to a citizen suit under the act, at the court's discretion. See S. Rept. 94-684, 94 Cong. 2 sess. (1976), pp. 14–16. Cf. S. Rept. 94-1011, 94 Cong. 2 sess. (1976), recommending expanded authorization for attorneys' fees in suits under some of the Civil Rights Acts. For pressure on the organized bar to contribute to public-interest representation in the post-*Alyeska* period, see *Washington Post*, August 8, 1976.

desegregation has tested this tradition, and the judges have sometimes proved as resourceful as the English chancellors from whom their equitable powers spring. In the process, the willingness to entertain remedies as inclusive as those a legislature might provide has grown, even to the point where the judicially ordered consolidation of school districts or equalization of tax burdens across districts—wholly beyond imagination not long ago—become debatable measures, indeed litigated issues.[45]

All of this has taken place, perhaps could only take place, in a society given to an incomparable degree of legalism. In the United States, as Tocqueville observed long ago, "all parties are obliged to borrow, in their daily controversies, the ideas, and even the language, peculiar to judicial proceedings. . . . The language of the law thus becomes in some measure a vulgar tongue; the spirit of the law, which is produced in the schools and courts of justice, gradually penetrates beyond their walls into the bosom of society, where it descends to the lowest classes, so that at last the whole people contract the habits and the taste of the judicial magistrate."[46] The American proclivity to think of social problems in legal terms[47] and to judicialize everything from wage claims to community conflicts and the allocation of airline routes makes it only natural to accord judges a major share in the making of social policy. No doubt, this underlying premise in American thought was a necessary, though insufficient, condition for the expansion of judicial responsibility that has taken place over the last twenty years.

Expansion and Contraction, Constitutional and Statutory

The tendency to commit the resolution of social policy issues to the courts is not likely to be arrested in the near future. The nature of the forces undergirding the tendency makes them not readily reversible. Doctrinal erosion in particular is not easily stopped. Ironically, perhaps, the traditional judicial conception of precedent makes it more difficult for courts to change course dramatically than for the other branches

---

45. *San Antonio School District* v. *Rodriguez*, 411 U.S. 1 (1973); *Bradley* v. *School Bd.*, 338 F. Supp. 67 (E.D. Va. 1972), *reversed*, 462 F.2d 1052 (4th Cir. 1972), *affirmed by an equally divided Court*, 412 U.S. 92 (1973).

46. Alexis de Tocqueville, *Democracy in America*, vol. 1 (Knopf, 1945), p. 290.

47. Recently excoriated as the "myth of rights." See Scheingold, *The Politics of Rights*.

of government to do so. The generally greater stability of judicial personnel, appointed for life in the federal courts, appointed or elected to long terms in the states, also makes for continuity. The statutes already enacted and continuing to be enacted, lodging authority for policymaking in the courts by explicit provision or by default, are enough to propel judicial activity for some time to come. And the attractiveness of passing problems to the judges is unabated. The new responsibilities of the courts are not just the product of individual states of mind.

Even to the limited extent that judges can contract their recently expanded commitments, some curious twists are possible. Supreme Court Justices, appointed because a president thinks they will construe the Bill of Rights more narrowly than their predecessors, have a way of becoming entangled in institutional tradition. No contraction is likely to take place on all fronts.

Beyond that, expansive exercises in statutory construction may be untouched by a contraction in constitutional adjudication. As a matter of fact, judges who recoil at innovation in constitutional lawmaking may not see the same dangers at all in the interpretation of statutes. It is customary to think that judicial self-limitation in constitutional interpretation is important because constitutional law is a permanent inhibition on policy: a legislature cannot override an interpretation of the Constitution. In statutory law, judges may reason, basic policy choices have been made by other branches, and judicial construction may later be overridden by them. For these reasons, judges with a strong sense of institutional limitation are less likely to let it stand in the way of innovation short of constitutional interpretation.

The soundness of this conventional distinction between the scope of constitutional and non-constitutional adjudication need not detain us here. Whether or not decisions that rest on constitutional foundations are really more permanent than those that do not is beside the point— which is simply that traditional counsels of restraint that apply to the former do not apply to the latter. Judges concerned to avoid the excesses that are believed to have characterized the Supreme Court of the 1930s and 1960s may still embark on ambitious ventures of judicial reform in the name of statutory construction.

Let me give two examples. Both, as it happens, are from the civil rights field, and both are decisions of the Supreme Court, but they might just as easily have come from some other court acting in some other field.

The first is *Griggs* v. *Duke Power Co.*,[48] in which the Court unanimously read Title VII of the Civil Rights Act of 1964[49] to require the elimination of tests and diplomas as job requirements if they disqualify prospective black employees at a higher rate than whites, unless the employer can show that the test or diploma bears a "demonstrable relationship" to successful job performance.[50] Employment practices that have no discriminatory intent, the Court said, are to be measured by "business necessity."[51] Tests that prevent minority applicants from obtaining jobs in proportion to their numbers must be shown to "measure the person for the job and not the person in the abstract."[52] So the Court, in an opinion by Chief Justice Burger, interpreted the Civil Rights Act.[53]

The act had forbidden job discrimination on grounds of "race, color, religion, sex, or national origin."[54] An amendment, added on the floor of the Senate in order to clarify and reaffirm the rights of employers to use "ability tests" to screen potential employees, had insulated such tests from scrutiny, provided the tests were "not designed, intended or used to discriminate" on racial or other forbidden grounds.[55] That, at least, is what the senators thought.

In the event, the Supreme Court read the word "used" to mean used intentionally or unintentionally, and so to forbid tests like the aptitude test used in *Griggs* unless the employer could prove it measured job performance in the narrow sense.

There is convincing legislative history to show that Congress intended the opposite of the result reached in *Griggs*. This was a provision on which Congress was at pains to make itself clear. The sponsors of the testing amendment explicitly wished to insure that no court would prohibit a testing procedure to evaluate applicants because some categories of applicants might do better on them than others.[56] The senators plainly

---

48. 401 U.S. 424 (1971).
49. 42 U.S.C. §§ 2000e–2000e(15).
50. 401 U.S. at 431.
51. Ibid.
52. Ibid. at 436.
53. The Chief Justice wrote for all eight Justices who participated in the decision. Mr. Justice Brennan did not sit.
54. 42 U.S.C. § 2000e–2.
55. 42 U.S.C. § 2000e–2(h).
56. See the abundant evidence in Hugh Steven Wilson, "A Second Look at *Griggs* v. *Duke Power Company*: Ruminations on Job Testing, Discrimination, and the Role of the Federal Courts," *Virginia Law Review*, vol. 58 (1972), pp. 844–74, at pp. 852–58.

believed that general intelligence and aptitude tests were job-related, and meant to exempt them from the act for that reason. It is not surprising, therefore, that the Court's handling of the legislative history is halting and embarrassed.

Griggs has already been interpreted very broadly by lower federal courts to require a number of significant changes in public and private employment practices.[57] There have been suggestions that *Griggs'* requirement of expensive validation of employment tests may cause firms to abandon testing and move to more subjective (and potentially more biased) methods of screening applicants[58]—or, on the other hand, to proportional hiring on a racial basis in order to avoid charges of discrimination.[59] Either way, the result contravenes the twofold legislative intention, which was to forbid preferential hiring on a racial basis and "to allow an employer's bona fide use of professionally developed tests despite their disparate impact on culturally disadvantaged minorities."[60]

In its skepticism of aptitude tests and formal credentials, *Griggs* accords with some recent research questioning the predictive value of such requirements for job performance.[61] But *Griggs* cannot be understood as a traditional exercise in statutory exegesis.[62]

The second example is *Lau* v. *Nichols*.[63] *Lau* arose under Title VI of

57. Ibid., pp. 847–51. The opinion has also been read by the New York City Commission on Human Rights to forbid layoffs based on job performance unless the criteria to evaluate it are "job-related" and "justified by business necessity." City of New York, Commission on Human Rights, Memorandum to Employees, December 16, 1974, p. 3 (processed). But see *Washington* v. *Davis*, 44 U.S.L.W. 4789 (U.S. Sup. Ct. 1976).

58. Wilson, "A Second Look at *Griggs* v. *Duke Power Company*," pp. 873–74.

59. Note, "Business Necessity Under Title VII of the Civil Rights Act of 1964: A No-Alternative Approach," *Yale Law Journal*, vol. 84 (November 1974), pp. 98–119, at pp. 116–17.

60. Ibid., pp. 104, 106.

61. See Christopher Jencks and others, *Inequality: A Reassessment of the Effect of Family and Schooling in America* (Basic Books, 1972), pp. 192–94. In the very long run, *Griggs* may also catalyze some far-reaching changes in the structure of educational institutions. See Sheila Huff, "Credentialing by Tests or by Degrees: Title VII of the Civil Rights Act and *Griggs* v. *Duke Power Co.*," *Harvard Education Review*, vol. 44 (May 1974), pp. 246–69.

62. It is interesting to note that the Court has recently declined to extend the rigorous *Griggs* standards for employment tests to cases arising under the Constitution rather than under Title VII. *Washington* v. *Davis*, 44 U.S.L.W. 4789 (1976). This may suggest that the majority is unhappy with what the lower courts have done with *Griggs*, and wishes to confine the impact of the decision. But it is also consistent with the thesis that some Justices are willing to be bolder in statutory interpretation than in constitutonal interpretation.

63. 414 U.S. 563 (1974).

the Civil Rights Act of 1964, which forbids discrimination on grounds of "race, color, or national origin" in "any program or activity receiving Federal financial assistance."[64] As a condition of federal aid, the Department of Health, Education, and Welfare had required school districts to "take affirmative steps to rectify the language deficiency" of "national-origin minority group children" unable to speak and understand English.[65] So enlarged by the regulations, the act was read by the Supreme Court, 9–0, to require the San Francisco school system to take some action to rectify the language deficiencies of some 1,800 Chinese-American pupils (most of them born in the United States) who do not speak English.[66]

The decision has already had important consequences across the nation. Indeed, it is one of the ironies of *Lau* that, though it was rendered in the case of Chinese-origin pupils, it will affect primarily the rights of Spanish-speaking children all over the United States. The decision has been widely interpreted—erroneously—as *requiring* "bilingual-bicultural" education, rather than remedial instruction in English.[67] Stimulated by *Lau*, the Texas legislature has recently enacted a law making bilingual education mandatory in schools with twenty or more children whose ability in English is limited,[68] and there are movements for bilingual education in several other states. The decision will doubtless affect instructional programs and language choice across the nation.[69]

Lau may be interpreted as a judicial experiment. The Court did not hold that any particular action was required of the school system—only that inaction was forbidden. The case was remanded to the district court for the fashioning of relief, and the Court may have thought there would be time enough for a second look after a decree was entered.

This may explain the offhanded way in which the case was disposed of, for the majority and concurring opinions contain no serious discus-

64. 42 U.S.C. § 2000d.

65. 35 Fed. Reg. 11595.

66. Mr. Justice Douglas, joined by Justices Brennan, Marshall, Powell, and Rehnquist, wrote for the Court. The remaining four Justices concurred in the result.

67. Dexter Waugh and Bruce Koon, "Breakthrough for Bilingual Education," *Civil Rights Digest,* vol. 6 (Summer 1974), pp. 18–26.

68. 2 Tex. Code § 21.109 (Supp., 1974); Bilingual Education Act, 20 U.S.C. § 880b (1970).

69. Cf. Roger M. Thompson, "Mexican-American Language Loyalty and the Validity of the 1970 Census," *International Journal of the Sociology of Language* (The Hague), no. 2 (1974), pp. 7–18.

sion of the central issues of the litigation: whether it constitutes discrimination to teach all pupils in English regardless of their fluency at the time they enter school, and whether, in any event, linguistic discrimination constitutes discrimination on the basis of "race, color, or national origin." Discrimination is generally thought of as differential treatment. What was complained of in *Lau* was the failure to differentiate in the instruction given pupils fluent in Chinese and not fluent in English. Similarly, linguistic loyalty and national origin are related but are not the same thing. No claim was made in *Lau* that Chinese-origin pupils were affected adversely by the policies of the school system—only that monolingual, Chinese-speaking pupils (most of whom had their "national origin" in the United States) were so affected. There is little in the language of Title VI that suggests it contemplates affirmative action to remedy linguistic deficiencies, and there is nothing in the legislative history that hints at such a purpose.[70]

These two seminal decisions of the Burger Court—neither of which drew a single dissent—should suffice to show that judicial participation in the making of social policy is no ephemeral development. It is part of a chain of developments that can survive the vicissitudes of constitional "activism" and "restraint." No one could mistake these decisions for "interstitial" statutory interpretation, since they are departures from the language and legislative history of the statutes they construe. Nor does it need to be stressed that these decisions were not solely the work of judges who "view themselves as holding roving commissions as problem solvers." That they do not so regard themselves attests to the structural, enduring character of the phenomena I have been describing.

Legitimacy and Capacity

The appropriate scope of judicial power in the American system of government has periodically been debated, often intensely. For the most part, what has been challenged has been the power to declare legislative and executive action unconstitutional. Accordingly, the debate has been cast in terms of legitimacy. A polity accustomed to question unchecked power views with unease judicial authority to strike down

70. See Gary Orfield, "Urban School Desegregation and the Politics of Busing" (Brookings Institution, in manuscript), chap. 10, "Desegregation and the Rights of Linguistic Minorities."

laws enacted by democratically elected legislatures. Where, after all, is
the accountability of life-tenured judges? This question of democratic
theory has been raised insistently, especially in times of constitutional
crisis, notably in the 1930s and again in the 1950s.

The last word has not been heard in these debates, and it will not
soon be heard. The structure of American government guarantees the
issue a long life. But, for the moment, the debate seems to have waned
with the growing recognition that there are elements of overstatement
in the case against judicial review. The courts are more democratically
accountable, through a variety of formal and informal mechanisms, than
they have been accused of being. Equally important, the other branches
are in many ways less democratically accountable than they in turn
were said to be by those who emphasized the special disabilities under
which judges labor. Hence the many academic discussions of the need
for "representative bureaucracy," for a less insular presidency, and for
reform of the procedures and devices that make Congress undemocratic
internally and unrepresentative externally. (That students of any single
institution often tend to see that institution as the flawed one is a useful
indication of the limited perspective that comes from singleminded attention to any one institution. It should properly make us chary of
drawing inferences about the courts without an institutionally comparative frame of reference.)

As the debate over the democratic character of judicial review wanes,
there is another set of issues in the offing. It relates not to legitimacy but
to capacity, not to whether the courts *should* perform certain tasks but
to whether they *can* perform them competently.

Of course, legitimacy and capacity are related. A court wholly without capacity may forfeit its claim to legitimacy. A court wholly without
legitimacy will soon suffer from diminished capacity. The cases for and
against judicial review have always rested in part on assessments of
judicial capacity: on the one hand, the presumably superior ability of
the courts "to build up a body of coherent and intelligible constitutional
principle";[71] on the other, the presumably inferior ability of courts to
make the political judgments on which exercises of the power of judicial
review so often turn.[72] If the separation of powers reflects a division of

71. Henry M. Hart, Jr., and Herbert Wechsler, *The Federal Courts and the
Federal System* (Foundation Press, 1953), p. 93.

72. See, e.g., *Dennis* v. *United States*, 341 U.S. 494, 570 (1951) (concurring
opinion of Jackson, J.): "No doctrine can be sound whose application requires us

labor according to expertise, then relative institutional capacity becomes relevant to defining spheres of power and particular exercises of power.

The recent developments that I have described necessarily raise the previously subsidiary issue of capacity to a more prominent place. Although the assumption of new responsibilities can, as I have observed, be traced to exercises of the traditional power to declare laws unconstitutional, they now transcend that power. Traditional judicial review meant forbidding action, saying "no" to the other branches. Now the judicial function often means requiring action, and there is a difference between foreclosing an alternative and choosing one, between constraining and commanding. Among other things, it is this difference, and the problematic character of judicial resources to manage the task of commanding, that make the question of capacity so important.

Amendment from the Judgment Seat

Before proceeding any further, let me try to recapitulate what I have said so far and where it seems to me to lead. I have argued that judicial intervention in matters of social policy has greatly increased and will not soon decrease. This expansion of judicial responsibility means, first, a broadening of the sphere of judge-made law, into areas that might once have been called "social welfare" and were not considered "legal" at all. It also means an expansion of the scope for judicial initiative within these areas. Courts are no longer as confined to the interstices of legislation as they once were—now the statute is often a mere point of departure—and they are no longer as inhibited as they once were from delving into supervisory or administrative responsibilities in connection with the remedies they award. They are more often found requiring detailed, specific, and affirmative action than previously. They are less constrained, too, by the limitations of the cases and the litigants before them. More openly, self-consciously, and broadly than before, the courts are engaged in efforts to shape or control the behavior of identifiable social groups, groups not necessarily before the court: welfare administrators, employers, school officials, policemen. The expan-

to make a prophecy of [international and national phenomena which baffle the best informed foreign offices and our most experienced politicians] in the guise of a legal decision. The judicial process simply is not adequate to a trial of such far-flung issues. The answers given would reflect our own political predilections and nothing more."

sion of the judicial sphere means there are more such groups whose behavior has become a subject of judicial attention.

This has not happened all at once, and the transition is anything but complete. Most courts, most of the time, are doing roughly what they did many years ago. Not a landslide but an erosion of some of the distinctive features of the judicial process is what seems to have been occurring.

What this means is that there is somewhat less institutional differentiation today than two decades ago. There is now more overlap between the courts and Congress in formulating policy and between the courts and the executive in both formulating and carrying out programs. That is, the types of decisions being made by the various institutions—their scope and level of generality—seem to be converging somewhat, though the processes by which the decisions are made and the outcomes of those processes may be quite different—as different as the groups who maneuver to place an issue before one set of decisionmakers rather than another, or who, defeated in one forum, turn hopefully to the next, believe them to be. Thus, to say that there is convergence in the business of courts and other institutions is not tantamount to saying that it makes no difference who decides a question. On the contrary, it matters a good deal, for the institutions are differently composed and organized. The real possibility of overlapping responsibilities but opposite outcomes makes the policy process a more complex and drawn-out affair than it once was.

The recency, the incompleteness, and the incremental history of these developments should not obscure their portentousness. It is just possible that these modifications in the scope of judicial power will one day amount to a major structural change. We regard as quaintly and unduly restrictive the medieval conception of legislation as mere restatement of customary law. Future generations may likewise view our distinctive association of adjudication with the grievances of individual litigants as an equally curious affectation.

It may be, of course, that something much less significant than this is in the offing. For the purposes of this discussion, it makes little difference. The changes of degree that are already visible are quite enough to raise important questions about the consequences of using the judicial process for the resolution of social policy issues.

If extensive judicial activity in matters of social policy is not a passing phenomenon, then Mansfield and Bentham have a new relevance for us. For we must confront Bentham's blunt assertion that "amendment from the judgment seat is confusion."

Nor is that all. Hybrid institutions run the risk of inheriting the disabilities of both parents. To the extent that institutional differentiation is in decline and courts are making policy of the scope formerly associated with legislatures, it must be asked not only whether Bentham's charge is true, but also whether Lord Mansfield's case against legislative foresight might not now be turned around on the courts. Do the putative advantages of "the common law that works itself pure" apply to judicial ventures into broad matters of social policy? Or do the courts now share the problem Mansfield attributes to Parliament: the inability to "take in all cases" in advance? Pound's "perils of prophecy," in other words, may now be on the other foot.

CHAPTER TWO

Attributes of Adjudication

There is an undeniable attractiveness to the judicial method. In its pristine form, the adversary process puts all the arguments before the decisionmaker in a setting in which he must act. The judge must decide the case and justify his decision by reference to evidence and reasoning. In the other branches, it is relatively easy to stop a decision from being made—they often effectively say no by saying nothing. In the judicial process, questions get answers. It is difficult to prevent a judicial decision. No other public or private institution is bound to be so responsive.

Such felt advantages of the judicial process help explain why pressing problems find their way to the judiciary. The lawsuit and the court decree are often thought to be more powerful moral influences than are alternative avenues of problem solving. Judicial decisions vindicate legal rights in a specific, authoritative way. They do so by an accessible process triggered by precise steps spelled out in advance. Judicial tests of relevance are rigorous, and therefore the judicial process is less subject to exogenous political influences than are the other branches. On these grounds, adjudication is a more direct, immediate, and rational mode of policymaking than can be offered by the legislative process.

Yet these justly venerated virtues of the judicial process may equally be viewed as vices. This is especially the case when we consider the aptness of adjudication for the resolution of major issues of social policy. The very fact that judges must act, must respond to complaints, means that they will find it difficult to devise a coherent program of action. In this sense, responsiveness implies ad hoc decisions, one case at a time. The requirement that judges justify their decisions by reference to reason may mean that adjudication is not appropriate for those problems

22

best resolved by a process of negotiation. Compromise outcomes are often not defensible by resort to reason.

Judges may be unencumbered by commitments to pet programs and untroubled by the presence of influential groups who are in a position to block action in other forums. The National Education Association was not the most powerful voice heard in *Lau* v. *Nichols*,[1] and the National Association of Manufacturers was in no position to thwart the Court's decision of *Griggs* v. *Duke Power Company*.[2] The fact that there are fewer participants in the adjudicative process than in the legislative process makes it easier for judges than for legislators to cut through the problem to a resolution. But it is precisely this ability to simplify the issues and to exclude interested participants that may put the judges in danger of fostering reductionist solutions.

More such coins could be turned over. But this is enough to suggest that the simplicity and straightforwardness of the judicial process, its strengths in some settings, may be its undoing in others. In particular, many aspects of adjudication that seem well suited to the determination of particular controversies seem unsuited to the making of general policy.

This is a theme to be pursued in this chapter at some length. The purpose is to explore areas of potential judicial incapacity, as a prelude to case studies designed to illuminate the performance of the courts when they undertake the making of social policy.

This skeptical perspective is justified on both descriptive and prescriptive grounds. Institutions are often a step behind the tasks they must perform. This is especially likely to be true if new tasks have been added to the old, rather than displacing them, so that the problem is not simply one of transformation but of performing both tasks. Moreover, institutional lag is likely to be greater if new tasks have been added by the imperceptible process of accretion, utilizing the same forms as have long been used. This is very much the situation of the courts. Their policymaking functions have gradually been superimposed on a structure that evolved primarily to decide individual cases.

Retooling institutions that are out of phase with their new responsibilities is, of course, impossible without an assessment of current limitations. Again, therefore, the accent on the limitations of adjudication can be constructive as well as critical.

1. 414 U.S. 563 (1974).
2. 401 U.S. 424 (1971).

The point can surely be made that, if courts cannot do certain things well, other institutions may perform the same tasks even less capably. (Indeed, one reason for judicial involvement in social policy matters has been the reticence of other policymakers to address them at all, and their occasional proclivity to push them onto the courts.) No institution can do everything, and for some tasks legislative and bureaucratic institutions may be even less well suited than the courts are. On some matters, an imperfect judicial performance may be the best that is currently available, if there is to be any official performance at all. Whether judicial action is desirable will depend on a number of factors, of which limited capacity will be only one. But such occasions for action furnish no reason to gloss over the limits of judicial capacity. On the contrary, they provide ample reason to augment that capacity where possible. And, it seems to me, they counsel courts to weigh the appropriateness of judicial action against the possibility that action to be taken may proceed from defective diagnosis or be deflected in the course of execution.

In truth, there is as of now no basis for firm conclusions about the relative capacities of our institutions. There are few studies directed explicitly to the issue of capacity that would enable us to form sound comparative judgments one way or the other. Until we have such a comparative analysis, skepticism must not be permitted to harden into a final judgment.

It would be desirable, but at this moment scarcely possible, to study the capacities of all three branches (or of the different processes available in all the branches) simultaneously. The weak foundation on which such a study would rest would impair its utility, even leaving aside the massiveness of such an undertaking. This book, then, is about the judicial process. It proceeds from the premise that every process, every institution has its characteristic ways of operating; each is biased toward certain kinds of outcomes; each leaves its distinctive imprint on the matters it touches. The concern of this book is to trace the imprint of the judicial process on matters of social policy, taking pains to relate policy process to policy outcome.

But a study of the judicial process raises questions about the other processes. Most of these cannot be answered yet. But at various points I shall pause to make comparative reference to other institutions and the way they seem to handle comparable problems. Occasionally, I shall speculate on how a specific issue might have come out had it been processed in a different forum. Overall, however, this is an analysis of a single institution, and that makes it imperative to avoid creating fictitious, if only implicit, images of the capacities of other branches.

We shall return to institutional comparisons in the final chapter. For now, it is convenient to begin such an assessment with the personnel of adjudication, principally the judges themselves.[3]

The Personnel of the Adjudicative Process

In a complex, highly differentiated society, the generalist role is not to be deprecated. The interpreter, the person who stands at the synapses and makes connections between subsystems and subcultures, is a vital part of any policymaking process. Nevertheless the relative weight accorded to specialist and generalist opinion, and the kind of input made by each, can impart a distinctive cast to the resulting decision. One consequence of generalist dominance in a decision process, astutely pointed out by Robert Presthus,[4] is that, in the interstices where expertise is lacking, the generalist tends to fill in the gaps with his own "generalized normative axioms." It is not clear that the generalized normative axioms of the lawyers, which have so far cemented the cracks of judicial decisions, are well adapted to policymaking in all of the areas to which they have been applied.

The generalist character of judges commends them as community representatives for many of the duties they must perform, but it unfits them for processing specialized information. In fact, this is one of the jobs that many judges do with the least skill and the greatest impatience.

It has always proved difficult to integrate specialists into the adjudicative process. Specialized information is usually provided to judges through the medium of expert witnesses and consultants or through popularized written versions of the information. (We shall see examples

3. Although I shall make only occasional reference to the role of counsel, I do not wish to be understood as implying that the part played by counsel in the process of adjudication is minor. Counsel's role is anything but minor, though it is often neglected in studies of the judicial process, and the presence of counsel will certainly make itself felt in the case studies. For the role of government lawyers in administrative agency litigation, see Donald L. Horowitz, *The Jurocracy: Government Lawyers, Agency Programs, and Judicial Decisions* (Lexington Books, in press).

4. "Decline of the Generalist Myth," *Public Administration Review*, vol. 24 (December 1964), pp. 211–16, at p. 216.

of both in later chapters.) The expert witnesses are paid by the respective parties, and they are almost invariably partisan. The popularizations share the usual defects of the genre. They simplify, and sometimes they mislead.

Even purely legal specialists are often not allowed to speak for themselves in court. In a complex securities case, a large law firm will send someone from the litigation department to represent the client in court. The litigator will be advised by the securities specialist who has probably handled the client's business, short of litigation, for years, but the specialist may be confined to whispering, even in non-jury cases and even during conferences in the judge's chambers. The litigator, unfamiliar though he may be with the law of securities and the problems of the client, will act as spokesman for the client and interpreter of specialized information for the benefit of the judge.[5]

This division of responsibility is carefully geared to the character of the central actor: the judge. By virtue of the processes of recruitment and socialization and the apportionment of work, the judge of a trial or appellate court of general jurisdiction is a generalist par excellence. Those who appear before him must organize themselves and their information accordingly.

The basic outlines of the judicial selection process for the federal courts are by now quite clear, though the state court recruitment processes have been studied less.[6] The elaborate interplay between the White House, the American Bar Association's Standing Committee on the Federal Judiciary, the Senate Judiciary Committee, the Office of the Deputy Attorney General, and individual senators from states having judicial vacancies, has been fully described. We know, for example, that presidents consider the choice of Supreme Court nominees to be their prerogative, that senators have the same proprietary view of district court appointments in their states, and that court of appeals nominees fall somewhere in between.[7] We know, too, that the American Bar Association has argued for the importance of "professional" as against "po-

5. For a similar phenomenon among government lawyers, see Horowitz, *The Jurocracy.*

6. On the federal courts, see Joel B. Grossman, *Lawyers and Judges: The A.B.A. and the Politics of Judicial Selection* (John Wiley, 1965); Harold W. Chase, *Federal Judges: The Appointing Process* (University of Minnesota Press, 1972); Chase, "Federal Judges: The Appointing Process," *Minnesota Law Review,* vol. 51 (December 1966), pp. 185–221; Sheldon Goldman, "Judicial Appointments to the United States Court of Appeals," *Wisconsin Law Review* (Winter 1967), pp. 186–214.

7. Grossman, *Lawyers and Judges,* p. 27.

litical" qualifications, and that, while there is about an even chance that a lower-court nominee will come from the ranks of public or party office-holders, the ratio of private practitioners appointed to the bench has slowly increased.[8]

This pulling and tugging suggests that it makes a difference whether the American Bar Association or an individual senator is more influential in judicial selection. For some purposes (especially degree of party activism) it does, but there is another way to look at the recruitment process. It makes sense to view it as a mutual veto system, a system likely to throw up candidates who are not unacceptable to the main actors. The policy views of a prospective nominee have generally not played a prominent part in the selection of lower federal judges, but administrations have usually eschewed the nomination of those they regard as holding extreme views.[9] The selection process can thus be viewed as one of narrowing down and pushing toward the least common denominator candidate. In terms of expertise, it makes little difference whether a political officeholder or a favorite private practitioner of the American Bar Association is selected. A practitioner able to obtain a high ABA rating is likely to have had some litigation experience or general corporate practice and to be exactly the kind of generalist who appears before judges.

If this suggests judicial self-perpetuation, that begins to approach the mark. About 40 percent of the Department of Justice files of the judicial appointees of the Eisenhower and Kennedy administrations contained letters from sitting judges recommending the then-prospective candidate.[10] In both administrations, moreover, more than half the appointees to the court of appeals had themselves had prior judicial experience.[11] Judges beget judges.

This is what is known about the recruitment process. What is not really known is just how this process affects the composition of the federal judiciary. There are, as I have said, grounds for suspicion that the multiple players active in the selection process are likely to screen out

8. Ibid., pp. 32–33, 205–06; Goldman, "Judicial Appointments to the United States Court of Appeals," pp. 194–95; Goldman, "Characteristics of Eisenhower and Kennedy Appointments to the Lower Federal Courts," *Western Political Quarterly,* vol. 18 (December 1965), pp. 755–62.

9. Goldman, "Judicial Appointments to the United States Court of Appeals," pp. 203–04.

10. Ibid., p. 190.

11. Goldman, "Characteristics of Eisenhower and Kennedy Appointments," pp. 761–62.

specialists and approve of nominees with broad general experience. In this connection, it is interesting that an attempt to correlate judges' basic background characteristics like political party, religion, and prior judicial experience with their judicial decisions led to inconclusive results.[12] A very limited range of variance was explained by these social background variables. The reason, presumably, is that there is a great deal of homogeneity on the federal bench—much more than there is diversity—and the process of recruitment may help to explain why this should be so.

Whatever the impact of the recruitment process, the socialization of judges and the apportionment of responsibilities among them impede the development of pools of expertise that might be useful in the handling of social policy matters. These two factors are closely related, because the process of socialization is heavily directed to the manifest responsibilities of the job.

The key to the on-the-job socialization of a federal judge is the breadth of his docket. Judges are rotated from problem to problem. There are few things they see enough of to make them real specialists. (The few that come to mind are criminal prosecutions, negligence cases, and prisoners' petitions.) The basic problem for the new judge is to develop the breadth he will need. A study of thirty new federal district judges is instructive in this regard.[13] Almost half of this small sample consisted of "lawyer-generalists" before appointment, seven had been state-court judges, four had been United States Attorneys, and only six had been in specialist private practice. Despite the preponderance of generalists, the overwhelming majority "pointed to many areas of federal law that they were expected to be familiar with as a judge but for which their pre-judicial careers had not prepared them."[14]

Here the contrast with congressmen is pronounced. Congressmen often specialize, and more senior and influential congressmen tend to

12. Joel B. Grossman, "Social Backgrounds and Judicial Decision-Making," *Harvard Law Review*, vol. 79 (June 1966), pp. 1551–64.

13. Robert Carp and Russell Wheeler, "Sink or Swim: The Socialization of a Federal District Judge," *Journal of Public Law*, vol. 21 (1972), pp. 359–93. For the formal aspects of judicial socialization (training seminars, for example), see Beverly Blair Cook, "The Socialization of New Federal Judges: Impact on District Court Business," *Washington University Law Quarterly* (Spring 1971), pp. 253–79.

14. Carp and Wheeler, "Sink or Swim: The Socialization of a Federal District Judge," pp. 367–68. See also Glenn R. Winters and Robert E. Allard, "Judicial Selection and Tenure in the United States," in Harry W. Jones, ed., *The Courts, the Public, and the Law Explosion* (Prentice-Hall, 1965), pp. 172–73.

specialize more. The House of Representatives has been a notoriously decentralized body. Much decisionmaking authority has resided in committees. This decentralization has fostered specialization. The growth of seniority and the related increase in safe seats over the last several decades have also permitted increased specialization.[15] Senior congressmen tend to be "primarily concerned with [their] committee work, and rarely develop legislation which is before another committee."[16] There is an informal rule in the House against serving on more than one major committee. "This rule enforces specialization and encourages technical expertise in a small range of issues and reliance on shortcuts in most other areas."[17]

Not only is there specialization in practice; there is also a congressional norm of specialization. In a sampling of members of the House of Representatives, 80 percent agreed that a congressman should be a specialist, and 95 percent agreed that the important work of the House was done in committee.[18] The need for specialization was attributed to the heavy and varied workload of the House.

The same situation, therefore—heavy and varied workload—gives rise to opposite adaptations on the part of judges and congressmen. Where a congressman finds rewards in carving out a special niche for himself and acquiring credentials that differentiate him from his many colleagues, a judge finds rewards in becoming omnicompetent and more like his colleagues.

Much of the difference can be attributed to the parceling out of

15. See Nelson W. Polsby, "The Institutionalization of the House of Representatives," *American Political Science Review*, vol. 62 (March 1968), pp. 144–68. On seniority, see Charles S. Bullock III, "House Careerists: Changing Patterns of Longevity and Attrition," *American Political Science Review*, vol. 66 (December 1972), pp. 1295–1300. For the more limited but still discernible specialization that occurs in some state legislatures, see H. Owen Porter and David A. Leuthold, "Acquiring Legislative Expertise: Appointments to Standing Committees in the States" (paper presented at the 1974 annual meeting of the American Political Science Association; processed); Charles M. Price and Charles G. Bell, "Socializing California Freshman Assemblymen: The Role of Individuals and Legislative Sub-Groups," *Western Political Quarterly*, vol. 23 (March 1970), pp. 166–79, at pp. 172–73.

16. Susan Webb Hammond, "The Changing Role of the Personal Professional Staff in Congressional Decision-Making" (paper presented at the 1974 annual meeting of the American Political Science Association; processed), p. 20.

17. Nelson W. Polsby, *Congress and the Presidency* (2d ed.; Prentice-Hall, 1971), p. 89.

18. Herbert B. Asher, "The Learning of Legislative Norms," *American Political Science Review*, vol. 67 (June 1973), pp. 499–513.

tasks. If judge-shopping by litigants is to be avoided and the goal of equality before the law fostered, then cases must be assigned to judges on a random or near-random basis. Furthermore, judicial decisionmaking at the district-court level is generally solitary decisionmaking: district court cases are ordinarily heard by a single judge. Both of these factors put the accent on omnicompetence, since a judge must be prepared for virtually any kind of case and cannot rely on the expertise of his colleagues. In the court of appeals, cases are also assigned on a random or near-random basis, and although that court sits in panels of three judges, the continuous reshuffling of panel members leaves little room for a division of labor or the development of spheres of expertise.

In Congress, on the other hand, the size of the body and the collegial character of all decisions permits and encourages such a division of labor. No congressman need fear that an issue outside his sphere of competence will be thrust upon him. He need decide nothing alone. Each can confidently rely on expert colleagues to counsel him in fields with which he is not familiar, secure in the knowledge that they will reciprocally consult him in areas of his special competence.

Of course, some congressmen never specialize, and some judges are indeed known as experts on particular legal subjects. But the thrust of the two institutions is quite different. Whereas both congressmen and judges start out as generalists, they tend to move in opposite directions, narrowing down in the one case, broadening out in the other. There is no judicial counterpart to the congressman who has made problems of education or health care his own special preserve. Even if there were, the chances would be slim that a suit raising such issues would find its way to him. On most of the important social policy issues that come to them, judges are bound to be novices.

The contrast with administrators is different once again. Career administrators, especially at the bureau level and below, tend to be highly specialized. Political appointees who serve in the departments and agencies tend, however, to be quite inexperienced in the programs they are expected to manage, and furthermore they often do not stay long enough to master them. Where the judge, with long tenure but short case assignments, is rotated from problem to problem, the political executive, with concentrated assignments but short tenure, is rotated from job to job.

The difference is that the political executive, generalist though he is, has informational resources close at hand that are denied the judge, and, moreover, he relies on them.[19] To be sure, the political appointee may quickly be captured by the career bureaucrats on whom he depends, and they in turn may be beholden to the interests outside their agency which they are to serve or regulate. The point here is that the unusual independence and isolation of judges is attended by the difficulties they have of informing themselves.

The generalist skills of lawyers and judges, it may be argued, are their most valuable attribute in the making of social policy. If expertise were the sole criterion of capacity to make good policy, then the established bureaucracies, interest groups, and legislative committees that possess the expertise would have made it, and there would be no need to involve the courts. Yet we know that the most specialized of all government decisionmakers, the operating bureaus of government departments, often suffer from a limited vision and a propensity to become committed to one and only one version of several alternative policies.[20] The increasing resort to the courts reflects the felt need to break loose from expertise and to gain the benefits of a more distant, uncommitted perspective on policy problems.

Perhaps so, but there is a difference between a fresh perspective and an ignorant one. That judges are generalists means, above all, that they lack information and may also lack the experience and skill to interpret such information as they may receive. On many matters, after all, the expert may know nothing of the particulars before him; what he does know, however, is the general context, and he can locate the issue in its proper place on the landscape. Judges are thus likely to be doubly uninformed, on particulars and on context. This makes the process by which they obtain information crucial, for social policy issues are matters far from the everyday experience of judges.

The adjudication process conspires in a dozen small and large ways to keep the judge ignorant of social context. This may, of course, be regarded as the vestigial influence of the earlier, less ambitious functions of adjudication, structured as it was to make law only as a byproduct of responding to individual conflicts. Vestigial or not, it is with us still, and it will be examined more directly in a moment.

Before doing so, however, there is another attribute of lawyers and

19. Herbert Kaufman, *Administrative Feedback: Monitoring Subordinates' Behavior* (Brookings Institution, 1973), pp. 51–52.
20. See Anthony Downs, *Inside Bureaucracy* (Little, Brown, 1966), pp. 103–07.

judges that requires mention. It is the non-probabilistic character of legal reasoning. This side of legal thinking has been described perceptively, if acerbically, by Victor Thompson, on the basis of his experience in the Office of Price Administration during World War II.[21] Thompson notes the lawyer's propensity to invent hypothetical enforcement problems with no necessary referents in actual behavior, and the related tendency to invest great quantities of time and energy attempting to draft regulations to cover all contingencies (including, presumably, the hypothetical ones). This Thompson sees as behavior stemming from the desire of lawyers to carry out their functions in a "watertight" way, to plan for remote contingencies as if they were searching a title or drafting a will. In fact, he argues, the tendency to concentrate on the small minority of potential violations of law (perhaps 5 percent) was counterproductive in the context of the rationing program. The success of the program turned not on preventing the 5 percent from violating the rules but on making it possible for the other 95 percent to comply with them. The "desire to cover the last possible case"[22] sometimes made it harder to secure compliance in the run of cases, because it imposed additional and complex requirements to facilitate the detection of violators.

To be sure, a contrary argument can also be made. In the rationing program, so heavily dependent on public perception of fairness and equal sacrifice, the conspicuous presence of a small minority of violators could have poisoned the morale of those 95 percent otherwise disposed to comply. But this, it seems to me, is beside the more general point. Legal reasoning does tend to be every-last-case reasoning, rather than run-of-the-cases reasoning. Whatever the rationing problem may have required, most problems of planning and social policy require a mind-set fixed on the behavior of most of the people, most of the time.

I am not sure I can specify the origins of non-probabilistic legal reasoning, and this is not the place to try. But adjudication does seem to reinforce this mode of thought. In litigation, the traditional unit of analysis is the individual case, and standards of individual compliance tend to be absolute. In such a setting, it makes sense to exclude every last possibility of deviation. It is to the process of adjudication that we now turn.

21. Victor Alexander Thompson, *The Regulatory Process in OPA Rationing* (King's Crown Press, 1950), pp. 207–20.
22. Ibid., p. 220.

The Adjudicative Process

Each decision process leaves its distinctive mark on the issues it touches. Each of them snatches a few transactions from the flow of events, brings them to the foreground and blurs others into the background. Each applies its own mode of analysis to these magnified phenomena. Each has its own set of tools that it uses to devise solutions to problems it has analyzed. No one tool kit is exactly the same as any other. Equally important, each decision process decides some things and leaves other things undecided. There are significant and characteristic patterns of non-decision, as there are patterns of decision.

Adjudication, of course, has its own devices for choosing problems, its own habits of analysis, its own criteria of the relevance of phenomena to issues, its own repertoire of solutions. These hallmarks of adjudication have, as I have already suggested, a common origin: judicial preoccupation with the unique case. This admirable preoccupation imparts to the judicial process many of the characteristics that differentiate it in degree or in kind from the legislative and administrative processes, both of which accord greater explicitness and legitimacy to their general policymaking functions.

In what follows, I attempt to elicit some of these distinctive characteristics of adjudication.[23] Adjudication is naturally a large subject, and it will be necessary to speak in rather sweeping, often unqualified, terms. Some of the enumerated consequences of these characteristics for social policymaking amount to propositions that can be stated with a high level of confidence; others are simply inferences from the structure of litigation. There are often explicit comparisons to the legislative and administrative process. I shall have occasion to reappraise the characteristics of adjudication in a more refined way and to make a few more

23. There have been a few previous attempts at partial inventories. See, e.g., Robert H. Jackson, *The Struggle for Judicial Supremacy* (Knopf, 1941), chap. 9 ("Government by Lawsuit"); Richard S. Wells and Joel B. Grossman, "The Concept of Judicial Policy-Making," *Journal of Public Law*, vol. 15 (Spring 1966), pp. 286–310; Philip L. Bereano, "Courts as Institutions for Assessing Technology" (paper presented at 1972 annual meeting of the American Association for the Advancement of Science; processed); J. Woodford Howard, Jr., "Adjudication Considered as a Process of Conflict Resolution: A Variation on Separation of Powers," *Journal of Public Law*, vol. 18 (Spring 1969), pp. 339–70; and Lon L. Fuller's still-unpublished classic, "The Forms and Limits of Adjudication" (ca. 1961; processed).

comparative judgments in the concluding chapter, after examining the adjudicative process at work at rather close range.

1. *Adjudication is focused.* The usual question before the judge is simply: Does one party have a *right?* Does another party have a *duty?* This should be contrasted with the question before a "planner," whether legislative or bureaucratic: What are the *alternatives?* These are quite different ways of casting problems for decision. For the judge, alternatives may be relevant, but they are relevant primarily to the subsequent issue of what "remedies" are appropriate to redress "wrongs" done to those who possess "rights." In other words, the initial focus on rights tends to defer the question of alternatives to a later stage of the inquiry and to consider it a purely technical question.

As this suggests, the initial focus on rights is also a serious impediment to the analysis of costs, for, in principle at least, if rights exist they are not bounded by considerations of cost. If a person possesses a right, he possesses it whatever the cost.

Costing may, to be sure, creep into litigation through the back door, in a variety of disguises. One of the masks it wears is the "balancing of convenience" that occurs in deciding whether an injunction will issue and to what activities it will extend. Judges, confronted with a plaintiff's assertion that he has a right to a hearing before a governmental body acts in a matter affecting his interests, have been known to inquire how many such additional hearings would be required if the plaintiff's right to one were recognized and how much disruption that might inflict on the work of the governmental body. But they tend to regard such questions as tangential and, if pressed on this front, are likely to recoil from a judgment that would make rights stand or fall on considerations of such an order.

Adjudication, then, is narrow in a double sense. The format of decision inhibits the presentation of an array of alternatives and the explicit matching of benefits to costs.

The contrast between rights and alternatives suggests the much broader framework in which non-adjudicative policymakers function. This is best seen in what the lawyers and judges call remedies. As indicated above, there is some flexibility in tailoring a remedy to the nature of the wrong it is designed to correct, but for the most part this flexibility extends only to the terms and timing of the injunction to be issued. For, paradoxically enough, though they have the fewest coercive resources at their command, the courts have only the option of issuing coercive orders: injunctions that direct parties to do or refrain from doing something.

Legislators and administrators, on the other hand, have a wider range of tools in their kit. They may resort to the same kinds of sanctions judges invoke, or they may use taxation, incentives and subsidies of various kinds, interventions in the marketplace, the establishment of new organizations or the takeover of old ones, or a number of other ways of seeking to attain their goals. The judiciary, having no budget (save for administrative expenses), no power to tax[24] or to create new institutions, has much less ability to experiment or to adjust its techniques to the problems it confronts. The courts can forbid, require, or permit activity, but in general they cannot permit activity conditionally (for example, by taxing something so as to discourage it). Many of the tools that are favored by economists in particular are missing from the judicial black bag.

There is a caveat that must be added, however. Although judges do not have the power to tax or spend, sometimes the decrees they issue have the effect of requiring expenditure. Their decisions can therefore get caught up in the budgetary process, and may stimulate exercises of the appropriation power. Whether a decree will be complied with by spending or not spending and, if by spending, by reallocating a fixed sum or by expanding the total sum available, affects in a fundamental way the outcome of judicial action. Significantly, however, the choice of this response remains outside the control of the court.

2. *Adjudication is piecemeal.* The lawsuit is the supreme example of incremental decisionmaking. As such, it shares the advantages and the defects of the species. The outcome of litigation may give the illusion of a decisive victory, but the victory is often on a very limited point. The judge's power to decide extends, in principle, only to those issues that are before him. Related issues, not raised by the instant dispute, must generally await later litigation. So it is at least in traditional conception.

Incrementalism may be entirely appropriate for some kinds of policy. For others, it may be simply too slow or too disjointed.

Incrementalism is, of course, well suited to decisionmaking when information is scarce. Since adequate information is so often scarce when decisions must be confronted, many decisions are of an incremental

24. But see *Butz* v. *City of Muscatine*, 8 Wall. (75 U.S.) 575 (1869).

character, regardless of where they are made. The less the change imposed by the decision, the less the potential error. With courts, this is an
especially important consideration. Judges do not choose their cases and
so may often have to act in matters in which they lack complete confidence in their information base. Step-by-step adjustment can thus be
viewed as a protective measure responding to the limited control courts
have over the choice of issues they decide. I shall say more about these
features of adjudication later in this chapter.

Related to limited information is the enhanced ability to backtrack
when just a few steps have been taken: "at the heart of incrementalism
lies the notion of reversibility."[25]

In the case of courts, however, reversibility presents some very special
problems. Courts do sometimes alter a course they have recently embarked on, but the change is not generally in response to new information
about the consequences of the course chosen. Courts are not possessed
of great ability to detect the need for backtracking—a point I shall also
return to later.

Moreover, there are special inhibitions on changing judicial course.
These derive principally from the doctrine of precedent. However innovative or experimental it is in fact, adjudicative policymaking is sancti-
fied as law, which is in principle permanent. The courts, therefore, have
only limited ability to admit candidly the tentative nature of conclusions they have reached. To say that a person or group "has a right" is to
take a position difficult to reverse. Courts are on this account loath to
give the appearance of fickleness that might attend unrestrained willingness to change course whenever circumstances seem to require
change.[26] In constitutional cases, these inhibitions are less prominent,
but they do not disappear altogether, so that when change comes it often
takes the form of engrafting qualifications onto old decisions rather than
starting fresh. Even judicial backtracking tends to be decremental.

The net result of these special limitations both of doctrine and of lack
of information is that the theoretical advantages of reversibility on the
basis of new factual material are not usually realized in judicial prac-

25. Daniel Metlay, "Error Correction in Bureaucracies" (unpublished talk, Brookings Institution, in manuscript, 1975), p. 1.

26. Judges who place a high value on the stability and predictability of legal
rules—"it is more important that the law be settled than that it be settled right,"
is one conventional way of saying this—may be giving expression to the fear of
fickleness.

tice. Changes of direction do, of course, occur, but only rarely do they occur when a court has both the information and the ability to admit in retrospect the failure of a given course of policy to affect behavior as intended.

At the same time, the piecemeal quality of judicial decisions has a number of important negative effects. Piecemeal decisions unsettle old patterns without providing unambiguous new patterns to which expectations can conform. Time and again, public and private decisionmakers have both underread and underreacted to and overread and overreacted to the implications of a new trend of Supreme Court decisions—only to find later that their adaptations had been, respectively, insufficient or excessive.

Examples are legion. *Watkins* v. *United States*[27] promised a new day in vindicating the rights of individuals against congressional investigating committees. Two years later, *Barenblatt* v. *United States*[28] brought an early dusk to the day that had just dawned. *Stanley* v. *Georgia*[29] seemed to make similar promises regarding obscenity, but the promises were not redeemed.[30] On the other hand, *Escobedo* v. *Illinois*[31] soon proved to be only a prologue to more far-reaching doctrinal development.[32] Discerning whether a decision is an opening wedge or a blind alley requires prophetic skills of a high order.

Piecemeal decisions also isolate artificially what in the real world is merged. It is a truism that everything is related to everything else, and of course this cliché proves too much, because no institution can or should attempt to deal with everything simultaneously. But the litigation setting creates the danger of doing too little at one time and thus magnifies the possibility of unanticipated consequences that a more comprehensive view might perceive and attempt to limit or control.[33]

---

27. 354 U.S. 178 (1957).

28. 360 U.S. 109 (1959). Also compare *Uphaus* v. *Wyman*, 360 U.S. 72 (1959), with *Sweezy* v. *New Hampshire*, 354 U.S. 234 (1957).

29. 394 U.S. 557 (1969).

30. Cf. *Miller* v. *California*, 413 U.S. 15 (1973); *Paris Adult Theatre* v. *Slaton*, 413 U.S. 49 (1973).

31. 378 U.S. 478 (1964).

32. *Miranda* v. *Arizona*, 384 U.S. 436 (1966).

33. Metlay, "Error Correction in Bureaucracies," p. 10, puts the point well: "A decisionmaking strategy which tends to fragment complex decisions into simpler components is also error prone. Such a partitioning may assume a degree of decomposability which does not exist. This may arise, for example, when the values of a

One aspect of this needs particular elaboration. Piecemeal decisions result in the seriatim consideration of policy priorities. The judge cannot frame his issue in terms of more health care versus less prison reform, though (depending on whether and how executives and legislators respond to his decision) this may be the exact result of a decision that purports to make choices in one of these areas or the other. Again, the focus on rights obscures the ultimate nature of the social policy choices being made, and so does the judges' lack of budgetary authority or responsibility. Unlike legislators, against whom some of the same criticism has been leveled (regarding the congressional budgetary process in particular), judges never need to tally up the expenditures required by their decisions and agree on a total taxing and spending figure. When they deal with issues in a series, their treatment of each is truly discrete.

3. *Courts must act when litigants call.* The passivity of the judicial process is one of its most prominent characteristics. Judges sit to hear disputes brought to them by parties; they do not initiate action. This makes the sequencing of judicially ordered change dependent on the capricious timing of litigants rather than the planning of a public body. It also makes it difficult to ascertain the extent to which the situation of the litigants faithfully represents or illustrates the dimensions of the problem they bring to court.

So central is this aspect of the judicial process that some writers have viewed it as a definitional property of adjudication: "a judge of an organized body is a man appointed by that body to determine duties and the corresponding rights upon application of persons claiming those rights. It is the fact that such application must be made to him, which distinguishes a judge from an administrative officer."[34] Courts, a critic has said, "are like defective clocks; they have to be shaken to set them going."[35]

It is, of course, the impartiality of the judges that restricts them to a passive, responsive role. If a judge were to play a part in initiating proceedings, that might imply that he had "a certain commitment and often

---

trade-off problem are treated independently. In such a case, the outcomes tend to be very loosely integrated or coordinated. The substantial interactions between the separate components of the policy often go unresolved. One would expect that the system would be prone to gradually evolving crisis in that problem area."

34. John Chipman Gray, *The Nature and Sources of the Law* (2d ed.; Macmillan, 1927), quoted in Fuller, "The Forms and Limits of Adjudication," p. 26.

35. Quoted in Fuller, "The Forms and Limits of Adjudication," p. 26.

a theory of what occurred."[36] With such preconceptions, how could he sit in judgment?

In addition, courts do not purport to possess the administrative machinery to know when "something is wrong"—indeed, wrong enough to require their intervention. For this reason, it is frequently said that courts are "poorly equipped to perform early warning functions since there are no motivated parties to clearly present the issue" before the harm is certain to occur.[37] Litigation generally occurs after the grievance has crystallized, when the harm is about to be inflicted and it is too late to plan to avert the unwanted occurrence. Because litigation is often a last resort, much may already have transpired. Every so often, however, a grievance triggers a lawsuit very early, before the shape of the conflict between the parties is clear. For such cases, the federal courts devised a cautionary rule, now much diluted, against entertaining controversies that have not yet "ripened."[38] Either way, adjudication proceeds by fits and starts, now too early, now too late, only occasionally well timed.

The sequence of judicial decisions also depends on the chance order in which grievances find their way to court. Theorists of social change have noted the importance of having some changes precede others.[39] The stability of the British polity has often been attributed in part to sequencing: England became a nation before she had a state; on the Continent the reverse was more common. The decisions of the Warren Court on the rights of criminal suspects have perhaps made easier police acceptance of the rights of political demonstrators; it seems doubtful that decisions on the rights of demonstrators would have had much effect on the police view of the rights of criminal suspects. Some changes, in other words, may pave the way for others, and the resulting social amalgam may depend heavily on the order in which issues are faced. The point here is simply that courts control their calendar but not their agenda. Accordingly, the sequencing of innovation is to a large extent left to the vagaries of private initiative.

To be sure, courts do occasionally signal their readiness to entertain

36. Ibid., p. 27.

37. Bereano, "Courts as Institutions for Assessing Technology," p. 5. See also Wells and Grossman, "The Concept of Judicial Policy-Making."

38. See *Poe* v. *Ullman*, 367 U.S. 497 (1961).

39. See Wilbert Moore, *Social Change* (2d ed.; Prentice-Hall, 1974); Leonard Binder and others, *Crises and Sequences in Political Development* (Princeton University Press, 1971).

an issue. But although the entry of the courts into new fields may stimulate the filing of new cases or new appeals, it does not necessarily generate cases in any particular order.[40] Lawyers, of course, can be acutely
aware of this and sometimes try to insure that the most favorable case
in the most favorable court reaches its destination ahead of less favorable cases in less favorable courts, pushing in the former, stalling in the
latter.[41] The most favorable case, of course, is not just the one that has
the most attractive factual setting; it may also be the one that seems to
require the least innovation, the smallest doctrinal jump, to achieve the
desired result.[42] It is much easier to build a bridge over a stream than
over a river.

But if lawyers know this—and the incremental, precedential character of the judicial process gives them ample reason to know it—it does
not follow that they can generally do anything much about it. Although
judges are dependent on parties and their lawyers to bring lawsuits,
parties and lawyers are dependent on judges to decide them. The tempo
of decision may be affected by efforts of counsel to speed it up, but in
the end there is no hurrying a judge determined to reflect long and hard
on his problem and no stalling a judge determined to act on a sense of
urgency.

Quite apart from this lack of control, there is typically a lack of coordination among cases as well. Lawyers see their cases as essentially
individual matters, and they are generally unwilling to collaborate to
the point of subordinating their cases for the sake of insuring that a
better case is brought or appealed. Where organizations are involved,
there is the added problem of gaining constituency authorization to
coordinate in this manner.[43] There have, of course, been exceptions, but
these generally occur where one organization is in control of litigation
in a whole field. Otherwise, communication becomes too difficult, discipline is impossible to impose, and targets of opportunity are hard to
resist. The National Association for the Advancement of Colored People

40. A more specific invitation, transparently issued in the course of a judicial
opinion, may elicit a case raising the exact issue to which the invitation refers, but
such invitations are rare and in any case do not generally alter the order of cases
apart from the one to which they refer.

41. See, e.g., Paul A. Freund, *The Supreme Court of the United States: Its
Business, Purposes, and Performance* (Meridian Books, 1961), pp. 145–70.

42. For an example of this sequencing problem, see John P. MacKenzie, "Testing the Right to Treatment," *Washington Post*, October 27, 1974.

43. Nathan Hakman, "Lobbying the Supreme Court—An Appraisal of 'Political
Science Folklore,'" *Fordham Law Review*, vol. 35 (1966), pp. 15–50.

embarked on a concerted and successful campaign to invalidate ordinances prescribing racial segregation in housing. When this was accomplished, the organization then proceeded to attack in the courts racially restrictive covenants. There was careful planning in the choice of cases, issues, and jurisdictions.[44] This concerted action could succeed because in the first half of this century only the NAACP had the interest and resources to operate in the area of housing segregation at all. A proliferation of diverse civil rights organizations might easily have undone its careful planning. Where there are no organizations operating or, on the other hand, several, coordination becomes very difficult.[45] For these reasons, most cases are not carefully stage-managed in relation to others; and, in the few instances where they are, usually "an unmanaged case gets there first," often the "wrong one."[46] For the most part, therefore, the sequencing of cases remains haphazard.

The passive role of the courts in choosing and deciding cases has another important consequence. Judicial decision becomes a chance occurrence, with no guarantee that the litigants are representative of the universe of problems their case purports to present. In fact, the guarantees are all the other way. As a matter of litigation strategy, plaintiffs' lawyers are likely to bring not the most representative case but the most extreme case of discrimination, of fraud, of violation of statute, of abuse of discretion, and so on.

That this is no idle concern is shown by, among others, two cases discussed earlier. In *Lau* v. *Nichols*,[47] the Supreme Court decided issues of language in education that may affect millions of Spanish-speaking children in the United States; the Court did so in a case brought by Chinese-speaking pupils. Furthermore, the record in *Lau* showed that the school system had done virtually nothing to assist pupils unable to function in classes run in English. Was the performance of other school systems equally unambiguous? Likewise, in *Griggs* v. *Duke Power Com-*

---

44. Clement E. Vose, "The NAACP's Legal Strategy to Overturn Restrictive Covenants in Housing," in Herbert Jacob, ed., *Law, Politics, and the Federal Courts* (Little, Brown, 1967), pp. 5–16. See also Vose, *Caucasians Only* (University of California Press, 1959).

45. For an illustration of what looks like interorganizational criticism regarding failure to coordinate strategy in choosing issues to litigate, see *"Kalur v. Resor,* Water Quality and NEPA's Application to EPA," *Environmental Law Reporter,* vol. 2 (March 1972), pp. 10025–28. I am indebted to Richard Liroff for this reference.

46. Hakman, "Lobbying the Supreme Court," p. 37.

47. 414 U.S. 563 (1973).

pany,[48] the Court ruled on the validity of aptitude tests not used for a discriminatory purpose but having the effect of disqualifying disproportionate numbers of minority applicants for jobs. The Court faced this question, however, in a case involving a company with a history of racial discrimination in employment, a company that had added the aptitude test requirement on the very date the law against employment discrimination became effective. The validity of aptitude testing for all employers was thus decided on a factual record evoking suspicion about the motives of the particular employer before the Court. Could the Court allow the employer to "get away with" its machinations?

Cases like *Lau* and *Griggs* evoke in judges the urge to "do something," whether or not the cases are representative. Skillful trial lawyers are alert for opportunities to elicit just this kind of damning background evidence, and experienced appellate lawyers are eager to sprinkle their briefs with such material in order to make the case appear to be one that calls out for action.

It is not, however, only the worst cases that come to court. Litigants with the inclination and resources to bring suit may give the court an equally incomplete but more favorable view of the practices they complain of. Rather than state this point abstractly, it is better to illustrate it by reference to two studies of housing and employment cases brought to commissions against discrimination.[49] Both commissions had adopted a quasi-judicial approach to their business, acting on the basis of individual complaints, much as courts do. For that reason, the distribution of their cases is of general interest.

In 1958, New York City enacted a fair housing ordinance. The ordinance had a wide sweep. It applied to 70 percent of all residential housing in the city. Between 1958 and 1961, 685 complaints were brought to the commission set up to administer the law. The vast majority (81 percent) of complainants were blacks, although there is reason to believe that Puerto Ricans, among others, also suffered housing discrimination. What is more striking about the composition of the cases, however, is that they were brought disproportionately by young, middle-class blacks. Thirty-seven percent of the black complainants were col-

48. 401 U.S. 424 (1971).

49. Harold Goldblatt and Florence Cromien, "The Effective Reach of the Fair Housing Practices Law of the City of New York," *Social Problems*, vol. 9 (Spring 1962), pp. 365–70; Leon H. Mayhew, *Law and Equal Opportunity: A Study of the Massachusetts Commission Against Discrimination* (Harvard University Press, 1968).

lege graduates, 22 percent had some college education, and another 32 percent were high school graduates. In other words, 91 percent had at least a high school diploma. As these educational data imply, the majority of black complainants were employed in managerial, professional, or other white collar occupations.

In addition, 56 percent of the complainants already resided in areas 75 percent or more white, and 94 percent of the housing they sought was in such areas.[50] Given these figures, it is clear that the cases brought under the New York City law by no means typified or represented the dimensions of the housing discrimination problem. It goes without saying that general solutions devised on the basis of the particular cases brought, while they might be quite appropriate for handling the problems of upwardly mobile blacks who wished to move from one white residential area to another, might be wholly misguided and inapt for the problems of the black working class in search of decent housing.

Much the same results emerge from a study of the equally passive, judicial enforcement policy of the Massachusetts Commission Against Discrimination. Again, housing complaints generally involved areas overwhelmingly white in composition, more than two-thirds of them 97 percent or more white.[51] The complainants were 91.5 percent middle-class.[52] Housing cases were brought "primarily by middle-class Negroes wishing to escape the ghetto and not by working-class Negroes seeking to improve ghetto conditions. . . ."[53]

Employment complaints in Massachusetts were skewed in a different direction, but skewed nonetheless. They did not mirror the prevailing patterns of employment discrimination. "Rather, the complaints reflected the current structure of Negro employment; they tended to be directed toward areas where racial barriers had already fallen."[54] The average firm against which a complaint was filed already employed 6.6 percent blacks, twice the black percentage of the area's population; and one-fourth of the firms against which complaints were filed employed at least 10 percent blacks.[55] Many individual firms and whole industrial sectors practicing the most blatant discrimination were not targets of

50. Goldblatt and Cromien, "The Effective Reach of the Fair Housing Practices Law of the City of New York," p. 369.

51. Mayhew, *Law and Equal Opportunity*, p. 167.

52. Ibid., p. 155.

53. Ibid., p. 165.

54. Ibid., p. 159.

55. Ibid., p. 165.

complaints; presumably black job seekers were not informed of opportunities in these firms and therefore did not apply for them.

A process that left the initiative in filing complaints to victims of discrimination thus yielded a disproportionate number of complaints against the very firms that did not discriminate, in effect practically immunizing the worst offenders from commission action. Antidiscrimination policy formulated on a case-by-case basis to deal with employers who already had hired minority employees would naturally tend to underestimate the dimensions of the problem and might, in addition, emphasize strategies quite inappropriate for breaking the patterns of discrimination practiced by the all-white firms. Remedies devised on the basis of the cases represented by the complaints might also, if they were effective, exacerbate the cleavage between segregated and integrated occupational sectors. Private initiative neither turned up a fair sample of the affected category of parties aggrieved nor provided an accurate picture of the social problem it was the commission's task to deal with. Distortion prevailed on both fronts.

There is, in short, no assurance that litigants constitute a random sample of the class of cases that might be affected by a decree. Because courts respond only to the cases that come their way, they make general law from what may be very special situations. Courts see the tip of the iceberg as well as the bottom of the barrel. The law they make may be law for the worst case or for the best, but it is not necessarily law for the mean or modal case.

The unrepresentative character of litigants raises another problem. Unlike legislation, litigation is not a finely tuned device for registering intensities of preference. Bargaining and compromise—at least bargaining and compromise beyond the confines of the individual case—are more difficult because of the adversary setting and the limited number of interested participants. Dependent as it is on an uncompromisingly partisan presentation, the adversary process is not conducive to the ordering of preferences. It compels the litigants to argue favorable positions with a vigor that may be out of proportion to their actual preferences and that may therefore mislead the judge; in any case, their preferences may have little support in the wider social group the litigants ostensibly represent.[56] In ascertaining the configuration and intensity of public preferences, the judge is, for the most part, left to roam at large.

56. To some extent, the device of the brief *amicus curiae* can mitigate the potential unrepresentativeness of the actual litigants, but *amici* do not have the

This problem is naturally exacerbated by the deliberately imposed isolation of judges from their communities. The prohibition on judges discussing pending cases with individuals or groups interested in the outcome is obviously designed to insure the independence and impartiality of the judiciary.[57] But what fosters the detachment of judges is necessarily at odds with their sensitivity to social forces.

4. *Fact-finding in adjudication is ill-adapted to the ascertainment of social facts.* The fact that judges function at some distance from the social milieu from which their cases spring puts them at an initial disadvantage in understanding the dimensions of social policy problems. The focused, piecemeal quality of adjudication implies that judicial decisions tend to be abstracted from social contexts broader than the immediate setting in which the litigation arises, and, as already indicated, the potentially unrepresentative character of the litigants makes it hazardous to generalize from their situation to the wider context.

The judicial fact-finding process carries forward this abstraction of the case from its more general social context. To make this clear, it is necessary to distinguish between two kinds of facts: historical facts and social facts. *Historical facts* are the events that have transpired between the parties to a lawsuit.[58] *Social facts* are the recurrent patterns of behavior on which policy must be based. Historical facts, as I use the term, have occasionally been called "adjudicative facts" by lawyers, and social facts have also been called "legislative facts." I avoid these terms because of the preconceptions they carry and the division of labor they imply. Nonetheless, by whatever designation they are known, these are two distinct kinds of facts, and a process set up to establish the one is not necessarily adequate to ascertain the other.[59]

---

ability to shape the issues or the factual record. In this they typically take a back seat to the parties. *Amicus* participation cannot redress the deficiencies caused by unrepresentative litigants, among other reasons because *amicus* participation so often begins on appeal, after the record is frozen.

57. On the need for certain elites to restrict their interactions with outsiders, see Downs, *Inside Bureaucracy,* p. 236. On the isolation of judges in particular, see Carp and Wheeler, "Sink or Swim."

58. I include in this any other factual matter subsisting between the parties and relevant to their controversy, even though not strictly an historical event, such as a status (e.g., trustee).

59. I leave to one side, of course, the difficult epistemological problem of whether past events can ever be "ascertained," "reconstructed," or "verified," or whether all such efforts are actually creative in character. Important as this issue may be, it raises problems of a completely different order from those presented by the difficulties of ascertaining social facts.

Social facts are nothing new in litigation. Courts have always had to make assumptions or inferences about general conditions that would guide their decisions. The broader the issue, the more such imponderables there are. The breadth of the issues in constitutional law has always made it a fertile field for empirical speculation. Does a civil service law barring alleged subversives from public employment have a "chilling effect" on free speech?[60] Is the use of third-degree methods by the police sufficiently widespread to justify a prophylactic rule that would exclude from evidence even some confessions that are not coerced?[61] Does pornography stimulate the commission of sex crimes, or does it provide cathartic release for those who might otherwise commit such crimes?[62]

Constitutional law is a fertile field, but it is not the only field in which such questions arise. If a court refuses to enforce against a bankrupt corporation an "unconscionable contract" for the repayment of borrowed money, will that make it more difficult for firms needing credit to obtain it and perhaps precipitate more such bankruptcies?[63] Does it encourage carelessness and thus undercut a prime purpose of the law of negligence if an automobile driver, a shopkeeper, or a theater owner is permitted to insure himself against liability inflicted as a result of his own fault?

These are, all of them, behavioral questions. They share an important characteristic: no amount of proof about the conduct of the individual litigants involved in a civil service, confession, obscenity, bankruptcy, or negligence case can provide answers to these probabilistic questions about the behavior of whole categories of people. As a matter of fact, proof of one kind of fact can be misleading about the other. What is true in the individual case may be false in the generality of cases, and vice versa. The judicial process, however, makes it much easier to learn reliably about the individual case than about the run of cases.

The increasing involvement of the courts in social policy questions has increased the number and importance of social fact questions in litigation. As the courts move into new, specialized, unfamiliar policy areas, they are confronted by a plethora of questions about human behavior that are beyond their ability to answer on the basis of common

60. *Keyishian v. Board of Regents,* 385 U.S. 589 (1967).

61. *Miranda v. Arizona,* 384 U.S. 436 (1966).

62. See the contributions to the debate over pornography in *The Public Interest,* no. 22 (Winter 1971).

63. *In the Matter of Elkins Dell Manufacturing Company,* 253 F. Supp. 864 (E.D. Pa. 1966).

experience or the usual modicum of expert testimony. A few examples, drawn from a social science manual for lawyers, will make the point:

Do the attrition rates for different racial groups applying for admission to a union apprenticeship program suggest a pattern of racial discrimination?

How would the elimination of a local bus system through bankruptcy affect low income people and the elderly poor in particular?

How are different income groups and communities of varying sizes differentially affected by the formula allocation of General Revenue Sharing funds?[64]

Obtaining answers to such behavioral questions has become exigent, and not only because the interstices in which courts make fresh policy keep expanding. If a judge or a jury makes a mistake of fact relating only to the case before it, "the effects of the mistake are quarantined."[65] But if the factual materials form the foundation for a general policy, the consequences cannot be so confined.

Traditionally, the courts have been modest about their competence to ascertain social facts and have tried to leave this function primarily to other agencies. They have shielded themselves by applying doctrines that have the effect of deferring to the fact-finding abilities of legislatures and administrative bodies, to avoid having to establish social facts in the course of litigation.

The reasons for this general modesty are well grounded. There is tension between two different judicial responsibilities: deciding the particular case and formulating a general policy. Two different kinds of fact-finding processes are required for these two different functions. The adversary system of presentation and the rules of evidence were both developed for the former, and they leave much to be desired for the latter.

In general, the parties can be depended upon to elicit all of the relevant historical facts, through the ordinary use of testimony and documentary evidence, and the judge or jury can be presumed competent to evaluate that evidence. Social facts, on the other hand, may not be elicited at all by the parties, almost surely not fully, and the competence of the decisionmaker in this field cannot be taken for granted.

64. Leonard Goodman and others, *Sources and Uses of Social and Economic Data: A Manual for Lawyers* (Washington, D.C.: Bureau of Social Science Research, 1973; processed), pp. xii–xiii.

65. Henry M. Hart, Jr., and Albert M. Sacks, "The Legal Process: Basic Problems in the Making and Application of Law" (tentative ed.; Harvard University, 1958; processed), p. 384.

These deficiencies of the adversary process have led to proposals for the employment of outside experts as consultants to the courts. So far relatively few impartial experts have been appointed, and the proof of social facts has largely been left to the traditional adversary method.

Expert testimony is the conventional way for the litigants to prove social facts, but its deficiencies are considerable. The experts are usually partisans, employed by the parties, and their conclusions tend to reflect that status. If the parties provide a skewed picture of the problem they purport to represent, their expert witness may do the same. Finally, reliance on expert witnesses hired by the parties makes the judge the prisoner of the parties' definition of the issues of social fact that are involved.

The rules of evidence are equally inapt for the verification of social facts. They are geared to the search for truth between the parties, not to the search for truth in general. Understandably, there is a prohibition on the introduction of hearsay evidence. Courts must act on what happened, not on what someone said happened. The emphasis in judicial fact-finding on choosing between conflicting versions of events by assessing the credibility of witnesses also places a premium on requiring witnesses to have firsthand knowledge of the events about which they testify. Sensible though the hearsay rule may be, however, it makes the ascertainment of scientific facts of all kinds, including social science, very difficult. Books and articles constitute inadmissible hearsay; they are not alive and cannot be cross-examined.[66] Consequently, when behavioral materials are introduced into evidence, it is usually pursuant to some exception to the hearsay rule.

The relevant exceptions are several, and we shall consider them in the concluding chapter.[67] Some of them, it will be clear, give undue advantage to some kinds of materials at the expense of others. A good deal of material relevant to social fact issues tends to be sifted out by the hearsay rule, despite its exceptions.

The use of expert testimony involves another kind of exception. Duly qualified experts, unlike ordinary witnesses, need not confine themselves to testifying about facts. They may also state their opinion, which may be nothing more than a guess or a bias. Yet the studies on which

66. See Edwin W. Patterson, *Law in a Scientific Age* (Columbia University Press, 1963), pp. 17–18.

67. For a concise summary, see Goodman, *Sources and Uses of Social and Economic Data*, pp. I-1–5.

their opinion may be based remain inadmissible as hearsay (though they may be introduced to impeach an expert's opinion).

All of these cumbersome devices tend to make the judge dependent on secondary interpretations of the relevant empirical material and to discourage him from going directly to the material itself. As we shall see in later chapters, filtered knowledge has its problems.

If new rules and mechanisms do develop to aid in informing the courts about social facts, further problems will arise. The courts may have to administer a dual system of evidence—one part for historical facts, another for social facts—and there is the problem of what might be called contamination. Evidence introduced for one purpose may, as it often does, spill over to infect the other set of issues. Compartmental-ization to prevent contamination is one of the hardest jobs a judge must perform. This particular problem suggests again the underlying tension between deciding the litigants' case and making general policy.

How have social fact issues been handled by the courts in practice? They have been handled in much the same way that the rules of evidence and the adversary system have been adapted to accommodate social facts: by neglect or by improvisation.

A first, quite common way is to ignore them or to assume, sometimes rightly, sometimes wrongly, that the litigants' case is representative. This is patently inadequate.

A second way, more sophisticated but not always adequate, is to derive behavioral expectations from what might be called the logical structure of incentives. That is, courts may consciously formulate rules of law calculated to appeal to the interests of "legal man" in rather the same way as the marketplace is thought to appeal to the interests of "economic man." A rule is designed to shape (more than follow) the behavior of all those calculative creatures who wish to gain its benefits and avoid its penalties. The problem with this, of course, is that it is deductive rather than empirical. There is no assurance that the judge has correctly formulated the structure of incentives: his logic and the logic of the actors affected by rules of law may begin from different premises. The problem of ascertaining existing behavior is then com-pounded by the problem of forecasting future behavior.

A third way of dealing with social facts is to go outside the record of the case in search of information. This is what Mr. Justice Murphy did when he sent questionnaires to police forces in thirty-eight cities in order to determine the relationship between the admissibility of illegally obtained evidence and police training in the law of search and seizure.[68] The same impulse has sometimes moved other judges, restless in their ignorance of behavioral fact, to consult experts of their acquaintance, as Judge Charles Clark, then former Dean of the Yale Law School, consulted the Yale University organist about a music copyright case that was pending before him.[69] These attempts, primitive as they are, show the existence of a deeply felt need rather than a method of satisfying it.

What these examples also suggest is that the need for empirical data is often not even sensed until the case is on appeal. The traditional formulation of causes of action rarely incorporates social facts as an element of proof. When behavioral facts are implicitly incorporated (for example, "reasonable care of a prudent man under the circumstances"), these standards are often not met by evidence but left to the decision-maker to judge from his own experience.

The law thus tends to slight the need for behavioral material in a number of ways. In practice, this means that the option of utilizing such material falls on counsel. Generally, public-interest lawyers have been much more assiduous about introducing evidence of social facts than have other lawyers, and it is they who have often compiled voluminous records of expert testimony and memoranda. We shall peruse one such record in chapter 4.

That the process of adjudication places the emphasis heavily on the accurate ascertainment of historical facts, while it neglects and renders it difficult to prove social facts, is, of course, exactly what might be expected from its traditional responsibilities. That is to say, the fact-finding capability of the courts is likely to lag behind the functions they are increasingly required to perform.

To argue that this problem of capability exists is still to say nothing of the materials on which proof of social facts might be based. The problems here are considerable. There may be no studies that cast light on the issue in litigation. If there are, the behavioral issue may be framed in a way quite inappropriate for litigation. Studies may, of course, be specially commissioned for the purposes of the lawsuit. Even if the potential bias of such studies is overcome, the constraints of time and resources may dictate research methods much less than satisfying. On

68. See *Wolf* v. *Colorado,* 338 U.S. 25, 44–46 (1949) (dissenting opinion).

69. See Marvin Schick, *Learned Hand's Court* (Johns Hopkins Press, 1970), pp. 126–29.

large issues, existing data are likely to be fragmentary. Then the question becomes one of generalization from partial or tentative findings, or one of drawing inferences from proxies. This is no place for a full-scale consideration of the imperfect fit between law and social science. It is enough to say here that the problems of social science do not disappear in litigation, but are instead compounded by the litigation setting, the different ways in which lawyers and social scientists ask questions, and the time constraint.

This last point needs to be underscored. As I have said earlier, litigation is, for the most part, a mandatory decision process. Courts do not choose their cases; cases choose their courts. With certain exceptions, a case properly brought must be decided. Whereas a legislator or administrator has some freedom to shy away from issues on which his quantum of ignorance is too great to give him confidence that he can act sensibly, courts are not afforded quite the same latitude. That courts have difficulty finding and absorbing social facts in the context of a largely mandatory decision process puts them at a comparative disadvantage in social policymaking.

5. *Adjudication makes no provision for policy review.* As the judicial process neglects social facts in favor of historical facts, so, too, does it slight what might be called *consequential facts.* Judges base their decisions on *antecedent facts,* on behavior that antedates the litigation. Consequential facts—those that relate to the impact of a decision on behavior—are equally important but much neglected.

This, of course, is a result of the focus on rights and duties rather than alternatives. Litigation is geared to rectifying the injustices of the past and present rather than to planning for some change to occur in the future. The very notion of planning is alien to adjudication.

In the judicial process, the modification of behavior still tends to be treated as a question of compliance or enforcement. Difficulties of adjusting behavior to new rules of law are mainly regarded as being relevant to the nature of the remedy that is appropriate, as I indicated earlier. In the simpler world of the common law—in which the adjudicative process is still firmly rooted—compliance was merely a question of obedience. Ability to comply could be taken for granted. The judicial process has not really faced up to the issue of compliance costs in social policy cases. Still less has it considered the problem of unintended consequences of decisions.

Now it might be said with considerable justification that all decisionmaking processes are unduly based on what has happened in the past and insufficiently attuned to what might happen in the future, even to what might happen as a result of their action. Furthermore, there is nothing particularly unusual about the character of the unanticipated consequences produced by judicial decisions. A court decision may eliminate one obstacle to eligibility for welfare, only to cause welfare officials to tighten their enforcement of other eligibility requirements, thereby reducing the total number of beneficiaries.[70] A new building code that upgrades housing requirements in the interests of health and safety may have similar effects. It may contract the supply of decent housing, just as strict code enforcement by administrative authorities may induce landlords to abandon their properties.[71] The courts have no monopoly on unintended consequences.

There is no need to take issue with these points as general propositions, for what is at issue is not the propensity of decisions to have untoward effects. The point is rather that the courts suffer from an unusual poverty of resources to minimize the incidence of unintended consequences in advance and especially to detect and correct them once they occur.

The inability of courts to prevent unintended consequences flows in part from the allocation of work discussed earlier. The assignment of cases on a rotational basis impedes the growth of a pool of experience in particular kinds of problems that might sensitize a judge to difficulties he might face in later cases having similar characteristics. The experience is there, of course, but it is widely distributed among all the judges rather than concentrated along functional lines. Experience distributed so widely is hard to tap when decisions must be made by a single judge, as they generally are in the federal district courts, or by a panel of three judges, as they are in the federal courts of appeals.

Beyond this, it has been argued that lawyers (and presumably judges) have inordinate faith in the power of the written word to shape behavior and a concomitant tendency to minimize the likelihood of behavior that deviates from the requirements of properly drafted regulations.[72] There has indeed been a propensity, as I have said, to assume that properly

70. For an example of a decision that allegedly had such effects, see Harry Brill, "The Uses and Abuses of Legal Assistance," *The Public Interest*, no. 31 (Spring 1973), pp. 38–55, at pp. 43–44.

71. Cf. George Sternlieb, *The Tenement Landlords* (Rutgers University, Urban Studies Center, 1966).

72. Thompson, *The Regulatory Process in OPA Rationing*, pp. 213–20.

framed court orders would be more or less self-executing. This tendency detracts from what might otherwise be a more frequently perceived need to improve the judicial capacity for forecasting, as well as for follow-up.

It may be, however, that the judicial insensitivity to unanticipated consequences in advance of their occurrence is only marginally greater than that of other decisionmakers. All decisionmakers like to think that the choices they make will be translated into action, and they prefer not to think of the forces that may deflect their policies from their intended course. So it is just possible that the focus on rights rather than alternatives, the apportionment of work among judges, and the faith of lawyers and judges in the ability of a proper verbal formulation to induce action in accordance with it—it is possible that these characteristics simply exaggerate a uniform human tendency.

Perhaps so, but there is no mistaking the singular lack of judicial machinery to detect and correct unintended consequences after they have occurred. Here the deficiencies of adjudication are formidable.

If a party subject to an injunction does not comply with it, or if his compliance creates unforeseen difficulties for him or for other parties to the suit, the court that issued the decree may subsequently be advised that this is the case. Either the party subject to the decree or another party to the suit may return to court seeking enforcement, amendment, or dissolution of the injunction. The court is then informed of the consequences of its former action and may begin the consideration of alternatives. The key to this consideration is private initiative. Parties to the suit have an investment in its outcome and a reason to provide the court with an updating of results.

Private initiative breaks down, however, when the non-compliance is not that of a party but of one who may be only similarly situated. If courts make law rather than merely decide individual cases, then their decisions are expected to have ramifications that often extend beyond the parties, at least to all those who share the same characteristics. If decisions do not have those expected ramifications, or if the compliance of non-parties creates unforeseen consequences, the court is unlikely to be advised of such developments.

This is because courts have no self-starting mechanisms. They are dependent on litigants to ignite their processes. If litigants fail to take the initiative, because they do not have the resources or the energy or because they have moved on to other matters, then the effects of judicial action will probably pass unnoticed.

There have been times when the litigants did press forward, calling the courts' attention to the consequences of earlier decisions as they became manifest (though the process was certainly not put in these terms). When earlier decisions invalidating segregationist housing ordinances moved segregationists to adopt a new discriminatory technique —that is, racially restrictive covenants—the NAACP began a long struggle against this as well.[73] The organization's efforts, however, bore fruit only after the passage of decades. Though the pace of change has quickened since that time, it is still a long, arduous, and expensive process for litigants to pursue cases that would have the effect of apprising the courts of a string of consequences that attached unintentionally to their decisions. For the most part, such litigants are likely to consist almost exclusively of governmental bodies and highly specialized, dedicated organizations like the NAACP. Others are prone to fall by the wayside.[74]

The courts, then, depend on the vagaries of litigants and litigation for their feedback about the effects of earlier decisions. Slowly, through a line of cases—always interspersed in a large pool of cases of many other kinds—the realization that there are problems stemming from earlier decisions may strike the judges. If so, they may turn to corrective action, doubtless long after the initial decisions and long after people have adjusted their behavior to them. And all of this is, needless to say, very much a matter of chance.

There is, however, a distinction to be drawn and an exception to be stated. We must distinguish between corrective action taken as a result of newly received information about the consequences of a decision and corrective action taken as a result of a change of judicial outlook. The former is likely to follow the cumbersome route described above, but the latter need not. The first *Flag Salute Case*[75] had barely been decided when some members of the Supreme Court began to have second thoughts, which they conveyed in a dissenting opinion in another case.[76] After the resignation and replacement of one more Justice, the

73. Vose, "The N.A.A.C.P.'s Legal Strategy to Overturn Restrictive Covenants in Housing."

74. Cf. Joel F. Handler, "Social Reform Groups and the Legal System: Enforcement Problems" (University of Wisconsin–Madison, Institute for Research on Poverty, Discussion Paper no. 209-74, June 1974; processed).

75. *Minersville School Dist.* v. *Gobitis*, 310 U.S. 586 (1940).

76. *Jones* v. *Opelika*, 316 U.S. 584, 623–24 (1942) (dissenting opinion of Black, J., joined by Douglas and Murphy, JJ.).

first *Flag Salute Case* was reconsidered and overruled.[77] But this change of course had nothing to do with the receipt of information about the effects of the earlier decision. It was internally generated, and the publication of some Justices' misgivings in a later dissent virtually invited new litigation to challenge the earlier decision. The new lawsuit was not a vehicle to convey information; it simply provided the occasion for change. Hence the relative rapidity with which the change occurred (three years). By itself, a change of direction is no evidence that impact information has been received.

The exception is a narrow one. In those few decisions that excite great public controversy, the chances of feedback are likely to be somewhat greater than in most other cases. This is especially true if there are expressions of legislative approval or disapproval of the decision, though it is important not to overestimate the frequency of such expressions or to underestimate the inertial forces that make for legislative acquiescence.[78] If this approval or disapproval is translated into law, the resulting statutes are one consequence the courts may become apprised of, particularly because they may stimulate new litigation.

The distinction drawn, the exception stated, the general point remains. The courts are mainly dependent for their impact information on a single feedback mechanism: the follow-up lawsuit. This mechanism tends to be slow, erratic, unsystematic. Courts have no inspectors who move out into the field to ascertain what has happened. They receive no regular reports on the implementation of their policies. (It is, however, a mark of the increasing overlap between courts and administrators that some decrees now require periodic compliance reports, but only to monitor compliance by the parties.) The judges have no grapevine extending into the organizations and groups whose behavior they affect. Judicial proprieties foster isolation rather than contact. Neither do the courts learn about the effects of their decisions by conducting investigations or planning exercises; as I have said, they do not have these self-starting mechanisms.

In all of these respects, the information-gathering resources of administrators are vastly superior; those of legislators, modestly superior.[79]

77. *West Virginia Bd. of Educ.* v. *Barnette,* 319 U.S. 624 (1943).

78. See Nathan Hakman, "The Impact of Judicial Opinions: Another Critical Analysis of Political Science Folklore" (paper presented at 1974 annual meeting of the American Political Science Association; processed).

79. For a suggestive evocation of some of the ways administrators may obtain impact information, see Sir Geoffrey Vickers, *The Art of Judgment* (Chapman and

Neither labors under the same disabilities as the courts do: neither is passive, and neither is dependent on a single channel of information.

As the courts have no policy review process that would enable them to gather or utilize impact information, they also have no way of sensitizing lawyers and judges to the empirically questionable inferences courts draw in the course of making decisions. The absence of policy review means that the courts miss an opportunity for general learning about the relation of their decisions to their environment. The neglect of social facts and the neglect of impact facts are therefore mutually reinforcing. Without policy review, judicial decisions possess a finality that legislative and administrative decisions do not necessarily have. This finality, buttressed by the doctrine of precedent, amounts to an immunity from amendment in the light of impact facts. This means that the courts have very limited ability to monitor and control unintended consequences.

Processes, Issues, and Target Populations

The discussion up to this point has emphasized the general limitations of adjudication. That is as it should be, for many of the aspects of the judicial process that have been singled out for analysis would seem to render that process a dubious vehicle for handling "problems of great magnitude and pervasive ramifications, problems with complex roots and unexpectedly multiplying offshoots. . . ."[80] Nevertheless, it is fatuous to suppose that all social policy problems are of a piece and that these attributes of adjudication will impinge on them all in the same way. It is time to be more discriminating about the relation of adjudication to particular kinds of issues and the particular target populations to whom court decrees are addressed.

If "social policy" means policy designed to affect the structure of social norms, social relations, or social decisionmaking, even this rather amorphous definition yields some distinctions among issues. Certainly a good case can be made that, given the background of most judges and the likelihood that they are very much immersed in the general culture,

Hall, 1965), pp. 173–80. See also Kaufman, *Administrative Feedback*, pp. 24–41, on the multiple sources of information on bureaucratic compliance. On legislative information, cf. Polsby, *Congress and the Presidency*, pp. 88–89.

80. Alexander M. Bickel, *The Supreme Court and the Idea of Progress* (Harper and Row, 1970), p. 175.

the informational capacity of the courts is greatest in the area of social norms. The conventional wisdom, however, is that normative change is the most difficult to accomplish. There is some evidence, drawn from studies of the importation of foreign legal systems in modernizing countries, that instrumental behavior is more readily altered than is behavior that expresses the core values of a culture. The adoption of a new commercial code may transform existing contractual practices, whereas a new family code may not have a significant impact on family structure.[81] The same, presumably, would be at least equally true of judicial decisions. If, therefore, this distinction between normative and instrumental behavior were clearcut, it might be hypothesized that the courts are likely to be better informed and yet less effective in bringing about intended changes in normative than in instrumental behavior.

The problem, of course, is that the distinction quite readily breaks down. Certain commercial practices may be as deeply rooted in a particular culture as some aspects of family relations. The prohibition on taking interest on loans in Muslim societies is a clear example of such a practice. By the same token, the extent to which the French law against primogeniture was an effective disincentive to population increase and thus had a fundamental effect on French family life suggests that normative-instrumental distinctions are easily blurred. Much of human behavior in fact crosses such artificially constructed boundaries.

Unsatisfactory as such distinctions may be, they do emphasize the issue of how deeply ingrained is the behavior affected by judicial decisions. Typologies of policy issues are almost as numerous as the writers about them, but one common way of approaching the problem is to "locate" the behavior in community life. Leon Mayhew's study of the Massachusetts Commission Against Discrimination, discussed earlier, argues that the commission had a bigger impact on the housing problem than on the employment problem. Whereas work relations in industrial society are regarded as impersonal, housing still has a "communitarian" aspect to it.[82] Housing may actually have been a more intractable problem than employment, but it was easier to mobilize community feeling for fair housing than it was to evoke a sense of community responsibility for the conduct of large, impersonal business firms. From this Mayhew

81. Yehezkel Dror, "Law and Social Change," in Vilhelm Aubert, ed., *Sociology of Law* (Penguin Books, 1969), pp. 90–99. The point, however, is by no means settled. Cf. June Starr and Jonathan Pool, "The Impact of a Legal Revolution in Rural Turkey," *Law and Society Review*, vol. 8 (Summer 1974), pp. 533–60.

82. *Law and Equal Opportunity*, pp. 281–83.

concludes that law may have a greater impact in the "more communal" areas of social life.

What Mayhew finds mobilizable other writers find immovable. Franklin Zimring and Gordon Hawkins have suggested that how effective law will be in changing behavior depends on how central the behavior is in the life of the affected community.[83] In general, the more central—that is, the more significant, the more morally supported, the more connected to other behavior—the more resistant the conduct is likely to be to efforts to alter it.

These two hypotheses may not be as mutually exclusive as they seem. Mayhew may actually have been saying that there was moral ambivalence on the housing issue. If so, its "communitarian" quality (which is rather hard to pin down) may have made it easier to tap antidiscrimination sentiment. But if this is indeed the way to reconcile these opposing views, then all that is being said is that it is easier to bring about change in an area where change is already under way, the more so where there is a felt sense of community responsibility. This, one suspects, is a proposition that is neither easy to confirm nor of much operational utility to courts.

A less refined but potentially more useful distinction among issue areas is based on judicial familiarity. The closer the issue is to other issues courts have faced, or to other institutions courts have known, the more likely it is that the courts will gain a solid grasp of the situation as it emerges in litigation. Courts are, as I have suggested, vessels into which a legal and evidentiary case is poured; and they tend to give short shrift to social facts. This puts a premium on prior judicial experience. If, for example, the question is how to persuade or compel corporate organizations to include environmental impact in their calculations or how to induce government agencies to implement antidiscrimination directives in hiring and promotion, courts are not likely to possess expertise in the incentive structure of complex organizations. The adjudicative process is not likely to throw up sufficient material to enlighten them, and both lawyers and judges are likely to fill in the interstices with some highly stereotyped notions of "bureaucracy" drawn from their operational code. The less familiar the area, the less informed the decision: that is a proposition that will be examined.

So far we have been looking broadly at issue areas. It is also possible

83. "The Legal Threat as an Instrument of Social Change," *Journal of Social Issues,* vol. 27 (1971), pp. 33–48.

to distinguish more finely among issues on the basis of precise issue content.

There is, for example, a conventional legal distinction between procedural and substantive decisions. Certainly there are fewer judicial inhibitions on decisions that lay down purely procedural requirements than on those that impose substantive burdens. Part of the rationale for this distinction rests on the belief that courts have some special insight into the uses of procedure that is denied them when it comes to matters of substance. Again, it comes down to a question of familiarity. But whether decisions that are purely procedural are in fact more likely to be well informed, less likely to give rise to unintended consequences, and in general less subject to the limitations of the adjudicative process remains to be seen.

A distinction has also been drawn by Lon Fuller between cases that raise what he calls polycentric problems and those that do not.[84] A polycentric problem is one that is so "many-centered" that a pull at any one point changes an entire web of relationships. Such problems, Fuller suggests, involve enormous difficulties of forecasting effects and of structuring preferences. They are, therefore, more suitably resolved by sensitive managerial direction or by the reciprocities of the marketplace than by adjudication. As Fuller recognizes, however, all problems have polycentric elements, and it is difficult to decide when they predominate. Nevertheless, he concludes that the allocation of economic resources is one such task that is not suitable for the adjudicative format. The focused and piecemeal qualities of adjudication are likely to distort allocative choices, and the monitoring of the consequences of allocative decisions is a prodigious undertaking beyond the machinery of the courts.

Another content-based issue typology derives from the extent to which the decision is redistributive.[85] Some government policies distribute benefits to certain groups without affecting the share of benefits held by others. Other policies, however, allocate benefits among competing claimants. Although the informational resources of the courts

84. "The Forms and Limits of Adjudication," pp. 35–43.
85. Cf. Theodore Lowi, "Decision Making vs. Policy Making: Toward an Antidote for Technocracy," *Public Administration Review*, vol. 30 (May/June 1970), pp. 314–25; Lowi, "American Business, Public Policy, Case-Studies, and Political Theory," *World Politics*, vol. 16 (July 1964), pp. 677–715; Robert H. Salisbury, "The Analysis of Public Policy: A Search for Theories and Roles," in Austin Ranney, ed., *Political Science and Public Policy* (Markham, 1968), pp. 151–75.

may not vary from one type of policy to another, the consequences of decisions may vary considerably. Deflection of a decision into unanticipated channels may be more likely if there is more initial resistance to it; and resistance may be greater in the case of broad redistributive decisions than in the case of decisions that redistribute only within a narrow compass or decisions that do not redistribute at all. The monitoring capacities of the courts may also be taxed most heavily in the case of redistributive decisions.

This is enough to indicate that the various attributes of adjudication may be more adequate for certain kinds of policy decisions and less so for others. As we investigate concrete cases, it will be necessary to bear this in mind.

Similar caution is in order in approaching the audiences or target populations affected by a decree. These are the groups expected to modify their behavior in accordance with judicial decisions. They may or may not be formal parties to the suit. Hypotheses about the relationships of judicial decisions to target populations abound. Some relate the impact of a decision to the number of such groups, some to the identity of the groups.

In general, it has been thought that court decisions would be more effective if there were fewer target populations. (For the moment, we shall have to ignore the difficulty of ascertaining what the "impact" of a decision is or how "effective" it is.) As the number of groups whose behavior must be coordinated expands, so do the occasions for evasion of responsibility. More than that, the chances increase that the decision itself will strain the relationships of such groups among themselves and make the implementation of the decision difficult. Finally, the possibility also exists that unexpected combinations of behavior will ensue from a decision addressed to multiple audiences, thus magnifying the likelihood of completely unexpected outcomes.

Not only the number of categories of target populations but also the number of units of such populations has been viewed as decisive. Most writers have argued that compliance with a judicial decision is more likely if there is a single bureaucracy responsible for implementing it, rather than the public at large.[86] Another way of putting the same propo-

86. Harrell R. Rodgers, Jr., "Law as an Instrument of Public Policy," *American Journal of Political Science*, vol. 17 (August 1973), pp. 638–47.

sition is to say that the more centralized the responsibility (hence the fewer units), the more likely the compliance.[87]

If the addressees are relatively few, as in voting decrees issued under the Fifteenth Amendment, and in reapportionment decisions, the judiciary is in a relatively better position all by itself to render its law operational. . . . When the addressees are many, as in the school segregation and school prayer cases, the judiciary by itself tends to be relatively helpless.[88]

The identity of the target populations may also affect the way in which a decision is implemented. It is possible to scale target populations according to their "distance" from the courts. At one end of the scale can be placed those institutions and organizations that have a "legal" mission or orientation and that are more or less subject to the control of the courts. They may place a high value on conformity to law. They may, in addition, be sensitive to the reasoning underlying court decisions, and they may need the cooperation of the courts for the pursuance of their own goals. This is in contrast to organizations that do not define their goals in legal terms, are in court on rare occasions, are not dependent on the courts for their general success, and have difficulty understanding the basis of judicial decisions. The scale of target populations thus runs from proximate, dependent, and knowledgeable to distant, independent, and uninformed.

Some writers have theorized that distance of the audience from the source of judicial decisions is an important determinant of the outcome of such decisions.[89] In explaining the failure of the Norwegian Housemaid Law of 1948 to affect the relations between housemaids and their employers, Vilhelm Aubert notes that the relationship it was intended to alter was far from traditional regulation by law, and the target populations affected by the law were unaccustomed to adjusting their behavior in accordance with legal requirements:

The law addresses groups which traditionally have had little connection with laws and with public authorities. The recipients of the legal message consist of women who are not organized, and thus lack an intermediary link with the government. The law concerns an area traditionally protected against public inspection and control, the home. The place of work is isolated, and the nature of the work relationship is intrinsically difficult to regulate. It is

87. Joel B. Grossman, "The Supreme Court and Social Change," *American Behavioral Scientist*, vol. 13 (March/April 1970), p. 546.

88. Bickel, *The Supreme Court and the Idea of Progress*, p. 91.

89. See, e.g., James P. Levine, "Methodological Concerns in Studying Supreme Court Efficacy," *Law and Society Review*, vol. 4 (1970), pp. 583–92.

an area on the border-line between "work" and "private life," where it is
sometimes hard to distinguish between the worker and the (slightly inferior)
member of the family. . . .[90]

Here is a case of target populations very distant from law and from
courts.

I have deliberately avoided constructing a hard-and-fast list of hypotheses about the relationship of the adjudication process to types of
issues and target populations.[91] It will, in any case, prove quite impossible to confirm or refute very many specific propositions on the basis
of a few cases, and it is probably more fruitful to embark on case studies
with a fluid rather than a fixed idea of how these three sets of variables
may interact. With that said, it is appropriate to explain why the case-
study method was chosen and how it was pursued, describe what characteristics were sought in the cases selected for intensive study, and
then provide a preview of the cases in the order in which they will make
their appearance.

The Case-Study Method and the Cases Studied

The advantages of case studies for constructing a first set of approxi-
mate generalizations are considerable. Since the courts themselves deal
in the case as their unit of analysis and action, case studies enable us
to match the way the adjudicative process "saw" and handled a case
against alternative ways of viewing and processing the same case. The
aim is to trace the imprint of process on outcome. That means we are
interested in how things happen when the judicial process deals with
social policy questions: how a factual setting is established and interpreted, how issues are framed, how decrees produce results. For such
questions, a good deal of detail is indispensable, detail about the elements of decision and their interactions. This argues strongly for a view
of a whole, self-contained unit. An inestimable benefit of the case-study
method is, then, that each case provides "a connected body of information about a particular situation."[92]

90. "Some Social Functions of Legislation," in Aubert, ed., *Sociology of Law,*
p. 122.
91. Others have compiled such lists. See, e.g., Grossman, "The Supreme Court
and Social Change," pp. 545–49; Stephen L. Wasby, *The Impact of the United
States Supreme Court: Some Perspectives* (Homewood, 1970), pp. 243–68.
92. George C. Homans, *The Human Group* (Routledge and Kegan Paul, 1951),
p. 18.

Because the case-study method concentrates research resources and attention on a few cases, it permits a careful scanning and sorting of the various characteristics of the cases that come to court and of the process by which they are decided, in order to search out relationships among them that might otherwise go undetected. Restricted attention to a few cases also enables us to move backward quite some distance into the setting from which the litigation emerged, and likewise to move forward from the decision to identify all its effects. In fact, I shall make liberal use of the opportunity to look into social context and consequences in the cases to be examined.

If these are the advantages of the case-study method, the method also entails sacrifices. For one thing, it is not possible to project from single case studies how frequently a certain phenomenon recurs. For this, a random sample is required. Nor is it possible to impose controls adequate to insure that the conditions thought to produce given outcomes are specified exactly. Finally, a few case studies may not be representative of the universe of cases.

These pitfalls are not sufficient to offset the reasons for pursuing case studies. First of all, frequency is not an issue in this study. For our purposes, it does not matter how often the confluence of certain conditions produces a given result. What is important is that the result may be produced when the conditions interact.

This, however, makes the question of controls more significant. Controls are a problem with all case studies, at least until the conclusions of a few such studies are refined by later investigations. This is not a fatal difficulty here, because the aim is to arrive at a first set of generalizations about judicial capacity, and it should not disappoint us if these generalizations are refined or modified by subsequent efforts. Moreover, more than one of the cases casts light on several of the issues of concern here. This provides a rudimentary check on some of our formulations. Indeed, as we shall see in the concluding chapter, in many ways the case studies are cumulative; they reinforce each other and together suggest some of the characteristically judicial ways of dealing with social policy questions.

The problem of representativeness is also inherent in case-study investigations. There are two issues here. First, what is the universe of cases that the case studies might represent? Second, in what sense, if any, are the cases representative of that universe?

It would, of course, defeat the purpose of the inquiry to select cases typical of all the cases that come to court. I have already said that, most of the time, most courts still do what they have long been accustomed to doing. The "new responsibilities" of the courts are in this sense atypical of judicial work as a whole, but disproportionately important. Clearly, the relevant universe consists, not of all cases, but only of all social policy cases.

Is it possible to achieve representativeness, even of this limited universe, in a few case studies? If we mean representative in the sense that a carefully drawn random sample reproduces the relevant characteristics of the universe from which it is drawn, then a few case studies can never meet this standard. But there is a more modest meaning of the term representative. Case studies may be representative in the sense that they are simply not aberrational.

The test of whether the cases selected are representative in this sense is the test of plausibility and context. Does what we learn about each case fit what we already know about the judicial process and how it characteristically functions? If not, is there a coherent explanation for what happened, and does that explanation rest on factors that are likely to prove idiosyncratic or recurrent in litigation? The judicial process is not, after all, wholly strange or unfamiliar. It is among the most public of decision processes. To ask new questions about the capacity of courts is not to demand that we forget what we already know about their workings. It is, rather, to build on what we know. In fact, there already is established a rather rich context in which to fit what we learn as we go along. By the time we are finished with each case, we shall have a solid basis for deciding whether it was, in some significant way, atypical of the judicial process.

This is, of course, not to guarantee that any given outcome would inexorably emerge over and over again. One of the things that is clear about the judicial process is that it accords individual judges a considerable measure of latitude to choose among competing outcomes. The common constraints of the judicial process do not always override the element of individual choice. So it is not exact replicability of outcome that is the test of representativeness. All that is claimed is that what happened in each of the case studies can be explained on the basis of aspects of adjudication that are more or less familiar. For if they are familiar, then they are recurrent and therefore likely to play a broadly similar role in other, similar cases.

Some of the central questions of this inquiry involve the detection of things that may be difficult for courts to detect. If, for example, we are to investigate the extent to which the judicial process is inapt for the ascertainment of social facts or unable to foresee and discover certain consequences of judicial decisions, then it is necessary to detect in the case studies some of the things the courts themselves did not detect. Otherwise it will be impossible to assess the significance of what lies beyond the vision of the courts. For this reason, I took the opportunity to move backward into the environment from which the litigation springs and forward into the environment in which a judicial decision must operate. On the assumption that a fine net is required to be certain of catching everything germane, the rule of inquiry adopted here was to err on the side of inclusiveness.

As the investigation proceeded, it became clear that pursuing this tack did indeed expand the analytical yield. What was learned from each case increased markedly with the depth of the investigation. For example, many second-order consequences of decisions would probably have gone unnoticed had a less inclusive approach been adopted.

Each case, therefore, has been plumbed just as far as it seemed profitable to go. I share with the reader the full understanding that was gained of each case, so he can check the conclusions advanced against the composite picture provided. The significance of the points extracted from each case is difficult to appreciate without knowing the place they occupied in the case as a whole.

The choice of cases was biased in favor of somewhat sweeping decisions in which courts had done bold things. These, clearly, would test the limits of judicial capacity more sharply than decisions that more closely approximated traditional judicial work. Consequently, decisions were selected that either broke new ground or had important and immediate consequences for the policy being carried out by the parties to the suit.

At a minimum, I was interested in cases where social and "political reality" might diverge from "judicial reality"; where social science was involved; where there was an unfamiliar government program in litigation and where there was a familiar one; where the follow-up abilities of the courts were tested; where major national policy was being laid down; and where local disputes were being settled but with wider ramifications. I was interested in finding decisions that reallocated resources as well as those that asked institutions to modify their behavior, decisions that seemed to impose purely procedural requirements and those that demanded substantive change. I was looking for different numbers and types of target populations: lower courts and bureaucracies, organizations that function in close proximity to the courts and those that operate at some remove from them.

Because of the emphasis placed on understanding the case as a whole, less attention is devoted in the four case-study chapters to explicit discussion of the analytical issues raised by this chapter than to specific problems raised by the decisions themselves. In the concluding sections of some of the case studies and in the final chapter, this gap will be closed. Each of the five attributes of adjudication is illuminated by at least one of the case studies, some by more than one. Only one issue that has been discussed in this chapter is not really treated by the case studies: the issue of sequencing, which would have required a prohibitive investment of research resources in examining a run of cases, rather than a single case.

The *Area-Wide Council* case (chapter 3) involved the courts in defining the meaning of the "citizen participation" requirement of the Model Cities 'program. It thrust them into an unfamiliar issue area, as well as an ongoing political dispute.

Hobson v. *Hansen* (chapter 4) was an explicitly redistributive decision. The court ordered the District of Columbia school system to equalize per-pupil expenditures on teachers' salaries. This issue forced the court to decide empirically what the meaning of equality of teacher services really consisted of—a problem that tested the court's fact-finding capacities. The implementation of the decision by the school system raised questions about the ability of the courts to forecast even the immediate consequences of compliance.

In re Gault (chapter 5) was a Supreme Court decision that undertook to alter the procedures prevailing in the juvenile court. The decision was reinforced by, if not based on, the Court's understanding of how juvenile-court procedure affected juvenile delinquency. Gleaned as it was from social science literature, this understanding provides an interesting comparison to the *Hobson* court's understanding of the meaning of equal distribution of teacher resources. Beyond that, *Gault* imposed merely procedural requirements on courts and lawyers accustomed to interpreting and following procedural requirements. It was, presumably, a decision about matters with which the Court felt itself familiar.

Mapp v. *Ohio* (chapter 6) was a Supreme Court decision, the impact of which has long been debated. The Court forbade the use of illegally obtained evidence in state criminal trials, in large part because it hoped this would discourage illegal behavior by the police. The problematic character of the subsequent behavior of the police, which might be characterized as a bureaucracy dependent on the courts, has been a prominent theme in the ensuing debate. Less discussed but highly significant has been the way in which lower courts have carried out the *Mapp* decision, particularly when this is contrasted with the way the Supreme Court supposed it would be carried out.

Each of these cases evokes the various attributes of adjudication in differing proportions. But each in its own way—and each case compared to the others—can help clarify the capacities and incapacities of courts as social policymakers.

CHAPTER THREE

The *Area-Wide Council* Case:
The "Great Society" Comes to Court

The judicial process has a short attention-span. The claim of any piece of litigation on a court's time is strictly limited. Judges expect a varied menu, they expect their decisions to be the dispositive last word, and they tire quickly of repeated sequences of litigation before them. The judges move from controversy to controversy, typically lavishing on each a brief, albeit often intense, devotion to mastering the facts, formulating the issues, and devising an appropriate resolution.[1]

The judges' function is exercised not only intermittently but passively. That they deal in establishing and evaluating "facts" means that the events they judge have already transpired. The courts sit to evaluate action primarily undertaken and accomplished by others. Has the supplier breached his contract? Has the licensing board accorded due process? Has the defendant committed acts that amount to embezzlement? Has the seller tendered a marketable title? These questions, all of them in the past tense, presuppose a kind of tentative finality in the working out of relations between the parties—a finality subject to undoing only by court order. The court is traditionally not an active participant in events but a passive reviewer of them.

The passivity of the judicial function and its intermittent exercise are related. It is because all the relevant facts are already in place that courts are afforded the luxury of moving rapidly from one question to

1. Sometimes the brevity of judicial deliberation has generated criticism, though most of it relates to the Supreme Court. See, e.g., Henry M. Hart, Jr., "Foreword: The Time Chart of the Justices," *Harvard Law Review*, vol. 73 (1959), pp. 84–125; Federal Judicial Center, *Report of the Study Group on the Caseload of the Supreme Court* (Administrative Office of U.S. Courts, 1972).

another. It takes far longer to participate in action than merely to review it.

The presupposition of factual finality is reflected in a variety of legal doctrines, though perhaps most prominently in the administrative-law doctrine that a petitioner must exhaust all of his administrative remedies before a court will sit in judgment on government action unfavorable to him. If there is still a way open to the administrative agency to reverse itself, the courts will stay their hand to permit the attempt. Courts sit in review.

Sometimes, however, courts are called upon to judge action in progress. In some ways, this is a species of judicial function quite different from the more traditional function of judicial review. For one thing, it quite commonly involves judgment at more than one point along the way, for each decision is not necessarily dispositive of the controversy. For another, it often requires courts to monitor the results of the action they take in the midst of a controversy.

Courts, however, are notoriously short on machinery. Their own lack of a bureaucratic apparatus is one of the prime reasons why they are so often asked to correct the failings of bureaucracies: unburdened by cumbersome machinery, they are believed to be concerned with ends more than with means. Yet the lack of machinery also means that the supervisory capacities of the courts have not necessarily kept pace with the new supervisory duties that come their way.

There is, then, a strong tradition of courts accustomed to sit in judgment of action already completed, unused to the requirements of continuing surveillance, and expecting and receiving simple compliance with their orders. Against this background, it is instructive to consider what happens when courts become entangled in events that are still unfolding outside the courtroom. Can they understand the local situation adequately? Can they keep up with events taking place on the ground? Can they fasten a hold on those events so that judicial supervision will have its intended effects? What happens, in other words, when courts structured to deal with static, established facts are injected into a still-fluid political controversy? These are some of the questions posed by *North City Area-Wide Council v. Romney,*[2] a case that also raises a

2. Civil No. 69-1909, E.D. Pa., Nov. 12, 1969, *reversed,* 428 F.2d 754 (3d Cir. 1970), *on remand,* 329 F. Supp. 1124 (E.D. Pa. 1971), *reversed,* 456 F.2d 811 (3d Cir. 1971), *cert. denied sub nom. Rizzo v. North City Area-Wide Council,* 406 U.S. 963 (1972), *on remand,* Civ. No. 69-1909, E.D. Pa., Sept. 6, 1972, *affirmed,* 469 F.2d 1326 (3d Cir. 1972).

number of questions about the extent to which the federal courts can be
expected to make informed judgments about the administration of national social programs.

The National Program

The setting of the *Area-Wide Council* litigation was the Model Cities
program.[3] Established by Congress in 1966, Model Cities was very much
a central part of the "Great Society" proposed by the Johnson administration. A product of one of the innumerable "task forces" of the mid-
1960s, Model Cities was initially an attempt to unite urban renewal and
social programs in order to revitalize urban slum areas.[4] In the lofty
language of the act, the federal government was to provide funds to
cities "to plan, develop, and carry out locally prepared and scheduled
comprehensive city demonstration programs containing new and imagi-
native proposals. . . ."[5]

The main theme of the Model Cities program was coordinated planning at the local level. The earlier urban renewal program had emphasized physical rehabilitation, not social services. The war on poverty's
Community Action program, then under way, did not stress compre-
hensiveness. A concerted attack on the problems of the slums had to
concentrate on "the total environment" of that portion of the city that
was to become a "demonstration area" or, as it came to be called, "model
neighborhood." In the competition for funding, the plans of a city would
be judged in large part by whether they attempted to integrate an array
of facilities and services, physical and social, to benefit the target area.

The program envisioned a one-year planning period followed by five
years of implementation. By the end of 1968, some 150 cities had been
awarded planning grants, and before President Johnson had left office,
he had budgeted nearly a billion dollars for the program.[6] The act itself

3. Demonstration Cities and Urban Development Act of 1966, 42 U.S.C. §§ 3301
et seq.

4. The background and early operation of the program are admirably described
by James L. Sundquist, *Making Federalism Work* (Brookings Institution, 1969),
chap. 3, on which I have relied heavily.

5. 42 U.S.C. § 3301.

6. Sundquist, *Making Federalism Work*, p. 84.

encouraged the cities to think big: a program would not be eligible for funding unless it were

of sufficient magnitude to make a substantial impact on the physical and social problems and to remove or arrest blight and decay in entire sections or neighborhoods; to contribute to the sound development of the entire city; to make marked progress in reducing social and educational disadvantages, ill health, underemployment, and enforced idleness; and to provide educational, health, and social services necessary to serve the poor and disadvantaged in the area, widespread citizen participation in the program, maximum opportunities for employing residents of the area in all phases of the program, and enlarged opportunities for work and training. . . .[7]

Though the Model Cities Act made "widespread citizen participation in the program" a condition of assistance, it also rather clearly contemplated that the program was to help city governments solve their problems. The statutory emphasis on "widespread citizen participation" and "local initiative"[8] implied that, in the ordinary run of city government, these things could not be taken for granted. At the least, special efforts would have to be made to involve citizens of the target area in the program. At the most, wholly new structures might have to be devised to guarantee a preeminent role for residents of the affected area. But if so, where would that leave the city governments?

The act raised this troublesome question, but it did nothing to help answer it. Neither the nature of the local administrative machinery nor the meaning of "widespread citizen participation" was specified by the President or Congress.[9] That job was left to the Department of Housing and Urban Development, and it did the job only sparingly in the first two years of the program.

HUD was more explicit on the role of the "city demonstration agencies" (CDAs), the municipal offices that were to run the program for the cities, than it was on the meaning of citizen participation. HUD required that the CDA be tied in closely with the city's decisionmaking process and particularly with its regularly elected leadership.[10] Most cities cre-

7. 42 U.S.C. § 3303(a)(2).

8. The act required HUD to "emphasize local initiative in the planning, development, and implementation of a comprehensive city demonstration program." Ibid., § 3303(b)(1).

9. See the generalities discussed in *Housing Legislation of 1966*, Hearings before a Subcommittee of the Senate Committee on Banking and Currency, 89 Cong. 2 sess. (1966), p. 100.

10. Sundquist, *Making Federalism Work*, p. 83.

ated a separate CDA office, though its precise relation to the city government and the target neighborhood, and even its name, varied widely.

"Widespread citizen participation" was defined solely in platitudes. HUD's only official guidelines on the subject during the Johnson administration—CDA Letter Number 3—urged "the constructive involvement of citizens in the model neighborhood area" and "the affirmative action of the people themselves."[11] It required "some form of organizational structure, existing or newly established, which embodies neighborhood residents in the process of policy and program planning and program implementation and operation. The leadership of that structure must consist of persons whom the residents accept as representing their interests."[12] For the rest, there was no guidance about how the citizens' components were to be established (by election?) or what powers they were to have. Access to decisionmaking and information sufficient to enable residents to make proposals and react to others' proposals was required, but could the residents be permitted some degree of sole or concurrent control or veto power over the whole or parts of the program?

HUD gave no formal answers. All that was clear was what could have been inferred from the language of the act itself: "widespread" citizen participation was to be something less than the "maximum feasible" participation of the Community Action program. For by 1966, when Model Cities was enacted, the Community Action program had already given rise to a hostile reaction among mayors and other local government officials. A year later that reaction would produce a congressional backlash against the Community Action program in the form of the Green Amendment, an amendment designed to bolster the authority of local governments and established institutions at the expense of citizens' groups.[13] Even before the 1967 urban riots triggered the rethinking of citizen participation as embodied in the Community Action program, it was clear to Congress at least that if the participation of the poor was required to make Model Cities a success, too much participation and too much by-passing of city hall could only hurt the program.

So Congress came down firmly for enough but not too much. And

11. U.S. Department of Housing and Urban Development, "Citizen Participation—CDA Letter No. 3," MCGR 3100.3 (Nov. 30, 1967).

12. Ibid.

13. The amendment required all local Community Action funds to be controlled by public officials. Economic Opportunity Act of 1964, § 210, as amended, 42 U.S.C. § 2790.

HUD espoused this position as wholeheartedly as its precision warranted.

In fact, until 1969 HUD tended to support more rather than less citizen participation. Vague as the HUD standards were, they included provision for "professional technical assistance, in a manner agreed to by neighborhood residents. . . ."[14] What that meant in practice for many cities was the creation and funding by city governments of technical staffs, sometimes large and well-paid staffs, that reported directly to the neighborhood organizations. Perhaps more than anything else, the creation of these publicly funded staffs helped generate and sustain demands in various cities for neighborhood control of the program or various aspects of it. In addition, HUD let it be known that it envisioned citizen participation components that might adopt an adversary posture toward local government. "Negotiations" and "bargaining" with city hall were regarded as part of what was expected, and delegations of governmental authority to community organizations were not ruled out. Revisions were often required by HUD in city funding applications that failed to provide enough neighborhood input.[15]

Responding to HUD's posture, most cities tended to move toward what James L. Sundquist has called a "bicameral" structure of citizen participation.[16] The residents' organizations developed an administrative structure that more or less paralleled the cities' own Model Cities offices and were accorded something approaching a coordinate role in the program. Some mayors moved in this direction only grudgingly; others welcomed the opportunity to divest themselves of sole responsibility for the program and to remove themselves from the firing line.

The general thrust toward a large measure of autonomy and influence for citizens' organizations should not, however, obscure the wide diversity of patterns of participation that arose.[17] Model Cities was, after

14. CDA Letter No. 3.
15. For examples, see "Nashville Model Cities: A Case Study," *Vanderbilt Law Review*, vol. 25 (May 1972), pp. 727–844, at p. 773; Marshall Kaplan, Gans and Kahn, "The First Action Year of the Model Cities Program in Denver, Colorado: A Case Study" (unpublished report to U.S. Department of Housing and Urban Development, 1973; processed), p. 12.
16. *Making Federalism Work*, pp. 86–90.
17. See, e.g., the four "planning systems" identified by the Marshall Kaplan, Gans and Kahn study, "Ten Model Cities: A Comparative Analysis of Second Round Planning Years" (unpublished draft report submitted to U.S. Department of Housing and Urban Development, n.d. [1973?]; processed), pp. 16–20.

all, a large program, covering cities of many sizes in all regions of the country. Only 8,000 people lived in the model neighborhood area in New London, Connecticut; 140,000 lived in Houston's. The model neighborhood in Santa Fe consisted almost entirely of Spanish-surnamed residents; Cleveland's was 90 percent black.[18] Even cities of the same size in the same part of the country, or cities in the same state, might have quite different programs. Most cities had a single contiguous area as the model neighborhood; a few had more than one neighborhood. In some, participants in the Community Action program quickly became active in Model Cities as well; in others they ignored the new program, or their opponents became active in it. Some cities had relatively cohesive citizens' organizations; others experienced fragmentation and organizational competition. In some localities, citizens' organizations gained enough power to allow them to participate in CDA staffing decisions, power that was sometimes used to force CDA directors from office. Other city governments adamantly refused to relinquish power of this kind.

Everywhere, however, the scope, the form, and the amount of citizen participation became a critically important issue in the Model Cities program. The previous experience of many cities in the Community Action program, the opacity of the Model Cities Act on this question, the reluctance of HUD to be specific, the restrictiveness of some mayors, the permissiveness of others—all of these elements combined to insure that, as the national program unfolded, the role of neighborhood groups in implementing it would become a contentious issue in many cities, a burning one in some.

At least that was the situation until early 1969, when the Nixon administration took office. At that time, many cities had completed the planning process, but none had yet been awarded a grant to implement plans that had been drawn up. This gave the incoming administration a policy latitude it might not have had if the program across the country had been further along. The enthusiasm for Model Cities declined appreciably in Washington. There were suggestions the program might go under or be radically transformed. No new cities were added, and a certain tentativeness set in.

HUD's view of citizen participation underwent some important modifications. Roughly, the presumption in favor of more rather than less neighborhood participation was reversed. Where, before, revisions were

18. Figures from ibid., p. 46.

required in applications lacking a sufficiently large citizens' role, now applications were scrutinized to insure that too much authority was not in the hands of neighborhood organizations.[19] The ultimate responsibility of mayors and city governments was reaffirmed.[20] A heavy burden of justification was placed on cities that planned to bypass "established institutions" in the operation of their programs, whether they were to be run by CDA offices or citizen participation components, and the delegation of signoff authority to citizens' groups was generally discouraged.[21]

Eventually, in March 1970, HUD and the Office of Economic Opportunity issued a joint statement on citizen participation in Model Cities programs, CDA Letter Number 10B.[22] This was the first such formal statement from HUD on this subject since November 1967. The language was still less than precise, but, in view of the history of citizen participation, the thrust was plain enough. Citizen participation was to extend only to the identification of problems and priorities, access to the decisionmaking process, and involvement in "planning, monitoring, evaluating, and influencing" the program.

Omitted were the references of CDA Letter Number 3 to an official belief that "only the affirmative action of the people themselves" can improve "the quality of life" of the neighborhood's residents. Omitted, too, was any hint that residents could be delegated more than an advisory role or that they could be involved in "carrying out" proposals that were accepted as part of the program. Finally, the "technical assistance" afforded neighborhood organizations no longer had to be provided "in a manner agreed to by neighborhood residents": the city was merely responsible for making available some form of technical assistance—not necessarily independent staffs reporting to the community organization.

The Nixon administration tended to believe that city governments were abdicating too much responsibility for the Model Cities pro-

19. See, e.g., Marshall Kaplan, Gans and Kahn, "The First Action Year of the Model Cities Program in Denver," p. 32.

20. Address by Floyd H. Hyde, Assistant Secretary of Housing and Urban Development, at the Annual Meeting of the U.S. Conference of Mayors, Pittsburgh, June 17, 1969; Press Conference of George Romney, Secretary of HUD, April 28, 1969, reported in *Philadelphia Inquirer*, April 29, 1969.

21. Warren H. Butler, "Resident Participation: the Federal Perspective," *Denver Law Journal* (Special Magazine Issue, 1971), pp. 44–46.

22. U.S. Department of Housing and Urban Development, "CDA Letter Number 10B: Joint HUD-OEO Citizen Participation Policy for Model Cities Programs," MC 3135.1 (Supplement 1, March 1970).

gram to citizens' groups.[23] What HUD did in its guidelines, its public
statements, and its communications with individual cities was to shore
up the authority of city halls and demand the reduction of the authority
of the neighborhoods to an essentially advisory role. This produced
some unusual alliances—between a Republican administration and the
Democratic city governments it often shored up. The new policy was
simply another reconciliation of the built-in antinomy between "widespread citizen participation" and programs to help city governments
solve their problems in a coordinated way.

In spite of everything, the change in emphasis in Washington produced less change in local Model Cities programs than was expected
The leadership of an assistant secretary who had been the mayor of
a California city proved to be somewhat more sympathetic to the program that was under way than might have been predicted. Moreover,
it was too late to affect relations between citizens' organizations and
city governments in many cities. The pattern of those relations had
already crystallized. It was generally out of the question to consider,
for example, withdrawing the funding of technical staffs responsible to
the citizens' groups once those staffs had been established, funded, and
operating for some time. And so what was being done in general continued to be done, ukases to the contrary from Washington notwithstanding. Where changes in citizen participation relationships occurred,
they were generally the result of a new project proposal or of a change
in the balance of local forces. In Philadelphia, both played a role.

The Philadelphia Conflict

Unlike many cities, Philadelphia was quick to sense the possibilities
of the Model Cities program. By January 1967, the mayor had named a
City Development Coordinator to handle the program, and by March,
the city had filed an application with HUD for a planning grant. In
November 1967, the planning grant was awarded, and by December of
the following year Philadelphia had submitted its application for a five-
year operating program.

With some thirty component projects ranging from health care to
tenants' unions, and federal funding of more than $25 million for its
first year, the Philadelphia program was large and diverse. The desig-

23. See Butler, "Resident Participation."

nated model neighborhood was North Philadelphia, an extensive, predominantly black area with a population of about a quarter of a million.[24]
From the beginning, Philadelphia's leadership saw Model Cities as an
opportunity to augment the city's budget with a large infusion of federal
funds.

If city hall moved quickly and diligently, the citizens of the model
neighborhood did no less. By the end of January 1967, community meetings had begun. A month later the basic organization of the North City
Area-Wide Council (AWC) began to emerge in outline form. Essentially a federation of a large number of existing community organizations, the Area-Wide Council eventually had a board of ninety-two
directors. It had no competitors in the target community, which it divided into some sixteen "hubs" or areas.

From the outset, the AWC proposed to develop and rely on its own
staff, supported by Model Cities funds but responsible solely to AWC.
The staff ultimately grew to fifty-two members, far more than the city
had envisioned,[25] and operating expenses to more than half a million
dollars a year. With a strong staff and an unwieldy board of directors,
staff initiatives naturally played an overwhelmingly important role in
the development of the AWC's program. The Model Cities program
got moving so fast that it proved quite impossible in Philadelphia, as
elsewhere, to build the citizens' organization gradually from the ground
up. The speed of the undertaking, the complexity of the plans, and the
availability of federal funds for "technical assistance" all pointed to a
leading role for full-time staff in the development of community proposals.[26]

In this situation, the initiative fell to AWC Executive Director William
Meek, an articulate black social worker. Reflective, inclined to act on

24. The original area proposed was somewhat larger, with an estimated population of 300,000. HUD required a reduction in size to an area officially described as
embracing a population of 217,000, a figure within HUD's outer limit of 10 percent
of the total city population. *Philadelphia Evening Bulletin,* January 15, 1968. The
10 percent maximum was later rescinded by Secretary Romney, and some HUD
officials indicated they believed the population of the Philadelphia model neighborhood had been understated at the outset to conform to the 10 percent rule. Interview,
Washington, D.C., August 28, 1974.

25. In an early interview (September 22, 1967) with James L. Sundquist, a
Philadelphia official envisioned an AWC staff of about six people. I am grateful to
Sundquist for making the 1967 Philadelphia interview notes available to me.

26. For remarks critical of the AWC's relations with constituents in the hubs,
see *Philadelphia Evening Bulletin,* September 30, 1969.

theoretical precepts, Meek could not be accused of being a politician. Indeed, one of his key decisions in organizing the AWC was to avoid entanglement with local politicians. In solidly Democratic North Philadelphia, scarcely a ward leader was active in the affairs of the Area-Wide Council. The AWC aimed, in the words of one of its close allies, "to prevent North Philadelphia from being ripped off by politicians"[27]— this in a city in which the Community Action program had been very much under the influence of city hall. For the AWC, it was a fateful decision, one that maximized the independence of the organization at the risk of its survival.

The AWC strategy was essentially confrontationist. Not that technical work was neglected: it was not. The AWC staff was deeply involved in research; it spun off position papers and developed elaborate plans. But the AWC leadership saw the relationship with the city as essentially adversary and generally believed that the way to gain adoption of its proposals was to bring pressure to bear on city hall. It used the tested civil rights tactics of demands buttressed by demonstrations; it tended to emphasize planning and to disdain compromise. The first two Model Cities administrators,[28] both white, left their jobs after disputes with the AWC. Indeed, the AWC had demanded the resignation of the second.[29] The third administrator, who was black, also found the going difficult, and took advantage of an opportune moment to seek a judgeship. There were times, informants report, when he and William Meek spoke only through neutral third parties.[30]

Plainly, the AWC was not without influence. From the beginning, it sought and achieved "the authority, the financial resources, and the independence to bargain with the city on behalf of the community."[31] It aimed at an essentially coordinate role with the city government in the planning and execution of the program. At the least, this implied that the AWC would have a veto over anything to be done by the city in the model neighborhood. The stormy relations between the city and the AWC, with frequent breakdowns of negotiations, beginning as early

27. Interview, Philadelphia, July 19, 1974.

28. The equivalent of "CDA directors" in other cities. Actually, Model Cities fell under the portfolio of the Philadelphia Development Coordinator. By the time the third administrator was appointed, the program was his sole responsibility.

29. *Philadelphia Inquirer,* June 23, 1968.

30. Interview, Washington, D.C., August 28, 1974.

31. "Maximum Feasible Manipulation," as told to Sherry R. Arnstein, *Public Administration Review,* vol. 32 (September 1972), p. 379. This article presents the official AWC view of the controversy.

as 1967, were not unlike those in other cities with "bicameral" structures of citizen participation. Beyond that, "partnership status" meant that AWC would play a leading role in actually administering the program. The plan sent to Washington at the end of 1968 included provision for creation of some seven operating corporations to run virtually the entire program. Four of these "were to be community controlled in that the majority of their board of directors would be chosen by the AWC."[32] The AWC was to have a leading role in selecting directors of the others as well. Thus, the Philadelphia program raised precisely those questions about citizen participation that had been left unresolved by Congress and dealt with only generally by HUD.

Until 1969, as we have seen, HUD tended to favor extensive citizen participation and took no strong position against the delegation of operating authority to citizens' groups. Also until 1969, the city of Philadelphia Model Cities office tended to take the opposite view. Where it yielded, it did so only reluctantly, as in the inclusion of the seven corporations in the grant application. But during the tenure of the first three Model Cities administrators it never quite said, with the explicitness of a final decision, that the citizens' role was to be purely advisory. At least not until mid-1969.

In March 1969, weary of conflict after only nine months in office, the third of Philadelphia's Model Cities administrators resigned. He was succeeded by Goldie Watson, then occupying a patronage job in the city records office. Described by a former associate as "an absolute pragmatist," Goldie Watson was a veteran black politician in North Philadelphia, the first Model Cities administrator to live in the model neighborhood.[33] A long-standing ally of the mayor, she was in a position to lay down conditions for her acceptance of a sensitive job like that of Model Cities director—the mishandling of which could cause the mayor considerable political grief.

No one who knew Goldie Watson doubted what the thrust of her conditions would be. Mrs. Watson would be an unlikely candidate for a position in which a community organization would tell her how to run her office. Still less would she be indulgent of flamboyant rhetoric, complicated theories of the causes of poverty, or noisy demonstrations. For not only was Mrs. Watson a seasoned political leader; her personal

32. Ibid., p. 385.
33. Brief biographical sketches are contained in the *Philadelphia Evening Bulletin,* March 11, 1969; *Philadelphia Inquirer,* March 12, 1969.

life had taught her a number of lessons which seemed to assume the character of cardinal tenets with her. A teacher dismissed by the school system in 1954 in a surge of McCarthyism, she had fought tenaciously in the courts and in 1961 finally won reinstatement with back pay. Her political creed embraced the values of bluntness, doggedness, and observance of the rules of the game. "There are some things I don't believe in doing if they're unrealistic," she was once heard to say. Her directness, her discomfort with shared authority, her impatience to get on with a job and—not least—her own ambitions in North Philadelphia led her to demand and receive an assurance that the Model Cities program in Philadelphia would be hers in fact as well as in title.

This personal view was reinforced by Mrs. Watson's understanding of what had transpired under the program before she took it over. She knew that the Area-Wide Council had secured the removal of one Model Cities administrator and that it had successfully appealed a cut in the AWC's operating budget to the mayor, thus undercutting the administrator's authority.[34] There was to be no confusion of Model Cities with the poverty program: Model Cities, as she saw it, was "a mayor's program," and Goldie Watson was to act for the mayor.

Mrs. Watson had, as indicated, a special distaste for what she saw as sophomoric rhetorical solutions to problems. That alone would have sufficed to bring her into conflict with the AWC, which tended to see the problems of North Philadelphia less as matters of jobs, credit, delivery of services, and the like than as questions of powerlessness and the unresponsiveness of institutions. In addition, years earlier Mrs. Watson had had political contacts with AWC Executive Director Meek, in the course of arranging for a visit of the late Reverend Martin Luther King, Jr., to Philadelphia. By all accounts, the collaboration of the social worker and the politician was fraught with friction.

Mrs. Watson's assumption of the Model Cities administrator's office fundamentally changed the nature of relations between the city and the AWC. No longer was it a question of how much citizen participation and control there would be, or even whether some uneasy modus vivendi could be worked out. Nor was it even a question of whether an ad hoc organization or the city government would be the dominant influence. Now it was a question, simply put, of who would run the program: Meek or Watson, the black activists or the Democratic party, the starry-eyed staff of the Area-Wide Council or the "professionals" at city hall.

34. *Philadelphia Inquirer*, February 28, 1969.

No matter how the question is put, the mixture is explosive. Meek and Watson were both strong-willed. They had firm and quite different ideas about the program. The Democratic party had had a considerable role in the administration of the Community Action program. Now it was virtually excluded from the patronage possibilities of a $25-million-per-year program, one of whose statutory objectives was to employ local people in program projects. And finally, the AWC held a skeptical view of the role of "professionals" in solving community problems. Mrs. Watson's view, colored perhaps by her teaching background, was far more deferential to expertise. True, in one sense the conflict was over citizen participation. But it was also over basically divergent conceptions of the program.

While the dispute remained formally between the AWC and the city, slowly it grew to be a dispute between the AWC and a new competitor for its clientele as well. Goldie Watson was exceedingly well connected in North Philadelphia. She lived there; she owned a shop there; she managed election campaigns there; she dispensed party patronage there; and she had many friends there. Eventually she would utilize these assets in the struggle to control the Model Cities program.

In the meantime, her accession to office was marked by a sharp increase in conflict between the city and the Area-Wide Council. On her side, Mrs. Watson, impressed with the pliability of previous administrators and their precipitous departures, was determined to avoid the mistakes of her predecessors. Their experience and her own predilections led her to conclude that their common flaw had been a lack of firmness— a deficiency she soon set about to rectify.

For its part, the Area-Wide Council took note of the new situation. "We knew," acknowledged one AWC leader, "we couldn't attack Goldie as we did the white administrators. She had ties to North Philadelphia, and people knew she cared about doing something about the plight of black people there, even though we were on different tracks. She was well known, she had been a teacher, she had a business, and her husband was also popular. It was different."[35] In the judgment of some who observed the conflict at close range, the AWC seems to have redoubled its own resolve in response to the firmness it anticipated from Mrs. Watson.

The AWC's foreboding was warranted by events. The new administrator made clear her impatience with protest tactics, her disdain for

35. Interview, Philadelphia, July 19, 1974.

some of the work-product of the AWC staff (as embodied in the application submitted to HUD in December 1968), and her insistence on adherence by the AWC to strict standards of financial accountability. Above all, Mrs. Watson told the Area-Wide Council, according to a later city hall statement, that it

would have to face up to the fact that its role was advisory—that it was nonsense to pretend that elected officials ever intended to give up their right to make the final decisions related to the program. The new administrator took these positions *before* HUD began to insist that she do so. She was able to do so because her political strength as an individual in the model neighborhood was far greater than that of the Area-Wide Council as an organization.[!][36]

As Mrs. Watson was assuming office in Philadelphia, the Nixon administration was getting its bearings in Washington. By March 1969, HUD's new policy on citizen participation was emerging. HUD insisted that existing institutions (particularly city governments) play the primary role in operating Model Cities programs, and it especially wanted to exclude citizen participation organizations from responsibility for operating the programs.[37] Citizens' groups in a number of cities had proposed the creation of citizen-dominated corporations to implement Model Cities plans. In a March 1969 letter to Model Cities mayors, HUD ruled these arrangements out, except in the rarest circumstances.

The Philadelphia application submitted to HUD in December 1968 had, of course, contained plans to create seven operating corporations to be either controlled or strongly influenced by the AWC. Quite apart from this, HUD required that the scale of the Philadelphia application be revised downward—from $49 million to roughly $25 million. For reasons not entirely clear, the revised application, submitted on April 30 with Mrs. Watson's approval, continued to emphasize the new corporations, in the face of HUD disapproval of exactly this type of mecha-

36. "The View from City Hall," *Public Administration Review,* vol. 32 (September 1972), p. 397. This article presents the official city view of the controversy. See also "A Bill of Particulars Relating to the Performance of the Area-Wide Council as the Citizen Participation Unit of the Philadelphia Model Cities Program" (unpublished statement of the Philadelphia Model Cities Administrator, September 12, 1969; processed), p. 1: "the critical point is that the Administrator had deep concerns about the philosophy and operations of the Area Wide Council *before* the new federal guidelines became known in the latter part of May [1969]" (emphasis in the original).

37. Letter from Floyd H. Hyde to Mayor James H. J. Tate and other mayors, March 19, 1969, quoted in *North City Area-Wide Council* v. *Romney,* 329 F. Supp. at 1127.

nism. In due course, the revised application brought a predictably negative response from HUD, which demanded changes in the revised application that would downgrade the corporations, prevent the AWC from controlling them, and require the city to play a more active part in running them. In this way, HUD provided the *casus belli* in the conflict between the AWC and Mrs. Watson: "In City Hall and the office of the Model Cities administrator, the HUD position was seen as a means of clarifying relationships that had become unclear and unworkable."[38] A Republican administration in Washington had seen fit to strengthen the hand of the Democratic machine in Philadelphia.

The break came quickly. With each side blaming the other for the failure to consult, the city unilaterally responded to HUD's critique of its revised application by proposing an amendment retaining the corporations but allowing the AWC to nominate a maximum of one-third of their directors. Significantly, the remainder were to be nominated by Mrs. Watson or by citizens' groups chosen by her. The AWC, in short, was to have no real operating role. Instead, Mrs. Watson was to take charge of the implementation of the program. This amendment was filed with HUD on June 9, 1969. Three weeks later the AWC's contract was due to lapse. Pressing her advantage, Mrs. Watson made its renewal contingent on the AWC's acceptance of the city's amendments to the proposal and the new power relations these amendments implied.[39] The Area-Wide Council board voted to bring suit instead.

The decision to sue was a critical one for the Area-Wide Council. For although the AWC emerged victorious in the courts, it took nearly three years to achieve that result. During that time events occurred outside the courtroom that were ultimately to prevent the AWC from benefiting from the vindication gained inside the courtroom. The juxtaposition of these two sets of events is a major theme in this controversy.

It is probably not an overstatement to characterize the decision to sue as an action undertaken on principle. At the point of decision, the AWC could still have had a contract renewal, albeit on much less favorable terms. Some in the Area-Wide Council urged such a course, but for most it was out of the question:

We searched our souls. A few of us *were* ready to be bought off for that dollar figure [the $540,000 for the next year of AWC operating expenses].

38. "The View from City Hall," p. 398.

39. HUD actually added two other restrictions on July 3. These are described below. For Mrs. Watson's conditions for a new contract with the AWC, see *Philadelphia Inquirer*, July 2, 1969.

Some of us argued that it was better to accept a drastically reduced role in the program than to chuck it all after two years of blood, sweat, and tears.

After much discussion, we voted overwhelmingly to refuse the unilateral contract terms. Instead we decided to take both the city and HUD to court to demand that our right to participate meaningfully be restored.[40]

Why did they decide to "chuck it all" and go to court? No doubt the AWC leadership was under no illusions about Mrs. Watson's intentions and what it would be like trying to retain the independence of the organization under the changed circumstances reflected in the most recent amendments to the city's application. Doubtless, too, further restrictions on the AWC's role, added by HUD in early July 1969, gave a heightened sense of futility to the AWC leadership. But more was involved than that. Meek's vision of community-government relations was not merely a local one. He was in touch with his counterparts in citizens' organizations throughout the northeastern United States and was conscious of the impact the Area-Wide Council's action might have on the fortunes of poverty organizations elsewhere. He was eager to establish "a precedent" on the rights of citizens even if that entailed some immediate sacrifices for the AWC. In tracking the effect of Area-Wide Council litigation, it is interesting to see how this calculation worked out in the end.

The View from the Bench

The litigation focused on two closely connected decisions. The first was the city's decision, in response to HUD's prodding, to amend its revised application by reducing the role of the Area-Wide Council in the seven operating corporations that were to be established. The second was HUD's acceptance of the application as amended and its simultaneous imposition of two further conditions. One of them prohibited members of the corporate boards from simultaneously holding AWC membership after one year; the other prohibited the AWC from nominating any board members after the first year.

These two decisions, the complaint alleged, were illegal because the reduction of the AWC's role in the operating corporations violated the "widespread citizen participation" requirement of the Model Cities Act. The complaint asked the federal district court to order HUD to review

40. "Maximum Feasible Manipulation," p. 386 (emphasis in the original).

the Philadelphia plan again and not to require the revisions in the AWC's role that were ordered previously. It also asked, essentially, for reinstatement of the Area-Wide Council as the sole citizen participation organization, with appropriate funding.[41]

The district court dismissed the complaint, holding that the Area-Wide Council and the several residents of North Philadelphia who joined in the suit lacked standing to sue and that, in any event, there had been no violation of law by HUD or the city.[42] The AWC took an appeal to the court of appeals, which reversed the district court.[43] The court assumed that the plaintiffs had standing[44] and proceeded to HUD's argument that its program decisions were discretionary and therefore not subject to judicial review.

HUD argued that it had discretion to approve applications based on its determination of whether the plans meet statutory criteria. This discretion, in HUD's view, was not judicially reviewable. In the first place, the Model Cities Act contained no provision for judicial review, and the Administrative Procedure Act expressly precludes judicial review of action "committed to agency discretion."[45] HUD went on to contend that judicial review of whether a particular plan satisfied the "citizen participation" and "local initiative" requirements of the act would be particularly inappropriate. It would involve the courts in weighing how much participation is sufficient and would tie HUD's hands by freezing citizen participation requirements, preventing HUD from altering them as it gained more and more experience in administering "legislation as frankly experimental as the Model Cities Act. . . ."[46] HUD urged, in summary, that courts were simply not equipped to fashion standards for citizen participation.

The court of appeals gave the shortest of shrift to this argument, observing that "[u]nless the language or structure of a particular statute precludes judicial review, there is a presumption that administrative

41. Complaint, Appendix, pp. 19(a)–22(a), *North City Area-Wide Council* v. *Romney*, 428 F.2d 754.

42. The district court's opinion, dated November 12, 1969, was not reported.

43. 428 F.2d 754.

44. Two decisions of the United States Supreme Court, liberalizing the law of standing, had intervened. *Association of Data Processing Service Organizations* v. *Camp*, 397 U.S. 150 (1970); *Barlow* v. *Collins*, 397 U.S. 159 (1970).

45. 5 U.S.C. § 701(a).

46. Brief for the Federal Appellees, p. 19, *North City Area-Wide Council* v. *Romney*, 428 F.2d 754.

action is reviewable"[47] and holding that the issue in the case did not involve agency discretion but agency conformity to law.

Having disposed of the reviewability question in these brief terms, the court turned to the merits of the complaint, the first appellate court in the country to address the "widespread citizen participation" question. The court recognized the Area-Wide Council's "right to be consulted and to participate in the planning and carrying out of the program," noting that this right had been recognized in HUD's own declaration of citizen participation policy—CDA Letter Number 3.[48] Then the court moved on to the two critical decisions: the city's decision to amend the application and HUD's decision to accept the amended application and to impose additional requirements. These had been made without any citizen participation; their effect was to work a "major modification" of the Philadelphia program. "While not every decision regarding a Program may require full citizen participation, certainly decisions which change the basic strategy of the Program do require such participation."[49] Hence, the court found there had been a violation of the Model Cities Act.[50]

The case was remanded to the district court, which held a lengthy hearing on the allegations of the complaint. The district court found that HUD's demand for revisions in the Philadelphia plan was in accordance with a longstanding HUD policy against permitting citizen participation components actually to operate Model Cities programs; it cast the blame for the AWC's lack of participation in the revisions on the AWC itself, for it had been unwilling "to cooperate and negotiate"; and, finally, it found the Philadelphia program to be operating within the bounds of the "widespread citizen participation" required by the act.[51] Once again, the district court dismissed the complaint.

And again, the court of appeals reversed.[52] As in its previous opinion, the court laid the principal responsibility for the violation of the act at HUD's door. At her meeting with a HUD official, the court said, Mrs. Watson discussed HUD's "new policy" regarding citizen participation

47. 428 F.2d at 757, citing *Abbott Laboratories* v. *Gardner,* 387 U.S. 136, 141 (1967).

48. 428 F.2d at 757–58.

49. Ibid. at 758.

50. Interestingly, the court spoke only of a violation by HUD, without explicitly naming the city as a violator.

51. 329 F. Supp. 1124.

52. 456 F.2d 811.

in the operation of the Model Cities program. She "protested the new policy but apparently finally acceded to it." The court added in a footnote: "We do not intend to imply any weakness of character on the part of Mrs. Watson. Indeed, it seemed to have been a situation where [he] who pays the piper calls the tune."[53] The court's rather transparent view was that this was another case of unconscionable political and bureaucratic machinations emanating from Washington.

According to the court of appeals, the tune being called was discordant. It conflicted with the intention of Congress, as elaborated in the act and in HUD's own CDA Letter Number 3:

Perhaps the best expression of Congress' intent in passing the Act was employed by plaintiffs' counsel in oral argument in this court: *viz.*, "Power to the powerless," that is to say, it was the intention of Congress to cause the poverty-stricken citizens of our larger cities to improve their lot by their own efforts.[54]

For the court, this was no mere rhetoric. It later stated that the revised application of April 30, 1969, "clearly demonstrated the powerlessness of the citizens to influence decisions affecting their community as the factor most responsible for perpetuating the undesirable conditions existing in the target area."[55] Indeed, the court appears to have been enthusiastic about citizen participation in the operation of the program, for it went on to disparage HUD's contrary policy, which, it said, "seems . . . to have been directed toward excluding AWC from exercising a direct operational function as we think was required by CDA Letter No. 3."[56] Thus, for the first time, the court held not only that the Area-Wide Council had a right to participate in any changes, but that the changes themselves were illegal because the new HUD policy on which the changes were based was itself illegal.

The holding of the first court of appeals opinion had been entirely procedural: changes in the "basic strategy" of a program can be made only if there is citizen participation. The holding of the second opinion went further: citizen participation must extend beyond consultation into the operation of the program. Both opinions had applicability well beyond the Philadelphia program, but the second purported to constrain HUD far more than the first.

I say "purported to" because what happened after the opinion, in

53. Ibid. at 816.
54. Ibid. at 813–14.
55. Ibid. at 815.
56. Ibid. at 816.

Philadelphia as well as at HUD, is an entirely separate matter from what may have been contemplated by the opinion. Before turning to that, it is well to make more explicit some of the premises that underlay the decisions of the court of appeals.

First of all, the court tended to construe the Model Cities Act as if it were construing the Community Action program. It defined "widespread citizen participation" to require "citizen participation, negotiation, and consultation in the major decisions which are made for a particular Model Cities Program."[57] The subtleties of "widespread" versus "maximum feasible" citizen participation were lost on the judges. There is in fact no evidence that the rich background underlying these cryptically contrasting statutory phrases, or the differing extent to which the two programs were to be subject to city government control, was ever brought to the court's attention. Nor is this surprising. Neither the judges nor the lawyers had any reason to be versed in the nuances of the various social programs that occupy the time of politicians and bureaucrats. In the absence of any such guidance, the court of appeals tended to fall back on misleading half-truths about "the intention of Congress to cause the poverty-stricken citizens of our larger cities to improve their lot by their own efforts."

The lack of such guidance led the court to an unnecessarily dogmatic conception of "widespread citizen participation,"[58] a conception that took "participation" to mean participation in decisionmaking and "widespread" participation to mean participation in all major decisions. In the abstract, "widespread" is an expansive term. But, compared to "maximum feasible," it is quite clearly restrictive. In statutory interpretation, of course, context is everything: "Words in statutes are not unlike words in a foreign language in that they too have 'associations, echoes, and overtones.' Judges must retain the associations, hear the echoes, and capture the overtones."[59] Against the background of "maximum feasible participation" under the Community Action legislation, an interpretation of "widespread participation" that read it as requiring "extensive" but not necessarily "exhaustive" involvement of community organiza-

---

57. 428 F.2d 758.

58. Some of the many uncertainties of the concept of "political participation" are explored by Sidney Verba and Norman H. Nie, "Political Participation," in Fred Greenstein and Nelson Polsby, eds., *Handbook of Political Science*, vol. 4 (Addison Wesley, 1975), pp. 1–74.

59. Felix Frankfurter, "Reflections on Reading Statutes," in Alan F. Westin, ed., *The Supreme Court: Views from Inside* (Norton, 1961), p. 80, quoting Sir Ernest Barker, "Introduction" to Aristotle, *Politics*, p. lxiii.

tions would have been more in keeping with what Congress seems vaguely to have had in mind.[60] But courts generally construe only one law at a time.

The court of appeals never seemed to sense that there was a middle ground between no judicial review, on the one hand, and an expansive reading of the act, on the other. In its second opinion, the court went even further, holding that participation in the actual operation of the program was also required. This position was later retracted in the third and final *Area-Wide Council* appeal, discussed below. Taken literally, it would have meant that the national policy adopted by HUD in early 1969 and later partially codified in CDA Letter Number 10B was illegal. This view reflected the court's second set of assumptions—about the respective roles of law and policy in the Model Cities program.

Not only did the court fail to construe the Model Cities statute to reflect a greater concern with the problems and capacities of city governments than was manifested in the Community Action program; it also failed to accord HUD very much latitude to change policy.[61] Accordingly, the court treated CDA Letter Number 3, promulgated by the Johnson administration in 1967, as if it had the force of law. In fact, of course, it was only the vaguest kind of policy statement. Even by the time the *Area-Wide Council* litigation reached the court of appeals for the first time, CDA Letter Number 3 had been superseded in several material respects by CDA Letter Number 10B.

Of course, CDA Letter Number 10B had not been issued at the time of the events in question (June and July 1969), but it was, as I have said, a reflection of some of the policy changes that had been put into effect earlier in 1969. The court of appeals gave no legal force to those policy changes, holding flatly that they contravened CDA Letter Number 3.[62]

60. An earlier district court opinion, subsequently reversed, had indeed construed the phrase not to require citizen involvement in every single major decision. *Shannon* v. *United States Department of Housing and Urban Development*, 305 F. Supp. 205, 223–24 (E.D. Pa. 1969), *reversed*, 436 F.2d 809 (3d Cir. 1970).

61. These two aspects of the Third Circuit's outlook were related. "The very essence of the Act," the court said, "is participation by the inhabitants of the affected community. . . ." 456 F.2d at 818. That view of the act, of course, tends to support both an expansive interpretation of the participation provision and severe limitations on HUD's discretion to vary the participation requirements.

62. On the merits, this was a highly dubious interpretation of CDA Letter Number 3, rendered doubly questionable by CDA Letter Number 6, issued in October 1968 and stating that the CDA (City Demonstration Agency, a term which includes citizen participation components) was not to be "a multi-functional operating agency." U.S. Department of Housing and Urban Development, "Budget Submission Requirements—CDA Letter No. 6," MC 314.7 (May 1970).

In other words, the court accorded legal recognition to policy found in the initial flurry of CDA letters and nowhere else. There seemed to be no room in the opinions for policy development as the program got going, for changes to match the accumulation of administrative experience, or to follow changes in HUD leadership. The court's opinions gave great scope to law and none to policy.

Finally, as we have already seen, the court of appeals viewed Washington as the villain. It is difficult to say whether the judges were incensed at what they may have viewed as the Nixon administration's efforts to kill citizen participation or at the bureaucratic malevolence the federal courts increasingly have found in the administrative law litigation that comes before them, exemplified in this instance by HUD's apparent highhandedness. Either way, the city was not regarded as the prime mover; rather, the city was more likely seen as being caught between the AWC and HUD, resolving its conflict in favor of "he who pays the piper."

The litigation setting was so familiar as to encourage the court to see the conflict in these terms: an administrative agency, perhaps under "political pressure," denies citizens their rights under applicable statutes and its own guidelines. What this perspective omits, of course, is the conflict between Meek and Watson, the struggle between them for control of the Model Cities program in Philadelphia, the conflicts between community organizers and party organizers and between mass power and expertise, that lay at the heart of the lawsuit. The court also failed to see how convenient the pressure from HUD was for a Model Cities administrator eager to play her own independent political role in the model neighborhood, for, as I have noted, "In city hall and the office of the Model Cities administrator, the HUD position was seen as a means of clarifying relationships that had become unclear and unworkable."[63]

That is not to say that the court of appeals was unaware of these frictions. But it seemed to undervalue their importance, to regard them as irrelevant to the appropriate legal decision, as mere obstacles to the future implementation of a legally correct decision. The operative facts on which the court zeroed in were the two decisions: the city's decision to amend its revised application—a decision the court practically regarded as coerced by HUD—and HUD's own decision to accept the amendments and impose further restrictions on the powers of the AWC. Everything else was background.

63. "The View from City Hall," p. 398.

The appellate court diagnosed the problem as one of "powerlessness," but in fact a cogent argument can be made that the problem was not one of too little power but of too much competing power: the model neighborhood had not one but two routes to city hall, through Meek and Watson, and the two channels were competing for the right of exclusive access to the model neighborhood. This aspect of the dispute, not well communicated to or understood by the courts, shaped the outcome of the controversy decisively.

On the Ground

The federal courts took no longer than usual to hear and decide the *Area-Wide Council* case. Although some delays were encountered in the district court, the court of appeals heard the second appeal on an expedited basis. Nevertheless, from the time of the contested decisions made by HUD and the city in mid-1969 to the second decision of the court of appeals, two years and eight months had elapsed: the second decision was rendered at the end of February 1972.

During all this time, no injunction was in effect. Both district court decisions had been favorable to HUD and to the city. Yet no request had been made by the Area-Wide Council for injunctive relief pending appeal. Hence HUD and the city were free to move ahead with their plans despite the lawsuit and despite the first reversal by the court of appeals, which only went so far as to reinstate the complaint and remand the case to the district court for further proceedings.

Even had there been a request for an injunction pending appeal, it would have been difficult to frame an order that preserved the status quo in an equitable fashion until the controversy was disposed of. The Philadelphia program was scheduled to move forward. An injunction either would have (1) stopped the program for the duration of the litigation; or (2) permitted the local program to go forward but with no citizen-participation component; or (3) permitted the AWC to carry on as the citizen participation component as proposed in the revised application before it was amended to reduce the AWC role. The first and most sweeping course would have been an unlikely one for a court to adopt, harmful as it was to the intended beneficiaries of the Model Cities program. The second would have been contrary to the very thrust of the lawsuit, which was intended to reestablish a powerful role for the citizens' organizations; it was not necessarily better than no injunctive relief at all. The third course would have prejudged the appeal in the AWC's favor and would have been difficult to undo in the event the district court were ultimately sustained.

The point is that there really was no status quo to preserve in this case, as there sometimes is in more conventional injunction cases. There was no equivalent to ordering a seller of property, for example, not to convey it to anyone else while the court determines whether another party who asserts a lawful interest in it has rights that ought to be recognized—no equivalent, in other words, to freezing the situation so that a court decision does not come too late. In the Philadelphia case, any injunctive relief might have inflicted some new harm as great as the harm of which the AWC was complaining. This brings me back to what I said at the outset of this chapter: courts are accustomed to sit in review of action already completed or about to be undertaken. Here, the courts were called upon to judge action very much in progress.

During the pendency of the litigation, things did not stand still on the ground. Starved for funds, the Area-Wide Council began to disintegrate. Not long after the break between the city and the AWC, Mrs. Watson began to organize her own "neighborhood councils," retaining the same geographic "hubs" around which the AWC had been organized. The neighborhood councils, capped by a formal Advisory Citizens' Committee, replaced the AWC as the citizen participation component, but on a strictly advisory basis.[64] The AWC had asked for an injunction to prevent Mrs. Watson from organizing her own citizen participation group, but no injunction had been obtained in the first round of the litigation. By the time of the second appeal, the neighborhood councils were a fait accompli.

The neighborhood councils were funded, but neither they nor the Advisory Citizens' Committee were accorded the specialized staff capability the AWC had managed to build up. Technical and operational matters rested entirely with the Model Cities Administrator's office, where Mrs. Watson could insure that they were handled by the "professionals" whose judgment she tended to value highly. Consistent with HUD's requirements, contracts for operation of various projects under

64. See Erasmus Kloman, "Citizen Participation in the Philadelphia Model Cities Program: Retrospect and Prospect," *Public Administration Review*, vol. 32 (September 1972), pp. 406–08. The new structure and the projects of the Watson program are outlined in a handbook-brochure, "Philadelphia Model Cities Program: the Plan Is YOU!" (City of Philadelphia, n.d.).

the program were concluded with "established institutions." New corporations were not set up. The new citizen participation organization was thus wholly and explicitly confined to planning and evaluation. Mrs. Watson's vision of the program had triumphed.

Beginning with the funding of a number of highly visible projects calculated to win community support for the neighborhood councils, the AWC gradually faded. Many of its staff went on to other jobs,[65] some of them in other cities. Some AWC leaders defected to Mrs. Watson's Advisory Citizens' Committee, agreeing, in the words of the AWC, "to serve on that plantation-type structure which (like the old days of Urban Renewal) can only advise, while the politicians decide."[66] Using her considerable political skill, Mrs. Watson lured them with jobs and funding for projects, warning them that the AWC had embarked on a hazardous and uncertain course:

> We've got this $25 million. Now it took eight years for my case [against the school board] to get settled. Model Cities is a five-year program. This case will be in court forever, maybe after Model Cities is over. We are ready to move ahead now.[67]

It was not difficult to see where the power and opportunities lay. "Model Cities was the best action in North Philadelphia, and most of the Area-Wide Council people wanted to stay with it."[68] Trading on her network of friendships and connections in the model neighborhood and her control of the program, Goldie Watson was able to build a strong structure of elected neighborhood councils.

The demise of the Area-Wide Council was nearly total. "After the lapse of two and a half years since the termination of the AWC contract with the city administration, AWC had survived only as a skeletal organization. In fact, its main purpose had been to remain in existence to pursue its case in the courts and be revived in the event of victory."[69] The court of appeals had resuscitated "a corpse."[70]

The court of appeals, of course, was not ignorant of the existence of a new citizen participation component, but it seems not to have recog-

65. "Maximum Feasible Manipulation," p. 386.
66. Ibid.
67. Interview, Philadelphia, July 19, 1974.
68. Interview, Washington, August 28, 1974; also interview, Washington, June 21, 1974.
69. Kloman, "Citizen Participation in the Philadelphia Model Cities Program," p. 406.
70. Interview, Washington, April 3, 1974.

nized the extent to which power in the model neighborhood had changed hands. "Manifestly," it concluded,

the various programs have continued for a considerable length of time under the auspices of the Interim [Advisory Citizens'] Committee which eventually ceased to be "interim" and became a committee created from the target area. A misunderstanding of the law by the District Court has not inhibited the HUD programs. Nonetheless, we find ourselves unwilling to accept what we deem to be error to prevent or avoid the operation of the Act as intended by Congress. Perhaps a workable solution to the difficulties presented by the attitudes of the respective parties can be arrived at. It is possible and we hope probable that the passage of time may have sweetened the minds of the parties to this suit and their representatives.[71]

The court then proceeded to remand the case to the district court with instructions for it to enter an order reinstating the AWC as "the citizen participation organization for the Philadelphia Model Cities program."[72] The AWC was to be ordered to "negotiate in good faith with the existing citizen structure for the purpose of integrating that structure into the organization of the Area-Wide Council."[73] The city was also to negotiate a new citizen participation agreement with the AWC, without the 1969 amendments to the program that the court had found illegal; and both the city and HUD were directed to negotiate with the AWC "concerning all changes made in the Model Cities Program since May 27, 1969,"[74] the date of the HUD letter demanding changes in the revised application.

On paper, it was a sweeping victory for the Area-Wide Council. The district court had been decisively reversed. But the political developments of the preceding thirty-two months could not be reversed. The serious negotiations mandated by the opinion never really came off. There were some eventual meetings and some skirmishing but no agreement.

71. 456 F.2d at 818.
72. Ibid. Actually, the court of appeals ordered the reinstatement of the AWC "*insofar as it may be* the citizen participation organization for the Philadelphia Model Cities Program." Ibid. (emphasis supplied). When events later thwarted the reinstatement of the AWC, the court of appeals made much of the qualifying words of this sentence, stating that its earlier mandate "should not be construed . . . as a self-operating substitution of NCAWC for ACC." 469 F.2d at 1333. This, however, seems a purely retrospective view of the matter, for that court had ordered AWC "as such citizen representation organization" to negotiate with the ACC. 456 F.2d at 818.
73. Ibid.
74. Ibid.

Following the denial of a petition for certiorari,[75] the parties returned to the district court, which entered a judgment reinstating the AWC as the citizen participation component of the program, substituting it for the Advisory Citizens' Committee as a party to the contract, ordering the AWC to negotiate with the Advisory Citizens' Committee in order to integrate the latter into the AWC structure, and ordering the city to negotiate a new contract with the AWC.[76] The discussions between the Area-Wide Council and the city soon bogged down as before over the issue of control over the operations of the program, while those between the AWC and the Advisory Citizens' Committee could not resolve the question of the form of organizational integration.[77] Meanwhile, the AWC demanded a budget from the city, as provided by the district court's most recent order, and for its part the city declined to enter into any new contract until the AWC completed the court-ordered integration of the Advisory Citizens' Committee into its own organizational structure.

By the time these discussions were held, so much planning had gone forward and so many commitments had been made under the ongoing program that it was scarcely realistic to expect Mrs. Watson to undo them at a stroke, simply to accommodate a dormant rival organization. Nor, on its side, was the AWC willing to compromise away its hard-won, court-ordered rights. The AWC was genuinely fearful that a merger of the two organizations could only benefit Mrs. Watson, since she had the money and power to gain control of the membership. And so, the rival organizations confronted each other still, as they had over the years, each with power derived from a different source.

In this posture of stalemate, the parties were soon back in court, with the city urging that elections be conducted for the AWC board of directors. The district court acceded to that request in September 1972. The next month the parties were again in the court of appeals, for the third time in less than three years.

The court of appeals opinion begins: "This matter is before the court of appeals for the third time, and the end appears nowhere in sight."[78] Plainly, the court was tiring of the continuing supervisory responsibili-

75. 406 U.S. 963 (1972).

76. The district court's judgment is unreported.

77. A brief description of the negotiations may be found at 469 F.2d 1331–32. I have also relied on interviews for these events.

78. 469 F.2d at 1328.

ties imposed on it by its earlier decisions. Construing its own second opinion as requiring something other than the automatic substitution of the AWC for the Advisory Citizens' Committee,[79] the court held that if negotiations to integrate the two groups failed,

> some other step was required. The step chosen, elections in the target area for a NCAWC Board of Directors, was not inconsistent with our prior mandate, and was consistent with the statutory policy of "widespread citizen participation" in the Demonstration Cities and Metropolitan Development Act of 1966.[80]

The court dismissed as self-serving the Area-Wide Council's objections to the election, suggesting that they were rooted in the reluctance of the AWC's leaders to participate in the elections "because they might not be re-elected."[81] Impatient with the Area-Wide Council's adamance, the court of appeals added, curiously: "Our prior decisions did not hold that by intransigence NCAWC could force HUD to yield on this issue [of the AWC's participation in the actual operation of the program], and *did not suggest that HUD's position was inconsistent with the Act.*"[82] The protracted, continuing character of the lawsuit seems to have inclined the court toward a narrower view of the requirements of the Model Cities Act than the one it had earlier adopted.

Anxious to dispose of the controversy, the court of appeals affirmed the district court decision ordering elections, and early in 1973 the elections were finally held. Their outcome, of course, was not in doubt. William Meek had gone on to a university teaching job, and so the AWC was without its original leadership. Without funds for three and a half years, the Area-Wide Council was in no position to compete with an organization that had controlled the Model Cities program during that period. Mrs. Watson's candidates swept most of the hubs, her conception of citizen participation prevailed, and the controversy finally came to an end. The Area-Wide Council, twice vindicated in the federal courts, was beaten on the streets of North Philadelphia.[83]

In the end, Mrs. Watson's perseverence paid off. Nearly six years after assuming office, she still ran the Philadelphia Model Cities program, though she had since risen to the office of Deputy Mayor. "Goldie

79. A dubious interpretation. See n. 72, above.

80. 469 F.2d at 1333.

81. Ibid.

82. Ibid. (emphasis supplied). Compare 456 F.2d at 816.

83. On the perils of courts choosing sides in ongoing political contests where each side claims to be the "legitimate government" and the outcome on the ground is uncertain, see *Luther* v. *Borden*, 7 How. 1 (1849).

Watson," an acquaintance remarked, "is not someone you forget once you've met her."

One Case, One Place: Philadelphia and the Nation

The court's statutory exegesis was performed entirely in the abstract. Outside of Philadelphia, it knew nothing about patterns of citizen participation, though of course it was making law not just for Philadelphia but for the Model Cities program in general.

What this meant in practice was that the court could have no sense for what was unique about the Philadelphia case and what was not, and it consequently had no ability to anticipate what the impact of a decision one way or the other might be on the program as a whole. This matter was especially important because the *Area-Wide Council* case was the first in which a court of appeals construed the meaning of "widespread citizen participation." Presumably, the decision would be viewed with interest by other courts, by participants in other Model Cities programs, and by HUD.

The orientation of the court was to regard the *Area-Wide Council* case as a single controversy requiring resolution, not as an example of a pattern of controversies across the country and certainly not as an example of only one pattern among several. Yet it was both of these latter things as well.

In city after city, a kind of natural antipathy developed between the leader of a strong citizen participation group and the city CDA director or Model Cities administrator. This rivalry was fostered by the vagueness of the early HUD policy, which encouraged both sides to claim overlapping powers. Often, as in Philadelphia, what was at stake was not so much the substance of the program as the power of one side or the other to represent the target community in the program and to represent the program in the target community.

In this infighting, some standard repertoires developed. One of the strongest weapons in the citizen participation arsenal was the threat to demand the resignation of the CDA director. Like Philadelphia, many cities went through three or four CDA directors in a couple of years. On their part, the CDA directors cultivated the rather less successful technique of undermining the leaders of citizens' groups with their own boards of directors. A common way of sowing discord in a neighborhood organization was to complain of its inevitable "staff domination."[84] Mrs. Watson attempted to drive a wedge between Meek and his board by demanding board votes on some of the uncompromising positions Meek took in his dealings with her. Earlier Model Cities administrators in Philadelphia had used the same tactic.[85] But the tactic was hardly unique to Philadelphia.

In a few cities the warfare threatened to get out of hand. In Cleveland, the neighborhood organization succeeded in obtaining the dismissal of the CDA director, but his successor in turn secured the removal of the organization's board chairman. She, however, made a comeback, but this proved to be only temporary.[86] At its best, this kind of rivalry produced a system of mutual deterrence, sometimes mutual respect. At its worst, it gave rise to instability in one or both jobs, which threatened the continuity of programs.

Viewing the *Area-Wide Council* case as sui generis, the Third Circuit evinced no understanding of the recurrent character of these disputes, of which the Meek-Watson confrontation was but one illustration. Indeed, it paid little heed to the Meek-Watson side of the dispute altogether, for it saw HUD as the prime mover. Understandably, therefore, the court made no effort to consider the effect of its decision on the delicate relations between CDA directors and the leaders of citizens organizations.

But the decision could have a considerable, perhaps destabilizing, impact in cities where rivalries of this kind were present. For one of the recognized major decisions of a Model Cities program is the decision to hire and fire CDA directors. The expansive opinions in the *Area-Wide Council* case may easily be read to require citizen participation in these decisions, and that is precisely what was demanded in some cities.[87] In Ann Arbor, for instance, the citizens' organization, having brought down two CDA directors and having successfully recommended the appoint-

84. See, e.g., Michael A. Di Nunzio, "Resident Participation: the Cities' Perspective," *Denver Law Journal* (Special Magazine Issue, 1971), p. 42; Marshall Kaplan, Gans and Kahn, "The First Action Year of the Model Cities Program in Denver," p. 51.

85. See *Philadelphia Daily News*, December 13, 1967; *Philadelphia Inquirer*, May 26, 1968.

86. Marshall Kaplan, Gans and Kahn, "Ten Model Cities," pp. 185–89.

87. "Nashville Model Cities," p. 777; *Model Cities Policy Bd. of Ann Arbor v. Lynn*, 497 F.2d 924 (6th Cir. 1974).

ment of the third, then demanded his resignation as well, bringing suit to gain recognition of this right.[88]

If the Third Circuit had known of these disputes and their implications for Model Cities programs, would it still have formulated so expansive a conception of citizen participation? Had it understood their recurrent and essentially competitive character, would it have been more willing to recognize an umpiring role for HUD in such controversies? Perhaps it is indicative of the difficulties of reconciling the *Area-Wide Council* opinions with the denial of at least some of what the citizens' group was demanding in Ann Arbor that in the latter case the Sixth Circuit Court of Appeals, affirming a judgment against the citizens' group, wrote no opinion.

If Philadelphia typifies a pattern, it is only one pattern: there were others. But the court of appeals was equally unaware of these.

Often the relations between CDA directors and citizens' organizations were far from adverse. Sometimes they were closer than HUD would have wished. A number of mayors made early judgments that close identification with the fortunes of the Model Cities program might prove damaging to their political careers, especially if what were optimistically billed as "model neighborhoods" were later engulfed in civil disturbance—this being, of course, the time of the urban riots of the 1960s. Unable to avoid having a program at all, some mayors nonetheless sought to dissociate themselves from it. A common way of doing this, adopted in some major cities, was to abdicate authority over the program, under the banner of neighborhood control. Where this happened, CDA directors were typically under the control of neighborhood organizations, which were accorded important veto powers.[89]

As Sundquist has pointed out, programs in which CDAs were subject to resident control encountered severe problems of involving the various city agencies in the common effort required for the success of a coordinated program.[90] This problem would, of course, be exacerbated if it were accompanied by the kind of executive disinterest that often was at its source. In these cases, HUD often stepped in to force the city to play a more active part. CDA Letter Number 10A required the local

88. Ibid. Actually, the case is more complex than I have depicted it, because the policy board also challenged the validity of certain city ordinances relating to the program.

89. See, e.g., Marshall Kaplan, Gans and Kahn, "Ten Model Cities," p. 259.

90. *Making Federalism Work*, pp. 100, 108.

government to "assume early, continuous, and ultimate responsibility for the development, implementation, and performance of the Model Cities Program."[91]

In practice, what this signaled was HUD's willingness to monitor cities that had delegated basic power over the program to citizens' groups.[92] St. Louis, for example, seemed to HUD to present an egregious case of a mayor's surrender of responsibility in order to avoid being associated with the program. A disjointed program was presented to HUD, the community organization was given extensive veto power over project proposals and contracts, and the organization was formally made part of the city's "Model City Agency." Following suggestions from HUD that these arrangements were impermissible, the mayor wrote to ask for clarification. What he got back from Washington was an ultimatum that "ineffective performance in the program, resulting from improper or arbitrary use of any of the veto powers or lack of exercise of the Chief Executive's responsibility and authority with regard to the program may be sufficient grounds for suspension or reduced funding."[93] A subsequent letter enclosed draft amendments to St. Louis Model Cities ordinance—the minimum changes required to meet HUD policy.

Here, unlike the Philadelphia case, HUD was ordering a reluctant city to reduce citizen participation that was widespread and to increase its own role. Unlike Philadelphia, this time the piper was indeed calling the tune. The court of appeals, of course, had no way of differentiating these two cases, because it had no way of knowing of the pattern that St. Louis exemplified. Was HUD's action in St. Louis also forbidden by the opinions in the Philadelphia case? Would HUD have no role in balancing city authority against citizen power?

The *Area-Wide Council* case had implications for still another pattern of citizen participation. Philadelphia had one target area and one citizens' organization up to the time of the litigation. Certain other cities, however, had more than one model neighborhood and more than one citizens' group. This complexity, which generally derived from the dis-

91. U.S. Department of Housing and Urban Development, "Model Cities Policy Statements—CDA Letter No. 10A," MC 3135.1 (December 1969).

92. See Butler, "Resident Participation: The Federal Perspective," p. 37.

93. Letter, Floyd H. Hyde, Assistant Secretary of HUD, to Alfonso J. Cervantes, Mayor of St. Louis, January 9, 1970, p. 4; Cervantes to Hyde, December 18, 1970. Copies in HUD files. For the background to this exchange, I have relied on interviews in Washington, July 24, 1974, August 23, 1974.

tribution of political forces or of ethnic groups within the city, made it difficult to ascertain exactly who "the citizens" were.

The program in Youngstown, for example, embraced two quite different areas.[94] The Youngstown plan had originally proposed a single target area, the poor but politically influential northeast. Though part of the city, this area was more rural than urban. HUD objected to the plan, insisting that a more urban, more populous neighborhood on the south side be added.

The integration of these two areas in a single program was never really accomplished. Both areas complained of inadequate participation in the program. The northeast objected that both the CDA director and his deputy were south side residents. The south side, on the other hand, had a grievance about the composition of the citizen participation component. Fearful of being outnumbered, the northeast had asked for equal representation, whereas the south side residents wanted representation solely by population. Eventually, a compromise formula, giving the south side less representation than its population warranted, was worked out.

Under the circumstances, this was probably the most equitable and practicable arrangement available. But was it lawful under the doctrine of the *Area-Wide Council* case? The conception of citizen participation forged by the court of appeals was heavily imbued with representative, majoritarian assumptions, scarcely articulated because Philadelphia had only one model neighborhood and one citizens' organization. Where there was more than one neighborhood and more than one group, could "widespread citizen participation" under the act be based on elections not conducted on a one-man, one-vote basis?[95]

Cities like Los Angeles and Denver, with large numbers of both black and Spanish-speaking poor, also had two model neighborhoods, one for each group. Here, too, power sharing was the issue.

In Denver, the issue was especially acute because one neighborhood was added after the other.[96] For the most part, the Denver Community

94. Marshall Kaplan, Gans and Kahn, "Ten Model Cities," pp. 263–70. I am also indebted to Larry Reed for a discussion of the Youngstown and Nashville programs.

95. Cf. *Mahan* v. *Howell*, 410 U.S. 315 (1973); *Avery* v. *Midland County*, 390 U.S. 474 (1968).

96. Denver data are derived from Marshall Kaplan, Gans and Kahn, "The First Action Year of the Model Cities Program in Denver"; Al Williams, "Resident Participation: The Citizen's Perspective," *Denver Law Journal* (Special Magazine Issue,

Action program had been dominated by Mexican-Americans, who at first took less interest in Model Cities. The Model Cities program tended to be controlled by blacks, who had an overwhelming majority on the board of directors of a well-funded, well-staffed citizen participation component. As the Community Action program was being phased out and Model Cities was becoming more attractive, the Mexican-Americans became more interested in Model Cities. To accommodate both sets of interests required expansion of the target area and restructuring of the citizen participation organization. Both of these were accomplished under pressure from HUD and the city, after months of debate, cajolery, persuasion, and threat.

During this time, there was a possibility of stalemate comparable in some ways to the breakdown in relations that occurred in Philadelphia. Had the recognized citizens' organization been firm in its refusal to share power with the Mexican-American community, and had Denver, perhaps acting on HUD orders, canceled its contract with the organization over this issue, would there have been a violation of the "widespread citizen participation" requirement of the act?

In the end, it did not come to that, but problems remained. Although the target area was expanded, control over the citizen participation organization continued to rest with the black community. Did HUD or the city have power under the act to alter that situation? If the Mexican-Americans in Denver had brought suit to gain a larger share of participation, did the *Area-Wide Council* decisions support such a claim?

How target areas and citizens' groups were to relate to each other and to the city posed extremely difficult problems, as Youngstown and Denver suggest. The mandate of the Model Cities Act for "widespread citizen participation" and "local initiative in the planning" by no means resolved the question of how much participation, and by whom, was required at what stages of a program. The act did not provide guidelines to determine when a program was in danger of being taken over by one organization to the detriment of its competitors in the community. Umpiring competition of organizations with each other and with the city governments for decisionmaking authority would certainly seem to be HUD's responsibility, but the Third Circuit opinions placed formidable limits on what HUD could do in the area of citizen participation.

1971), pp. 44–46; Michael A. Di Nunzio, "Resident Participation: The Cities' Perspective"; interviews, Washington, June 21, 1974, July 31, 1974.

Although law can certainly grow out of a series of judicial opinions rendered one at a time, opinions rendered without rudimentary knowledge of the heterogeneity of local conditions run the risk of confusing decisionmakers and imposing on one type of situation requirements apt only for another. Given the diversity of situations across the country and the many forms in which issues of "widespread citizen participation" might have arisen, the *Area-Wide Council* decisions might have wreaked havoc with the national Model Cities program. They might have made the tenure of CDA directors more precarious than it already was. In the St. Louis type of case, the opinions would have undercut HUD's authority to make the local government much more responsible for planning and results. Broadly applied to a city like Youngstown, the decisions might have impaired the relations of the citizens' organizations, and in Denver they might actually have exacerbated already strained ethnic tensions.

These results did not come to pass, but for reasons that are not necessarily comforting. HUD continued its policy of scaling down the authority of citizens' groups, confining them to an evaluative role, and reinforcing the authority of cities. Few suits were filed, and none produced decisions as sweeping as those of the Third Circuit.[97] What is most difficult to measure, of course, is the extent to which the decisions had important but essentially negative results—that is, the extent to which they produced restraint on the part of CDA directors in dealing with citizens or prevented HUD from demanding some things it might otherwise have demanded. There may have been some of this, but probably not much. Outside Philadelphia, as well as in Philadelphia itself, the litigation ultimately had little effect.

The HUD reaction to the Philadelphia decisions was to ignore them in the administration of the national program. Outside of court, it scarcely took note of the decisions at all. HUD provided no guidance for its field offices on the meaning of the decisions for the programs in their regions. In some measure, this may reflect HUD's greater sensitivity than that of the court to local variations in Model Cities programs. The principles of the Philadelphia case were simply not formulated with

---

97. Those that were filed typically challenged some reduction in the former authority of the citizens' organization. See, e.g., *Bouchard* v. *Washington*, 356 F. Supp. 223 (D.D.C. 1973), *reversed*, 514 F.2d 824 (D.C. Cir. 1975); *Model Cities Policy Bd. of Ann Arbor* v. *Lynn*, 497 F.2d 924 (6th Cir. 1974).

other cities or other participation problems in mind. In the main, however, factors besides local variations were more important. It was never thought at HUD that Model Cities was a "legal" program in which the courts were to be major participants, and the litigation staff in the HUD general counsel's office did not have the influence to overcome this view even if it had wanted to. "No one paid any attention to the decision," a HUD official recalled; it was viewed as "an oddball case."[98] In the words of another, the hope was that it would "go away" if ignored.[99]

The decision could be ignored, in large part because it came from a federal court of appeals. Decisions of a court of appeals bind lower courts and administrators only in the circuit over which the court presides. Other courts of appeals are free to disregard prior decisions of circuits besides their own, though generally they do not do so. Plainly, the power to disregard decisions of other circuits is a useful safeguard against the possibility that ill-considered decisions will become the law of the land before there is an opportunity for a second look at the problem. At the same time, however, the limited authority of the courts of appeals provides many opportunities for administrators to avoid the impact of judicial decisions unless and until the Supreme Court finally rules on the question.

In the event, the *Area-Wide Council* case did go away. Though cited from time to time by citizens' groups in their conflicts with officials, the case seems not to have become a major weapon in their hands. This may have been due in part to HUD's determination to push on with its policy, whatever the Third Circuit said about it, and HUD wrote the checks. Citizens' groups could choose to go to court, but they risked their subsistence. If they knew the Philadelphia case in detail, they probably knew that the Area-Wide Council was dying even as it was winning in court. This was not an attractive fate for organizations with instincts for survival.

But much more subtle forces were also at work, these having to do with the natural history of the program. By the time of the decisions, the Model Cities program was well under way. In the contest for power, most of the maneuvering was already over. Citizens' groups and CDA directors had, for the most part, reached their accommodations, "struck their deals," as a HUD regional administrator put it.[100] The court de-

98. Interview, Washington, April 3, 1974.
99. Interview, Washington, July 24, 1974.
100. Interview, Washington, August 28, 1974.

cisions came too late to change the tenor of relations in most cities. The Area-Wide Council's desire to establish "a precedent" for other cities came in the end to nought. In the national program, as in the Philadelphia program, the court of appeals decisions were overtaken by events.

CHAPTER FOUR

Hobson v. *Hansen*: The Calculus of Equality in School Resources

As the *Area-Wide Council* case shows, the relation between events in and out of the courtroom can be complicated. It is often difficult for a court to ascertain precisely what role each party has played in the events that precede the litigation, and it is even more difficult to foresee the effect that the litigation will have on subsequent behavior. The *Area-Wide Council* case returned to court a third time because, without disobeying any court order, one of the parties was able to maneuver effectively enough on the ground to thwart what had been decided in court. Ultimately, these actions produced a fait accompli that had to be recognized by the same court that had earlier contemplated a quite different result.

If the *Area-Wide Council* case returned to court because the court had demonstrated only a limited capacity to influence the balance of political forces outside, *Hobson* v. *Hansen*[1] has returned, and may return again, for different reasons. *Hobson* recognized the right to equal distribution of school resources within a single school district. The *Hobson* court has demonstrated a considerable capacity to influence the behavior of the parties outside the courtroom. The parties took action in compliance with the orders of the court, and the action taken

1. 265 F. Supp. 902 (D.D.C. 1967), *appeal dismissed,* 393 U.S. 801 (1968), 269 F. Supp. 401 (1967), *affirmed sub nom. Smuck* v. *Hobson,* 408 F.2d 175 (D.C. Cir. 1969), *further relief ordered,* 320 F. Supp. 409 (1970), 320 F. Supp. 720, 327 F. Supp. 844 (1971), *unreported opinion and order denying plaintiffs' motion to hold the defendants in contempt,* Civ. No. 82–66, D.D.C., Feb. 17, 1973.

Though this usage does violence to the strict chronology of decisions, I shall refer to the two main decisions, reported at 269 F. Supp. 401 and 327 F. Supp. 844, as *Hobson I* and *Hobson II*, respectively.

has had effects. No party to *Hobson* has been able to thwart what was decided in court, and fast-moving events on the ground have not outpaced slower-moving events in the courthouse, as they did in the *Area-Wide Council* case. But the court has had difficulty estimating in advance the magnitude or even the exact direction of those effects. Consequently, one of its orders produced results that fell far short of what had been anticipated. This made necessary a second order, the implementation of which took a permissible but unexpected form that yielded rather perverse results. There now seems to be agreement among the parties that recalibration of the decree may be necessary once again.

Hobson raises a number of interesting questions about the ability of courts to measure the relationship between action to be taken and results to be achieved, and to gauge in advance what form the process of implementing its orders will take. Some of the court's problems of anticipation have derived from the way in which it defined the rights of the parties. There are thus important links between legal conceptions and social consequences. The process of defining rights bears heavily on the process of implementing them.

In the process of defining rights in *Hobson*, expert advice played an important role. The opinion in the second *Hobson* case was the product of an intriguing fusion, really a juxtaposition, of social science data on one side with the court's own "common sense approach" and "straightforward moral and constitutional arithmetic" on the other.[2] *Hobson II* thus affords a glimpse of the scope and limits of expert advice in litigation, as well as of the difficulty of anticipating how those subject to a judicial decree will adapt to it. On both counts, the sense may have been common, but the arithmetic proved to be anything but straightforward.

The District of Columbia Schools and the Hobson Suit

The District of Columbia maintained dual, racially separate school systems until 1954, when the Supreme Court ordered desegregation.[3] In the first decade following the Court's decision, however, racial segregation in the schools was not reduced significantly. The persistence of segregated education was due in part to policies pursued by the school

2. 327 F. Supp. at 859.
3. *Bolling v. Sharpe*, 347 U.S. 497 (1954).

board and in part to changes in residential patterns in and around the District of Columbia.

One of the board's policies that maintained much of the segregation allowed students to remain at the school they had attended in the 1953–54 school year, even if it were not the school to which they would be reassigned by the desegregation plan. Another practice that perpetuated segregation was the board's use of "optional zones." This policy permitted students to transfer from schools in their own geographical area to schools with low enrollments in other, mainly white, neighborhoods. These students were required to supply their own means of transportation. Whites made disproportionate use of this option, thereby avoiding integration.[4]

The more significant explanation for continued racial segregation, however, lies with forces beyond the board's control. The years after 1954 saw an increasing pattern of de facto segregation in housing and a rapid decline in the number of white children in the city schools. When the schools opened in the fall of 1954, there were 3,500 fewer white children enrolled than in the previous academic year, when 56.8 percent of the student population was white. By 1964, ten years after integration was formally begun, 126 of the 185 public elementary schools in the District were 90–100 percent black, while thirteen elementary schools were 90–100 percent white. By 1965, the proportion of white students in District public schools was slightly over 10 percent.[5]

To the limited extent that desegregation did occur, the board faced another problem. The range of academic performance was extremely wide. The school administration's response to this problem was a practice known as "ability grouping" or "tracking."[6] The tracking plan was proposed by Carl Hansen, Superintendent of Schools since 1957. Although the tracking plan was to group students according to ability rather than race, the effect of the plan was to resegregate them. Critics charged that children were being placed in tracks for reasons other than ability, that once children were placed in a particular track they were rarely transferred, and that children were being stigmatized by their

4. Joan C. Baratz, unpublished draft manuscript (hereafter cited as Baratz draft), p. 9, based on official school system figures. I am indebted to Dr. Baratz for guidance and information at several points in this chapter. See also Baratz, "Court Decisions and Educational Change: A Case History of the D.C. Public Schools, 1954–1974," *Journal of Law and Education*, vol. 4 (January 1975), pp. 63–80.

5. Baratz draft, p. 10.

6. Ibid., p. 12.

placements. The apparent rigidities and inequities of the tracking plan became a source of controversy shortly after its inception.

Pupil segregation was not the only racial grievance in the District of Columbia schools. A "color-blind" policy of teacher assignment was also resulting in the segregation of faculties along racial lines.[7] Inner-city schools were overcrowded, and patterns of resource allocation appeared to discriminate against schools in the black and poor neighborhoods. In 1966, Julius Hobson, Sr., a government employee and civil rights activist who was later elected to the school board, filed suit in federal district court against the Board of Education and the Superintendent of Schools, claiming that their policies were denying black and poor children their constitutional right to equal educational opportunity. Hobson also challenged the constitutionality of the act of Congress requiring that school board members be appointed by judges of the federal district court.[8] This challenge was severed from the main lawsuit, and a three-judge district court was convened to hear it. Because of the nature of the challenge, however, all three judges in this case were circuit judges, uninvolved in the appointment process. With Judge J. Skelly Wright dissenting, the court sustained the constitutionality of the statute, holding that Congress could grant appointive powers to federal judges in the District of Columbia.[9] At the request of the Judicial Conference of the District of Columbia Circuit, however, Congress subsequently amended the statute to provide for an elected Board of Education.[10]

Hobson's remaining claims were heard by a single judge, Circuit Judge Wright.[11] Judge Wright held a lengthy hearing and filed an exhaustive opinion and decree enjoining continued implementation of certain school board policies and ordering adoption of certain others.[12] I shall refer to this decision as *Hobson I*.

The court was readily able to identify a number of board policies that fostered continued segregation, in part, at least, intentionally.[13] One

7. Apparently, high-seniority white teachers had chosen to remain at or transfer to predominantly white schools.

8. D.C. Code of 1961, § 31-101.

9. 265 F. Supp. 902 (D.D.C. 1967).

10. D.C. Code of 1973, § 1-1101. A copy of the resolution may be found in *Smuck* v. *Hobson*, 408 F.2d 175, 194 (D.C. Cir. 1969) (Appendix to opinion of Danaher, J.).

11. Sitting by designation under 28 U.S.C. § 291(c).

12. 269 F. Supp. 401 (D.D.C. 1967).

13. Ibid. at 415–19.

was a policy permitting liberal transfers of white students to predominantly white schools on an easily made showing that integration would cause them "psychological upset." Similarly, the court found evidence of occasional gerrymandering of school boundaries for racial purposes, and it concluded that the purpose of "optional attendance zones," at least in several areas, was to allow white students a choice of schools where the neighborhood school was predominantly black. The court also found the segregation of teachers and principals that continued after 1954 to be unconstitutional.[14]

Tracking presented more difficult questions, and the court felt compelled to study tracking practices in great detail.[15] The school system had chosen a tracking arrangement that involved "the greatest amount of physical separation by grouping students in wholly distinct, homogeneous curriculum levels."[16] The effect of tracking was to separate academically developed, middle-class white children from academically deprived, poor black children, and the court inferred that the adoption of the tracking system in 1955 was probably based in part on racial considerations.[17]

But the court did not take the next step and find the tracking system a form of de jure segregation. Rather, it held that, whatever the purpose of tracking, its segregative effect (by race and class) was unconstitutional. The defects in the particular track system adopted by the school system were its inflexibility (little mobility occurred between tracks), the lack of remedial programs to help students on the bottom tracks, and the use of inappropriate tests to gauge ability. The track system was held to be a mode of government classification of students that was irrational and therefore violative of equal protection.

In tracking, as in school boundaries and faculty segregation, the court found at least traces of action intentionally undertaken to promote segregation. In the other aspects of school policy canvassed by Judge Wright, no segregatory intention was discerned. Yet the intentional segregation already identified formed the backdrop for the court's consideration of other practices under attack. For the court was by then quite ready to believe that, even if the school administration did not always intend to perpetuate segregation, it was nevertheless not unhappy when that result followed from its policies.[18]

14. Ibid. at 421–31, 501–03.
15. Ibid. at 442–92.
16. Ibid. at 443.
17. Ibid.
18. Ibid. at 419, 503.

Still, the court was obliged to judge policies that unintentionally redounded to the disadvantage of the poor and black by a standard different from the standard used to judge policies calculated to produce such adverse effects. Intentionally discriminatory policies constituted, per se, a violation of the Equal Protection Clause; unintentionally discriminatory policies might or might not violate equal protection, de-depending on the significance of the non-racial purposes and effects flowing from them.

Judge Wright proceeded to articulate a strict standard of judicial review of policies unintentionally producing negative effects on "disadvantaged minorities." To meet constitutional requirements, the court held, such policies must not merely rest on a "rational basis," the traditional standard to judge the validity of governmental classifications under the Equal Protection Clause. Rather, the court applied a stricter standard, formerly invoked when manifestly discriminatory classifications were involved or when non-discriminatory classifications had adverse discriminatory effects on "critical personal rights," such as the right to vote or the right of a defendant to appeal a criminal conviction.[19] The stricter standard adopted by the court requires "overriding justification" from those who have adopted the policy:

If the situation were one involving racial imbalance but in some facility other than the public schools, or unequal educational opportunity but without any Negro or poverty aspects (e.g., unequal schools all within an economically homogeneous white suburb), it might be pardonable to uphold the practice on a minimal showing of rational basis. But the fusion of these two elements in de facto segregation in public schools irresistibly calls for additional justification. What supports this call is our horror at inflicting any further injury on the Negro, the degree to which the poor and the Negro must rely on the public schools in rescuing themselves from their depressed cultural and economic condition, and also our common need of the schools to serve as the public agency for neutralizing and normalizing race relations in this country. With these interests at stake, the court must ask whether the virtues stemming from the Board of Education's pupil assignment policy (here the neighborhood policy) are compelling or adequate justification for the considerable evils of de facto segregation which adherence to this policy breeds.[20]

19. See Note, "Judicial Supervision of the Color-Blind School Board," *Harvard Law Review,* vol. 81 (1968), pp. 1511–27.

20. 269 F. Supp. at 508 (emphasis supplied). The court did not apply the strict "compelling justification" standard consistently in its opinion. In its evaluation of the tracking system, the court oscillated between the "rational relation" and "compelling justification" standards (compare ibid. at 511 with 513). But since it concluded that the District's tracking system was wholly irrational, the result would be the same under either standard.

The court thus assimilated education to the so-called critical rights, but it laid equal stress on the presence of "disadvantaged minorities" unable to protect themselves through the political process, toward which the court twice expressed a singularly skeptical view. "Judicial deference" to legislative and administrative judgments ordinarily

is predicated in the confidence courts have that they are just resolutions of conflicting interests. This confidence is often misplaced when the vital interests of the poor and racial minorities are involved. For these groups are not always assured of a full and fair hearing through the ordinary political processes, not so much because of the chance of outright bias, but because of the abiding danger that the power structure—a term which need carry no disparaging or abusive overtones—may incline to pay little heed to even the deserving interests of a politically voiceless and invisible minority.[21]

The term "power structure"—a term nowhere defined, except implicitly to exclude the judiciary—may not be "disparaging or abusive," but neither is it flattering, for the court observes elsewhere in the opinion:

In sum, all of the evidence in this case tends to show that the Washington school system is a monument to the cynicism of the power structure which governs the voteless capital of the greatest country on earth.[22]

Governmental policies which can survive the test of mere "rationality" do not necessarily emerge unscathed when a "compelling justification" must be provided for them. This was the case with the school board's strong neighborhood school policy. Since school assignments were superimposed on patterns of residential segregation, the overall effect was to segregate the races in school as well. Inferring that the school administration was "affirmatively satisfied with the segregation which the neighborhood policy breeds,"[23] Judge Wright deplored the school system's failure to locate schools deliberately along racial-neighborhood boundaries or to take other measures to foster integration within the framework of a neighborhood school policy. To be sure, the neighborhood school policy was found to be "rational," in that it served valid public objectives. But that did not render the policy immune from judicial interference, for it produced harmful consequences that required "compelling justification."

The court found as a fact that integrated education produces better educational results for black children. On that basis, Judge Wright con-

21. Ibid. at 507–08.
22. Ibid. at 407.
23. Ibid. at 419.

cluded that black pupils were harmed by de facto segregation. He based this finding on the testimony of two expert witnesses, who in turn based their testimony on some rather limited observations and test scores, and on a concession on that point by the District's Superintendent of Schools, appearing as a witness.[24] Suffice it to say on this point there is much evidence that tends not to support the court's finding, at least in the unequivocal way it was formulated.[25] Commenting on the disparity between some educational studies and the court's finding of fact, one law review notewriter concludes: "Viewed as a finding of fact made by a judge constrained to consider only the evidence presented by the parties, it cannot be said to be erroneous."[26] This is so, of course, only if behavioral facts are to be established in litigation in the same way as are historical facts.[27]

The net effect of balancing the harm from de facto segregation against the benefits of neighborhood schools was to push the court toward the conclusion that the neighborhood school policy was not sacrosanct. Consequently, the court decided that, to foster integration, it was permissible to order the voluntary busing of children from overcrowded black schools to undercrowded white schools. As we shall see, a subsidiary purpose of the voluntary busing was to achieve a more equal per-pupil resource allocation.

The court recognized, however, that, given the overwhelming black majority in the District of Columbia schools, large-scale racial integration was an unlikely outcome. It therefore embarked on an examination of the distribution of resources between white and black schools.[28] The court pinpointed a number of inequalities. Overcrowding was greater in predominantly black schools. Predominantly white schools employed, on the whole, more experienced teachers, more teachers with advanced degrees, and fewer temporary (less qualified) teachers. Per-pupil expenditures were significantly higher in the mainly white schools west of Rock Creek Park—a park that is to some extent a racial dividing line

---

24. Ibid. at 419–20.

25. See, e.g., Christopher Jencks and others, *Inequality: A Reassessment of the Effect of Family and Schooling in America* (Basic Books, 1972), pp. 97–103, 153–55.

26. Note, *Harvard Law Review*, vol. 81, at p. 1515.

27. Even then, there might be doubts. The admissions of the Superintendent of Schools were no doubt admissible, but hardly conclusive. See 4 Wigmore, *Evidence* § 1059 (Chadbourn rev.; Little, Brown, 1972); *Matter of Komfo Products Corp.*, 247 F. Supp. 229 (E.D. Pa. 1965).

28. 269 F. Supp. at 431–42.

in the city—partly because of overcrowding east of the park, perhaps partly because of economies of scale in the larger schools east of the park, and partly because of the salary differentials deriving from years of teaching experience, advanced degrees, and temporary or permanent status.

A number of resources were relatively equally distributed. Black students were found in disproportionately large numbers in both the oldest and newest buildings in the city, but the school system's building program was heavily concentrated east of Rock Creek Park. There was some inequality of library resources, but efforts to correct it seemed well advanced. Textbooks and supplies were not unequally distributed, according to the evidence adduced. And special federal programs to aid underprivileged areas did purchase extra equipment and services in some schools east of the park.

Although the court did not advert to conditions nationwide, the District of Columbia schools tended to mirror the emerging national profile of expenditure inequality.[29] More experienced, highly paid teachers are often able to use their seniority to claim positions in schools in affluent neighborhoods. Similarly, teachers who have been in the system longest are likely to be concentrated disproportionately in neighborhoods with stable or declining enrollments; newer schools or schools in neighborhoods that have experienced considerable in-migration not unexpectedly tend to have more than their share of younger, less highly paid teachers. Of such non-teacher resources as books, supplies, and equipment, however, poor and black pupils are apparently rarely deprived.

The resource inequalities the court found in *Hobson* were not attributed to deliberate discrimination but to factors that were "relatively objective and impersonal."[30] Again, however, that did not insulate them from judicial review under the standard announced by the court:

if whites and Negroes, or rich and poor, are to be consigned to separate schools, pursuant to whatever policy, the minimum the Constitution will require and guarantee is that for their objectively measurable aspects these

29. For a study of resource allocation patterns in nine large cities, see John D. Owen, "The Distribution of Educational Resources in Large American Cities," *Journal of Human Resources,* vol. 7 (Winter 1972), pp. 26–38. For summaries of research, see Jencks, *Inequality,* pp. 24–26; D. Brock Hornby and George W. Holmes III, "Equalization of Resources Within School Districts," *Virginia Law Review,* vol. 58 (1972), pp. 1119–56, at pp. 1121–22. On interdistrict inequality, see Note, "A Statistical Analysis of the School Finance Decisions: On Winning Battles and Losing Wars," *Yale Law Journal,* vol. 81 (1972), pp. 1303–41.

30. 269 F. Supp. at 442.

schools be run on the basis of real equality, at least unless any inequalities are adequately justified.[31]

On the other hand, the court did not see any immediate necessity to rectify unequal per-pupil expenditures directly. Tracking and optional zones were enjoined outright; a program of transportation to white schools for black students on a voluntary basis was ordered to be established; and a program of "color-conscious" teacher assignments was ordered to effect faculty integration.[32] Expenditure equalization, it was assumed, would follow the reduction of overcrowding of black schools due to voluntary busing and to the redistribution of teachers whose salary levels varied widely.[33] Consequently, the otherwise far-reaching decree in the first *Hobson* decision did not contain provision for direct equalization of expenditures.

The decree precipitated a conflict between the Board of Education and the Superintendent of Schools. The policies of the Superintendent, Carl Hansen, had been repudiated by the decision in the *Hobson* case, and Hansen himself had been rebuked by the court at a number of points in the opinion. Naturally, he urged the board to appeal, but it declined to take his advice, whereupon he resigned. An individual board member, however, did take an appeal, and he was joined by Hansen and the parents of certain school children, who sought to intervene to pursue the appeal.

Sitting en banc, the court of appeals generally approved the district court's decree.[34] The orders abolishing optional zones and requiring faculty integration and voluntary busing to relieve overcrowding were affirmed. The order abolishing tracking was construed narrowly to refer to the track system "as it existed at the time of the decree,"[35] and implicitly not to prevent the school system from adopting a revised track system. So construed, that order, too, was affirmed.

Three judges dissented. Conceding that "wrongs have been exposed,"[36] they suggested that Congress had changed the entire situation by providing for an elected Board of Education about to take office. The dissenters urged that the decree be vacated so that the political process could take over and the newly elected board could start fresh.

31. Ibid. at 496.
32. Ibid. at 517–18.
33. Ibid. at 515.
34. *Smuck* v. *Hobson*, 408 F.2d 175 (D.C. Cir. 1969).
35. Ibid. at 189.
36. Ibid. at 193.

From *Hobson I* to *Hobson II*

The decree took effect, and the school system took steps to implement it. The tracking program and optional attendance zones were abolished. Changes in school boundaries were made to place school enrollments nearer to capacity. Where boundary changes could not relieve the overcrowding, as in Anacostia, children who volunteered were bused to schools in the white neighborhoods west of Rock Creek Park, where enrollments were below capacity. To integrate faculties, the board first designated schools in which the ratio of black to white teachers deviated by more than 10 percent from the citywide ratio as "target" schools. Teachers were then transferred on a voluntary basis to or from the target schools, and new teachers in the system were assigned to schools on a "color-conscious" basis until the faculties in these schools were brought to within the 10 percent limit.[37]

Some of these changes ran into administrative problems.[38] Because of a congressional prohibition on the use of certain federal funds to achieve integration, school officials had difficulty in freeing the money to transport children to schools west of the park. Some of the sending schools had advantages, such as free breakfasts and lunches, denied to the receiving schools, and this appears to have inhibited some parents from busing their children. Some teachers who had formerly taught only upper-track students did not adjust easily to less-advantaged children. But, in the main, these changes proved feasible.

The decree probably accelerated the decline in white enrollment in the District's schools, though perhaps not as much as had been feared. White enrollment in elementary schools was 6,692 in 1967, and it decreased to 5,629 in 1968.[39] This was a decline of 16 percent, approximately twice the rate of decline of the preceding year and of the following several years. It is impossible to state with certainty that the decree in *Hobson I* underlay many of the parental decisions reflected by these figures, but it seems likely that it did. No comparable effect seems to have been produced by the second *Hobson* decree, four years later, though by then only 4,000 white pupils were left in the District elementary schools.

37. Interview, Washington, D.C., March 13, 1974.
38. Baratz draft, pp. 22–24.
39. Ibid., p. 65 n. 47.

One anticipated effect that was not achieved by the implementation of the *Hobson I* decree was equalization of per-pupil expenditures. The court, it will be recalled, had assumed that expenditure equalization would be a secondary consequence of the other measures required by the decree, especially those designed to relieve overcrowding east of the park and to achieve faculty integration. If these measures worked, pupil–teacher ratios would be evened out and highly paid teachers would be distributed more evenly through the system. It did not happen that way.

Relatively few pupils were bused. As of January 1971, only 502 elementary-school pupils were being bused from schools east of the park to schools west of the park.[40] The system contained more than 80,000 black elementary-school pupils. To some extent, the use of busing to relieve overcrowding was becoming superfluous as new school buildings east of the park had been constructed. For the rest, it was said that parental enthusiasm for the long trip across the city was not great.

By the same token, the attempt to integrate faculties encompassed no special effort to redistribute highly paid teachers. Teacher transfers for integration were voluntary, and thus were unrelated to patterns of salary imbalance. Likewise, new teachers who were assigned with a view to integration tended to be inexperienced and therefore low on the salary scale.

As things turned out, Judge Wright had grossly overestimated the amount of voluntary busing that would take place and had misjudged the kinds of teacher transfers and assignments necessary to achieve a modicum of faculty integration. As a result, these measures had no discernible impact on the allocation of school resources.

Average teacher costs west of the park remained about 10 percent above teacher costs east of the park.[41] The maldistribution of both pupils and highly paid teachers was, of course, also reflected in unbalanced pupil–teacher ratios and teacher costs per pupil. Elementary schools west of the park—with aggregate pupil composition 74 percent

40. Memorandum, Bradford A. Tatum to Dorothy L. Johnson, March 29, 1971, copy attached to Fourth Joint Memorandum of Plaintiffs and Defendants, filed April 15, 1971, *Hobson v. Hansen*, 327 F. Supp. 844.

41. Tables S-6, S-7, attached to the Third Joint Memorandum of Plaintiffs and Defendants, filed April 13, 1971; tables S-8, S-9, attached to the Second Joint Memorandum of Plaintiffs and Defendants, filed April 12, 1971, *Hobson II*.

white[42]—enjoyed pupil–teacher ratios in the range of 18 or 19, depending on whether kindergartens were included and on whether counselors and librarians were counted as teachers.[43] The remainder of the District was in the 21–22 range, but one area, Anacostia, was as high as 22–24.[44] Per-pupil expenditures on teacher costs were 26.7 percent greater west of the park than they were in the rest of the District, and nearly 40 percent greater west of the park than in Anacostia.[45]

Total expenditures per pupil also showed great disparities. A number of schools were in the $300–$400 range, while others were in the $900–$1,100 range.[46] This apparently enormous spread reflected only regularly budgeted funds. As in the case of per-pupil teacher costs, funds derived from a variety of federal compensatory programs were excluded from the calculations. Most notable among these programs were Title I of the Elementary and Secondary Education Act of 1965 and the impacted areas program.[47] West-of-the-park schools did receive some federal impact aid,[48] but not Title I assistance, which is wholly directed at disadvantaged students. The effect of this supplementary aid was to narrow the expenditure gap between schools west of the park and others. However, since Title I aid is by law intended to be compensatory,[49] this could afford small comfort to the school system, which seemed to be using it to displace ordinary expenditures.[50] In this respect, the District of Columbia was acting no differently from the vast majority of school systems across the country, which appeared to be using Title I funds in this way.[51]

In mid-1969, Julius Hobson, by then an elected member of the school board, returned to court to seek enforcement of the order rendered in

42. Table S-14, attached to the Second Joint Memorandum of Plaintiffs and Defendants, ibid.

43. Tables S-6, S-8, note 41, above.

44. Ibid.

45. Tables S-7, S-9, note 41, above.

46. See appendix B, p. 4, to Plaintiffs' Memorandum to the Court, filed December 8, 1970, *Hobson II*.

47. 20 U.S.C. §§ 241a–241l; 20 U.S.C. §§ 236–244.

48. See 20 U.S.C. § 244(8). But this aid was supposed to be directed heavily at underprivileged attendance areas of the District. See *Hobson I*, 269 F. Supp. at 440.

49. The statute provides that it should "supplement not supplant" regular funds. 20 U.S.C. § 241e(a)(3)(B).

50. See *Hobson I*, 269 F. Supp. at 496.

51. See Hornby and Holmes, "Equalization of Resources Within School Districts," pp. 1121, n. 12, 1132, n. 78.

Hobson I.[52] The following May, Hobson, represented by new counsel, filed an amended motion zeroing in solely on equalization of expenditures.[53] He asked the court to order equalization of all per-pupil expenditures from the regular school budget within a tolerance of plus or minus 5 percent of the mean for all elementary schools.

The case again came to Judge Wright, who had apparently tried without much success to be relieved of his designated assignment to the district court.[54] On September 1, 1970, Judge Wright ordered the school system to show cause why it should not equalize regular budget expenditures *for teacher costs* at each school within 5 percent, and the following year he ordered that the system should indeed equalize its expenditures for teachers' salaries and benefits.[55] The plus-or-minus 5 percent deviation from the mean was adopted as the permissible outer limit, subject to certain exceptions for special or compensatory education of deprived, retarded, or handicapped children or other "exceptional" students or for variations solely accounted for by economies or diseconomies of scale. These exceptions might be allowed only "on an individual school basis shown to this court in advance."[56]

The doctrinal foundation for this decision had been laid four years earlier in *Hobson I*. While not ordering a direct remedy for the expenditure inequalities it uncovered at that time, the court had nevertheless condemned them as unconstitutional since there had been no "convincing justification" forthcoming for them.

This holding formed the starting point for the court's analysis in *Hobson II*. Presented with evidence of continuing and in some respects accelerating inequalities in teacher costs, the court immediately held that these inequalities made out "a *prima facie* case of racial discrimina-

52. Motion for Further Relief and for Enforcement of the Decree, filed July 30, 1969, *Hobson v. Hansen*, 269 F. Supp. 401.

53. Amended Motion for Further Relief and Enforcement of the Decree, filed May 19, 1970, *Hobson v. Hansen*, 269 F. Supp. 401.

54. On August 6, 1969, less than a week after Hobson's motion for further relief had been filed, Chief Judge Bazelon of the District of Columbia Circuit had terminated the designation of Judge Wright to sit as a district judge in the *Hobson* case. By then there were several district judges on the bench who had been appointed after the district court was relieved of responsibility for appointing school board members, and hence could sit in *Hobson* unencumbered by any past involvement, however remote, in the affairs of the school system. But, the following May, Judge Bazelon set aside the termination of Judge Wright's designation, in view of the additional motions then pending.

55. *Hobson II*, 327 F. Supp. at 863–64.

56. Ibid. at 864.

tion. . . ."[57] Such a prima facie case called either for rebuttal or "compelling justification," absent which a remedial order would be entered.

The burden thus shifted to the school system, which found itself unable to persuade the court that the disparities were randomly distributed, or that the correlation between neighborhood income level and teacher expenditures throughout the District was actually negative. Nor was the school system more successful in arguing that economies of scale could explain the disparities. Higher salaries for more experienced teachers did explain a great deal of the variation, but the court rejected the contention that teacher experience was unrelated to educational quality, on empirical grounds and on a number of legal grounds. A similar argument that pupil–teacher ratios, however unequal, had no impact on educational performance was rejected on the ground that the school system failed to prove this empirically. Unrebutted and unjustified, the prima facie case of racial discrimination ripened into a firm finding and the resulting equalization order.

In the next several sections *Hobson II* will be examined in considerable detail. First, I shall show how the issue was reformulated in stages from equalization of all resources to equalization of per-pupil expenditures on teachers' salaries and benefits, for the narrowing of the issues had an impact on the policy outcome. Then I shall turn to the court's handling of the empirical data presented to it, both on the significance of the expenditure disparities and on the alleged relationships between those disparities and "educational quality." Finally, I shall describe what the school officials did when confronted with the order to equalize and what difference their constraints and choices made.

Narrowing the Issues

Hobson I dealt with equalization of educational resources in general, and the motion that triggered *Hobson II* asked the court to order per-pupil equalization of all regularly budgeted expenditures. *Hobson II* ended, however, with a narrowly framed decree that embraced only resources that had previously been unequally distributed, that extended only to elementary schools, and that required the equalization of expenditures per pupil only for teachers' salaries and benefits, within a tolerance of plus or minus 5 percent of the mean.

57. Ibid. at 850.

The court's opinion provides some insight into the process from which this order emerged. The shift from total expenditures per pupil to expenditures per pupil on teacher costs only was explained as an effort to relieve school officials of responsibility for expenditure variations

truly beyond their control. Examples are differences in the amount and cost of vandalism occurring at different schools, in the age of different school buildings and the consequent cost of upkeep, and in the size of school plants and consequent variations in cost of operations attributable to economies of scale. . . . [T]he court therefore sought to focus the attention of the parties on those aspects of school management which appeared to contribute to the apparent disparities in per-pupil expenditure and which also appeared to be *within* defendants' control.[58]

Of course, many items that were excluded from the court's inquiry— such as books and salaries of non-classroom personnel—were very much within the school system's control, and some of these did contribute to the disparities in per-pupil expenditure. How, then, did the *Hobson II* order take on its remaining characteristics?

Counsel played a leading role in the narrowing process. When Hobson's lawyers examined the evidence, it was concluded that, outside of the allocation of resources, there was insufficient evidence of noncompliance with the first decree.[59] The first step was to focus on the equalization of resources, and the next was to decide *which* resources. There was no evidence of discrimination in apportionment of capital expenditures. Quite the opposite: all the building was being done east of the park, especially in Anacostia.[60] Counsel considered numerous possibilities: equalization of test scores of teachers' verbal ability (believed to be related to pupil performance), equalization of each element in the resource mix (textbooks, library books, etc.), equalization of years of teacher experience, and equalization of pupil–teacher ratios.[61] In the end, it was decided to focus on per-pupil expenditures as a whole, both because these were identified in the *Hobson I* opinion as a measure of resources, and because they provided "the kind of objectively measurable standard that we could come up with which would be administrable

58. Ibid. at 847 n. 3 (emphasis in the original).

59. Transcript of an interview, Peter F. Rousselot, Counsel for Plaintiffs in *Hobson II*, with an interview team from the Syracuse University Research Corporation, Washington, D.C., May 28, 1974 (hereafter cited as Rousselot interview), pp. 10–11. I am grateful to Mr. Rousselot for making a transcript of this interview available.

60. Ibid., p. 16.

61. Ibid., pp. 14–15.

by a court and which would not be rejected on the grounds of being an invasion of educational policy or being judicially unmanageable."[62]

Since there was little evidence of significant resource discrimination at the junior and senior high school levels, the plaintiffs focused on elementary schools.[63] The 5 percent figure also came from plaintiffs' counsel, who feared the possibility of evasion if there were no "clear" and "reasonable" standard by which to measure compliance. Obviously, the 5 percent figure had "no certain constitutional source,"[64] but it seems to have evoked little controversy.

This leaves the significant question of how and why the court directed its attention only to teachers' salaries, rather than to aggregate per-pupil expenditures, including textbooks, library resources, and the salaries of administrators, counselors, librarians, and clerical and custodial personnel. This decision was not made at the suggestion of counsel. Hobson's lawyers and those they consulted believed

it would be a major achievement to get an equalization in resources by that measure [aggregate per-pupil expenditures] and that to go beyond that for perhaps the more specific thing, such as honing in on different [i.e., specific] resources, would be too high a mountain to climb, might be unwise, and might be too constricting [on the school administration?].[65]

Limiting the equalization issue to teachers' salaries was done on the court's own initiative.

Some items in the resource mix seem to have been excluded because they were already more or less equally distributed. Textbooks and supplies were in this category by the time *Hobson I* was decided,[66] and library books were apparently on the way to being equalized.[67] If the court considered custodial and clerical services at all, these services may have been thought too far removed from educational performance and too susceptible to distortion by economies of scale, though this is surmise.[68]

62. Ibid., p. 13. The decision was made in close consultation with lawyers and economists affiliated with the Harvard Center for Law and Education.

63. Ibid., pp. 18–19.

64. Telephone interview, Washington, D.C., November 11, 1974. The figure of plus or minus 5 percent from the mean is, however, also the criterion for judging compliance under Title I. See 45 C.F.R. § 116.26(c).

65. Rousselot interview, pp. 13–14.

66. 269 F. Supp. at 436.

67. Ibid. at 433.

68. See *Hobson II*, 327 F. Supp. at 862–63: "the court finds that plaintiffs' initially requested relief requiring equalization of total expenditures per pupil across the system would sweep too broadly and would require the school administration

The most important unknown is salaries for librarians and counselors. These salaries, the available data indicate, were not equally distributed. Indeed, they appear to have been as unequally distributed as teachers' salaries.[69] But the court excluded them from its order—only implicitly, to be sure, but clearly enough for both sides of the litigation to agree on that interpretation of the decree. Plaintiffs' counsel has advanced an explanation for their exclusion:

I think the reason is that on the basis of Judge Wright's decision in *Hobson I* and on the basis of Judge Wright's familiarity with education, he felt that teachers were far and away the most important resource in the system, and that's also the conclusion of studies like the Coleman report—and he also felt that the expenditure per pupil measure was an objectively measurable and judicially manageable way to equalize this important resource. Once he made that decision, he probably felt that it was more sustainable on appeal and also it was the major resource in dollar terms as well.[70]

Although librarians and counselors were unequally distributed, plaintiffs' counsel did not object to Judge Wright's decision to exclude them from the proceedings. Plainly, this was a tactical decision:

The impetus for focusing on teacher salaries only, as opposed to teacher salaries plus librarian salaries or all those things separately, came from the judge and not from the parties. When the judge did that (in September, 1970, I believe it was), we then really focused for the first time on that and focused on whether we wanted to fight the judge or whether we wanted to go along with that refinement. He had done that on the basis of pleadings of ours which said, "They've got a point about heating and so on. Let's take those out." But we wanted them to either leave everything else in as a lump or perhaps separate and equalize separately. He said, "Let's go with teachers," and we then made a judgment that "he's made up his mind that teachers are the most significant resource in dollar terms and, we think, in educational terms. They are more significant than librarians and counsellors. If he's willing to go on this basis—and he coupled this with a show-cause order—this is where we are going to go, and it's not, as a matter of litigation strategy, going

---

to equalize some inputs which have little or nothing to do with educational opportunity. But upon careful consideration, the court does find that the equalization order approach is a good one, provided it is focused upon expenditures per pupil for teachers' salaries and benefits, so as to cover only inputs which do have a direct bearing on the quality of a child's education." See also ibid. at 847 n. 3, where costs of upkeep are discussed solely in terms of school-to-school variations attributable to differential vandalism rates, economies of scale, and other factors beyond the "control" of school authorities.

69. Compare tables S-6, S-7, with tables S-8, S-9, note 41, above. See Joan C. Baratz, "Resource Allocation in Selected D.C. Schools: A Case Study (1971–1974)," chapter 5 of a forthcoming book, pp. 14–15.

70. Rousselot interview, pp. 35–36 (emphasis in the original).

to gain for us anything to fight with one of the most liberal judges in the country to try to get more. Let's take it with this. This is a big step. We've probably won the case with the show-cause order because we don't think they can show cause, so let's ride with that."[71]

Nor did counsel for the school officials object. Doubtless they assumed it would be easier to contest a claim focusing on one expenditure item than on many (who could predict what inequalities might turn up in a wide-ranging examination?). More importantly, if an order were eventually to be entered against the school system, then the narrower its focus, the more limited its impact would be, and the better it would be for the interests of the school system. This would be standard defendants' reasoning.

Prospectively, these may not have been unreasonable assessments by counsel for both sides. But events did not bear them out in a number of important respects. As we shall see, no appeal was taken from *Hobson II.* What the court of appeals would or would not sustain became an academic question. Furthermore, the narrow order entered against the school system was not necessarily in the interest of school officials, teachers, or pupils, for, as we shall see, it restricted the range of means by which equalization might be effectuated. A broader equalization order might have been preferable for the officials subject to it than was the order that followed from the exclusive focus on teachers' salaries. (A narrower order, decomposing per-pupil expenditure on teachers' salaries into its constituent elements, would have had quite different results again.)

Litigation strategy and tactics thus affected the way the right was defined and the way the order was shaped. The general litigation setting was also influential. From the judge's perspective, there was no need to order the equalization of those resources that were already equally distributed: only inequalities had to be remedied. Courts sit only to right wrongs, not to right rights. Therefore, one by one, equally distributed resources were excluded from the scope of the lawsuit. And having identified teacher costs as the unequally distributed item in the resource mix, the court held there was a right to an equal per-pupil allocation of teacher services, as measured by teacher costs. The court had no occasion to decompose this right into its constituent elements: (1) expenditures on classroom teachers, (2) expenditures on special-subject teachers, and (3) pupil–teacher ratios. It was lump-sum equality of

71. Ibid., pp. 28–29.

previously unequally distributed resources that was to be achieved, and it was for school officials to determine the mix of these elements. The fact that equalization occurred in the framework of litigation, rather than in some other setting, had an important bearing on what kind of equalization it would be, what scope it would have, and how it might be carried out.

Law and Science at the Threshold

The issue of *Hobson II* was the lawfulness of disparities in per-pupil expenditures on teachers' salaries. In *Hobson I,* the court had already found what it regarded as systematic discrimination favoring west-of-the-park schools in the distribution of resources, and held the maldistribution to be unlawful. Now, confronted with further evidence of unequal expenditures, the court held that the "figures make out a compelling *prima facie* case that the District of Columbia school system operates discriminatorily along racial and socioeconomic lines," adding that " 'figures speak and when they do, Courts listen.' "[72]

The question, of course, was whether the figures had anything to say. The school system argued first that no unfavorable inference could be drawn from the disparity favoring the 13 west-of-the-park schools, out of a total of 130 schools, for it was one of several such random disparities. Indeed, the school system also argued, in the District as a whole the correlation between income of a school neighborhood and teacher expenditures at the school was actually negative. And, finally, the system contended that the west-of-the-park disparity was largely attributable to diseconomies of scale, enrollment in the west-of-the-park schools being disproportionately small. If any of these contentions had been valid, then the prima facie case of discrimination would have been rebutted.

The court had little difficulty with the first argument. The schools west of Rock Creek Park "constitute both a geographic and historical entity,"[73] and that was sufficient to render unlawful any discrimination in their favor, apparently even if statistically insignificant.

The court gave equally short shrift to the negative correlation asserted to exist, District-wide, between income and per-pupil teacher expenditure: "Even if defendants have computed the correlation correctly, all

72. 327 F. Supp. at 850, quoting *Brooks* v. *Beto,* 366 F.2d 1, 9 (5th Cir. 1966).
73. 327 F. Supp. at 850.

they have demonstrated is that random high per-pupil expenditures in favor of some children from poor, black neighborhoods east of Rock Creek Park at the expense of other children from poor, black neighborhoods east of Rock Creek Park are so great that they obscure the systematic discrimination in favor of white children from wealthy neighborhoods west of Rock Creek Park."[74] The issue, however, is at once more basic and more complex than this formulation would suggest.

Economists employed by both sides had argued vigorously over whether the correlation between income and per-pupil expenditure on teachers' salaries was weakly positive (plaintiffs) or weakly negative (defendants)—the outcome turning on the methodological issue of whether a rank-order correlation or a Pearson product-moment correlation was the appropriate way to measure this kind of association.[75] Judge Wright dismissed this as an "abstruse statistical dispute between the parties,"[76] but he then went on to relate expenditures to income as between west-of-the-park and east-of-the-park schools.

The economists' neighborhood income data derived from 1959 census tracts, unadjusted for demographic change since then. Apart from that, what the court and the economists were both doing—each in a separate way—was relating *neighborhood* income to *school* expenditures. For a variety of reasons, however, neighborhood income is not necessarily a reliable proxy for the income of the school population. The wealthy population west of the park (or elsewhere in the city) may well be disproportionately beyond the child-rearing years: white and wealthy may also mean disproportionately white and elderly. Suburbanization has also resulted in a large outflow of white pupils from the District schools. Of the white children of school age who remain in the District of Columbia, most do not attend the public schools. Some 55 percent of the white school-age population of the District attends private or parochial schools, compared to 8 percent of the black school-age population.[77] Under these circumstances, basing decisions about school population on neighborhood income is unjustifiable.[78]

74. Ibid. at 851–52.

75. See Stephan Michelson, "A Research Report for Plaintiffs," appendix C, pp. 33–35, to Plaintiffs' Memorandum to the Court, filed December 8, 1970, *Hobson* v. *Hansen*, 327 F. Supp. 844.

76. 327 F. Supp. at 851.

77. I am indebted to Joan C. Baratz for these data, which are taken from District of Columbia Public Schools, "Data Resource Book: School Year 1972–73" (November 17, 1972; processed).

78. See, e.g., Motion to Intervene, filed on December 1, 1972, by parents of Adams Community School pupils, p. 2, *Hobson* v. *Hansen*, 327 F. Supp. 844:

Although Judge Wright spoke of "low income *area* schools,"[79] the relevant measure is the income of the school population. But data on this did not exist. The school system proposed pupil participation in the free-lunch program as a surrogate measure, eligibility for participation being based on family income. Using these data, the economists consulted by the school system found that the mean per-pupil expenditure on teacher costs was slightly higher for free-lunch children than for non-free-lunch children, though they also found higher per-pupil teacher expenditures for white than for black children.[80]

The free-lunch data were attacked by the economists commissioned by the plaintiffs on the ground that there was likely to be a divergence between rates of eligibility and participation, with some principals involving more eligible children than others, and perhaps the highest-income members of the eligible class participating disproportionately.[81] The response of the court was to ignore the free-lunch data entirely and single out the favored position of pupils in predominantly white schools west of the park. "The wealthy and the white," the court concluded, "are virtually guaranteed more money—in almost every instance substantially more than five percent above the citywide average."[82]

No attempt having been made by the court to relate income to expenditures, the court's conclusion on this score was unsupported by factual material. Of course, this did not affect the finding that a white child in the District of Columbia school system stood a considerably better chance than a black child of being enrolled in a school with a higher-than-average per-pupil expenditure on teachers' salaries. Yet the

---

"Early this year impact aid questionnaires were received from 400 of Adams' 504 children. Of the 400 received, 136 or 34% indicated that the family adults concerned receive public assistance or are unemployed.

"However, in . . . the documents prepared for submission to the court by the school administration, Adams school's median income is listed as $13,785. This erroneous figure is obtained by using 1970 census tract data based on the school attendance area. Adams' attendance area includes the very wealthy 'Kalorama' area West of Connecticut Avenue although few if any actual children attend the school from this area."

79. Ibid. at 852 (emphasis supplied).

80. Dave M. O'Neill and others, "An Analysis of Variation in Teacher Expenditures Per Pupil Among D.C. Elementary Schools," pp. 18, 20, attached to Defendants' Reply Memorandum to the Court, filed January 18, 1971, *Hobson II.*

81. Michelson, "A Research Report for Plaintiffs," pp. 38–40. Michelson elaborates his objections to free-lunch participation as an income proxy in his article "For the Plaintiffs: Equal School Resource Allocation," *Journal of Human Resources,* vol. 7 (Summer 1972), p. 291.

82. 327 F. Supp. at 852.

premise of the litigation was differential expenditure based on both race and income, and the equalization decree applied to all schools, including all-black schools. On the threshold issue of socioeconomic discrimination, neither the economists nor the court was in a position to decide.

Neither side, however, seemed daunted by this fruitless exchange of computer printout. With equal enthusiasm, both proceeded to debate the extent to which salary differentials could be attributed to economies of scale. Schools west of the park have generally lower enrollment than schools east of the park. If costs per unit of output (in this case, per-pupil costs) decline as the scale of operation increases, then the higher per-pupil expenditure for schools west of the park might be a function of the size of the school. The court had earlier excluded from the litigation operating costs of school buildings, because they were subject to variations attributable to economies of scale.[83] Now the question was whether personnel costs might be subject to similar variations. If economies of scale explained the disparity in per-pupil expenditures on teachers' salaries, as the school system claimed, then the disparity might be beyond the control of school officials and thus, in the court's view, not discriminatory. The issue was therefore important.

The case for economies of scale was not difficult to formulate in the abstract.[84] Optimal pupil-to-teacher ratios were easier to arrange in large schools. With only voluntary busing to west-of-the-park schools, those schools were not merely smaller in capacity, but their capacity utilization rate was also lower than that of schools east of the park.[85] Thus, there were fewer pupils among whom fixed costs could be spread. In small schools, special-subject or "resource" teachers (for reading, music, art, etc.) had to be allocated on a partial-day basis; presumably, they could be scheduled more economically in large schools where they were not itinerant. Consequently, the utilization of both classroom and special teachers might be more economical in large schools.

Framed in this way, the issue appeared to present a straightforward empirical problem: how much of the disparity in per-pupil expenditures on teachers' salaries and benefits was explained by economies of scale? The analysis of the data did indicate that large schools were able to

83. Ibid. at 847 n. 3.

84. The argument was first made by June O'Neill and Arlene Holen, *Washington Post*, October 15, 1970.

85. Table S-16, attached to the Fourth Joint Memorandum of Plaintiffs and Defendants, filed April 15, 1971.

realize certain salary economies denied to small schools, but how large those economies were depended on the resolution of both legal and factual questions, the answers to which were by no means clear.

For example, was "scale" to be defined by school capacity or by number of students in attendance? Were controls to be instituted for disparate pupil–teacher ratios and average teacher salaries? Capacity utilization rates were lower west of the park. Thus, if the number of students in attendance were the measure of scale, schools west of the park were relatively smaller in scale than they would be if measured by their actual capacity. Similarly, pupil–teacher ratios were lower, and average salaries were higher, west of the park.

The analysis performed by the plaintiffs' economist, Stephan Michelson, seemed to demonstrate that size of the school, as measured by number of pupils, accounted for perhaps one-third of the disparity in per-pupil expenditures in teachers' salaries.[86] Such a finding would make a strict equalization order (or one within the plus or minus 5 percent range) unfair to smaller schools. But controlling for average teacher salary, capacity utilization, and pupil–teacher ratios east and west of the park reduced the explanatory power of size considerably, so that, in the plaintiffs' calculations, size alone explained only 15 percent of the per-pupil expenditure disparity on teachers' salaries.

This technique, of course, raised the issue of what significance to attach to the controlled variables. If they were not themselves discriminatory, then there was no need to control for them. But the plaintiffs argued that "the distribution of overcrowding and pupil–teacher ratios again favors the whitest and wealthiest areas of the City and constitutes discrimination for which defendants are responsible."[87] If this were so as a matter of law, then it was appropriate to control for capacity utilization and pupil–teacher ratios; and if more experienced, more highly paid teachers provide a better education, then a distribution of these teachers that was favorable to west-of-the-park schools could not be considered a neutral attribute.

Were the defendants held "responsible" for these differences? The answer is not clear. Ultimately, the court seemed to accept the plaintiffs' argument that size was not "a 'neutral' factor in D.C. elementary schools,"[88] for the court accepted Michelson's controlled—and reduced—

86. "A Research Report for Plaintiffs," chap. 6.
87. Ibid., p. 9.
88. Ibid.

estimate of the extent to which economies of scale could legitimately be said to account for expenditure disparities. In the words of the court:

The Michelson analysis demonstrates that, when variables other than size—such as average teachers' salaries, teacher–pupil ratio, or capacity utilization—are also considered, then size alone can be said to explain only somewhere between 7.5 per cent and 15 per cent of the observed differences in per-pupil expenditures for teachers' salaries. Thus defendants' initial claim that the differential is legitimate because it arises solely, or even substantially, from their alleged ability to run comparable quality schools more cheaply if they are larger has been convincingly refuted. . . .[89]

Yet the court's judgment was more equivocal when it considered separately each of the variables controlled by the Michelson analysis: pupil–teacher ratios, capacity utilization, and average teacher salaries. It is worth considering them in order.

The court never ordered the equalization of pupil–teacher ratios, and indeed the salary equalization that was ordered can be achieved without equalizing pupil–teacher ratios. Nevertheless, the court clearly disapproved of unequal pupil–teacher ratios. At least it disapproved of unequal ratios to the extent of not regarding lower ratios as a legitimate economy-of-scale item, for the opinion in *Hobson II* states that the larger classes east of the park, while more economical, may also be lower in quality.[90]

However, no similar disapproval of differences in capacity utilization east and west of the park was manifested in either *Hobson I* or *II*. Differences in capacity utilization were related to declining enrollments west of the park compared to expanding enrollments east of the park (until recent years). Where that led to real overcrowding, the court was disposed to grant relief. But the busing scheme that was ordered in *Hobson I* to reduce overcrowding at the most heavily utilized schools was to be purely voluntary at the sending end—which is to say that it guaranteed no particular capacity utilization outcome at either end.

The plaintiffs also controlled for average teacher salaries, which were higher in the small schools for which scale diseconomies were asserted. As in the case of pupil–teacher ratios and capacity utilization rates, they argued that this was not a neutral disparity, but one for which the school system should be held responsible. Again, the court's response was equivocal.

The differential in average teacher salaries could be decomposed

89. 327 F. Supp. at 853.
90. Ibid. at 853 n. 18; see also ibid. at 857.

into two components. The first was longevity. Older, more experienced, and therefore more highly paid teachers were disproportionately concentrated in older, smaller, west-of-the-park schools. The question was what inference to draw from this undisputed fact. The defendants' economists concluded that the major share of the salary differential traceable to experience could be attributed to the disproportionate presence of teachers west of the park who had seventeen years of service or more.[91] The relevance of this datum is that the plaintiffs had suggested in another connection—and the court agreed—that perhaps only the first few years of experience have a bearing on the quality of teacher performance.[92] If true, this would lend support to the defendants' assertion that the portion of the salary disparity attributable to longevity was not discriminatory, even in its effects.

The court received this argument sympathetically:

As to the first component of teaching cost—average teacher salary—Dave O'Neill [the economist consulted by the school system] finds there can be economies of scale. According to Dave O'Neill, variation in average teacher salary with size reflects "only the fact that old teachers tend to be in old (and therefore small) buildings." He criticizes the Michelson technique quite convincingly when he writes that "the fact that there is a built-in negative correlation between average teacher salary and school size has introduced much confusion into previous discussions."[93]

This observation seems at odds with the court's conclusion that average teacher salary is a variable that is properly controlled in estimating the effects of scale on expenditure disparities.

The second component of the disparity in average teacher costs was the greater sum spent on special-subject teachers west of the park. It was contended that this differential in turn was particularly susceptible to diseconomies of small scale, for special-subject teachers assigned to several small schools must consume time in traveling that special-subject teachers in large schools are able to spend in the classroom. The court regarded this as possible:

Small schools everywhere in town tend to have more special teachers than large ones; and because special teachers in small schools tend to be itinerant, the time they spend travelling may mean that students in large schools re-

91. O'Neill, "An Analysis of Variation in Teacher Expenditures," p. 16. O'Neill reiterates this point in his article, "For the Defendants: Educational Equality and Expenditure Equalization Orders," *Journal of Human Resources*, vol. 7 (Summer 1972), p. 321.

92. I deal extensively with this issue in the next section.

93. 327 F. Supp. at 853 n. 18.

ceive just as much classroom time per special teacher as students in small schools do. If this is true, Dave O'Neill concludes, "then it would appear that, as between sides of the park, significant differentials in the quality of schooling do not emanate from the [special teacher] differential." Although interesting, Dave O'Neill's economies of scale argument is speculative and unproved. At the moment, we cannot know how much of the existing variation in expenditures for special teachers is absolutely necessary because of economies of scale and how much could have been eliminated by more economical scheduling of special teachers.[94]

In this as in other matters, Judge Wright left the burden of proof squarely with the defendants.

However, the court left the door just slightly ajar:

Without prejudging this issue, the court will note at this point that an equalization order could be framed in such a way as to leave open exceptions to the permissible range of variation where defendants can prove that these were due purely to economies of scale.[95]

The final order did leave this option open to the school system, for it provided an exception where proof could be furnished "showing that a variance above or below the five per cent limit is accounted for *solely* on the basis of economies or diseconomies of scale."[96] (I discuss below the merits of resolving uncertainties by carving out exceptions to the decree.)

Thus, the plaintiffs' assumption that there was something invidious about the comparative underutilization of capacity west of the park, the failure to even out pupil–teacher ratios, and the failure to redistribute older teachers (and special-subject teachers) was not accepted unequivocally. When the court dealt in particulars, it condemned outright only disparate pupil–teacher ratios. But the court nonetheless accepted a computation that assumed all of these disparities to be illegitimate. This inconsistency raises a doubt about the extent to which the legal implications of the plaintiffs' economy-of-scale computations were fully understood by the court.

The use of econometric analysis on the threshold issues in *Hobson II* illustrates the limitations, both evidentiary and legal, of expertise in litigation. Appropriate data on which to evaluate the relation of family income to per-pupil expenditure were lacking. The most reliable data related to neighborhood income rather than family income of pupils. Proxy data on pupil-family income were presented, but their reliability

94. Ibid.
95. Ibid.
96. Ibid. at 864 (emphasis in the original).

was challenged. The court ultimately fell back on its own understanding of the city.

Data were available on the issue of economies of scale, but important factual and legal gaps remained. Each legal question turned on the resolution of an empirical question, which then turned out to have another legal question embedded within it. The legal question of inequality depended in part on the empirical question of economies of scale. Whether there were genuine economies of scale depended in turn on the legal question of exactly what scale-related disparities the school system was to be held "responsible" for.[97] But what disparities the system was to be held responsible for depended on the empirical question of whether the disparities had any effect on education.[98] This factual question was finally resolved by resort to a legal question: who bore the burden of proof on such questions?[99]

It is not my purpose at this point to dwell on the inappropriateness of resolving these issues on the basis of burden of proof. I shall have something to say about this in the next section. All that needs to be said here is that, if indeed substantial economies of scale did exist, there is a real possibility that an equalization order could, while changing the direction of inequality, render expenditure patterns more rather than less uneven. The important point is that technical issues like economies of scale concealed legal issues. The extent to which this was so seems not to have been fully appreciated by the court, particularly when it dealt with the appropriateness of controlling for scale-related disparities. After all the computations have been performed, what stands out starkly

97. The very definition of "scale" depended on whether the system was to be held responsible for variations in capacity utilization.

98. In the case of pupil–teacher ratios, whether the education in larger classes is inferior to that in small classes; in the case of the distribution of experienced teachers, whether experience (especially seventeen years or more) is associated with teacher performance; in the case of special teachers, whether the concentration of special teachers in small schools means they are spending more instructional time there or whether they spend their time traveling from school to school.

99. Burden of proof issues were resolved against the defendants, because the plaintiffs had made out a prima facie case by proving the existence of resource disparities. On the educational effects of variations in pupil-to-teacher ratios, see, for example, 327 F. Supp. at 857. Even assuming a prima facie case had been made out, requiring the defendants to justify the disparities, there is a serious question about whether the defendants' burden extended this far. Once the existence of economies of scale was shown, conventional apportionment of the burden of proof might well have required plaintiffs to show that scale-related disparities had educationally harmful results.

is just how impossible it was to resolve any of the threshold questions on the basis of the data alone. Figures sometimes speak, but courts must also listen for the silences.

Judging "Educational Quality"

Confronted with a nearly all-black school system—and a heavily segregated one at that—in *Hobson I*, Judge Wright stated that

if whites and Negroes, or rich and poor, are to be consigned to separate schools, pursuant to whatever policy, the minimum the Constitution will require and guarantee is that for their objectively measurable aspects these schools be run on the basis of real equality, at least unless any inequalities are adequately justified.[100]

The opinion went on to recognize that this statement articulated a "modern separate-but-equal rule," deriving from the equal protection doctrine that "government action which without justification imposes unequal burdens or awards unequal benefits is unconstitutional."[101]

The admirable clarity of this formulation masks the difficult dilemmas of its application. What, after all, is the concrete meaning of "real equality" or "unequal burdens . . . or benefits"? Plainly, no reasonable reading of the Equal Protection Clause can view it as requiring equality of educational results, since no school system can guarantee any particular outcome—although some lawyers have argued for educational "malpractice" suits against school systems that fail to achieve particular results.[102] For purposes of *Hobson II*, Judge Wright zeroed in on equality of educational resources. But, even here, problems remain. "If resource equality is the goal, the 'educational resources' that must be equalized still are undefined. Is it expenditures? teacher experience? academic qualifications? ability to run an orderly class? ability to run a creative class? Equality in some of these resources may preclude equality in others."[103]

The court in *Hobson* might simply have concluded that expenditure disparities across the board, or for all instructional costs, or just for

100. 269 F. Supp. at 496.
101. Ibid. at 497.
102. See Stephen D. Sugarman, "Accountability Through the Courts," *School Review*, vol. 82 (February 1974), pp. 233–59.
103. Hornby and Holmes, "Equalization of Resources Within School Districts," p. 1144.

teachers' salaries, conferred "unequal benefits" in "objectively measurable aspects," and, for that reason alone, were unlawful. Even in *Hobson I*, however, the court did not do this. It extended the inquiry and found that the unequal expenditures were purchasing unequal teacher resources, as measured by experience, graduate education, and permanent status.[104] Judge Wright, himself a former teacher (1931–35), specifically rejected the argument of school officials that teacher experience was not necessarily related to teacher performance:

it remains beyond denial that, other factors equal, experience is a real asset for a teacher, as it is for any professional. The Washington school system's pay scale, in proportioning salary to the number of years of teaching experience, is a testimonial to this fact. Moreover, it cannot be questioned that the initial few years of teaching make an enormous contribution to a teacher's competence.[105]

For Judge Wright, therefore, equality of resources meant equality of those resources that have a bearing on the quality of education.

The prima facie case having been made, the school officials attempted in *Hobson II* to meet their burden of proof by demonstrating that the disparities in experience (which were heavily responsible for expenditure disparities on teachers' salaries) had no effect on the quality of education. To their attempt the court gave four answers. First, it dismissed the school authorities' argument on law-of-the-case grounds, the issue having already been adjudicated against the defendants in *Hobson I*.[106] Second, the court held the school board's own budget statements against it.[107] (Not surprisingly, the board had justified requests for higher salaries on the ground that they purchased the services of better teachers.) Third, the court evaluated the studies summarized by the economists on both sides and concluded that some positive relationship between teacher experience and student performance had been demonstrated. Then, fourth, the court added, "teacher experience has not been proved to be unrelated to educational opportunity,"[108] so the defendants had not met their burden of proof on this issue.

It is important to note that, of the reasons adduced for rejecting the defendants' argument that the disparities in teacher experience had no

104. 269 F. Supp. at 434–36.
105. Ibid. at 434.
106. 327 F. Supp. at 854.
107. Ibid. at 855.
108. Ibid. For similar reasons, the court rejected the argument that pupil–teacher ratios were irrelevant to educational performance.

educational significance, only the third dealt with the issue on its merits. The first ground rested on considerations of judicial economy, repeated litigation of the same issue being disfavored by the law; the second on an inconsistent position taken by the school system in another setting; and the fourth on the burden of proof.

The effect of rejecting the contention of the school authorities was to include salary increments based on teacher experience in the equalization formula of the decree. However, in implementing Title I of the Elementary and Secondary Education Act of 1965, which also required equalization, as a condition of eligibility for grants, the Office of Education had decided to exclude longevity pay.[109] Hence Judge Wright's decision placed the school system in the difficult position of having to comply with the requirements of two divergent formulae.

Ultimately, the justification for this was constitutional. The Equal Protection Clause, as the court saw it, demanded equalization of those items of expenditure that bear on educational quality. If salary increments for experience affect quality, they must be equalized. Thus, the legitimacy of the order really turns, not on the law of the case, or on the rhetoric of school officials in budget hearings, or on the burden of proof, but on the accuracy of the court's factual finding that a positive relationship exists between teacher experience and student performance.

For this reason, it is worth comparing the analysis of the plaintiffs' economist, Stephan Michelson, with the findings of the court on the relation of teacher experience to student performance. First, Michelson:

Defendants argue that experience pay should not be counted when equalization questions are raised because experience has not been shown to be "productive" in terms of student achievement. . . . In actual fact, experience of teachers consistently shows a positive relationship with achievement test scores, both within and between cities. . . . In work which Henry Levin and Michelson are jointly pursuing, every attempt is made to minimize the effect of teacher experience. This is because that effect is, no doubt, biased upwards by the mechanism to which defendants refer . . . : teachers selecting the higher achieving students. However, neither these researchers nor defendants have demonstrated that this bias is great enough to reduce the real effect of experience to zero.

Levin's cost-effectiveness analysis makes no such claim. His results are that school systems seem to be paying *too much* for experience, not that they should pay nothing. . . .

In more detailed analysis, Levin found that experience and effectiveness did seem to be related, and in the way one would expect: the first few years

109. 45 C.F.R. § 116.26.

have great advantage, and then the increment in teacher effectiveness from more experience diminishes. Levin never does get a negative result; that is, experience never is *detrimental* to producing achievement in students. In separate articles printed together, Levin and Michelson present probably the most elaborate statistical work yet produced on the question of isolating effective school characteristics. In slightly different simultaneous equations estimations on the same data these authors find considerable effect of teacher experience in producing sixth grade verbal achievement. Once again, these estimates are biased upwards, but we do not know how much. Not even the most ardent anti-octogenarian has claimed that the first few years of teaching experience is valueless.

Defendants' appeal to the literature, in short, does not aid their argument. Researchers consistently find some relationship between experience and achievement, though not as great a one as is paid for.[110]

Now the court:

as the court reads them, the rather inconclusive educational studies tell us only that teachers seem to be *over*compensated for experience relative to their productivity. That is, researchers consistently find some relationship between experience and achievement, though not so great as is traditionally paid for. In the absence of more conclusive studies, large differentials such as exist in the District of Columbia cannot be condoned.[111]

Two things stand out when these passages are compared. First, the possibility that experienced teachers choose "higher achieving students" —"upward bias"—though mentioned briefly by Michelson, disappeared entirely in the court's opinion. Second, the conclusion was advanced and accepted almost verbatim that "researchers consistently find some relationship between experience and achievement, though not so great as is traditionally paid for."

What, exactly, do the studies show? I shall first review briefly the studies cited by Michelson and then turn to the literature in general.

The Levin cost-effectiveness analysis[112] begins with two sets of data. The first shows that the verbal score of a teacher is a better predictor of student performance on verbal tests than is the experience of the teacher. The second set shows that higher teacher verbal scores are a teacher characteristic that is inexpensive for school systems to purchase. From this Levin concludes that it is significantly more cost-effective for school systems aiming to improve students' verbal test scores to attract

---

110. "A Research Report for Plaintiffs," pp. 24–26 (footnotes omitted; emphasis in the original).

111. 327 F. Supp. at 855 (emphasis in the original).

112. Henry Levin, "A Cost-Effectiveness Analysis of Teacher Selection," *Journal of Human Resources*, vol. 5 (Winter 1970), pp. 24–33.

teachers with greater verbal skills than to attract teachers with more experience. Levin makes no claim that the results are without upward bias; indeed, he states that upward bias is a distinct possibility because of inadequate controls on the characteristics of the black students whose scores appear to be affected by teacher experience.[113]

The second Levin study cited by Michelson for the proposition that teaching experience has "a considerable effect . . . in producing sixth-grade verbal achievement," as measured by test scores, presents results only for white students.[114] The Michelson study cited for the same proposition presents data on white and black pupils, but the results differ significantly by race.[115] "Teacher experience," Michelson concludes, "does not help black children—at least not experience in the teachers blacks have. . . ."[116] Different resources, he suggests, probably affect black and white children differently.[117] If, as the Michelson litigation analysis contends, "experience of teachers consistently shows a positive relationship with achievement test scores," then Michelson's own study cited in support of that statement is in fact a glaring exception to it. More than that, it is a highly relevant exception, inasmuch as the student body of the District of Columbia elementary schools by 1971 was 95 percent black, and the lawsuit focused on resource discrimination against poor, black students.

Thus, by the time the studies were utilized by the court, much had been lost in the translation. As indicated, the significance of upward bias was lost on the court, even though it is a persistent theme in the literature. What it means is that the variables may be circular: what looks like teacher experience affecting student performance may really be student performance attracting experienced teachers.[118] That this is

113. Ibid., p. 32 n. 15.

114. Henry M. Levin, "A New Model of School Effectiveness," in U.S. Office of Education, *Do Teachers Make a Difference? A Report on Recent Research in Pupil Achievement* (1970), p. 69.

115. "The Association of Teacher Resourceness with Children's Characteristics," in ibid., chap. 6.

116. Ibid., p. 139. Compare Levin, "A New Model of School Effectiveness," in ibid., p. 29.

117. "The Association of Teacher Resourceness with Children's Characteristics," in ibid., pp. 140–41. At page 140, Michelson hints that the positive results for white pupils are partly attributable to the "association of quality teachers with quality students"—in other words, upward bias.

118. "Is more teaching experience associated with higher achievement because experience really matters or do teachers with more experience use their seniority rights as leverage in obtaining assignments that enable them to teach brighter chil-

not a fanciful concern is made clear by the widespread tendency of teachers to use their seniority to claim attractive assignments.[119] If this propensity is indulged frequently enough, the ostensibly dependent variable may end up influencing the ostensibly independent variable, and this is what a number of studies suggest:

Another complementary interpretation is that resource allocation responds to achievement in some communities but not others. Thus some communities allow experienced teachers to move to better schools, creating a spurious impression that experience causes high achievement. Other systems do not allow experienced teachers to move, so there is no association between teacher experience and student achievement.[120]

If the omission of upward bias from the *Hobson II* opinion can be put down to judicial impatience or inexperience or inadvertence, the same cannot be said for the divergence between what the court decided the studies had found and what they had in fact found. This divergence seems to have been produced by the court's excessive reliance on the Michelson summary, rather than on the original studies that were summarized.

One further point should be added. The school officials' economist had calculated that the disparity in total teacher expenditure per pupil could be decomposed into nearly equal disparities in number of teachers per pupil and in average teacher salary. The average teacher salary disparity east and west of the park was heavily attributable to the disproportionately high salaries paid to teachers with seventeen years or more of experience: west-of-the-park schools were surfeited with these "super-longevity teachers."[121] Both plaintiffs' and defendants' economists seemed to think—and the court also believed—that only the first few years of teaching experience might have an effect on student performance. If that were true, then some 80 percent of the variation in average teacher salaries was unrelated to student performance.[122] If the defendants were also correct in their contention that special teachers are unusually subject to economies of scale in scheduling,[123] then only a

---

dren?" Gerald Grant, review of Frederick Mosteller and Daniel P. Moynihan, eds., *On Equality of Educational Opportunity* (Random House, 1972), in *Harvard Education Review*, vol. 42 (February 1972), p. 115.

119. See Owen, "The Distribution of Educational Resources in Large American Cities."

120. Jencks, *Inequality*, p. 97 (footnote omitted).

121. O'Neill, "For the Defendants," p. 321.

122. Ibid., p. 318.

123. See pp. 131–32, above.

small portion of the total disparity in per-pupil expenditures on teachers' salaries bore any relation to pupil performance, as measured by standardized tests.

Needless to say, these are iffy propositions, and in general the court handled them by deciding that, since they were not proven, the defendants had not met their burden of proof. But the court did act on the asserted relationship between teacher experience and student performance. It is therefore necessary to look more closely at that critical relationship.

The appropriate caveat for anyone reviewing the school-resource studies has been sounded by Stephan Michelson—not the adversary Michelson of the litigation analysis, but the skeptical Michelson of the academy. "Personally," he said, "I think the educational production function literature is theoretically absurd and empirically irrelevant— and, as I have emphasized when participating in its profusion, useful only to generate ideas, not conclusions."[124]

Whether the literature is "absurd" or "irrelevant," it certainly has been inconclusive. Beginning with the Coleman Report in 1966,[125] there has been considerable debate on the impact of school resources on student performance. Two central problems have plagued the studies from the beginning. The first relates to what outputs are being measured. Standardized tests are the usual indicators of student performance, but these measure only a limited range of skills and they may do so only imperfectly and unevenly for some student populations. The second problem relates to relationships among inputs. The Coleman Report found that student background was a more powerful predictor of performance than were school resources. Since then the debate over this finding and the methods by which it was obtained has been unceasing. What is more, the difficulty of instituting proper controls has been approached in a number of ways, but never entirely satisfactorily. In the despondent words of one researcher, "the present rudimentary state of our quantitative models does not permit us to disentangle the effects of home, school, and peers on students' achievement."[126] In particular, "at the

124. "For the Plaintiffs," p. 286. For a concise view of some of the methodological problems of the literature, see John E. McDermott and Stephen P. Klein, "The Cost-Quality Debate in School Finance Litigation: Do Dollars Make a Difference?" *Law and Contemporary Problems*, vol. 38 (Winter–Spring 1974), pp. 415–35.

125. James S. Coleman and others, *Equality of Educational Opportunity* (Government Printing Office, 1966).

126. Alexander M. Mood, "Do Teachers Make a Difference?" in U.S. Office of Education, *Do Teachers Make a Difference?* p. 6.

present moment we cannot make any sort of meaningful quantitative estimate of the effect of teachers on student achievement."[127]

It may not be only methodological inadequacy that is responsible for the spotty, inconclusive character of the studies. Particular combinations of input variables may combine uniquely to produce results different from other mixes. Particular categories of students may benefit from some resources that do not affect other categories of students at all.[128] But school resources in general—teachers' experience, salary, degree level, and verbal ability, as well as class size, pupil–teacher ratio, physical plant, facilities, and materials—are rarely important determinants of measured student performance.[129] "No school resource is consistently related to student outcomes."[130] Although some studies do find certain resources related to outcomes, they often reach inconsistent results when they divide the student population into two groups or more.[131] "The specific school resources that have a 'statistically significant' relationship to achievement change from one survey to the next, from one method of analysis to another, from one sort of school to another, from one type of student to another."[132] Furthermore, "the gains associated with any given resource are almost always small," small enough to be pedagogically trivial.[133]

Teacher experience and graduate degrees—the attributes partly responsible for the District of Columbia expenditure disparity—fare no better in the studies than do other school resources:

The resources for which school systems have traditionally been willing to pay a premium—teachers' experience, reduced class size, and teachers' advanced degrees—do not appear to be of great value. Inexperienced teachers do not appear to produce students whose outcomes are significantly worse than the outcomes of students whose teachers are experienced, other things being equal. Similarly, students whose teachers have advanced degrees or

127. Ibid., p. 7.

128. Thus, Eric Hanushek, "The Production of Education, Teacher Quality, and Efficiency," in U.S. Office of Education, *Do Teachers Make a Difference?* pp. 92–94, finds children of working-class whites affected by certain teacher characteristics (especially teachers' verbal scores and the recency of their postgraduate education), middle-class whites less affected by these attributes, and Mexican-American children not affected discernibly at all. See also Michelson's findings on white and black pupils, note 115, above.

129. Harvey A. Averch and others, *How Effective Is Schooling? A Critical Review and Synthesis of Research Findings* (Rand Corporation, 1972), p. 44.

130. Ibid.

131. Ibid., p. 45.

132. Jencks, *Inequality*, p. 96.

133. Ibid.

who are in small classes do not do better, other things being equal, than students of teachers lacking advanced training or [students] attending large classes.[134]

"Experienced teachers," reports another summary, "are more competent than average in some systems, less competent than average in other systems."[135] The inference to be drawn from such findings, one researcher concludes, is that "the things that schools are buying do not appear to be valuable in the educational process."[136]

If that is so, it raises the question of why school systems reward teacher experience and graduate education. Leaving aside the possibility that school administrators are either worse- or better-informed than the researchers, coherent explanations for their behavior can be advanced. The market in teachers, of course, need not be a perfectly competitive market, in which quality is measured by price. Collective bargaining by trade unions, while it maximizes a variety of important values, may introduce distortions into market relations. Beyond that, school systems may be paying for loyalty and continuity, in order to minimize turnover costs. These may include costs that are tangible, such as recruitment expenses, and intangible, such as the potential costs of staff instability in the schools.[137] Then, too, experienced teachers, though not necessarily more competent than inexperienced teachers, may have more alternative job opportunities, including opportunities in other school systems that reward seniority. Consequently, the price of retaining an adequate supply of teachers may be higher at the higher levels of experience. School systems may also be paying teachers partly in accordance with some perceived, probabilistic approximation of the teachers' financial need, whether or not in accordance with their productivity. Given the prevalence of salary rewards for seniority in industry after industry, teachers' pay scales are far from aberrant in this respect. It is just that productivity—in the narrow sense in which that

134. Averch, *How Effective Is Schooling?* p. 48. On the specific issue of class size, see Dwight H. Lindbloom, *Class Size as It Affects Instructional Procedures and Educational Outcomes* (Educational Research and Development Council of the Twin Cities, 1970); Dee Schofield, *Class Size* (National Association of Elementary School Principals, Leadership Digest Series, no. 3, 1974); Ian Templeton, *Class Size* (Educational Management Review Series, no. 8, 1972).

135. Jencks, *Inequality,* p. 96.

136. Hanushek, "The Production of Education, Teacher Quality, and Efficiency," p. 90.

137. But see Emmett Keeler and John McCall, *A Note on the Effectiveness of Teacher Experience* (Rand Corporation, 1973), an inquiry into the relation of teacher turnover and student reading ability.

term is used by the researchers—may not be regarded as the sole measure of a teacher's utility to the school system.

If longevity reflects something other than the superior productivity
of more experienced teachers, it may still be possible to hold that per-
pupil expenditures on teachers' salaries must be equalized—but certainly not on the ground that the disparity is related to differences in
student performance. For the alternative bases of salary scales that I
have just hypothesized may be related in critical ways to the maintenance of an ongoing school system, but their effect on student performance would seem to be attenuated at best. The court, however, did not
reach this question, because it rejected all except productivity explanations for longevity pay.[138]

Teacher experience and education do not seem to be related to student performance, but that is not necessarily true of all teacher attributes. Beginning with the Coleman Report, several investigators have
found teacher verbal test scores to be positively associated with student
performance on verbal tests.[139] Like other such findings, the findings are
not consistent and are subject to upward bias, as verbally facile teachers
may seek out verbally facile students to teach. But suppose for a moment
that teacher verbal scores are a genuinely productive educational resource. Levin has calculated that many of the most verbally facile
teachers leave teaching within the first three years.[140] He has also shown
that verbal facility is much less rewarded in salary than is experience,
the latter being an explicit component of salary scales. That being so,
holding all else constant, the equalization of per-pupil expenditures on
salaries could easily result in an unequal distribution of an attribute
associated more significantly with student performance than is teacher
experience.

The upward bias caveat must be reiterated. The point is not to prove
that verbal scores are "better" resources than experience is. Rather, the
point is that, if, as a number of researchers have asserted, verbal scores
are better resources than experience is, then a concern for the equal

138. Judge Wright rejected out-of-hand all non-productivity explanations for
longevity pay as *"post hoc* rationalization . . . extremely speculative . . . essentially
makeweights." *Hobson II,* 327 F. Supp. at 856 n. 22.

139. See, e.g., Mood, "Do Teachers Make a Difference?" p. 2; Hanushek, "The
Production of Education, Teacher Quality, and Efficiency," p. 86. On the relation
of teachers' math test scores to student performance, see Demetrios P. Prekeges,
Relationship Between Selected Teacher Variables and Growth in Arithmetic (U.S.
Office of Education, 1973).

140. "A Cost-Effectiveness Analysis of Teacher Selection," p. 33.

distribution of school resources is not satisfied by eliminating salary disparities or the experience disparities they tend to reflect. Indeed, on these assumptions, since verbal facility is particularly concentrated in beginning teachers, the more productive proxy attribute to be equalized would be youth rather than age.

The same point can be made about another school resource: special-subject teachers. Some studies have found that the number of special-subject teachers seems to be positively related to student performance on standardized tests.[141] Again, it is not certain whether controls have neutralized the effect of student background variables on these results. Very likely not. But assume for the moment that the presence of special teachers does affect pupil performance. One of the effects of the equalization decree in *Hobson II* has been to deprive the most disadvantaged schools of special-subject teachers in the name of equalizing per-pupil expenditures on teachers' salaries. Hence, in the name of equalizing resources, it is just possible that *Hobson II* has marginally increased inequalities of educational opportunity.

When all is said and done, no one really can say flatly what school resources have an impact on pupil performance. The inconsistency among the studies—and among the results for particular student populations in the same study—does suggest that part of the reason for the uncertainty may lie in the futility of searching for the one resource that improves the performance of students. If we assume that different kinds of students are affected by different kinds of resources, the inconsistent results of the studies become more understandable. And if this does prove to be the case, it argues for a policy of flexibility in the allocation of school resources and against rigid allocative formulae like the one adopted in *Hobson II*. Certainly, there is no warrant in the studies or in the most probable inferences to be drawn from them for the equalization of expenditures on teachers' salaries on educational output grounds.

As noted, that is not the conclusion the court reached from the research summary it was presented. On the contrary, the court held that teacher experience was positively related to student performance, and it even went on to hold that the higher achievement test scores in west-of-the-park schools

reflect the result of the discrimination against east of the Park children in per-pupil expenditure. The burden of establishing that these test results reflect

141. See James W. Guthrie, "A Survey of School Effectiveness Studies," in U.S. Office of Education, *Do Teachers Make a Difference?* pp. 32–33.

something other than the proven discriminatory distribution of educational opportunity falls upon defendants. And once again defendants failed to meet their burden.[142]

Once again, the court resorted to the burden of proof to resolve an important issue—in this instance, requiring school officials to prove that unequal test scores were not caused by the unequal expenditures on teachers' salaries. As in the case of the relation of teacher experience to student performance, the school officials were required to prove a negative, the affirmative proposition being highly dubious to begin with.

This raises the more general question of the place of burden of proof in the litigation. Inasmuch as the empirical studies are inconclusive, if the case turns on the relationship of expenditures to educational quality, whoever has the burden of proof has lost the lawsuit. Shifting the burden of proof thus constitutes a decision on the merits.[143]

The matter goes beyond this, however, for findings of fact by the trial judge will be sustained on appeal unless the findings are "clearly erroneous."[144] In the area of school resources, it is very difficult to say that any finding of fact is clearly erroneous or clearly correct. As things now stand, a failure like that of the defendants in *Hobson* to prove the negatives they were called upon to prove means that the allegations will be found to be true even if they are not, and that the finding will be sustained on appeal.

In short, a court, using behavioral studies, can find as a "fact" what the studies cannot and do not show with anything approaching the degree of consistency required to generate confidence in the findings, and no one can impeach the results. This is what happened in *Hobson II*.

Social science cannot really be said unequivocally to have produced the result reached by the court in *Hobson II*. But it does seem to have

142. 327 F. Supp. at 858.
143. A point made by Hornby and Holmes, "Equalization of Resources Within School Districts," pp. 1143–44.
144. Federal Rules of Civil Procedure, Rule 52(a). Although lower courts are still divided over the applicability of the "clearly erroneous" rule to findings of fact based on evidence other than testimony, the Supreme Court has indicated that it does apply to findings based on documentary evidence. See *United States* v. *Singer Manufacturing Co.*, 374 U.S. 174, 194 n. 9 (1963). The doubt arises because of the faith placed by the rule in the trial judge's unique opportunity to observe witnesses in person and sort out the truth on the basis of his observation. A comparably unique opportunity is obviously not afforded him in the case of documents, which can be read equally well by appellate judges, but considerations of judicial economy—the desire to avoid duplication—may argue for the blanket application of the "clearly erroneous" rule to documentary, as well as testimonial, evidence.

hardened the court's determination to do what it did, to have imparted to the decision the veneer of extralegal legitimacy, and to have helped shield the decision from potential review on appeal. As I shall show in the next chapter, some of these functions of social science in litigation are not unique to *Hobson v. Hansen.*

Narrowing the Implementation

As we have seen, the equalization issue got progressively narrower during the course of *Hobson II*, so that what began as an effort to equalize all resources ended in a decree equalizing only per-pupil expenditures on teachers' salaries. Decisions made both by counsel and by the court contributed to this result, and the litigation setting of the conflict played a prominent role.

As soon as the decree was issued, a similar process of narrowing the options for implementing it was set in motion. The principal decision-makers were the Board of Education and school officials. The result of the forces that operated was to dictate implementation of the decree by one method only—transferring teachers—and later almost entirely by transferring special-subject or resource teachers.[145] The effects of the decree were powerfully shaped by this sequential process of peeling away alternatives.

The first problem faced by the Board of Education was whether to take an appeal. In a closed session, the board's lawyer explained the possible grounds for an appeal.[146] Believing the decree to be unworkable or fearing that Judge Wright was attempting to run the District's schools, some board members favored taking an appeal. But the new Superintendent and most board members understood that it would prove embarrassing to appeal a decision favoring poor, black students. Perhaps also chastened by the earlier affirmance of *Hobson I* in the court of appeals, and by the knowledge that findings of fact are difficult to overturn on appeal, the board voted to comply with *Hobson II* rather than appeal.

The decision was ironic in view of the contemporaneous assessment by Hobson's lawyer of the prospects for upholding the decree on appeal:

145. That is, teachers of art, music, foreign languages, mathematics, reading, language arts, physical education, and science.

146. Baratz draft, pp. 34–37.

Very chancy. My recollection is that at the time there was a vacancy on the D.C. Circuit, and that we had eight judges sitting, and we felt that the only way we could sustain it in the D.C. Circuit was to get a 4–4 tie.[147] So, we expected to sustain it on that basis. We felt we had four votes. . . . I think we felt we might lose in the Supreme Court, which was the reason we were anxious that there not be an appeal. I think we thought we had nowhere to go but down.[148]

How prescient this assessment was we shall see later.

Once the choice had been made to comply, the board was faced with a further series of choices.[149] The board could order the school administration to move students (by mandatory busing), move teachers (by compulsory transfers), or do both (by closing certain schools or redrawing school boundaries). The board had redrawn some boundaries after *Hobson I*, and it decided not to do so again after *Hobson II*. School closings, unpopular in any event, would not have reduced the number of teachers who had to be transferred, and so were ruled out, as was mandatory busing. This left only the option of transferring teachers, and the board resolved to comply by transferring as few teachers as possible. This effectively eliminated the possibility of equalizing pupil–teacher ratios, which would have required massive transfers. The board explicitly recognized this when it made provision in its policy guidelines for the school administration to place "only moderate emphasis on equalization of teacher experience and pupil–teacher ratios across the city" in drawing up a compliance plan.[150]

The first set of transfers in 1971 was accomplished in two steps. The first was to redistribute special-subject teachers (art, foreign languages, language arts, mathematics, music, physical education, reading, and science). The general thrust of this action was to reduce the west-of-the-park share of special-subject teachers in favor of east-of-the-park (particularly Anacostia) schools.[151] Thereafter, some 300 classroom teachers were transferred, and the first round of adjustments was completed.

It was only a matter of months, however, before it became clear that substantial further adjustments were necessary to secure compliance.

---

147. *Hobson I*, it will be recalled, had been heard by the full court of appeals, rather than by a three-member panel, and Rousselot was obviously anticipating another in banc hearing for *Hobson II*.

148. Rousselot interview, pp. 48–49.

149. These are well described in the Baratz draft, pp. 37–38.

150. "Report to the United States District Court from the District of Columbia Board of Education, Pursuant to Civil Action No. 82-66" (1971; processed), p. 3.

151. See ibid., table III-1, p. 47.

Those adjustments consisted almost entirely of transfers of about 100 special-subject teachers in the spring of 1972.

Since that time, compliance with the decree generally meant, in operational terms, large annual transfers of resource teachers. The school system learned—and never forgot—that it could implement *Hobson II* by successive rounds of resource-teacher transfers, thereby avoiding the greater disruptions thought to attend the transfer of classroom teachers. This pattern was broken, reluctantly, at the end of 1974, when the school administration proposed to transfer a small number of classroom teachers.[152] The administration has said, however, that it transfers classroom teachers only when transfers of special teachers are inadequate to secure compliance,[153] and even in 1974 and 1975 many more special-subject teachers than classroom teachers were transferred.[154]

Why has this been so? In the first place, after the first equalization, the yearly adjustments required at any given school are generally small. Special-subject teachers, being itinerant, often devote only a fraction of their work week to each of the several schools in which they may work. (Part of the reason seems to be the desire of central administrators to retain control over special-subject teachers; if they were assigned to a school on a full-time basis, they would presumably report to the principal of the school.) Therefore, a school that is out of compliance by only a few thousand dollars can most easily be brought into compliance by the transfer of a fraction of a salary. The only teachers susceptible to such fractional transfers are special-subject teachers. The utility of such transfers in terms of administrative convenience is overwhelming.

Several other reasons point in the same direction. Union rules discourage the transfer of teachers who have accumulated seniority.[155] Hence the most likely candidates for transfer would be younger, less experienced, less highly paid teachers. But such transfers would be futile for salary-equalization purposes, and principals also understand

152. *Washington Post,* November 8, 1974.

153. District of Columbia Public Schools, "Report to United States District Court, *Hobson v. Hansen*" (July 11, 1972; processed), pp. 4–5.

154. The *Washington Post,* April 20, 1976, reported that twenty-five full-time and ninety part-time teachers were transferred in 1974 and that twenty-five full-time and fifty-one part-time teachers were transferred in 1975, for equalization purposes.

155. See Article IV(D) of the contract between the Board of Education and the Washington Teachers' Union.

quite well that they can buy more teacher-resources with a young staff than with an old staff. Consequently, they are reluctant to lose the less senior teachers who would be most eligible for transfer. Union seniority rules also protect from transfer regular classroom and special-subject teachers who are assigned to a single school on a full-time basis. They do not protect itinerant special-subject teachers, because seniority is based on length of exclusive assignment to a single school.[156] In addition to this, both classroom teachers and principals enjoy a closer relationship with other classroom teachers in their school than they do with the special-subject teachers who may spend only a day or two each week at the school and who are not really responsible to its principal. Finally, schools are frequently able to compensate losses in special programs through sources of income other than the regular school budget funds that are subject to equalization. Losing a special-subject teacher thus does not necessarily mean losing the special subject itself.

These considerations apply primarily to decisions to adjust to decreases in the budget for salaries. When a school enjoys an increase in its budget, another factor becomes important. Assume, for example, that a school with one thousand students is allotted enough money to add one teacher to its staff. Assume also that there are forty classroom teachers in the school, giving the school an average class size of twenty-five students. Should the school request a classroom teacher or a resource teacher? A consideration of the alternative gains to be made suggests that the decision is likely to be in favor of taking on the additional resource teacher. If the school requests another classroom teacher, it will reduce its average class size from twenty-five to twenty-four and four-tenths students. If, on the other hand, the school requests another resource teacher, it can develop a French program, organize a school orchestra, or vastly expand its program of art instruction. Given the alternative gains of increasing the classroom or resource staff, principals are more likely to request a resource teacher.

For all of these reasons, special-subject teachers are the most movable and most vulnerable category of personnel, at the margin the most convenient teacher resource for a school to lose and the most valuable to gain. Juggling special-subject teachers is the least painful way to comply with *Hobson II*. It is also a mode of compliance plainly permitted by the court's definition of the right and framing of the remedy.

156. Interview, Washington, D.C., November 7, 1974.

What Wright Hath Wrought

We have seen that the *Hobson II* equalization formula can be decomposed into three elements: number of pupils, salaries of classroom teachers, and salaries of special-subject teachers. For equalization purposes, the school system has for the most part surrendered control over the movement of pupils and classroom teachers. Whatever "the equal protection of the laws" means abstractly, in the District of Columbia schools it currently means transferring enough resource teachers annually, or more often if necessary, to equalize dollar values.

Whether and how many resource teachers must be involuntarily transferred depends on the voluntary movements of classroom teachers and pupils in and out of particular schools. For instance, if one or more very experienced, highly paid classroom teachers retire or resign from a school and are replaced by less senior, less well-paid classroom teachers, the school stands to gain a significant increment in resource teachers, provided its enrollment is constant. Likewise, if the faculty is stable, a school with a declining enrollment stands to lose resource teachers, while a school with an expanding enrollment stands to gain them, regardless of the race or socioeconomic status of its pupils. The major direct effect of *Hobson II* is to make the special-subject program of the schools depend upon the vicissitudes of population movements that affect their enrollment and on the teacher attrition rate that affects their salary structure.

In many cases, pupil population movements are considerable. Of the 117 elementary schools in existence in both 1971 and 1974, 104 lost enrollment during that period, while only 13 gained. An annual change in enrollment in the 3–6 percent range is quite common, and changes of as much as 10–15 percent a year are not unheard of.[157] Since the margin for compliance is small, schools that are in compliance in one year can be radically out of compliance by the next unless transfers are ordered.

Enrollment projections from one school year to another are hazardous. Compliance must be based on actual enrollments, not projected

157. See District of Columbia Public Schools, "Teacher Expenditures and Enrollment by Schools," table I (November 20, 1974; processed); ibid., "Pupil/Teacher Ratios," table IV (January 10, 1973; processed); ibid., "Pupil/Teacher Ratios," table IV (June 1, 1972; processed). All of these tables are annexed to reports submitted by the Superintendent of Schools to the Board of Education.

enrollments. The original decree in *Hobson II* had required the school system to submit annual compliance reports by each October 1. But, because school enrollments generally do not stabilize until October, in 1972 the school officials moved successfully to amend the decree to permit filing of the report by December 1 instead. In practice, then, school programs are not definite until December of the school year in which they are implemented. Several programs already under way have been canceled when the resource teachers executing them were withdrawn by the school administration. The present situation means that equalization is achieved at the expense of significant disruptions in the middle of each school year, when transfers are announced. This aspect of equalization is widely condemned by parents, principals, and teachers alike.

The desire to minimize the annual mid-year disruption has reinforced the determination of school officials to shift the minimum number of resource teachers required to achieve compliance. Considerations of educational program, which would be served by a careful, perhaps extensive, rematching of transferred teachers with the needs of sending and receiving schools, often give way before the paramount interest of equalizing dollar-values of services.

In order to gauge the distributional effects of *Hobson II* on the school system, the distribution of classroom and resource teachers in 1971 (before the decree) and 1974 (three years after it) was ascertained, and this was related to a number of other variables, especially enrollment changes and certain surrogate indicators of poverty of school populations. All data were furnished by the school system of the District of Columbia. A brief outline of the results follows.

A significant change has occurred in the distribution of resource teachers from small to large schools. Small schools were accused of having more than their fair share of resource teachers before the decree; alternatively, legitimate economies of scale were postulated as the explanation. Either way, as table 1 shows, there is no longer a significant correlation between school size and the number of resource teachers per pupil. There remains, however, a small negative correlation between school size and the number of classroom teachers per pupil, but this is weaker than it was in 1971. Overall, large schools gained teacher services following the decree; small schools lost teacher services.

Just as we would expect, the distribution of resource teachers has changed more dramatically since the decree than has the distribution

Table 1. *Correlation of Teacher–Pupil Ratios with School Size as Measured by Enrollment, 1971 and 1974*

	Correlation coefficient	
Ratio	1971 (117 schools)	1974 (117 schools)
Resource teachers to pupils	−0.67 (0.001)	−0.03 (n.s.)
Classroom teachers to pupils	−0.42 (0.001)	−0.18 (0.024)

Figures in parentheses are significance levels.
n.s. Not significant.

of classroom teachers. The correlation of the ratio of resource teachers and classroom teachers to students with school size appears in table 1 for the 117 elementary schools in existence in both 1971 and 1974.

The distribution of both classroom and resource teachers has also been made significantly more equal, as judged by clustering within one standard deviation of the mean. As table 2 shows, about one school in four was more than one standard deviation from the mean in both the per-pupil distribution of classroom and resource teachers in 1971. While this was not an exceptionally high number (one school in three outside this range would usually be considered "normal"), there was a considerable reduction, especially in the classroom teacher category, between 1971 and 1974.

What this overall equalization obscures, however, is the character of extreme cases, which can be defined arbitrarily as those schools more than one standard deviation on either side of the mean. (These cases, it turns out, are not only definitionally extreme, but also differ from the non-extreme population on many other variables.) When these cases are examined, it becomes clear that the schools that have fewer than the mean number of resource teachers per pupil are more severely disadvantaged now than were comparable schools before the decree was rendered. Schools with an above-average number of teachers seem no less advantaged now than their counterparts were before the decree. Table 3 compares the mean ratios of resource teachers to each 100 pupils for all schools and for schools more than one standard deviation from the mean, for 1971 and 1974.

Table 3 indicates that the ratio of resource teachers to students for all schools declined between 1971 and 1974. The number of schools

Table 2. *Percentage of Schools in Which Teacher–Pupil Ratios Varied by More Than One Standard Deviation from the Mean, 1971 and 1974*

	Percentage of schools	
Ratio	1971 (117 schools)	1974 (124 schools)
Resource teachers to pupils	25.6 (0.004)	18.5 (0.004)
Classroom teachers to pupils	23.1 (0.005)	2.4[a] (0.01)

Figures in parentheses are standard deviations.
a. This is 12.9 percent using 1971 standard deviation.

defined as disadvantaged was nearly identical in 1971 (twelve) and 1974 (thirteen). For these disadvantaged schools, the average ratio of resource teachers to students declined markedly over the three-year period. In 1971, disadvantaged schools had on the average one resource teacher for every 200 pupils; in 1974, a similarly situated school had one resource teacher for every 500 pupils. Because the number of schools defined as advantaged in 1971 (nineteen) and 1974 (ten) differs substantially, it is difficult to draw any conclusions from the average ratio of resource teachers to students in those two years. The ratios of resource teachers to pupils at the advantaged schools remain at about the same level in both years. The advantaged category has become considerably smaller, but the gap between the overall ratios and the ratios at the advantaged schools has widened. The disadvantaged schools have clearly suffered losses. The many complaints from schools at this extreme about the total deprivation of resource programs flowing from equalization are understandable.

Was the distribution of resource teachers more or less responsive to changes in enrollment than the distribution of classroom teachers? The correlation of teacher–pupil ratio in 1974 with the percentage change in enrollment between 1971 and 1974 was −0.18 for resource teachers (significance level 0.001) and −0.41 for classroom teachers (significance level 0.029). This suggests that those schools suffering the most rapid decline in enrollment are losing teachers at a proportionally slower rate than those schools suffering a less rapid decline. Of the two categories of teachers, the ratio of resource teachers to the number of students appears to rise or fall in response to changes in enrollment far more than does the ratio of classroom teachers. The percentage changes

Table 3. *Ratio of Resource Teachers to Pupils, 1971 and 1974*

Type of school	1971		1974	
	Number of schools	Average number of resource teachers per 100 pupils	Number of schools	Average number of resource teachers per 100 pupils
All schools	117	0.96 (0.004)	124	0.76 (0.004)
Advantaged schools[a]	19	1.63	10	1.67
Disadvantaged schools[b]	12	0.50	13	0.19

Figures in parentheses are standard deviations.
a. Defined as schools in which the ratio of resource teachers to pupils was more than one standard deviation above the mean.
b. Defined as schools in which the ratio of resource teachers to pupils was more than one standard deviation below the mean.

that constitute the independent variable in the calculation are losses in enrollment; only 13 of the 117 schools existing in both 1971 and 1974 did not suffer a net loss in students over the three-year period. What the statistics indicate about relative changes in the distribution of both types of teachers is, in sum, that as an individual school's enrollment declined, its loss of resource-teacher services was nearly proportional to its loss of students, while its loss of classroom teachers was less responsive to falling enrollments. This finding is consistent with the school administration's policy of relying almost exclusively on transfers of resource teachers in complying with *Hobson II*.

The same results are suggested more directly by the correlations of percentage change in teachers per pupil with percentage change in enrollment. The greater the decline in enrollment, the greater the increase in the teacher–pupil ratio, which is to say that schools experiencing the most rapid declines in enrollment have a more favorable teacher–pupil ratio than those suffering less rapid enrollment declines. But, again, the relationship is not the same for classroom and resource teachers. Resource teachers are not nearly as often as oversupplied to schools with declining enrollments, the most probable reason being that the school system responds to changes in enrollment with changes in the allocation of resource teachers. The statistical basis for these observations is that the correlation of percentage change in teacher–pupil ratios between 1971 and 1974 with the percentage change in enrollment during the same period was -0.22 for resource teachers (significance level 0.008) and -0.42 for classroom teachers (significance level 0.001).

Finally, consideration was given to the relationship of classroom and resource teachers per student to two poverty proxies: whether a school was a designated "Title I" school and the proportion of students in the school eligible to receive a free lunch under the federally subsidized program. Both of these measures are at best rough approximations. Both depend on self-reported and potentially self-serving or otherwise inaccurate data. Nevertheless, they are the only indicators available.

Title I designation is a dichotomous variable: a school either is or is not designated a Title I school. Two criteria are used by the school system for the purpose of designation: an income factor based on the 1970 census (weighted 60 percent), and eligibility of students for the free lunch program (weighted 40 percent).[158]

Eligibility for the free lunch program is based on a survey of parents' income scaled by family size. A family of five with an annual income of $6,480 was eligible to participate in the program for the 1974–75 school year.[159]

The per-pupil distribution of classroom and resource teachers for 1974 was examined to determine whether there was any relationship between either poverty indicator and teacher distribution. There was none. The ratios of both resource and classroom teachers to pupils in 1974 were not correlated with either of the poverty proxies. The next step was to look at the percentage change in per-pupil distribution of teachers from 1971 to 1974, to determine whether, as Judge Wright hypothesized, schools with a disproportionate number of poor pupils would especially benefit from the redistribution of teachers resulting from *Hobson II*. The court's assumption was that poor schools were formerly deprived of teacher resources and would therefore now benefit. At least on the basis of these quite fallible poverty proxies, this does not seem to have occurred. The change, from 1971 to 1974, in the ratios of both resource and classroom teachers to pupils was likewise uncorrelated with either of the poverty proxies. It should be noted, however, that the measure of teacher resources here is the distribution of teachers per pupil, rather than per-pupil expenditure on teachers' salaries and benefits, as in *Hobson II*. Teacher changes are sensitive to enrollment

158. For current procedures, see District of Columbia Public Schools, "Selection of Eligible ESEA, Title I Attendance Areas of the District of Columbia for FY 1976" (1975; processed).

159. See District of Columbia Public Schools, Food Services, "Administrator's Handbook on Policies and Procedures of Food Services Programs" (August 1974; processed).

changes but not, so far as can be judged, to the poverty of pupils in the schools.[160]

As expected, smaller west-of-the-park schools have experienced a reduction of teacher services over the last several years. Expenditures on resource teachers now favor those schools formerly at the bottom in per-pupil expenditures, and some of the schools formerly at the top have no special-subject teachers at all.[161] But many schools in poor neighborhoods have also experienced falling enrollments and consequent reductions in their special-subject budgets. The resource programs of other schools have benefited from equalization because their enrollments are expanding or declining at a rate slower than the citywide rate.

One relatively large school, located in a high-income, predominantly white section of the city, has had a steadily increasing enrollment over the last several years. There was a net enrollment increase of 13.6 percent between January 1973 and November 1974, and it was anticipated that for 1975–76 there would be another increase of several percentage points. Although the school lost one classroom teacher with the first implementation of the equalization plan in 1971, subsequent equalization rounds have been benign. In 1973, the school gained enough additional funds to hire its second full-time music teacher, and it now has a complete resource program, including a school orchestra and French instruction for third grade pupils and above. For this school, equalization has meant enrichment programs.

Another school is located in a primarily black, low-income area of the District. Enrollment at this school has been falling steadily. Since 1967, it has lost about half of its student body, which then numbered more than 1,000 pupils. From fall 1972 to fall 1974, the school experienced a 24 percent decline in enrollment. The annual decreases have been met

160. The correlations of teacher–pupil ratios in 1974 with the poverty proxies in 1974 were as follows:

	Title I proxy	Free lunch proxy
Classroom teachers	0.03	0.01
Resource teachers	0.03	0.04

The correlations of the percentage change in teacher–pupil ratios from 1971 to 1974 with the poverty proxies in 1974 were as follows:

	Title I proxy	Free lunch proxy
Classroom teachers	0.00	0.01
Resource teachers	0.10	0.04

None of these correlations were significant.

161. Baratz, "Resource Allocation in Selected D.C. Schools," pp. 25–26.

by reducing classroom staff solely through attrition and reducing special-subject staff by involuntary transfers. At one time, the school had a complete resource program, conducted by full-time special-subject teachers. Now it lacks such a program in some areas, and covers others on only a part-time basis.

In addition to its decline in enrollment, this school is saddled with a highly paid faculty. A decade ago, it was a "demonstration school," and special efforts were made to develop a strong staff. Teachers were encouraged to seek graduate training, which was then reflected in their salaries. (Some 50 percent of the teachers held masters degrees, and the average teacher salary was in the $12,000–$15,000 range.) With equalization, the highly paid staff quickly became a liability. Transfers of classroom teachers provide no answer because of seniority rules, and so the school pays for its high salary structure and its declining enrollment with the disintegration of its resource program.

It should be noted that there is a basic asymmetry between schools with rising and falling enrollments. Schools with rising enrollments can sometimes add both classroom and resource teachers, for new classroom teachers are likely to be hired at the lowest end of the salary scale and therefore may not consume all of the mean per-pupil expenditure on teachers' salaries. Schools with falling enrollments, on the other hand, cannot lose teachers from the highest end of the salary scale because of seniority rules. Hence they are unable to salvage their resource program by moving to less highly paid classroom teachers. Needless to say, principals of schools with expanding enrollments tend to be more favorably disposed toward equalization than principals of schools with declining enrollments, and those with lower-salaried classroom teachers report an easier adjustment to equalization than those with higher-salaried classroom teachers.

Having witnessed the demise of their resource programs, some principals have suggested an equalization plan that would guarantee to all schools a minimum level of resource services, regardless of size or salary structure. The case for this is buttressed by the irrational distribution of resource teachers that is often a result of the policy of equalizing dollar values solely by transferring resource teachers. By "irrational," I mean two things, one quantitative, one qualitative. The quantitative irrationality occurs at the disadvantaged extreme, which has been made more unequal in the face of increasing overall equality in the distribution of resource teachers. The qualitative irrationality, which shows up in interviews but not in the correlations, occurs in the distribution of resource teachers primarily on the basis of dollar values and only secondarily (and weakly so) on the basis of resource programs. Whereas some schools have had virtually no resource program, others have had special-subject teachers "falling all over each other," in the words of one principal.

The distribution of special-subject teachers raises a basic question about *Hobson II*. The court was concerned with equalization of expenditures. It held that there was a "right" to the equal distribution of "measurable resources," and the resource on which the court finally focused was teachers' salaries considered in the aggregate. Assuming that there has been "compliance" with the decree, the resulting redistribution of expenditures on teachers' salaries has been achieved in the extremely disadvantaged schools at the expense of minimal programs in a number of special-subject areas. There has been, in other words, a conflict between minimum standards and redistribution. Since classroom and special-subject teachers do not really perform the same functions, they are incommensurables. For equalization purposes, however, they have been treated as if they were fungible entities, either of whose salaries could be used to satisfy the requirements of the decree.

As far as access to resources is concerned, the Equal Protection Clause has traditionally been construed to put a floor under the deprived, not a ceiling over the privileged.[162] Those seeking minimal facilities may have an equal protection claim no less legitimate—perhaps more legitimate—than those seeking full redistribution. Concretely, the claim of pupils deprived of a resource program may well have its own constitutional foundation.

There is another basic point about *Hobson II* that the dollar-value distribution of resource teachers exemplifies. Once the court determined that a "right to equal expenditures" existed, the costs of that decision became irrelevant. Once the right was defined to embrace all regular budget expenditures on teachers' salaries, inequalities in particular components of the salary mix could safely be disregarded in the implementation of the right as defined by the court.

The scope of the right that the court finally settled upon—narrower than all resources, broader than just classroom teachers' salaries—did

---

162. See Hornby and Holmes, "Equalization of Resources Within School Districts," p. 1139. For example, on minimal access to the courts, see *Boddie v. Connecticut*, 401 U.S. 371 (1971); *Griffin v. Illinois*, 351 U.S. 12 (1956).

not derive from any abstract principle. It was, as I have shown, the result of the litigation strategy of counsel and the court's perception of what expenditures seemed to be out of balance, educationally relevant, and within the school system's control. Had the right been defined either more broadly or more narrowly, the school system's room for maneuver in the implementation would have been completely different, and the distribution of resource teachers would also be different. Similarly, at the implementation stage, had the union's seniority protection embraced itinerant resource teachers, or the school board's reluctance to redraw school boundaries been less pronounced, or a number of other post-decree conditions been different, the equal protection of the laws would have a different operational meaning in the District of Columbia schools from the meaning it now has.

If the transfer of resource teachers according to budgetary criteria seems to amount to a trivialization of the equal protection principle, the methods adopted by the most resourceful school principals to avoid losing special-subject teachers show just how elusive the quest for equality can become. Principals faced with the loss of resource programs are not entirely without the ability to prevent this from happening. Some principals have been able to lower their per-pupil expenditures by raising enrollments or at least mitigating enrollment declines. Inasmuch as school boundaries are not easily manipulated for this purpose, the only way to enlarge enrollment is to create a new grade, either pre-kindergarten or perhaps seventh or eighth grade or both. A few principals have been able to retain valued teachers in this way.

Others have maintained programs and teachers by obtaining outside funding for them. One such source of funding is the parent-teachers association. Especially in schools with a student body that is both large and affluent, parent contributions through the association may be substantial enough to fund at least a portion of a teacher's salary.

Federal and foundation grants are the other principal source of outside funds employed to pay the salaries of teachers who would otherwise be transferred because of equalization. There is no easy way of knowing just how prevalent this is, but there is no doubt that at least some principals have been spurred by *Hobson II* to make a modest debut in the world of grantsmanship.

Expanding enrollment by creating new grades has the effect of spreading existing resources thinner, thwarting the redistribution of teachers by serving additional pupils. Obtaining outside funds to substitute for the regular budget funds that are subject to equalization requirements is another matter. This amounts to expanding the pie without sharing the extra slice. It does not thwart the transfer of resources to deprived schools, but it replaces the resources that are transferred with resources not subject to transfer. It can be viewed as a way of avoiding equalization or as a way of creating resources the school system would not otherwise have.

However one chooses to look at federal and foundation grants at the individual school level, it is difficult to avoid the conclusion that certain funds at the school system level are also available to avoid the impact of *Hobson II* if school officials wish to use them that way. To be sure, some federal funds, such as Title I and impact aid, are allocated on the basis of formulae that, if followed, make it difficult to use the funds to compensate schools adversely affected by *Hobson II*. But that is not true of all non-regularly budgeted funds. In particular, funds made available by the Emergency Employment Act—these are District of Columbia funds but not in the school budget—have been occasionally used to pay teachers' salaries in order to cushion the effect of equalization.[163] The distribution of teachers depicted in the tables above reflects only teachers supported by regularly budgeted funds. The total distribution of teachers is not reported.

Since *Hobson II* applies only to regularly budgeted funds and not to federal grant funds, the school system's ability to undo the equalization of regularly budgeted funds through the use of discretionary funds raises serious questions about the efficacy of any decree that does not touch discretionary funds. However, any decree that did succeed in eliminating the discretion provided by a grant program might of course run afoul of whatever educational objectives underlay the grant of that discretion to begin with.

In the end, the dilemma seems insoluble. It is not possible to know whether school officials have in fact used federal funds to cushion the impact of equalization. But it is quite clear that, when all federal funds (or all federal funds excluding Title I and impact aid) are included, there remain gross disparities in total per-pupil expenditures, though total per-pupil teachers' salary expenditures have not been calculated separately.[164]

163. District of Columbia Public Schools, "Federal Grant Supplement FY 1974" (December 1973; processed), pp. 149–50.
164. District of Columbia Public Schools, "Expenditures by Elementary School

Beyond the fairly clear and direct consequences of *Hobson II*, it is somewhat more difficult to assess the influence of the decision. It becomes impossible to determine whether some events that occurred or failed to occur would have taken the same course without the decree. More than that, some effects proved to be ephemeral, and some others that seem more enduring may yet prove to have been merely transitional. Still, one is struck by the range of activities touched in one way or another by *Hobson II*: school board–superintendent relations, administrative modernization, community control of schools, attempts at other innovations.

Immediately following the decision to implement the decree by transferring teachers, the board voted for a plan that involved hiring some 300 additional teachers.[165] This plan had been opposed by Superintendent Hugh Scott, and when he failed to hire the extra teachers, relations between the board and the superintendent reached a low point, from which they did not recover. Scott's contract was not renewed. As in the case of Superintendent Hansen, who resigned when the board refused to appeal *Hobson I*, the implementation of *Hobson II* has periodically added another strain to the tensions that tend to characterize board-superintendent relations in the District of Columbia.[166]

Perhaps the most significant long-range effect is the administrative change fostered by the decree. One aspect of this change, a vastly improved information system, was a result of the improved data base that the equalization program required. As part of the annual equalization report, required by the decree, the school system was required to compile and maintain data on pupil and teacher characteristics and on various categories of expenditures. Because this information must be presented to the court by December of each year, the school administration must continually update it. Had it not been for the equalization order, progress toward a more streamlined information system would probably have been much longer in coming.

Because it required expenditure accountability on a school-by-school basis, *Hobson II* also provided the impetus for the transition to school-by-school budgeting, a system designed to allow principals, staff, and

---

FY 1975," table II (November 20, 1974; processed). This table is annexed to a report submitted by the Superintendent of Schools to the Board of Education.

165. Baratz draft, pp. 40–46.

166. For a later episode, see *Washington Post*, December 3, 1974. Scott's successor, Barbara Sizemore, was dismissed by the board.

parents flexibility to determine the mix of teachers' services they want
to buy with the budget allocation they receive from the school administration. The new system is supposed to facilitate community involvement in budget decisions. In practice, however, the degree of flexibility
and the patterns of participation vary. Schools with expanding enrollments and expanding budgets report that they have newfound flexibility
in planning; schools with declining enrollments and declining budgets
report that they have newfound responsibility for making distasteful
decisions about budget cuts. Schools with flexible principals, active parents' groups, and expanding budgets also report a high level of community involvement; schools without these attributes report that most
decisions are made by the principal.

Both the improved information system and school-by-school budgeting might eventually have been developed had Julius Hobson never
gone to court. Nevertheless, by forcing the school system to report on
each school separately, *Hobson II* was a major catalyst of these changes.

Paradoxically, however, the decision created immediate problems for
a class of schools that already had a large measure of decentralized
authority: "community schools." These were experimental schools with
their own locally elected boards of education and considerable administrative power, including the hiring of new staff. *Hobson II* and the way
the Board of Education decided to implement it required the school
administration to have the ability to transfer teachers throughout the
system in accordance with expenditure criteria. The immediate effect
was to prevent the school administration from honoring its commitment
to permit local community boards to hire their own teachers.[167] When
some community boards objected, it was proposed that the Board of
Education request Judge Wright to exempt community schools from
the decree, but the board never did so. Control over hiring is not currently an issue for community schools, because, with generally declining enrollments, so little new hiring is taking place. School-by-school
budgeting permits schools to specify the kinds of teachers they want to
retain or lose, but the equalization decree requires teacher assignments
to be made with an eye to expenditures at each and every school. Consequently, *Hobson II* seems incompatible with decentralized hiring
decisions.

It is also very difficult to reconcile the equalization ordered by *Hob-*

167. Letter from Hugh Scott, Superintendent of Schools, to Rebecca Gray, July
26, 1972.

son II with the rather different equalization formulae of Title I of the Elementary and Secondary Education Act of 1965.[168] The purpose of the Title I equalization is to insure that Title I funds are not used to displace but to supplement regular school-system expenditures. Like *Hobson II*, it requires equalization within a range of plus or minus 5 percent of the mean expenditure. But there are three differences. First, the regulations promulgated under Title I require equalization of a number of separate items: pupil–teacher ratios, ratios of pupils to non-teacher instructional personnel, per-pupil expenditures on instructional personnel salaries, and per-pupil expenditures on instructional materials. Thus, Title I requires more specific equalization than does *Hobson II*, and it extends to pupil–teacher ratios, thereby limiting the choice of means of implementing *Hobson II*. Second, salaries of instructional personnel include those of librarians, counselors, principals, and other non-teaching staff. Third, the equalization of per-pupil expenditures on teachers' salaries under Title I excludes salary increments for longevity, which Judge Wright explicitly refused to exclude because he believed longevity to be related to teacher quality.

Despite these differences, the school system so far has not been found to be out of compliance with Title I, even though it has lavished its attention upon compliance with *Hobson II*. For one thing, the reports are due at different times of the year, which makes some last-minute shifting of personnel possible. Nevertheless, the divergence in formulae makes it exceedingly difficult to be in compliance with both sets of requirements simultaneously, especially if educational program is also to play a role in allocative decisions, and the Office of Education has on one occasion threatened to withhold funds.[169] In the somewhat unlikely event that the school system is in compliance with both—an event best described as a bare mathematical possibility—the probability is extremely high that this has been achieved by a distribution of teacher resources that can take little if any account of any assignment criteria other than the distribution of dollars.

There was a time, too, when it was thought that the then-proposed decree in *Hobson II* might be incompatible with the "Clark Plan," adopted by the Board of Education in 1970. The Clark Plan was designed to boost pupil achievement as measured by performance, and to

168. 20 U.S.C. § 241e(a)(3); 45 C.F.R. § 116.26. See Hornby and Holmes, "Equalization of Resources Within School Districts," pp. 1130–31.

169. Baratz draft, pp. 56–57.

that end had proposed to reward teachers by salary increases for the improved performance of their pupils on standardized tests. If the Clark Plan had provided the intended teacher incentive, the result might have been less equal, not more equal, concentration of salary resources.[170] To this argument Hobson's counsel rejoined that the Clark Plan incentives could be effectuated, but that successful, highly paid teachers would then have to be evenly distributed through the system by transfers.[171] Judge Wright agreed.[172]

In the event, it never came to that, because the Clark Plan was ultimately abandoned by the school system for other reasons. Nevertheless, the whole issue of whether and how the school system can use the teachers' salary structure for its own educational purposes, consistent with *Hobson II*, remains very much in doubt. How any merit pay scheme would work without a transfer being the ultimate reward for superior teacher performance—or, for that matter, how an incentive scheme to lure exceptional teachers into inner-city schools could function—these are issues that have not yet been reconciled satisfactorily with *Hobson II*.

In general, *Hobson* has had the effect of discouraging exceptional educational arrangements. The planners of the Fort Lincoln new town project in the District of Columbia believed, for example, that the very special and expensive school arrangements planned for that experimental project would have run afoul of *Hobson*.[173] This was one of several reasons the project did not go forward for some years. Indeed, the Board of Education has never taken advantage of the exceptions permitted by the decree in *Hobson II* for schools affected by genuine economies of scale and for schools providing compensatory education for educationally deprived, retarded, handicapped, or otherwise "exceptional" pupils. To take advantage of these exceptions, the board would have to justify them to the court. This would mean publicizing exceptional allocations, which would likely involve the school board and administration in a lengthy struggle to keep the list of exceptions smaller than the list of schools in the equalized category. The court evinced no understanding of the administrative and political costs of requiring ex-

170. See Robert W. Hartman, "Two Major School Plans May Be Incompatible," *Washington Post*, September 13, 1970.

171. Plaintiffs' Memorandum to the Court, pp. 12–13, filed December 8, 1970, *Hobson v. Hansen*, 327 F. Supp. 844.

172. 327 F. Supp. at 861–62 n. 28.

173. Martha Derthick, *New Towns In-Town* (Urban Institute, 1972), p. 36.

ceptions to its decree to be justified separately and publicly. Allowing exceptions to a decree to be made on a showing of justification is not the same thing as excepting something from the decree in the first instance.

Toward *Hobson III*

There has been considerable unease with the effects of *Hobson II*. Hobson himself was quickly disappointed. His hope, apparently, had been to achieve what his amended motion requested—equalization of all expenditures—as a prelude to conferring on individual schools the power to spend their fixed, equal allocation as they saw fit.[174] A number of economists have argued the case for "power to the school principals" on the basis of their presumed superior ability to match resources with pupils in a differentiated way;[175] this was essentially Hobson's goal. Not long after the *Hobson II* decree was rendered, it became clear that the decree required more, rather than less, centralized control over the hiring and assignment of teachers. This was, as has been suggested, partly a result of the way the issues were shaped to eliminate non-teaching expenditures from the decree. Hobson has said that plus or minus 5 percent is too small a tolerance and that "equalization should involve the total budget, not just teacher salaries."[176]

If this is the view of the victorious party, it is more than shared by the losing parties. Neither the Board of Education nor the school administration wishes to continue the present rigid system of annual transfers. As long ago as November 1973, the then Superintendent of Schools stated her intention to propose to the court a plan to widen the scope of the equalization decree to include more than just teachers' salaries, thereby providing somewhat more leeway than the decree presently does. (Teachers' salaries paid from regularly budgeted funds comprise some 85 percent of total regularly budgeted expenditures.) Subsequently, the superintendent issued a number of statements suggesting that the school administration would propose to the board and to the court a new plan for "incommensurability" to replace the decree in

174. Baratz draft, p. 46.
175. Michelson, "The Association of Teacher Resourceness with Children's Characteristics," pp. 150–55.
176. Quoted by William Raspberry, *Washington Post*, November 11, 1974.

Hobson II.[177] What this term means is anything but clear, though it surely implies a program of matching resources to pupils using some measure of valuation other than the common currency of dollar values.[178] That, of course, was exactly what the school authorities said they were doing before *Hobson.*

No such proposal was ever made to the court. Presumably, school officials, who have not fared well in court, are loath to return to court, at least without some signal from Hobson that he will concur in a request to modify or vacate the decree. The judicial machinery will not be invoked to monitor and review the results of its orders (as distinct from compliance with them), however dubious the orders may be, unless and until one of the parties sees a tactical advantage in doing so.

There is more than one way to modify the decree. The court could widen the scope of the decree to include in the equalization mix all expenditures (save beyond-control and economy-of-scale items) or at least all expenditures closely related to instruction (including textbooks, library books, instructional supplies, and salaries of principals, counselors, and librarians). This would provide decisionmakers with more choices among alternative ways to comply with the decree, for different schools could have different resource mixes, and it would be consistent with at least one formulation of the court's goals: "the law requires either that experienced teachers be distributed uniformly among the schools in the system *or* that some offsetting benefit be given to those schools which are denied their fair complement of experienced teachers."[179] But if teachers do occupy a unique place in the resource mix, then no other benefit may be truly "offsetting."

Alternatively, the court could narrow the decree further and require, somewhat as the Office of Education does with different categories under Title I, separate equalization of each of the components of per-pupil expenditures on teachers' salaries: classroom teachers' salaries, resource teachers' salaries, and perhaps pupil–teacher ratios. This would eliminate the capricious implementation of *Hobson II* through annual transfers of resource teachers, and would recognize claims to minimal resource programs. It would certainly not enhance the school system's

177. See, e.g., *Washington Post*, October 1, 1974.

178. The "incommensurability" concept is articulated by David Hawkins, "Human Nature and the Scope of Education," in Lawrence G. Thomas, ed., *Philosophical Redirection of Educational Research* (University of Chicago Press, 1972), pp. 287–326.

179. 327 F. Supp. at 855 (emphasis supplied).

flexibility or do away with the need for periodic transfers for equalization purposes. Nor, without a change in the requirement that longevity pay be included in the formula, would this modification render it easy to comply with both Title I and *Hobson II*. But it, too, would be consistent with the reasoning of *Hobson II*: this modification simply amounts to decomposing the right to equal per-pupil expenditures on teachers' salaries into its constituent elements and holding that there is a right to each of them separately.

A third way to modify the decree would be simply to adopt the Title I regulations wholesale and incorporate them into the decree. This would simplify compliance and minimize periodic disruptions due to teacher transfers.

That these basic modifications of the remedy remain possible the best part of a decade after the suit was filed suggests that no redefinition of the "right" or recalibration of the "remedy" is necessarily the last, unless a shortage of litigant and judicial energy makes it so. A definition of the right at any level of generality leaves open an implementation of the remedy that follows from it according to the structure of pressures and opportunities that impinge upon those who must implement it. Even with the utmost good faith, school officials will of course respond to the incentives of their environment. As Michelson has said of *Hobson II*: "Restraining one factor of production may serve to increase the cost and change the form of discrimination, but not necessarily to eliminate it."[180]

But if this much readjustment is periodically required in the light of the intervening behavior of school officials, it raises serious questions about the extent to which the problem can fairly be regarded as judicial. It consumes, simultaneously, too much and too little judicial energy— too much in the sense that the courts might more profitably spend their time on other problems; too little in the sense that judicial correction is only intermittent (in, say, four-year cycles) rather than sustained, too intermittent to prevent wholly fatuous compliance, and that judicial energy may eventually falter and abandon the problem at some arbitrary cut-off point.

And there is the question of what "right" means if a right defined in one way in *Hobson I* is defined still another way in *Hobson II* and yet another in *Hobson III*. Does it not then begin to lose the stable, intrinsic,

---

180. "For the Plaintiffs—Equal School Resource Allocation," *Journal of Human Resources*, vol. 7 (Summer 1972), pp. 283–306, at p. 285.

unfailing quality that may indeed be a definitional property of a right, especially a constitutional right? It may be one thing to expand or contract the scope of a right or set of rights from one case or one context to another; but fickleness may reach entirely different proportions when this is done in successive cracks at the same problem, each of them, in the accustomed manner of judicial opinions, purporting to be definitive.

To be sure, *Hobson II* may be the last of the *Hobson* cases on resource equalization. But there has been another development that may help bring the parties back to court before too long. The law has recently moved considerably beyond *Hobson* v. *Hansen*, and ultimately this may stir one side or the other to move the court to vacate or modify the decree in the light of intervening doctrinal developments.

In *Keyes* v. *School District No. 1*,[181] the Supreme Court held that where there is proof of intentional racial segregation in part of a public school system, the burden shifts to the school authorities to show that patterns of racial segregation elsewhere in the system were not also motivated by an intention to segregate. In this respect, Judge Wright may have been a bit too circumspect in confining his analysis of de jure segregation to the activities demonstrably affected by the intention to segregate. Under *Keyes*, all of the District of Columbia school system may have been presumptively segregated on a de jure basis at the time of *Hobson I*.

On the issue of resources, however, Judge Wright found the inequalities to have been inadvertent, so *Keyes* would presumably not have much impact. But other developments since *Hobson II* would. There is little doubt now that the requirement of "compelling justification" for unequal resource allocation was excessive. Both foundations of this strict standard have been eroded: deprivations inflicted inadvertently on "disadvantaged minorities" are no longer to be viewed as suspect in the way that intentional racial classifications are; and education is not to be regarded as a "critical personal right" of constitutional dimensions.

A year after *Hobson II*, the Supreme Court decided in *Jefferson* v. *Hackney*[182] that government programs having an unintentional racially differential effect need only meet the test of rationality. At issue in *Jefferson* was the validity of a state formula that distinguished among welfare programs in the amount of funding. The relatively disfavored

181. 413 U.S. 189 (1973).
182. 406 U.S. 535, 547–49 (1972).

programs had disproportionately higher numbers of minority participants. The Court sustained the formula as "not irrational."[183]

Jefferson involved welfare benefits. In *Hobson*, the court singled out
education as a "critical personal right"; until recently, welfare was often
categorized not as a right at all but as a privilege. Perhaps *Hobson*
could be distinguished on that basis.

Any such hope faded with *San Antonio Independent School District
v. Rodriguez.*[184] There the Supreme Court finally confronted the "right-
to-education" issue and held squarely that the Constitution conferred
no such right. Classifications impinging on the educational process are
therefore not to be subjected to the "strict scrutiny" of the "compelling
justification" standard but to the more permissive scrutiny of the "rational basis" standard.

However, *Rodriguez* presented the issue in the context of interdistrict rather than intra-district expenditure inequalities. Since there
was no proof that the poor lived in disadvantaged districts, or that rich
and poor within a district were treated differently, the Court was unable
to identify the "disadvantaged minority" identified in *Hobson*. This
difference between *Rodriguez* and *Hobson* is probably not crucial, however, for the Court held that, "at least where wealth is involved, the
Equal Protection Clause does not require absolute equality or precisely
equal advantages."[185] (On this score, *Rodriguez* seems to interpret the
"critical personal right" cases relied on in *Hobson* to give rise to an equal
protection claim only when there is "an absolute deprivation of the
desired benefit,"[186] such as complete denial of access to a court or to the
ballot, rather than simply an unequal distribution.) The Court in
Rodriguez did not have occasion to deal with the specifically racial
character of the "disadvantaged minority" identified in *Hobson*, but it
gave no reason to doubt the continued vitality of *Jefferson v. Hackney*:
strict scrutiny of "suspect classifications" does not appear to extend to
unintended or inadvertent discriminatory effects.[187]

It seems clear from *Rodriguez* that the equal protection analysis of

183. Ibid. at 549.
184. 411 U.S. 1, 29–39 (1973).
185. Ibid. at 24.
186. Ibid. at 23.
187. Quite the opposite. The Court cited three "suspect classification" cases,
all of them involving intentional rather than inadvertent action: *Graham* v. *Richard-
son*, 403 U.S. 365 (1971); *Loving* v. *Virginia*, 388 U.S. 1 (1967); *McLaughlin* v.
Florida, 379 U.S. 184 (1964). 411 U.S. at 16 n. 40.

both *Hobson I* and *Hobson II* has been repudiated by the Supreme Court. Less than two years after the decree was rendered, *Hobson II* had lost its constitutional underpinning.

This is one of the dangers of pathbreaking social policy decisions rendered by federal district courts. Their decisions are more vulnerable to changes in legal doctrine than are decisions of the appellate courts. Litigants who comply rather than appeal may end up running their affairs on the basis of decisions that are no longer law.

The irony of complying with a decision that may have been overruled has escaped the school system for quite some time. Perhaps it will continue to elude school officials. Perhaps, as impatience with the results of the decree grows on both sides of the litigation, the parties will return to court. A cynic has observed that the most important effect of *Hobson I* was *Hobson II*. It seems at least possible that the most important effect of *Hobson II* will be *Hobson III*.

CHAPTER FIVE

In re Gault: On Courts Reforming Courts

The *Area-Wide Council* and *Hobson* cases were judicial ventures far from the ordinary run of judicial experience. The Model Cities program and the issue of expenditure equality surely qualified as unfamiliar territory. One might therefore hazard the guess that, if the courts only stay closer to home, to issues and institutions they know and understand, they will be better able to anticipate the effects of their decisions and control them later. That, at any rate, was the hypothesis with which I began the investigation of *In re Gault*,[1] a decision in which the Supreme Court undertook to impose some important changes on the juvenile courts of the nation.

Gault was preceded by the portentous case of *Kent* v. *United States*,[2] decided by the Supreme Court in 1966. Construing the provisions of the District of Columbia Juvenile Court Act in the light of constitutional requirements, the Court required juvenile courts to hold hearings, accord counsel, and state reasons whenever they entertained the possibility of waiving their jurisdiction over juveniles and remitting them to the adult criminal courts. The opinion created an atmosphere of uncertainty and suspense over the constitutional status of juvenile proceedings in general, since those proceedings had customarily been conducted without the procedural paraphernalia usual in criminal trials.

The suspense was short-lived. A year later, the groundwork laid, a majority of the Supreme Court rang in the new regime of juvenile law in a sweeping opinion requiring written notice of any proceedings that might result in confinement of a juvenile; the right to counsel, provided at state expense in the event of indigency; the privilege against self-

1. 387 U.S. 1 (1967).
2. 383 U.S. 541 (1966).

171

incrimination and safeguards to insure that waivers of the privilege are voluntary and informed; and the right to confront and cross-examine witnesses testifying under oath. This was *In re Gault*.[3]

It would be too much to call these specific requirements a revolution in juvenile proceedings. Some legislatures, some courts, and some individual judges had already gone a long way toward meeting some or all of these requirements. The revolution, if there was any, was not in the formal requirements laid down but rather in the assumptions that had given rise to judicial proceedings without these requirements. It was a change of the spirit that the Supreme Court imposed, more than a change of the rules. It seems appropriate, therefore, to begin a discourse on *Gault* with a consideration of the Supreme Court's own assumptions as it embarked on this reforming venture.

A Skeptical Theology

More than most opinions of the Warren Court, *Kent* and *Gault* already seem like period pieces. Authored by Mr. Justice Fortas, the opinions are suffused with the meliorism of the mid-1960s. This was, after all, the time of the great programs and the great commissions: the Crime Commission, the Civil Disorders Commission, the Campus Unrest Commission, the Violence Commission. It was a time when the nation was being told that sharp precipices lay ahead unless the country turned onto other roads, and a time when a number of such turns were taken.

In general, the *Kent* and *Gault* opinions share this perspective—that things are wrong, but not so wrong that they cannot be righted if the problems are faced squarely. And in the case of juvenile courts, *Gault* faces them: the opinion makes a frontal attack on the central myths of the juvenile court movement. But in the course of challenging the untested assumptions of that movement, the Court acted on some untested assumptions of its own.

Three sets of assumptions can be identified. First of all, the Court had some definite ideas about the state of the juvenile courts. In addition, the Court entertained some deeply embedded conceptions about

3. In the years following 1967, the limits of the *Gault* principle were tested. The requirement of proof beyond a reasonable doubt was imposed where the juvenile is charged with an offense that would be a crime if committed by an adult. *In the Matter of Winship*, 397 U.S. 358 (1970). But the Court declined to require jury trials for such cases. *McKeiver* v. *Pennsylvania*, 403 U.S. 528 (1971).

the functions and behavior of lawyers and the likely impact of the presence of lawyers on juvenile proceedings. Last, though they were less prominent and certainly not dispositive, the Court expressed some views about the prospects for improvement of juvenile courts—views informed by what it took to be the state of knowledge about the relations of juvenile courts to juvenile delinquency.

The opinions in *Kent* and *Gault* exhibit the skepticism of established institutions that was so widely prevalent in the mid-1960s. Skepticism, and not hostility, for the Supreme Court did not view the juvenile courts with a jaundiced eye; it did not see them as malevolent, oppressive instruments of class or race discrimination. There is a long excursus in the *Gault* opinion on the evolution of the juvenile court as an institution. The emphasis is on good intentions gone awry. The protective blanket of the juvenile court, designed to shield those of tender years from the harshness of the criminal law, had kept from the young the protections of due process while imposing sanctions comparable to the criminal sanction:

A boy is charged with misconduct. The boy is committed to an institution where he may be restrained of liberty for years. It is of no constitutional consequence—and of limited practical meaning—that the institution to which he is committed is called an Industrial School. The fact of the matter is that, however euphemistic the title, a "receiving home" or an "industrial school" for juveniles is an institution of confinement in which the child is incarcerated for a greater or lesser time. His world becomes "a building with whitewashed walls, regimented routine and institutional hours. . . ." Instead of mother and father and sisters and brothers and friends and classmates, his world is peopled by guards, custodians, state employees, and "delinquents" confined with him for anything from waywardness to rape and homicide.[4]

Although juvenile courts do not classify offenders as criminals, the term "delinquent . . . has come to involve only slightly less stigma than the term 'criminal' applied to adults."[5] The confinement and stigma to which juvenile offenders are exposed suggest that the protective blanket of the juvenile court has worn thin. It has not kept them from exposure to essentially criminal liability.

Furthermore, the Court calculated, the sacrifice of procedural regularity has been made without offsetting gains in the rehabilitation of delinquents and the prevention of their anti-social behavior from becoming chronic. Despite the claims of the proponents of juvenile courts,

4. 387 U.S. at 27 (footnotes omitted).
5. Ibid. at 23–24 (footnote omitted).

the Supreme Court was unfavorably impressed with the apparently high rates of juvenile crime and recidivism. Results of that kind could, in the Court's view, scarcely justify a continuation of the "unbridled discretion, however benevolently motivated,"[6] possessed by juvenile judges.

Throughout, the argument is that the performance of juvenile courts has not been what it might be, that high-handedness and arbitrariness have been tolerated in the name of "the best interests of the child." The emphasis is on the need for dispassionate analysis: "Neither sentiment nor folklore should cause us to shut our eyes, for example, to such startling findings" as those on rates of juvenile recidivism.[7] The need is to examine "whether fact and pretension, with respect to the separate handling and treatment of children, coincide."[8]

The thrust of the early juvenile court movement is, according to the Court, captured in the reciprocity by which the juvenile surrendered the procedural safeguards attending criminal trials in return for essentially parental concern and expert treatment. The Court's self-conscious realism leads it to challenge this catechism, on which juvenile court practice is founded. In *Kent,* the Court remarked on what a bad bargain it is:

> While there can be no doubt of the original laudable purpose of juvenile courts, studies and critiques in recent years raise serious questions as to whether actual performance measures well enough against theoretical purpose to make tolerable the immunity of the process from the reach of constitutional guaranties applicable to adults. There is much evidence that some juvenile courts, including that of the District of Columbia, lack the personnel, facilities and techniques to perform adequately as representatives of the State in a *parens patriae* capacity, at least with respect to children charged with law violation. There is evidence, in fact, that there may be grounds for concern that the child receives the worst of both worlds: that he gets neither the protections accorded to adults nor the solicitous care and regenerative treatment postulated for children.[9]

Gault pursues much the same theme. The aim of the exercise is to separate "fact" from "pretension." One such pretension, exposed as "folklore," is that juvenile court proceedings are so informal they "reduce crime or rehabilitate offenders."[10]

6. Ibid. at 18.
7. Ibid. at 21.
8. Ibid. at 22 n. 30.
9. 383 U.S. at 555–56 (footnotes omitted).
10. 387 U.S. at 22.

Kent and *Gault*, then, are concerned with relating process to results Claims about performance are scrutinized, myths unmasked. It is a realistic jurisprudence that these opinions put forward.

If the Court's view of the juvenile court is highly skeptical, its view of the role of lawyers in juvenile court is not. The view can be stated simply, because it was not elaborately reasoned. Indeed, in *Kent* the Court states without elucidation that the other rights accorded juveniles are without meaning "unless counsel is given an opportunity to function."[11] For the Court, what functioning as a lawyer means is self-evident.

Later in the opinion, in the course of holding that counsel must be afforded access to the child's social welfare records that are before the judge, the Court goes on to say that counsel must be able to examine, criticize, and refute these reports before any decision on waiving jurisdiction can be based on them.[12] Apart from these brief references, *Kent* contains no description of what the effective assistance of counsel entails. There is little doubt, however, that the Court envisioned the same probing, challenging, contentious behavior that Kent's own counsel had exhibited—behavior that brought the case all the way to the Supreme Court.

In *Gault*, there are further allusions to much the same assumed reality. Due process requirements are anticipated to "introduce a degree of order and regularity . . . and in contested cases will introduce some elements of the adversary system. . . ."[13] Among the functions of counsel is "to insist on the regularity of proceedings. . . ."[14] One role counsel is certain to play, the Court assumes, is to aid in implementing the privilege against self-incrimination that the Court simultaneously grants to juveniles.[15] In the Court's view there is no question that counsel will often restrain the transmission of information from the juvenile to the juvenile court by advising him of his right to silence and helping to make it a reality. The assumed effect of counsel is to limit the information passed from the juvenile to the juvenile court and, by requiring the state to prove its case, to produce far more formality in juvenile court proceedings than previously existed.[16]

11. 383 U.S. at 561.
12. Ibid. at 563.
13. 387 U.S. at 27.
14. Ibid. at 36.
15. Ibid. at 55.
16. 387 U.S. at 38–40 n. 65.

The third set of assumptions deals with the Court's assessment of the impact of alternative procedures on the juveniles affected by them. In this, as also in its assessment of the performance of juvenile courts, the majority relies frequently on extrajudicial commentaries on delinquency. Two in particular stand out: the then-recent report of the Crime Commission, which is cited nine times in the *Gault* majority opinion, and a pamphlet on delinquency policy by Stanton Wheeler and Leonard Cottrell, cited seven times. Both of these works are cited for a number of behavioral propositions. For example, Wheeler and Cottrell are said to

observe that when the procedural laxness of the *"parens patriae"* attitude is followed by stern disciplining, the contrast may have an adverse effect upon the child, who feels that he has been deceived or enticed. They conclude as follows: "Unless appropriate due process of law is followed, even the juvenile who has violated the law may not feel that he is being fairly treated and may therefore resist the rehabilitative efforts of court personnel."[17]

A stronger statement to the same effect is quoted from the Crime Commission report:

[T]here is increasing evidence that the informal procedures, contrary to the original expectation, may themselves constitute a further obstacle to effective treatment of the delinquent to the extent that they engender in the child a sense of injustice provoked by seemingly all-powerful and challengeless exercise of authority by judges and probation officers.[18]

On the question of self-incrimination, Wheeler and Cottrell are invoked again for the proposition that

In fact, evidence is accumulating that confessions by juveniles do not aid in "individualized treatment," as the court below put it, and that compelling the child to answer questions, without warning or advice as to his right to remain silent, does not serve this or any other good purpose.[19]

Such a disjunction between the encouragement to confess and the subsequent discipline is likely to produce, the Court infers, hostility and resentment that impede rehabilitation.

It would be wrong to overemphasize the role of these behavioral findings in moving the Court to action. They were not decisive. But neither did they provide merely post hoc rationalization. The expert authority

17. Ibid. at 26, quoting Stanton Wheeler and Leonard S. Cottrell, Jr., *Juvenile Delinquency: Its Prevention and Control* (Russell Sage Foundation, 1966), p. 33.

18. 387 U.S. at 26 n. 37, quoting U.S. President's Commission on Law Enforcement and Administration of Justice, *The Challenge of Crime in a Free Society* (Government Printing Office, 1967), p. 85.

19. 387 U.S. at 51.

to which the Court recurs reinforces its view that formal procedure is not only legally essential but may actually have marginally therapeutic effects on the delinquency problem itself. That is the crux of this third set of assumptions.

It is easy to summarize the Supreme Court's views on juvenile courts, as revealed in *Kent* and *Gault*. Juvenile courts are often arbitrary, as well as generally ineffective in helping to control delinquency. They can be made at least less arbitrary by surrounding them with a panoply of procedural protections, especially the right to counsel. This would no doubt make their proceedings far more formal than they have been, but that cost may be offset or even more than offset by benefits in revised juvenile attitudes toward the juvenile court. Fair procedure may well produce a feeling of having been dealt with fairly. A sense of having been treated fairly is likely to be conducive to rehabilitation. It is comforting to know that what is required to redress arbitrariness will probably be at least somewhat beneficial in controlling delinquency as well.

The Court found the informality of the juvenile court no longer tolerable. It found juvenile courts frequently arbitrary in the name of informality, and it regarded even the intended informality of their proceedings as probably dysfunctional to the rehabilitation of offenders. Either way, change was indicated.

How the Supreme Court "knew" that juvenile courts often behaved arbitrarily is an interesting question of judicial epistemology, but this I shall only touch on in the concluding chapter. Here I want to dwell on the Court's speculations about the relation of procedural informality to the rehabilitation of offenders, not because the Court itself dwelled on it at length—it did not—but because it casts light on the Court's social science and how that affected the structure of choices before the Court. Then I intend to move from input to impact, to anticipated and actual results of having lawyers in juvenile court. Finally, I shall have some things to say about the effects of the *Gault* decision in forums other than the courts.

The Juvenile Court as a Problem Child

Alarmed by the recidivism figures, the *Gault* majority concluded that the present arrangements for "parental guidance" and "expert treatment" must not be working effectively to rehabilitate juvenile offenders. The quid pro quo for informality in juvenile proceedings had thus broken down. If juvenile offenders are not being "treated" effectively, at least they ought to be tried and punished fairly.

There were, however, alternative ways of interpreting the recidivism figures. Recidivism rates might be even higher, were it not for the informal procedures of the juvenile court.[20] More likely, offenders may recidivate despite the guidance they receive in juvenile court or, for that matter, despite any disposition they might receive in any court. The judicial process may simply have no bearing on recidivism one way or another. For, though high recidivism rates often "have been interpreted as an indication of the inefficiency of the juvenile court as a delinquency prevention and treatment agency," they might "equally be used to indicate the stubbornness of the social pressures that determine delinquent conduct despite efforts at treatment and control."[21]

None of these hypotheses could have been confirmed or rejected in the then-present state of knowledge about delinquency. Not merely were there no controlled experiments to test them; there was not even circumstantial evidence from which to draw inferences about the probable significance of recidivism rates for the functioning of juvenile courts. Yet the offhand speculations of Wheeler and Cottrell, who were far more modest than the Court about what they did not know, were taken as "evidence" or "conclusions." The stronger, more positive statements of the Crime Commission were accepted as if they were supported by evidence, though the Crime Commission cited none.

Actually, the commission's statement can be traced back to the report of its Task Force on Juvenile Delinquency and Youth, where the same statement is made almost verbatim, with a rather crucial exception: the commission said there was "increasing *evidence*" that informal procedures constitute an obstacle to treatment, whereas its task force said there was "increasing *feeling* on the part of sociologists and social welfare people" that informal procedures constitute an obstacle to treatment.[22] The task force went on to say that "[a]s in most matters dealing

20. A similar hypothesis is offered by W. Vaughan Stapleton and Lee E. Teitelbaum, *In Defense of Youth: A Study of the Role of Counsel in American Juvenile Courts* (Russell Sage Foundation, 1972), p. 170.

21. Harry Manuel Shulman, *Juvenile Delinquency in American Society* (Harper, 1961), p. 82, n. 40.

22. U.S. President's Commission on Law Enforcement and Administration of Justice, Task Force on Juvenile Delinquency, *Task Force Report: Juvenile Delinquency and Youth Crime* (Government Printing Office, 1967), p. 31 (emphasis supplied).

with juvenile delinquency, there is *no reliable evidence* as to whether or how accurate these observations are."[23] In the commission report, no such caveat is to be found. Needless to say, there is good reason to regard commission reports on social problems with at least as much skepticism as the Court lavishes on juvenile courts.[24]

The importance of such skepticism is underscored by the plausibility of a hypothesis diametrically contrary to those of the Crime Commission, of Wheeler and Cottrell, and, by derivation, of the Court. It is possible to assume that what happens in court does have some impact on what later happens on the street—as I have said, an assumption open to question—and still not conclude that the informal procedure of the juvenile court is inimical to rehabilitation. It could surely be argued that the atmosphere of adversariness typical of the full-fledged criminal trial does not generally convince the defendant that he has been dealt with fairly, for he may possess strong psychological defense mechanisms to help him avoid confronting his own guilt.[25] Instead, the combative trial atmosphere, with its emphasis on challenge and rebuttal and on denial of responsibility, may reinforce the defendant's hostility

23. Ibid. (emphasis supplied). The task force was correct. No evidence is to be found in the two studies it cites. One of these, David Matza, *Delinquency and Drift* (Wiley, 1964), p. 136, argues that juveniles detect "inconsistency" between the helping rhetoric and punitive behavior of juvenile judges, but makes no assertion that this is traceable to informal procedure and no showing that it affects rehabilitation. The second study (Elliot Studt, "The Client's Image of the Juvenile Court," in Margaret Keeney Rosenheim, ed., *Justice for the Child: The Juvenile Court in Transition* [Free Press of Glencoe, 1962], pp. 200–16) is more to the point. This sensitive essay suggests that "there is too great a disparity between the informality of the process [in juvenile court] and the seriousness of what actually happens in the life of the family. The client may well experience feelings of worthlessness and helplessness. 'Going to court' becomes not a sober accounting for one's own behavior before the community but a horrifying precipitation into insecurity against which the client learns to defend himself by manipulation. *One possible consequence* of such an experience *may be* the crystallization of delinquent identification and an intensified commitment to the familiar delinquent culture." Ibid., p. 204 (emphasis supplied). Contrast this careful statement with the commission's discovery of "increasing evidence" that informal procedures are a barrier to treatment.

24. See the illuminating analysis by Martha Derthick, "On Commissionship—Presidential Variety," *Public Policy*, vol. 19 (Fall 1971), pp. 623–38.

25. For the view that pleading guilty rather than going to trial may facilitate rehabilitation by requiring an unambiguous admission of guilt, see Donald J. Newman, *Conviction: The Determination of Guilt or Innocence Without Trial* (Little, Brown, 1966), p. 96. For other comments on the relation of procedure to rehabilitation, see ibid., pp. 45–47.

toward the community's agents, thereby retarding rather than fostering rehabilitation.

In short, the disjunction between the trial and the disposition may be even sharper when the trial is a fully adversary proceeding than when it is an informal, loosely conducted hearing. We shall see later that this hypothesis, though not stated so elaborately, is widely held by many juvenile court judges and lawyers. This view has greatly affected the implementation of *Gault* in the lower courts. Thus, this secondary theme in the Court's opinion has a major effect in practice.

Meticulous insistence on procedural regularity may be at odds with other aspects of delinquency prevention. A goal that has been rather widely accepted among lawyers and sociologists is the avoidance of what is called labeling. Even more than most branches of social science, the study of juvenile delinquency has produced a plethora of untested theories, of which labeling theory is one of the most prominent. Its basic assumption is that a juvenile who has been labeled a delinquent will subsequently be viewed by parents, teachers, employers, police, and others as a delinquent, will view himself as a delinquent, and will then act out this role. A preventive strategy thus avoids labeling except as a very last resort.

In operational terms, labeling theory has led to an emphasis, over the last decade or so, on diversion of juveniles away from the formal court machinery—which is assumed to be the chief labeling agent— and into various programs of informal probation and the like. The under-lying premise of the theory is that the response of the authorities to anti-social behavior may confirm the delinquent in his status, in his eyes and in the eyes of others. It follows from this that the more elaborate the authoritative procedure for arriving at determinations of delin-quency, the more powerful will be its influence in conditioning future behavior. Preceded by a meticulous process reserved for cases war-ranting severe community condemnation, the judgment of the authorities may then be more likely to be accepted, both by the juvenile and by the community, the latter of which will in turn adjust its behavior toward him accordingly. As Anne Rankin Mahoney has argued:

The very fact that a person is labeled by a procedure that he considers legitimate or just, may have an even greater negative impact on him than it would have had if he had perceived it as unjust. A label fairly affixed may be taken more seriously than one attached in a clearly unfair way. An unfair label is easier to deny psychologically. A community which believes its juvenile court is fair is likely to take its judgments seriously. Thus, probably one of the worst things we can do, if we are really concerned about the effects of labeling, is to develop a court which community members and defendants believe is really fair. A just procedure is highly desirable for other reasons, but it will not necessarily decrease the negative effects of labeling.[26]

It is not necessary to oppose fairness to unfairness, as Mahoney does, to appreciate the potential impact of procedure on labeling. A label elaborately affixed may be more powerful and enduring than one casually affixed—though it is necessary to reiterate that the validity of labeling theory itself has not yet been demonstrated.[27] From the standpoint of labeling theory, it can be hypothesized that there are positive virtues in the procedural offhandedness of the traditional juvenile court. And with this observation the argument comes full circle. For, though they did not phrase it in terms of labeling, proponents of the early juvenile court movement and the laws they promoted aimed, among other things, "to remove the stigma of criminal involvement and to provide the essentials of guidance and care which presumably were not given by the natural parents" of delinquent children.[28]

This is how the hypotheses on the impact or lack of impact of procedure on recidivism and rehabilitation might have looked at the time the *Gault* case was decided. Several of the theories are so reasonable that it seems difficult to choose among them. Certainly it is difficult to make the case that they are less probably valid than the hypothesis put forward cautiously by Wheeler and Cottrell, propounded with such confidence by the Crime Commission, and elevated by the Court into the structure of a constitutional determination.

Since *Gault*, however, evidence has begun to accumulate on the relationship of prospects for rehabilitation of juvenile offenders to the operations of the courts in which they find themselves. Such data as are now available suggest that courtroom procedure, formal or informal, adversary or not, probably plays little or no role in conditioning the offender's receptivity to reformative efforts.

The studies conducted so far indicate that juvenile-court proceedings are not regarded as unfair by the juvenile offenders who experience

26. "The Effect of Labeling Upon Youths in the Juvenile Justice System," *Law and Society Review*, vol. 8 (Summer 1974), pp. 583–614, at p. 590.

27. Pieces of the theory are beginning to be chipped away. See, e.g., Jack Donald Foster, Simon Dinitz, and Walter Reckless, "Perceptions of Stigma Following Public Intervention for Delinquent Behavior," *Social Problems*, vol. 20 (Fall 1972), pp. 202–09.

28. Stapleton and Teitelbaum, *In Defense of Youth*, p. 15.

them. Summarizing their findings, Stapleton and Teitelbaum state that "relatively few juveniles processed through the Zenith and Gotham courts [courts that held, respectively, an "adversary" and a "traditional" conception of their role] regard the system as 'unjust.' "[29] By "relatively few," Stapleton and Teitelbaum mean between 5.4 and 8.5 percent of all the juveniles "using unfavorable words."[30] Whatever the unfavorable words applied to, so low an incidence of perceived injustice (less than 10 percent in each of four subsamples) is impressive.

Two other studies point to the absence of evidence linking perceptions of unfairness to the procedure by which a disposition was made. Offenders, it would seem, do not perceive juvenile-court hearings to be unfair. In fact, the hearing process, as distinct from its outcome, is not a particularly prominent feature of the offender's attiude toward his offense or his punishment.

In one of the studies, conducted by Eloise C. Snyder,[31] the offenders had been placed on probation, most for the first time. Their hearings, held in Columbia, South Carolina, had all been conducted before *Gault* and without counsel. Interviewed a few weeks later, the offenders recalled feeling considerable fear at the time of the hearing. Despite the fact that they admitted committing the offense, they did not report feeling any guilt about it. Even though these were pre-*Gault* hearings, probably conducted quite informally, and even though the offenders did not seem especially remorseful, none found the hearing to be unfair. On the contrary, "[a]ll children felt . . . that the actual hearing was fair; most seemed quite seriously affected by it."[32] The offenders also reported having favorable attitudes toward the judge because of his concern for them. Their most vivid recollection of the hearing—and the thing about it that made them "feel best"—was the judge's decision, in these cases to place them on probation.

The second study was conducted by Martha Baum and Stanton Wheeler in Boston, Massachusetts.[33] It involved interviews with 100 offenders confined for the first time, the interviews conducted, as in South Carolina, relatively soon after the juvenile-court hearing. The offenders

29. Ibid., p. 171.
30. Ibid., p. 181, n. 61.
31. "The Impact of the Juvenile Court Hearing on the Child," *Crime and Delinquency*, vol. 17 (April 1971), pp. 180–90.
32. Ibid., p. 183.
33. "Becoming an Inmate," in Wheeler, ed., *Controlling Delinquents* (Wiley, 1968), pp. 153–85.

reported having little recollection of the proceedings, "largely because," as in the Snyder study, "they were waiting to hear the central message—commitment or no commitment."[34] The youths in this study regarded their commitment as punitive and unpleasant, despite the therapeutic rhetoric of delinquency prevention. Most of them, moreover, did not expect to be committed. It is all the more significant, therefore, that these offenders, too, accorded considerable legitimacy to the judge's decision to commit them. Fifty-four percent felt the decision was "fair," 14 percent "somewhat fair," 8 percent "balanced fair-unfair," only 18 percent "unfair," and 6 percent "somewhat unfair."[35] Eighty-three percent of the offenders felt their difficulties were mainly their own fault. These offenders found no real injustice in the decision to commit them or in the way it was made. Their conclusion squares with the research findings of other studies of offender attitudes toward juvenile courts,[36] as well as of adult offender attitudes toward their punishment.[37]

These studies came too late to help the Court. The admittedly tentative, often frankly speculative, essay by Wheeler and Cottrell and the much more positive recommendations of the Crime Commission preceded and were utilized in the Court's decision. Baum and Wheeler's study was published a year after the Court's decision, and the other studies followed within a few years. One hypothesis on which the Court seized, treating it as if it were supported by evidence, turns out to be one of the rare hypotheses in the juvenile delinquency field on which persuasive disconfirming evidence began to accumulate shortly after the Court's decision. A related hypothesis the Court put forward—that encouragement to confess, followed by stern disciplining, is likely to generate resentment—remains untested, but the later research casts doubt on its validity as well. In short, hardly had the Court rendered its opinion when it became empirically suspect.[38]

34. Ibid., p. 165.
35. Ibid., p. 171.
36. See Brendan Maher and Ellen Stein, "The Delinquent's Perception of Law and the Community," in Wheeler, ed., Controlling Delinquents, p. 211: "Few responses implied that the delinquent felt he had been dealt with unfairly in the court."
37. Jonathan D. Casper, "Did You Have a Lawyer When You Went to Court? No, I had a Public Defender," Yale Review of Law and Social Action, vol. 1 (Spring 1971), pp. 4–9, reprinted in George F. Cole, ed., Criminal Justice: Law and Politics (Duxbury Press, 1972), pp. 236–46.
38. If juvenile-court procedure has little impact on the perceptions of offenders, juvenile-court dispositions may make a difference. There is a hint of this in the South

The point is not really which hypothesis is right. The point is that the Court chose among conflicting hypotheses without knowing it was doing so. Indeed, it chose a hypothesis filtered through the lenses of popular commentaries and commission reports, the latter of which often speak with an assurance inversely proportional to the empirical support undergirding their conclusions. *Gault* raises the question of how courts obtain their behavioral information and how it is likely to be filtered.

Gault also raises the question of what courts do with such behavioral information as they obtain. For assuming the Court's social science to be dubious still leaves open the further question of whether that dubious social science really matters. I think it does.

I have already said that the Court's behavioral findings were not dispositive, but that does not make them unimportant. It is one thing if all considerations relevant to a decision seem to point one way; it is another if they seem to point in different directions or in no clear direction at all. In the latter cases, there will have to be weighing of preferences and costing them against countervailing considerations. That process was avoided by the happy confluence of law and social science in *Gault*.

As things stood, there was nothing to choose. The costs of continuing the old system appeared high, the benefits slight. Everything seemed to fall into place. Had the Court been as skeptical of social science as it was of juvenile courts, the *Gault* opinion would have had a quality of toughminded policy choice that the issues in the case warranted. But no sooner had the majority insisted on its skepticism for the one than it abandoned it for the other.

Carolina and Massachusetts studies. In the South Carolina study, the offenders had been placed on probation; these youths tended to deny their own responsibility for their actions and to locate responsibility in the influence of peers or in the provocations of victims. In the Massachusetts study, the offenders had been committed; they tended to blame themselves for their predicament and to view their commitment as punishment for wrongdoing, punishment that might help them avert a recurrence. The respondents in both studies focused, not on courtroom procedure, but on the disposition made by the judge. Whether the difference between probation and commitment has any effect on later evaluations of the delinquency by the offender seems plainly an issue in need of investigation. It may well be that such substantive matters as the proportionality of the disposition to the offense or the ratio of an offender's arrests to the frequency of his offenses play a greater role than does courtroom procedure in influencing prospects for rehabilitation. Arrest and punishment may bring home the personal costs of engaging in delinquent activity. At least this hypothesis seems more plausible than any that relates modes of procedure to susceptibility to rehabilitation.

There is another issue, too. If what I have said so far is right, the Court was echoing propositions not yet established, with more confidence in their probable truth than was warranted. By echoing them, it gave them greater currency. It endorsed one version of the facts, a version that may turn out to be utterly false. The court was writing an essay on what right-thinking people ought to believe about juvenile courts and about their relationship to juvenile delinquency. In particular, it was telling a society that is continually "judicializing" itself (that is, converting more and more procedures into the adversary model) that, apart from its merits as an instrument of procedural justice, the adversary process can exercise a benign influence on the relationship between the adversaries.

It is in this sense that the *Gault* opinion has been called the product of a "social movement."[39] That phrase imparts more coherence to the proponents of juvenile court reform than is probably warranted, but it does rightly emphasize that the origins of *Kent* and *Gault* lie in the preferences articulated by reformers, not in the truths discovered by science.

The Role of Lawyers

Nor was there any uncertainty about what the expected contribution of lawyers was to be. For the Supreme Court, the lawyer's role is to implement the privilege against self-incrimination and to prevent arbitrariness by the skillful exploitation of ceremony. Formal procedures are the lawyer's stock-in-trade, and the Court assumed there would be more formalization of the juvenile court's procedure, and presumably more contested dispositions, as lawyers became involved on a routine basis.

Frequency of Representation

It is now becoming clear that this assumption was mistaken. First of all, although the number of cases in which lawyers actually appear in juvenile court, even in proceedings that might result in commitment of the juvenile, is unknown, there is reason to think that lawyers still appear much less often than might have been expected. In Providence,

39. Albert K. Cohen, "An Evaluation of *Gault* by a Sociologist," *Indiana Law Journal*, vol. 43 (Spring 1968), pp. 614–18.

Rhode Island, for example, lawyers represented juveniles in 5 percent of all pre-*Gault* cases. After *Gault*, this had risen to only 15 percent. Comparable figures for Portland, Maine, were 2 percent, pre-*Gault*, and 20 percent, post-*Gault*.[40] In California, where the right to counsel was provided by statute in 1961, appearances of lawyers rose from a county-to-county median of 3 percent before the law to only 10 percent by 1965. There was a wide differential from county to county and a lesser range from one type of case to another within counties. In Sacramento County, California, as of 1962–63, counsel appeared in 16.5 percent of all truancy and incorrigibility cases and 21.4 percent of all cases charging a juvenile with a violation of criminal law.[41] In the Columbus, Ohio, juvenile court, which seemed receptive to *Gault*, representation by counsel in delinquency and incorrigibility cases rose from 13 percent in the immediate pre-*Gault* period to 29 percent in the immediate post-*Gault* period, though counsel appeared more often in more serious cases.[42] Juveniles were represented by counsel in 36.7 percent of the cases that reached formal adjudication in an urban upstate New York county, but this figure includes "persons-in-need-of-supervision" cases, in which counsel was present fully 50 percent of the time.[43] A study of another county found attorneys to be present in 24 percent of delinquency cases.[44] In short, even in formal delinquency hearings, lawyers are clearly the exception rather than the rule.

If counsel is now required, it is natural to ask why counsel appears so infrequently. There are several answers to this question, and they all tell something about the implementation of externally formulated social policy in an ongoing institutional setting.

40. Richard J. Maiman, "Private Attorneys in Juvenile Court: The Impact of *In re Gault*" (paper presented at annual meeting of American Political Science Association, 1974; processed), p. 3.

41. Edwin M. Lemert, *Social Action and Legal Change: Revolution Within the Juvenile Court* (Aldine, 1970), pp. 172, 175. California was one of several states that adopted a *Gault*-type regime for juvenile courts in the years before *Gault* was decided. In discussing the impact of counsel on juvenile courts in the pages that follow, I occasionally refer to the "pre-*Gault*" and "post-*Gault*" periods. For those states that implemented the right to counsel by law before *Gault*, this terminology of course refers to the date of that enactment rather than the date *Gault* was decided.

42. Charles Reasons, "*Gault*: Procedural Change and Substantive Effect," *Crime and Delinquency*, vol. 16 (April 1970), pp. 163–71, at p. 168.

43. David Duffee and Larry Siegel, "The Organization Man: Legal Counsel in the Juvenile Court," *Criminal Law Bulletin*, vol. 7 (July–August 1971), pp. 544–53, at p. 551.

44. E. Ferster, T. Courtless, and E. Snethen, "The Juvenile Justice System: In Search of the Role of Counsel," *Fordham Law Review*, vol. 39 (1971), pp. 375–412.

To begin with, the reaction to *Gault* was far from uniform.[45] No doubt some juvenile-court judges used the opportunity to expand and upgrade their courts. They scrupulously fulfilled the requirements of the opinion and accepted the new burdens imposed on their courts. Others, especially in smaller cities, towns, and rural areas, saw the requirement of counsel as burdensome and costly: their compliance was "partial and inconsistent, with minimal psychic commitment or conviction that the changes were necessary."[46]

It is not difficult for judges to act on this ambivalence or hostility toward counsel in the juvenile-court setting. For, in one key respect, juvenile court is unlike other courts. Probation officers and judges are often fairly certain of dispositions of cases in advance of hearings on them. A common tendency is to let the disposition dictate the findings, rather than vice versa.[47] Not surprisingly, this makes it very difficult for a lawyer to conduct an effective adversary defense, as we shall see. It also makes it quite easy for a judge to handle a large part of his docket— that part in which he has decided against incarceration—without counsel. Thus, a judge in northern California states: "If a felony charge is involved, I advise minors and parents of their right to counsel. However, I don't do this for the 'Mickey Mouse' offenses. . . ."[48] In Portland, "intake officers" screen a large fraction of cases, disposing of many by informal probation:

an intake officer who wishes to continue a case informally is likely to avoid mentioning counsel at all unless the juvenile or the parents deny the charge or ask to be represented. This rarely happens, however, because the accusatory and coercive aspects of the proceeding are skillfully underplayed by the intake officer. By such "selective application" of the counsel warning the Portland intake officers are able to dispose of a large majority of their post-*Gault* cases in a pre-*Gault* manner.[49]

In Providence, virtually every juvenile referred to the court appears before a judge, but the result is the same. A common practice is to place the juvenile on some form of probation. This typically happens rather quickly and without mention of the right to counsel.[50] The lenient dispositions often found in juvenile court lend themselves to proceedings without counsel, for, as we have seen, the disposition is likely to be of

45. See Lemert, *Social Action and Legal Change,* pp. 158–71, for comparably variable responses to the California law requiring counsel.

46. Ibid., pp. 168–69.

47. See, e.g., ibid., pp. 176, 178, 206.

48. Quoted in ibid., p. 170.

49. Maiman, "Private Attorneys in Juvenile Court," p. 4.

50. Ibid.

much greater importance to the juvenile than the manner in which it was reached.

Where courts do advise parties of the right to counsel, the advice may be given in an incomplete way (omitting, for example, that free counsel will be provided in the event of indigency) or in a way otherwise calculated to discourage the exercise of the right.[51] Juvenile court judges who are inhospitable to lawyers can often find ways to keep them out of their courtrooms. These ways find their justification in the oft-reiterated belief of many judges that the child's best interests are not served by an adversary hearing. Non-adversary hearings are often accepted by parents who believe with the judges that the best interests of their miscreant children lie in submitting them to the court and its remedial facilities, rather than in turning the encounter into a combat.

The Lawyer's Posture

Beyond the frequency or infrequency with which counsel appears is the issue of how lawyers operate when they do appear in juvenile court. There is increasing evidence that the presence of lawyers does not necessarily alter the pre-*Gault* operating assumptions of those juvenile courts that entertain a heavily therapeutic orientation toward their work. Even in less traditional juvenile courts, the presence of lawyers often seems to facilitate rather than impede informal disposition—that is, disposition short of the full-fledged, formal adversary hearing.

A number of forces combine to produce this result. There is a deeply embedded notion, espoused as much by lawyers as by anyone else, that a juvenile who gets into trouble ought not to escape without some reproof from the juvenile court. Many lawyers have a marked distaste for helping juveniles to "beat a case."[52] Fearing that if they are able to get a meritorious case dismissed "they may be contributing to a future criminal career,"[53] many lawyers are reluctant, as one lawyer put it, to "raise technicalities for any child."[54] Another lawyer is more explicit:

51. See ibid., pp. 5–8; Norman Lefstein, Vaughan Stapleton, and Lee Teitelbaum, "In Search of Juvenile Justice: *Gault* and Its Application," *Law and Society Review*, vol. 3 (May 1969), pp. 491–562; Lemert, *Social Action and Legal Change*, pp. 176–77.

52. Sanford J. Fox, "Juvenile Justice Reform: An Historical Perspective," *Stanford Law Review*, vol. 22 (June 1970), pp. 1187–1239, at p. 1236.

53. Anthony Platt and Ruth Friedman, "The Limits of Advocacy: Occupational Hazards in the Juvenile Court," *University of Pennsylvania Law Review*, vol. 116 (May 1968), pp. 1156–84, at p. 1184.

54. Ibid. at p. 1183.

"At times the attorney may plead a juvenile guilty even though he feels that at a trial he can obtain a not guilty finding through a technical defect in the prosecution's case, since in his opinion the child's welfare is better served by exposing him to the rehabilitative opportunities offered by the juvenile court."[55] The assumption is that " 'how to help' should be the keynote—not 'how to defend.' "[56]

Such views are widely held by defense counsel in juvenile court.[57] Whether public defenders or private practitioners, lawyers are likely to see themselves as a hybrid species: part advocate, part social worker.[58] Sharing the general assumptions of the court and probation staff, lawyers sometimes express only token opposition to the commitment of their clients to custody.[59] Studies of lawyers in juvenile court are rich with illustrations of this proclivity. Consider the following statements of two public defenders:

Ordinarily I stipulate that the probation officer's report is acceptable in the jurisdictional hearings. Otherwise he would have to bring in witnesses. In many such cases, perhaps most, the evidence would not support the judgment, but I hate to see a young kid get the idea that he can get away with something. One 15 year old boy who broke into a bar and took a case of beer told me in an interview that his problem was that he got caught. I became indignant and asked him if he wasn't too young to drink. The boy said, "No, only too young to buy." I decided he needed to be jolted—maybe with a stay in detention—so I encouraged him to admit his guilt in court. No corpus delicti needed to be established. If it had been an adult case I would have taken the position that the D.A. could not prove his case, because the beer was never found and not even reported until a month after it disappeared.

In many cases I just put the boy on the stand and let him explain his feelings. When the judge asks for comments I don't make any. But in some cases I act. My attitude is that if a minor gets more than is coming to him I step in and correct it.[60]

These sentiments and the behavior that follows from them do not originate solely with defense lawyers. The assumptions and style of juvenile-court judges tend to push lawyers away from an adversary role

55. Quoted by Maiman, "Private Attorneys in Juvenile Court," p. 16.

56. Ibid.

57. Maiman found that, in the two cities he studied, "counselors" greatly outnumbered "advocates" in juvenile court. Ibid., p. 14.

58. Anthony Platt, Howard Schechter, and Phyllis Tiffany, "In Defense of Youth: A Case Study of the Public Defender in Juvenile Court," *Indiana Law Journal*, vol. 43 (1968), pp. 619–40.

59. See Robert M. Emerson, *Judging Delinquents: Context and Process in Juvenile Court* (Aldine, 1969), pp. 138–39.

60. Quoted by Lemert, *Social Action and Legal Change*, pp. 178, 201.

conception. There is frequent pressure from juvenile-court judges on lawyers to insist less on their clients' rights and more on what they regard as their welfare.[61] The juvenile court often believes a severe chastening is the key to deterring new offenders. Consequently, courts are loath to encourage denials of the charges and eager to use courtroom procedure to put the juvenile in the status of wrongdoer and have him acknowledge his errant ways.[62] Admissions by the juvenile legitimate the court's "helping role."[63] In addition, they are sometimes the only admissible evidence before the court.[64] In a word, a great many juvenile-court judges have "a non-adversary conception of the attorney's role,"[65] and it leads them to press lawyers toward a cooperative stance.

For all of these reasons, juvenile judges are likely to discourage the interposition by lawyers of complete defenses. The emphasis, instead, is on excuses, justifications, and mitigating circumstances.[66] Plainly, this puts the accent on non-legal defense strategies, and specifically on the "pitch"—a presentation designed to establish that the juvenile is not a "bad kid" or that there is some reasonable excuse for his behavior or that there is some reputable "sponsor" willing to assume responsibility for him.[67] It also leads lawyers to seek ways, such as informal probation, that avoid formal disposition of the charges against the juvenile.

By virtue of both the predilections of lawyers and the pressures of judges, counsel often assumes a non-adversary posture in juvenile court. This results in a large number of essentially uncontested dispositions. According to one study, more than half of the juvenile cases in which lawyers appear in Portland and Providence are disposed of by guilty plea or informal probation, even though cases involving private attorneys are more often contested than cases in which the juvenile is unrepresented.[68] The admission of guilt is a common defense practice in juvenile court.[69]

61. Monrad G. Paulsen, "Juvenile Courts and the Legacy of '67," *Indiana Law Journal,* vol. 43 (Spring 1968), pp. 527–57, at pp. 536–37.

62. See, e.g., Emerson, *Judging Delinquents,* pp. 183–92.

63. Edwin M. Lemert, "Records in the Juvenile Court," in Stanton Wheeler, ed., *On Record: Files and Dossiers in American Life* (Russell Sage Foundation, 1969), p. 367.

64. Lemert, *Social Action and Legal Change,* p. 185.

65. Stapleton and Teitelbaum, *In Defense of Youth,* p. 64.

66. Emerson, *Judging Delinquents,* p. 143.

67. Ibid., chap. 5.

68. Maiman, "Private Attorneys in Juvenile Court," p. 9.

69. See Stapleton and Teitelbaum, *In Defense of Youth,* p. 116.

As might be expected, there are some differences, depending on the inclinations of lawyers and courts. In the Portland-Providence study, lawyers were divided into "counselors" and "advocates" according to their orientation toward the appropriate role of the juvenile court and toward the role of lawyers appearing in it. In both cities, lawyers who do not entertain a fully developed adversary conception of their role ("counselors") are more than twice as likely not to go to trial or secure a dismissal as those who do entertain an adversary role conception ("advocates").[70] Similar differences appear between courts operating on different assumptions. A comparative study of lawyers in two juvenile courts, one "traditional" and treatment-oriented, the other "adversary" and adjudication-oriented, found that twice as many cases were contested in the adversary court (70 percent) as in the traditional court (36 percent).[71] Thus, a lawyer who deliberately assumes an adversary stance can indeed turn the proceedings into an adversary contest in a juvenile court disposed to permit such tactics, but it is much more difficult to do so in a court that believes its function to be therapeutic rather than punitive.

A great many lawyers and judges, then, are wedded to a hypothesis about the relation of procedure to rehabilitation diametrically opposite to the hypothesis advanced by the Supreme Court. This divergence in belief has proved to be one of the most potent obstacles to the implementation of *Gault* in a generally adversary fashion.

The Effect of Lawyers on Dispositions

The scant data now available suggest that, in some courts, juveniles with lawyers fare better than those without lawyers, particularly in avoiding commitment to an institution.[72] This in itself does not neces-

70. Maiman, "Private Attorneys in Juvenile Court," p. 17.

71. Stapleton and Teitelbaum, *In Defense of Youth*, p. 116. These are remarkably similar to the figures reported by Maiman, "Private Attorneys in Juvenile Court," p. 17. Needless to say, the terms "adversary" and "traditional" are not perfectly descriptive and should be viewed as relative rather than dichotomous. With this qualification in mind, these terms are employed through the rest of this chapter.

72. Stapleton and Teitelbaum, *In Defense of Youth*, p. 71; Maiman, "Private Attorneys in Juvenile Court," p. 9. See also Edwin M. Lemert, "Legislating Change in the Juvenile Court," *Wisconsin Law Review* (Spring 1967), pp. 421–48, at p. 441, reporting more favorable dispositions with counsel than without, but apparently in neglect rather than delinquency cases. See Lemert, *Social Action and Legal Change*, pp. 192–94.

The ultimate impact of lawyers on cases is not really measured by aggregate

sarily indicate the use of adversary tactics: it is perfectly consistent
with the facility of lawyers for making pitches for their clients or for
negotiating compromise outcomes. But these same data also indicate
that outright dismissals may be more frequent where counsel partici-
pates. Unfortunately, it is impossible to determine the extent to which
any of these favorable outcomes is an artifact of the kinds of cases in
which lawyers are involved or of the personal and social characteristics
of those juveniles who obtain representation. This much is clear: there
are markedly different rates of representation by counsel for different
types of offenses.[73] This variance, of course, is consistent with what we
already know about the differential frequency with which judges and
probation officers advise parents of the right to counsel in different kinds
of cases.

If juveniles with lawyers fare better in some courts than juveniles
without lawyers, that is not the universal tendency. In one study, juveniles who were represented by counsel actually received significantly
more severe dispositions (more commitments, fewer dismissals) than
those who were unrepresented.[74] This relationship persisted even when
the severity of the offense charged was controlled. Incarcerations of
unrepresented juveniles were very rare—a fact that strongly suggests
that the court was culling the docket for serious cases likely to receive
severe dispositions and then requiring counsel in those cases but not
others.[75] Other data hint at the same phenomenon.[76] As I have suggested, this kind of prejudgment makes a lawyer's conduct of an adversary defense exceedingly difficult, for the adversary system can hardly

---

figures on dispositions of cases where juveniles were and were not represented.
These figures may mask a large number of changes in result that are offset by
changes in the opposite direction and hence do not show up in the aggregate figures.
There is reason to think that this does happen in juvenile court, and that representation can affect many individual outcomes not fully reflected in the aggregate data.
For example, as will be shown, the presence of counsel in some cases may help
preserve the right to remain silent, while in others it may help to insure a waiver;
in both, the result may turn on whether or not the juvenile chooses to tell his story.
Consequently, Gault may have a greater impact on individual cases than the disposition figures indicate, but there is no way to determine the extent to which this
is true. The aggregate figures are the best available.

  73. Lemert, Social Action and Legal Change, p. 175; Duffee and Siegel, "The
Organization Man," p. 551; Reasons, "Gault," p. 168.
  74. Duffee and Siegel, "The Organization Man," p. 550.
  75. See note 47 and accompanying text, above.
  76. Reasons, "Gault," p. 169.

function unless the decisionmaker is prepared to suspend a judgment he might otherwise reach before all the evidence is in.[77]

The dispositions obtained by counsel seem also to depend on the style of the court. The comparative study of a traditional and an adversary court referred to above found that, in the court that entertained a therapeutic conception of its function, lawyers tended to obtain slightly less favorable outcomes (fewer dismissals, more commitments) than were obtained by unrepresented juveniles.[78] This may, of course, be a function of the severity of the cases that find their way to lawyers in such a court. In the more adversary courtroom setting, however, lawyers obtained more dismissals and fewer commitments than unrepresented juveniles.[79] Clearly, it is not lawyers alone, but also the milieux in which they function, that determine the effect of legal representation.

Even in the adversary-style court, along with the greater frequency of dismissals, there was a noticeable trend toward informal dispositions. To be sure, some kind of informal probation or court supervision was much more common in the traditional-style juvenile court, where very nearly a third of all cases were disposed of by such a technique, whether lawyers participated or not.[80] In the adversary court, such dispositions were very rare where no lawyers participated, but significantly more frequent where lawyers were involved.[81]

The number of dismissals in cases where lawyers were present in the adversary court was unusually high. Just over half of all such cases were dismissed. This probably reflected several unusual conditions. First, dismissal rates in that court were generally high: even unrepresented juveniles had their cases dismissed 39 percent of the time, twice as often as unrepresented juveniles in the traditional court. Second, the lawyers who participated in the study were instructed to "consistently conduct themselves in a generally adversary fashion, especially at the adjudication hearing, rather than adopt a more treatment-oriented posture or any combination of approaches."[82] This instruction doubtless led

77. See Lon L. Fuller, "The Adversary System," in Harold J. Berman, ed., *Talks on American Law* (Vintage Books, 1961), pp. 30–43. See also John Thibaut and others, "Adversary Presentation and Bias in Legal Decisionmaking," *Harvard Law Review*, vol. 86 (December 1972), pp. 386–401.

78. Stapleton and Teitelbaum, *In Defense of Youth*, p. 71.

79. Ibid.

80. Ibid.

81. Ibid.

82. Ibid., p. 58.

them to seek dismissal whenever that was an arguable disposition. Third, the study was conducted not long after *Gault* was decided. Pre-*Gault* cases in a great many courts were often loosely prepared and presented by the prosecutor or probation officer, and hence subject to dismissal at the insistence of aggressive counsel.[83] As adjustments to the post-*Gault* regime are made, cases will presumably be better prepared or better screened, and fewer dismissals can be expected. The result of this will in all probability be a greater prevalence of compromise outcomes in juvenile court. Indeed, there have already been serious discussions among lawyers and other specialists in juvenile justice about the uses and abuses of plea bargaining as a result of the increasing frequency of attorney representation in juvenile court.

Plea Bargaining for Juveniles

In the past, plea bargaining as such has often been impeded in juvenile court. In many jurisdictions, there has customarily been no prosecutor to bargain with. The juvenile court judge himself conducted the trial, and his role in many cases extended to eliciting the prosecution's evidence. While he may in some sense be acting as prosecutor in these cases, the very idea of plea bargaining is negotiation for a disposition in advance of the judge's participation. Consequently, the judge is hardly a likely participant in such negotiations. In courts without prosecutors, therefore, plea bargaining has been rare.

Plea bargaining has also been made difficult by the fact that, in many jurisdictions, the juvenile is not charged with a number of counts, some of which can be dropped in return for a guilty plea to others. The equivalent of adult conviction for specific offenses is the single pronouncement of delinquency and a disposition in accordance with the perceived needs of the offender rather than with the nature, number, and severity of the offenses. The either-or quality of the charges and the propensity to calibrate the sentence according to what is perceived as the welfare of the offender both impede plea bargaining.

Despite the obstacles to negotiation, plea bargaining remains possible, and increasingly so. Juvenile courts are usually aided by a screening facility called the "intake office" or some comparable designation. The range of discretion lodged in this office is typically very great. De-

83. Cf. Lemert, *Social Action and Legal Change*, p. 185; Daniel L. Skoler, "The Right to Counsel and the Role of Counsel in Juvenile Court Proceedings," *Indiana Law Journal*, vol. 43 (Spring 1968), pp. 558–82.

pending on the jurisdiction, perhaps half, perhaps more than half of all cases are adjusted at the intake stage, thereby obviating the need for a court appearance.[84] Several options are open to the intake officer: he may dismiss the case or simply send the juvenile home with a warning; he may place him on informal probation—that is, supervised release not ordered by the court itself—or refer him to some special facility or agency set up to handle a given class of cases; or he may petition for a formal hearing in juvenile court.[85] The existence of these graded alternatives opens up the possibility of negotiated disposition, for if the juvenile appears repentant, or if there is a lack of evidence that makes the hearing a risky or uncertain course, or if the intake officer wants to avoid labeling a first offender as a delinquent, the intake officer may be favorably disposed toward an informal resolution of the problem.

For their part, the juvenile and his parents are often content to accept a probationary arrangement or a dismissal contingent on the juvenile's participation in some remedial program if that means—as it does—that no finding of delinquency will be entered. As Lemert says,

Despite the greater formality and legalism of the present-day juvenile court, much of its work even in large and populous counties continues to be informal. Many cases are either dismissed by probation officers after intake interviews, and after citation hearings, or placed on informal probation. Some judges still "put over" hearings or grant continuances to help reach the diverse ends sought by probation officers. While more and more of these cases are dismissed for lack of evidence, still there are many "good" cases in which the probation officer is tempering the wind to the shorn lamb, choosing leniency over severity. Here he is in a strong position to induce "co-operation" from minors or parents by the actual or implied threat to activate a petition. His tools are moral suasion and bargaining, underwritten by the ubiquitous threat, "unless you do this we will have to do this."

When an attorney enters a case he may do nothing other than satisfy himself that the facts are beyond dispute and that the probation officer is offering

84. See Note, "Juvenile Delinquents: The Police, State Courts, and Individualized Justice," Harvard Law Review, vol. 79 (February 1966), pp. 775–810, at p. 788; Donald R. Cressey and Robert A. McDermott, Diversion From the Juvenile Justice System (University of Michigan, National Assessment of Juvenile Corrections, 1973), pp. 11–12. The vast majority of state laws provide for administrative screening of petitions before formal court proceedings can begin. Statutory criteria for screening cases out are loose or nonexistent. See Mark M. Levin and Rosemary C. Sarri, Juvenile Delinquency: A Comparative Analysis of Legal Codes in the United States (University of Michigan, National Assessment of Juvenile Corrections, 1974), pp. 26–27.

85. See, e.g., Cressey and McDermott, Diversion From the Juvenile Justice System, pp. 19–20.

a more lenient disposition than could be gained by negotiation or a formal hearing. Thereafter he may drop out of the case or simply not appear if there is a hearing. It is in cases where a contest is possible that an attorney's presence changes the pattern of informal interaction. However, it is a distortion to say that the legal license to contest cases has prompted a significant number of attorneys to resort to adversary proceedings for juveniles.[86]

In general, only uncontested cases are filtered out at the intake stage, so that an informal disposition of this kind can be regarded as a form of admission of guilt in exchange for lenient treatment with no formal stigma attached.[87] This is the equivalent of what has become known in adult criminal courts as plea bargaining. To the extent that lawyers are present at this early stage, the possibility of such an exchange may be raised much more frequently than previously; for it is by now well known that one of the commonest functions of lawyers in criminal courts is not to insist on a trial but to insist on concessions in return for the plea of guilty that is the usual prelude to the disposition of the offender.[88]

Recent statutory developments in juvenile-court law may also facilitate such negotiated outcomes. Attempting to avoid placing the stigma of "delinquent" on all who pass through the juvenile court, more than half the state legislatures have created lesser categories of juvenile offenders.[89] This, of course, opens the possibility of bargaining for what amounts to a reduction of the charge, from "delinquency" to, for example, "unruliness" or "incorrigibility." Again, the presence of lawyers, coupled with this increased legal flexibility, makes a bargained outcome more likely.

The *Gault* opinion enhances the possibility of plea bargaining in ways other than merely making a lawyer part of the legitimate *dramatis personae* of the juvenile court. For one thing, *Gault* makes it more important to have a prosecutor handle and present cases, lest defense lawyers learn of the loose and legally vulnerable way in which they may be presented by probation officers.[90] Where prosecutors have taken over,

86. Lemert, *Social Action and Legal Change*, pp. 197–98 (footnote omitted).

87. Cf. Cressey and McDermott, *Diversion From the Juvenile Justice System*, p. 44.

88. In his study of plea bargaining, Donald J. Newman found that defendants who were represented and those who were not both generally pleaded guilty, but the former more often extracted concessions in exchange for their plea. "Pleading Guilty for Consideration: A Study of Bargain Justice," in George F. Cole, ed., *Criminal Justice: Law and Politics* (Duxbury Press, 1972), pp. 183–96.

89. Levin and Sarri, *Juvenile Delinquency*, p. 12.

90. Cf. Skoler, "The Right to Counsel and the Role of Counsel in Juvenile Court Proceedings," pp. 576–77.

there is an additional actor to negotiate with at the hearing stage, one who has a strong interest in avoiding overcrowded dockets. *Gault* also gives the offender something to exchange for leniency. He can forgo his rights, previously not always recognized, to put the state to its proof and to remain silent during the proceedings if concessions are forthcoming, and he can insist on them if they are not:

Occasionally attorneys can get dismissals, once in a while by instructing minors and parents to refuse to make statements. More often they succeed in getting allegations reduced in number or modified to conform to legal usage, so they can then argue for a more favorable disposition. They also have some negative power to alter dispositions simply by an implied threat to contest evidence and thereby slow down the work of the court. Occasionally this is bare-faced bargaining at the hearing.[91]

Thus, while "opportunities to use adversary skills in juvenile court are limited,"[92] the possibility of conducting a full-fledged hearing is not wholly theoretical. Quite the opposite: the possibility of adversary tactics, enhanced by *Gault*, conditions the bargaining process:

Attorneys can influence the court by instructing their juvenile clients to tell the probation officer nothing. . . . If minors stay silent, the probation officer is sometimes put in an awkward position, because he has to place a bare-bones report before his judge, who may show his ire at having to make findings or a disposition with so few facts.[93]

This does not exhaust the repertoire of the juvenile-court practitioner. In some big-city courts, one of the commonest ways of gaining bargaining leverage and simultaneously signaling the prosecutor that negotiations are in order is to file a motion to suppress evidence allegedly obtained in violation of the juvenile's constitutional rights.[94] Since the constitutional rights of alleged juvenile offenders were in the past severely circumscribed, the motion-to-suppress weapon was scarcely available before *Gault*.

As in all plea bargaining, uncertainty of outcomes provides an incentive to both sides. Lawyers are reluctant to take "a lead-cinch loser" to trial if there is any doubt about the appearance and testimony of witnesses. If the severity of the probable disposition is great, a juvenile defense lawyer has a good reason not to go to trial. In some juvenile

---

91. Lemert, *Social Action and Legal Change*, p. 194.
92. Ibid.
93. Ibid., p. 198.
94. I am indebted to Professor Robert O. Dawson for this information and the information in the following paragraph.

courts, the existence of compromise devices like consent decrees, which typically hold cases in abeyance for what amounts to a period of probation, with dismissal on a showing of good behavior, facilitates the process of negotiation. Often, too, there is a good chance of getting the charges reduced within the delinquency category (say, from robbery to larceny) to reduce the seriousness of the case, especially because the disposition—commitment to custody or no commitment—may turn on the nature of the charges. Obviously, whether the offender will be committed to custody or not is a matter as important in juvenile court as it is adult criminal court.

There seems to be evidence of precisely this phenomenon after *Gault* in at least one jurisdiction where figures are available. In Columbus, Ohio, *Gault* was accompanied by a general reduction in the seriousness of offenses.[95] Auto thefts showed a particularly marked decline—a drop of 66 percent from the year immediately before to the year immediately after *Gault*. About half of this decline was taken up by an increase in cases of operating an automobile without the owner's consent, a lesser charge. Counsel appeared in both types of cases about three times as frequently after *Gault* as before, and it seems probable that much of the decline in the more serious charges and of the increase in the less serious is attributable to negotiated reductions obtained by counsel.

The same study also showed a 16 percent decline in total cases heard by the judge and the referee. The referee's caseload declined by 10 percent, the judge's by fully 28 percent. Since only the judge heard contested cases, the inference seems reasonable (though the data do not permit proof) that ways were being found to reduce the number of contested cases. Given the accompanying reduction in the seriousness of charges, one way of reducing the incidence of contested cases was probably to reduce charges in return for admissions of guilt.

The general thrust of *Gault* is to push juvenile court proceedings toward the model of adult criminal proceedings. Given this thrust, it is reasonable to expect that many of the same practitioners will appear in both courts and carry into juvenile court the same practices they engage in regularly in criminal court.[96] Plea bargaining and informal disposition in general are such frequently used tools of the criminal-law

95. Reasons, "*Gault*," pp. 167–68.
96. Cf. Platt and Friedman, "The Limits of Advocacy," p. 1181, finding that juvenile-court lawyers in Chicago in 1966 were "small fee practitioners who make their living from minor criminal and civil matters."

trade that, once the juvenile court mystique was pierced in *Gault*, these tools would surely find their way into the lawyer's kit used to work on the problems of children.

Though it is well known that the majority of juvenile-court dispositions are essentially uncontested, that, of course, does not mean that they are necessarily negotiated. Reliable figures on the frequency of plea bargaining are hard to find, but the earlier-cited comparative study of lawyers in two juvenile courts begins to suggest the possibilities.

In both the traditional and the adversary court, the incidence of plea bargaining was not especially high, presumably because, as we have noted, lawyers in this experimental study were instructed to conduct themselves in an adversary fashion, thereby minimizing the possibility of compromise outcomes.[97] Nevertheless, there were significant differences between the two courts in the reported frequency of negotiated pleas. Plea bargaining was more common in the adversary court that functioned more or less on the *Gault* model than it was in the traditional court that stressed informal proceedings, took a parental or therapeutic view of its responsibilities, and concentrated on the offender more than on the offense. In the former, plea bargaining could be identified in 19 percent, in the latter 3 percent, of all cases.[98] It is worth reiterating that, because of the experimental setting, these figures probably understate the incidence of plea bargaining in contexts where lawyers have available to them the usual range of tactics and approaches.

As juvenile courts become more adversary—that is, more like criminal courts for juveniles—there may be more bargaining and less formality in both procedure and disposition. This may be paradoxical, but it is certainly explicable. Formal procedures may take longer. Sheer workload considerations therefore impel the participants toward shortcuts. Then, too, as Stapleton and Teitelbaum have pointed out, traditionally minded juvenile judges find it difficult to perceive the need for compromise, inasmuch as they feel charged with looking after the best interests of the child.[99] Formal proceedings, by contrast, introduce an element of risk, in which prosecution and defense chance all-or-nothing outcomes if they go to trial. The desire to reduce the stakes is a powerful impetus toward compromise. Yet, if there is such a risk, it is often calculable. The more formal the procedure, the easier it is to see the aggregate pat-

97. Stapleton and Teitelbaum, *In Defense of Youth*, p. 58.
98. Ibid., pp. 134–38.
99. Ibid., p. 138.

tern of results and the variables associated with particular outcomes. Lawyers on both sides can, within limits, begin to predict what would be the "correct" outcome if the case went to trial. As in all settlement negotiations, they can conduct their negotiations by projecting likely outcomes and then applying a discount for uncertainties of testimony and the like. Thus, the combination of risk and certainty militate in favor of compromise. The order that *Gault*-type reforms have introduced into juvenile proceedings has had the effect of making it quite superfluous to resort to the formal proceedings in every case.

What all this suggests is that the Supreme Court in *Gault* may have traded in one set of issues for another. Some of the arbitrariness the Court assumed to be endemic to juvenile proceedings may be gone. But, as the proceedings become more adversary and more like criminal proceedings, the private, out-of-court, for the most part unreviewable settlement of delinquency matters, handled by prosecuting and defense attorneys and merely ratified by judges, may assume a more prominent place in the way in which the problems of juveniles are handled.

Counsel and the Right to Remain Silent

It is not at all clear that the effect of *Gault* on implementation of the privilege against self-incrimination has been what the Supreme Court intended it to be. The Court had questioned whether confession served any useful purpose, and it regarded counsel as guarantor of the right to silence. Of course, the majority was not so naive as to think that defense counsel should never urge his client to disclose facts about himself or the alleged offense. But the Court presumably contemplated disclosure only when disclosure was in the tactical interests of the client.

What juvenile courts contemplate seems to be quite different. Admission of wrongdoing by juveniles has long been common in juvenile court,[100] and is regarded by some judges as the sine qua non of the court's therapy. As indicated earlier, there has always been considerable pressure on juveniles to tell all in a kind of ritual of cleansing. In addition, courts have customarily been eager to know as much as possible about the context of the delinquency: the home life, school experience, and prior misbehavior of the juvenile. As we have seen, lawyers, too, often have a sense that they ill-serve a reformable client if they insist on all the client's rights. This combination of forces produces a thrust

---

100. Monrad G. Paulsen, "Juvenile Courts and the Legacy of '67," *Indiana Law Journal*, vol. 43 (Spring 1968), pp. 527–57, at p. 547.

toward truthtelling that is quite at odds with the privilege against self-incrimination, strictly construed.

Concretely, what this sometimes means is that lawyers may attempt to persuade their clients to admit their guilt for the sake of the client's own interests, either to avoid the punishment that some judges will mete out to unrepentant juveniles or to take advantage of the court's rehabilitative facilities. No doubt, this happens much more frequently in the more traditionally "therapeutic" juvenile-court settings.[101] A lawyer who is prepared to go to trial or is aiming at a good plea bargain will probably counsel his client to keep silent, but a lawyer who is counting on the goodwill of a judge who wants to know the full story will probably counsel his client to make a humble disclosure or will do nothing to prevent it.[102]

Study after study reports that the lawyer is expected to act as an interpreter between the court and the family.[103] On the one hand, he is to explain the juvenile court's "philosophy" and its decision to the child's parents. On the other, he is to provide information to the court that will aid in its decision process. He is often urged to disclose everything he has learned about the case and to cooperate with the court in devising an appropriate solution for his client's problems.[104] In the words of one judge, lawyers

can get information in many cases we can never get. . . . People will tell lawyers things they would not tell members of the court, especially myself. . . . Lots of parents come in here and tell us nothing but lies. Lawyers can get a lot more than we can, and it would be a great benefit to us if we could get them to realize that we are not going to use it to hurt but to help their clients.[105]

The result of court urgings of lawyers "to make a 'contribution' to the court's efforts to handle cases"[106] may well be that the pressure to tell

101. Stapleton and Teitelbaum, *In Defense of Youth*, pp. 116–19; Note, "Juvenile Delinquents," pp. 797–98.

102. This practice has rarely been challenged. But in *In re Bacon*, 240 Cal. App. 2d 34, 49 Cal. Rptr. 322 (1966), the claim was made that juveniles were deprived of the effective assistance of counsel because counsel had permitted the delinquency to be established from their testimony, rather than putting the state to its proof. The claim was rejected, but the vitality of this decision in the light of *Gault* is very much in doubt.

103. Stapleton and Teitelbaum, *In Defense of Youth*, p. 161; Platt and Friedman, "The Limits of Advocacy," p. 1176; Lemert, "Legislating Change in the Juvenile Court," p. 431; Note, "Juvenile Delinquents," p. 798.

104. Stapleton and Teitelbaum, *In Defense of Youth*, p. 38.

105. Quoted by Emerson, *Judging Delinquents*, p. 22.

106. Ibid.

all will be more effective with lawyers than without. More, rather than less, information will flow from the juvenile and his family to at least traditionally minded juvenile courts than might otherwise be the case, given the common reticence of the affected parties to make disclosures directly to the judge.

Now it may be argued that this kind of disclosure strays rather far from the *Gault* Court's concern with implementing the privilege against self-incrimination. First, the privilege relates only to involuntary self-incrimination, not to information the parties choose to disclose. Second, not all information is protected from disclosure. Background information of the kind typically passed from lawyer to judge and court staff may not be within the ambit of the privilege, because it may not relate to commission of the offense.

These objections, however, are difficult to sustain. A juvenile and members of his family may disclose things to a lawyer with no inkling that the lawyer will pass them on to the court. Even after the fact, they may not know the information has been transmitted to the judge or court staff if it has been communicated informally rather than in open court. In these circumstances, it can hardly be said that there has been a "knowing waiver" of the right to keep silent.

Furthermore, in juvenile court, background material is often crucial to the court's disposition. The juvenile court is engaged in an effort at categorizing acts and people.[107] Is the offender "normal," "criminal," or "disturbed"? How serious is the "trouble"? In this process of categorization, the juvenile's biography and his family background play a central role. As juvenile courts have argued for decades, their focus is not only on the offense but also on the problem from which the offense springs. That being so, what might be unincriminating background disclosures in an adult criminal court can really assume the character of highly damaging admissions in juvenile court. There is, then, no assurance that the presence of counsel effectively protects the right to silence, and no assurance that the disclosures that are elicited by counsel are urged on the client for purely tactical (as opposed to therapeutic) reasons.

Summary

We have seen that counsel tends to appear relatively infrequently in juvenile courts, and that this is largely attributable to the ability of

---

107. For this aspect of the juvenile court's work, see especially ibid.

those courts to resist reform of their procedures. When counsel does appear, he does not necessarily behave in an adversary fashion, if that is taken to mean challenging the factual allegations essential to a finding of delinquency. Disposition without an adversary hearing remains the norm, because judges and lawyers tend to think that adversary tactics do not generally accord with the best interests of juveniles. Cases in which juveniles are represented by lawyers are often disposed of more favorably to the juveniles than those in which they are unrepresented, though this may reflect the kinds of cases in which there is representation, and less favorable outcomes have been reported where lawyers represented juveniles in traditional or therapeutically oriented courts.

Whether or not there is an advantage to representation by counsel, the presence of lawyers in less traditional, adversary courts does seem to create an atmosphere conducive to negotiation. In those courts, plea bargaining has begun to flourish. On the other hand, the presence of lawyers seems to have helped more traditional courts to operate more effectively in their accustomed but quite non-adversary way, particularly by eliciting and communicating information about the juvenile to the court and by explaining the court's actions to the juvenile and his parents. These courts welcome a lawyer's pitch for his client, and may accord leniency, but not as a matter of right.

Gault does seem to have had effects on juvenile courts, but the predominant effect has not been to create a strongly adversary procedure in which factual allegations are contested, the prosecutor is put to his proof, and the finding of delinquency is vigorously resisted. Doubtless, *Gault* has homogenized courtroom procedure, at least to the extent of reducing the distance between the most traditional and the most adversary courts. Even before *Gault*, there was movement in some states toward the adversary proceeding that partakes of many of the same features as the adult criminal trial.

But there remains a differentiation of styles among courts and among individual judges.[108] The style of judicial behavior limits and channels the tactics employed by counsel. Courts that regard their function as therapy rather than punishment discourage aggressive tactics and disdain compromise. Courts that allow counsel the latitude to function

108. Paul Tappan has pointed out, interestingly, that much of this polarity was urban versus rural. Rural courts, with small caseloads and little therapeutic ideology, often conducted their business like adult criminal courts. Tappan, *Juvenile Delinquency* (McGraw-Hill, 1949), pp. 179–80. But see Lemert, *Social Action and Legal Change*, pp. 169–71, on "cow county" juvenile courts.

as in adult courts permit aggressive tactics, but find that they are not necessarily resorted to very frequently. Both types of courts have managed to absorb the impact of counsel by allowing lawyers to perform their role in ways that are helpful to the courts in disposing of cases in a manner consistent with their respective conceptions of their function. Plainly, the recipient of the order to change has had infinitely more ability to guide the direction of change than has the progenitor of change.

Gault is only a decade old, and it may be that juvenile courts are ineluctably headed for the adversary model with the passage of more time, the infusion of more lawyers, and turnover among judges committed to the pre-*Gault* way of doing things. Perhaps juvenile courts will eventually become simply junior versions of adult criminal courts, although the urge to treat, guide, and admonish young offenders, rather than to punish them, has so far been powerful and persistent. If juvenile courts do more or less uniformly become like adult criminal courts, then, as I have suggested, an increased emphasis on negotiated dispositions in the bulk of cases can be expected. To be sure, this may be accompanied by insistence on procedural regularity (in the form of trials or dismissals) at the margins, for the availability of a formal procedure is a logical precondition to the parties' decision to avoid it. The conduct of all negotiations is conditioned by forecasts of what the likely resolution would be, should negotiations fail.

Gault and the Work of Juvenile Courts

So far, I have discussed some of the empirical foundations of the *Gault* decision and traced the reception of the decision as it was reflected in the handling and disposition of cases. *Gault*, however, has had a more wide-ranging impact than this. In tandem with other forces, it has probably altered the actual distribution of cases that find their way to juvenile court. To demonstrate this conclusively, far better trend data on the work of juvenile courts would be needed than currently exist. It would also be necessary to disentangle the effects of *Gault* from those of other forces working in the same direction. Nevertheless, it is worthwhile attempting to sketch some of the main lines of *Gault's* structural impact, together with some of the evidence bearing on it.

This impact can be concisely described. First, *Gault* encouraged the trend toward establishing separate categories of juvenile offenders in order to provide separate handling and treatment of those juveniles who are, in the statutory phrase, "in need of supervision" but who have not committed acts of a criminal character. Second, *Gault* reinforced the view of many delinquency professionals and reformers that those juveniles described as being in need of supervision do not really belong in the juvenile court at all, and *Gault* helped stimulate efforts to divert them from the legal process. Third, partly as a result of the first two trends, but also as a direct result of the application of criminal procedure to delinquency matters, *Gault* helped alter the character of the delinquency adjudication. Gradually, adjudication as a delinquent is, in several ways, becoming tantamount to conviction of a juvenile for a crime. The same legal standards are being applied to delinquency proceedings as to criminal proceedings, the same kinds of offenders are being tried, and the same stigma is being attached to both. Reiterating the caveat that the evidence for these propositions is tentative and circumstantial, let us now look more closely at each of them.

The Creation of Separate Categories

It has long been believed that juvenile courts must deal with behavior that, if committed by an adult, would not be subject to legal sanction. Consequently, all state and federal jurisdictions in the United States permit juvenile courts to assume jurisdiction over juveniles who have not committed crimes, and traditionally they have permitted delinquency adjudications for such non-criminal conduct as truancy, "idling," "immorality," or "habitual disobedience" to parents or guardians. Until 1959, juvenile codes made no attempt to distinguish between delinquency based on essentially criminal and non-criminal conduct.[109] The familiar concept of delinquency as a condition rather than an offense rendered such a distinction superfluous.

Responding in part to the same misgivings about juvenile courts that the Supreme Court was later to express in *Gault*, state legislatures began around 1959 to create a separate category for non-criminal juvenile offenders, reserving "delinquency" in the main for criminal offenses. The non-criminal category was created for "unruly," "incorrigible," "habitually disobedient," "wayward," or "ungovernable" children or those who were "in need of supervision" (variously called PINS, CHINS, MINS, and JINS, depending on whether the law denominates the offender a

109. Levin and Sarri, *Juvenile Delinquency*, p. 12.

person, a child, a minor, or a juvenile). As of January 1, 1972, twenty-four states plus the District of Columbia had created such a separate category, which I shall refer to as PINS.[110] About half of these jurisdictions had acted in the eight years before *Gault*, the other half in the four years after *Gault*. Since 1972 several more states have joined the ranks of those with separate PINS jurisdiction.

Creation of the PINS category was part of the same reforming trend of thought about juvenile courts and delinquency that informed the Supreme Court opinion in *Gault*. Many of the same reformist impulses were to be found in the views of the Crime Commission, which, as noted, were influential in shaping the *Gault* decision. State legislatures and the juvenile justice professionals who counseled them were fearful of the effects of labeling juveniles as delinquents, and they wished to reduce labeling to a minimum. They were concerned to segregate occasional or merely mischievous juvenile offenders from hardened juvenile offenders, and PINS laws often prohibited punitive confinement of a PINS altogether or specified separate facilities for PINS from those housing delinquents. Although *Gault* had nothing specific to say about the PINS laws already in existence, the echoing of the reformers' concerns in the majority opinion was no doubt a powerful force in gaining the PINS idea wider acceptance in state legislatures.[111]

Besides legitimizing change by endorsing the reformers' theories, *Gault* implicitly threatened the statutory status quo in states that had not yet separated PINS from delinquency jurisdiction. In 1962, the Supreme Court had cast constitutional doubt on the category of crimes committed not by doing something but by being someone—the so-called status crimes. In *Robinson* v. *California*,[112] the Court struck down a state law making it a crime to "be addicted to the use of narcotics." Juveniles who were adjudicated delinquents, not for criminal behavior, but for "incorrigibility" or "habitual disobedience," were arguably in the same category as Robinson, although claims were still made that delinquency was not a criminal proceeding. After *Gault*, the validity of these claims was very much in doubt. The confluence of *Robinson* and *Gault* strongly argued for separate, less punitive treatment of status delinquents, lest delinquency based on status alone be held unconstitutional.

110. Ibid.

111. Cf. J. Lawrence Schultz, "The Cycle of Juvenile Court History," *Crime and Delinquency*, vol. 19 (October 1973), pp. 457–76, at p. 473.

112. 370 U.S. 660 (1962).

Gault provided concrete incentives to separate PINS from delinquents and even suggested a course of action. *Gault* required counsel and the other constitutional safeguards it imposed only where there was the possibility of commitment to what was virtually a penal institution. The Court had stressed the fact that the kind of "training school" to which Gerald Gault had been committed was typically run along highly restrictive lines, the inmates consisting of, among others, rapists, murderers, and other felons. *Gault* implied that commitment of a juvenile to an institution that was the functional equivalent of a prison was the test of whether state juvenile codes were to be judged by the strict constitutional standards applicable to criminal statutes. The formality of the *Gault* requirements and the other constitutional requirements that seemed in the offing (restrictions on searches and seizures, proof beyond a reasonable doubt, perhaps jury trial) could be avoided in those classes of cases where commitment to the juvenile equivalent of prisons was prohibited or where commitment was limited to institutions that did not also house juveniles who had committed crimes.[113] After *Gault*, it took no great prescience to see that the Court might strike down laws allowing confinement of juveniles who had committed no crimes to institutions essentially penal in character. There were therefore several good reasons to sort out status offenders for treatment separate from the treatment accorded to juveniles.

Not surprisingly, legislatures that enacted PINS laws after *Gault* more often imposed restrictions on confinement than had legislatures that enacted PINS laws before *Gault*. The great majority of post-*Gault* PINS laws require the segregation of PINS from delinquents during pre-trial detention; before *Gault*, the great majority did not.[114] In terms of disposition after adjudication, there are also notable changes. Some states, before and after *Gault*, had prohibited commitment of PINS to any facility housing delinquent children.[115] Other states, before

113. In *Gault*, holding that juvenile confinement was the equivalent of adult imprisonment, the Court had emphasized both the loss of liberty and the indiscriminate mixing of minor offenders with hardened criminals. 387 U.S. at 27. State legislatures might therefore have thought one or the other of these features was decisive.

114. Computed from W. L. Grichting, "The Structure of Juvenile Codes in the United States" (unpublished paper, n.d.).

115. 31 Hawaii Rev. Stat. § 571-48(2); Kansas Stat. Ann. § 38-826(b); 29A Consolidated Laws of N.Y. § 754; 26 Md. Code Ann. § 70-19(a); Mass. Gen. Laws Ann., ch. 119, § 39G(c); S. Dak. Comp. Laws Ann. § 26-8-40.1.

Gault, had prohibited such confinement in the first instance, but if the PINS proved to be unamenable to treatment or rehabilitation, the court might then treat the child as a delinquent for purposes of disposition.[116] After *Gault,* this became the favored disposition formula.[117] In other words, state PINS laws enacted after *Gault* was decided rarely allowed PINS to be committed to an institution for delinquents, at least not without a second adjudication.

To the accepted policy reasons for separating PINS from delinquents, *Gault* added some reasons grounded in the desire of state officials to sustain the validity of their juvenile codes (in particular, to preserve their jurisdiction over status offenders) and to conduct as many proceedings as possible without the full panoply of constitutional safeguards made applicable by *Gault* and by later cases to delinquency hearings. For instance, the Supreme Court has required proof of delinquency beyond a reasonable doubt when a juvenile is charged with misconduct that would constitute a crime if committed by an adult,[118] but the Court has not yet held this standard applicable to PINS or other adjudications based on non-criminal conduct. Although post-*Gault* PINS statutes require "clear and convincing evidence" or proof beyond a reasonable doubt more often than did pre-*Gault* PINS laws, PINS adjudications in most states are based on the lesser standard of a "preponderance of the evidence"—the standard the Court has held impermissible in delinquency cases. Current practice thus bears out the expectation that, by separating PINS from delinquents, the broad sweep of the juvenile court's powers could be preserved, in some jurisdictions with a lesser degree of procedural formality than might have been required had status offenses and criminal offenses still been handled under the single rubric of delinquency.[119]

116. Calif. Welfare and Institutions Code § 730; 11 Colo. Rev. Stat. § 22-3-12; Neb. Rev. Stat. § 43-210.01.

117. 1A Fla. Stat. Ann. § 39.11; 5A N. Dak. Code Ann. § 27-20-32; Ohio Rev. Code Ann. §§.2151.353, 2151.354(c); 6 Tenn. Code Ann. § 37-232; 33 Vt. Stat. Ann. §§ 656, 662(d),(e). Compare 10 Okl. Stat. Ann. § 1137(a). See Robert J. Willey, "Ohio's Post-*Gault* Juvenile Court Law," *Akron Law Review,* vol. 3 (Spring 1970), pp. 152–87, at pp. 164–65.

118. *In re Winship,* 397 U.S. 358 (1970).

119. A similar result was accomplished in New Jersey by court rule. Shortly after *Gault,* the state Supreme Court promulgated a rule establishing two calendars for juvenile court cases, "formal" and "informal." Which calendar a case was assigned to depended on a preliminary determination by the court of whether there was a possibility of commitment to an institution. If not, the case went on the

There is no need to exaggerate *Gault's* influence. The PINS movement was well along before *Gault*, and many state legislatures might still have enacted PINS laws without *Gault*. But *Gault* was considered by a large number of juvenile court judges as imposing major new burdens on them. By distinguishing sharply in *Gault* between cases in which penal commitment was possible and those in which it was not, and in the later burden-of-proof case between criminal and non-criminal conduct, the Court gave authoritative judicial recognition to precisely the kinds of lines state legislatures were thinking of drawing and many juvenile justice professionals hoped they might draw. After *Gault*, "traditional" juvenile court judges and "progressive" juvenile court reformers could agree on the need for an in-need-of-supervision category.

The Diversion Movement

Among the myths the Supreme Court attempted to dispel in *Gault* was the view that, even when he punished a youth, the juvenile court judge was not just a judge but a surrogate parent and a social worker as well. *Gault* made it clear that, in the conduct of its judicial business, the juvenile court was to be considered a court like any other, subject to the same restraints that applied to all courts. *Gault* consequently made it more difficult to sustain the therapeutic mystique of the juvenile court, though many such courts have made heroic efforts to do so. As a result, it has seemed more and more anomalous to subject juveniles who have not engaged in criminal activity to the jurisdiction of a court that looks more and more like an ordinary criminal court. Hence the accelerated efforts to divert them:

We are witnessing a reevaluation of the role of juvenile justice. For juveniles whose offenses would be crimes if committed by an adult, there appears to be both an increasing stress on legalism and an abandonment of the traditional juvenile court philosophy that such juveniles are being helped rather than punished. For predelinquents, however, the old benevolent philosophy is being refurbished and perhaps reconstituted.[120]

The refurbishing is taking place outside the courtroom, in programs that

---

informal calendar and was handled without the *Gault* protections. However, "temporary" but sometimes lengthy commitments of unrepresented juveniles occurred even under that system. Larry Schultz, "The Problems of Problem Children," *The Nation*, October 29, 1973, pp. 426–29, at p. 427. These rules were superseded by the passage of a JINS law, which prohibited commitment of a JINS to an institution. 2A N.J. Stat. Ann. §§ 4-42 et seq. I am indebted to Marcia Richman of the New Jersey Public Defender's Office for this information.

120. Cressey and McDermott, *Diversion From the Juvenile Justice System*, p. 41.

attempt to keep "predelinquents" away from formal contact with the juvenile justice system.

As in the creation of the PINS category, avoidance of labeling has been an important moving force in attempts to divert juveniles out of the legal process. As *Gault* spurred the PINS movement, so has it helped the diversion movement along, both by legitimizing disquiet over the performance of juvenile courts and by calling attention to—and ritualizing—their punitive and stigmatizing functions. The seeming inappropriateness of submitting the problems of troublesome children and their families to the law has given rise to a plethora of experiments and programs to divert juveniles to non-judicial agencies and services. Such programs have been particularly extensive for non-criminal cases, in which the assumption is that the juveniles involved "are not yet 'hard core,' "[121] but in some instances programs have been extended to minor criminal activity as well.[122]

In addition, there are now many proposals to accomplish the ultimate in wholesale diversion—to abolish juvenile court jurisdiction over noncriminal behavior and end what is regarded as the pretense that a court is the best institution to deal with what are typically manifestations of serious family and community problems. "Poverty, unfit parents, broken homes, inadequate education, poor vocational training, and lack of opportunities," it is argued, "cannot be abolished by judicial decree."[123]

Some such proposals call for the outright repeal of the PINS jurisdiction,[124] a position now officially espoused by the National Council on Crime and Delinquency.[125] An alternative is to recognize a "right to treatment" for PINS as a condition of subjecting them to the jurisdiction

121. Ibid., p. 33.

122. See, e.g., Roger Barron and Floyd Feeney, "Preventing Delinquency Through Diversion: The Sacramento County Probation Department 602 Diversion Project, A First Year Report" (Center on Administration of Criminal Justice, University of California, Davis, 1973; processed).

123. Jill K. McNulty, "The Right to Be Left Alone," *American Criminal Law Review*, vol. 11 (1972), pp. 1–25, at p. 25.

124. See, e.g., ibid.; David Bazelon, "Beyond Control of the Juvenile Court," *Juvenile Court Judges Journal*, vol. 21 (1970), p. 42, reprinted in part in Sanford J. Fox, *Cases and Materials on Modern Juvenile Justice* (West Publishing, 1972), pp. 259–64.

125. Board of Directors, National Council on Crime and Delinquency, *Jurisdiction Over Status Offenses Should Be Removed From the Juvenile Court: A Policy Statement* (NCCD, 1974).

of the juvenile court.[126] Since it is most difficult to know what treatment might be helpful for most PINS—this having been the central problem of the juvenile court from the beginning—such a proposal might come in the end to the same thing: a proposal to abolish the PINS category altogether.

In the meantime, *Gault* and what has followed in its wake have made it more difficult to bring some such cases into juvenile court. In the past, as Edwin H. Lemert has said, if a child was regarded as needing help, some pretext could usually be found for bringing him before the court. Now, "some forms of juvenile deviant behavior must be ignored, or new ways found to handle them," one of them being to "redefine delinquency as a psychiatric problem. . . ."[127] This is not merely true in individual cases. Broad legal attacks are being leveled against the PINS and "beyond control" jurisdiction,[128] just at the time that this jurisdiction is becoming more and more prevalent among the states. The thrust of the recent legal attacks on PINS laws has been to attempt to draw a sharp line between the criminal and non-criminal jurisdiction of the juvenile court. If efforts to abolish the PINS jurisdiction succeed, this will, of course, be the most radical form of diversion from the juvenile justice system.

To be sure, surveys of custodial facilities for juveniles still find that the inmate population consists of astonishingly high percentages of juveniles who have committed no crimes.[129] But the courts and the re-

126. See Aidan R. Gough, "The Beyond-Control Child and the Right to Treatment: An Exercise in the Synthesis of Paradox," *St. Louis University Law Journal,* vol. 16 (Winter 1971), pp. 182–200.

127. *Social Action and Legal Change,* p. 197.

128. See, e.g., *Gesicki* v. *Oswald,* 336 F. Supp. 371 (S.D.N.Y. 1971), *affirmed per curiam,* 406 U.S. 913 (1972); *In re S,* 12 Cal. App. 3d 1124, 91 Cal. Rptr. 261 (1970), hearing denied by the California Supreme Court; *A* v. *City of New York,* 31 N.Y.2d 83, 335 N.Y.S.2d 33 (1972); *Lavette M.* v. *Corporation Counsel,* 35 N.Y.2d 136, 359 N.Y.S.2d 20 (1974).

129. One reckoning, based on 15–20 children's correctional institutions, showed that about 30 percent of the children confined there had not committed criminal acts. William H. Sheridan, "Juveniles Who Commit Noncriminal Acts: Why Treat in a Correctional System," *Federal Probation,* vol. 31 (March 1967), p. 26, reprinted in Fox, *Cases and Materials on Modern Juvenile Justice,* p. 254. A census of facilities housing delinquents (apparently including PINS) found that one-third "of all the persons for whom offense data were reported were in custody for commission of acts forbidden only to that portion of the population classified as juveniles." U.S. Department of Justice, *Children in Custody: A Report on the Juvenile Detention and Correctional Facility Census of 1971* (n.d.), p. 6. The National Council on Crime and Delinquency estimates that 45 to 55 percent of juveniles confined in

formers alike are gradually chipping away at the non-criminal jurisdiction of the juvenile court. *Gault* has made the attacks easier in several
ways: by stripping away the therapeutic pretenses of the juvenile court;
by forcing juvenile officials to face the "spectre of juveniles being submitted to all the disabilities of the adult model of criminal justice";[130]
by juxtaposing the formal apparatus of the post-*Gault* juvenile court to
complex family problems that scarcely seem to lend themselves to solution by adjudication; and by applying strict constitutional standards to
aspects of juvenile court practice that cannot stand scrutiny if measured
by those criteria.

At once skeptical and authoritative, the *Gault* Court helped set loose
an array of reforming impulses both inside and outside the juvenile
justice system. "Everywhere in the realm of juvenile justice there is the
belief that a new day is dawning."[131]

The Criminalization of Delinquency

The PINS laws and the diversion programs might aptly be called
parts of a movement to "decriminalize" status offenses and minor
breaches of criminal law by juveniles.[132] If this movement is reflected
in the handling of cases, the delinquency category will increasingly be
reserved for serious cases, involving, in the main, criminal behavior.[133]
As a matter of fact, bringing "only the most serious lawbreakers before
the juvenile courts, referring others to entirely voluntary agencies and
counseling, job placement, and 'peer-group activities,' "[134] is an explicit
plank in many reform platforms. The forecast of Donald K. Cressey and
Robert A. McDermott seems reasonable:

The near future should witness many structural changes in the realm of
juvenile justice. It appears that there will be a polarization of attitudes and

---

training schools or equivalent institutions are PINS. Milton G. Rector, *PINS Cases:
An American Scandal* (NCCD, 1974), p. 4. See also Rosemary C. Sarri, *Under
Lock and Key: Juveniles in Jail and Detention* (University of Michigan, National
Assessment of Juvenile Corrections, 1974), pp. 9, 18.

130. Cressey and McDermott, *Diversion From the Juvenile Justice System*, p. 61.
131. Ibid.
132. This is so, even though many of those who favor diversion wish to abolish
PINS jurisdiction. Proponents of PINS laws and proponents of diversion, though
often in disagreement over PINS, nevertheless agree at least on the need to take
status offenses out of the quasi-criminal delinquency category.
133. For a similar forecast, based solely on caseload considerations, see Benedict
S. Alper, "The Children's Court at Three Score and Ten: Will It Survive *Gault*?"
Albany Law Review, vol. 34 (Fall 1969), pp. 46–68.
134. Schultz, "The Cycle of Juvenile Court History," p. 474.

programs: Lawbreaking juveniles are likely to be processed along the lines of the adult model and hence will receive more due process and less humanistic consideration—after all, are they not merely small criminals? Juveniles who have been called "predelinquents," because they can't get along at home or in school, will be diverted.[135]

Whether this has already begun to happen is difficult to say on the basis of the available national statistics, which do not distinguish between delinquency and PINS, between criminal and non-criminal behavior, or between serious and minor cases. There has been a decline in the annual rate of increase in judicial dispositions of juvenile cases over the last several years. There has also been a decline in the ratio of judicial to non-judicial dispositions.[136] These figures are consistent with the trends I have outlined, but they certainly do not demonstrate the existence of these trends.

One study, though limited in time and place, did find some important changes.[137] Comparing the year before with the year after *Gault* in the Columbus, Ohio, Juvenile Court, Charles Reasons found, as indicated earlier, a 16 percent decline in total cases. He found an even more pronounced decline in incorrigibility (PINS-type) cases: 44 percent. This suggests more selectivity and screening of all cases, but especially of the non-criminal cases which, after *Gault*, it seems increasingly anomalous to bring into court. Whether or not a formal diversion program existed, plainly there was diversion going on in Columbus as a result of *Gault*.

Yet one aspect of the Columbus experience raises questions. The drastic decline in incorrigibility cases seems at odds with expert impressions that PINS-type cases have generally been on the increase compared to delinquency cases. In some jurisdictions, the category of incorrigibility has become a receptacle for cases that before *Gault* would have been processed as delinquency. But not in Columbus. The decline in incorrigibility cases in Columbus can, I believe, be explained. And the explanation suggests a distinction between the way two types of jurisdictions might respond to *Gault*'s pressures toward diversion: one by channeling relatively minor offenders out of the juvenile justice

135. Cressey and McDermott, *Diversion From the Juvenile Justice System*, p. 61.

136. I base these statements on the statistics published annually by the Office of Youth Development of the Department of Health, Education, and Welfare. These figures have a number of well-known deficiencies. I have also examined a number of state reports on which the national figures are based, but these are quite thin, and point in no clear direction.

137. Reasons, "*Gault*," pp. 167–69.

system altogether, the other by diverting offenders from the delinquency to the PINS-type category.

Columbus is among the former. From Reasons' figures, it seems that, even before *Gault*, delinquency was a category reserved for criminal behavior and incorrigibility for non-criminal behavior. The two did not overlap. If so, then the incorrigibility category was an unlikely receptacle for less serious cases screened out of the delinquency category: watertight compartments do not leak into each other. Screening of both kinds of cases should simply result in fewer cases altogether or, in other words, more diversion across the board—which is what the Columbus figures show.

Equally important, alleged incorrigibles were permitted counsel even before *Gault* in Columbus, so there was no motivation to avoid *Gault's* counsel requirement by categorizing cases as incorrigibility that earlier would have been called delinquency. Under these circumstances, the way to adapt to *Gault's* stricter counsel and other constitutional requirements was to reduce the caseload and make greater use of informal devices to avoid an increase in contested cases. This, too, was done in Columbus.[138]

In those jurisdictions where the same acts may form the basis for either a PINS or a delinquency charge, however, the existence of the PINS option makes it possible to reserve the delinquency category for cases involving relatively serious crimes to a greater extent than was the practice in the past, by shifting less serious cases from the delinquency to the PINS docket. The incentives to do so are particularly great where commitment of a PINS is prohibited, for in those jurisdictions PINS cases are sometimes tried without according the juvenile all the rights that apply in delinquency cases. Administrative convenience and the desire to preserve as much of the traditional ethos of juvenile hearings as possible both argue in favor of limiting delinquency cases to essentially criminal behavior. In those jurisdictions that still try PINS cases in a pre-*Gault* fashion, that is likely to mean expanded use of the PINS option. Hence the common belief that in recent years the use of the PINS category has been increasing despite the growth of diversion programs.

The evidence, scant though it is, suggests the coming criminalization of the delinquency category. Many cases that would earlier have been regarded as delinquency matters will be handled as PINS or, depending

138. See p. 198, above.

on the jurisdiction, not handled judicially at all. Many other cases that would earlier have been regarded as PINS will instead be diverted away from the juvenile justice system. In short, there will be relatively fewer delinquency cases, and those that there are will be more serious.

Formal adoption of an extensive diversion program should facilitate the conversion of the delinquency docket to something approximating a criminal docket for juveniles. The growth of PINS and diversion programs should also lead officials to view the remaining delinquency cases more seriously and to treat them accordingly. Awareness of the existence of diversion outlets is likely to alter the judge's view of those who are not diverted and who therefore come before him. Since decision-makers at the end of the line know of the efforts of their colleagues to screen cases out, juveniles who pass through all the filters without being channeled away from the legal process tend to be regarded as serious cases. For example, in two cities with diversion programs, those offenders who

"make it" to the intake unit through a maze of diversion units are apt to be viewed as "losers." Consequently, intake officers probably feel under pressure to "do something" with such cases. Whatever the motivation, in [one of these cities] there has been a decrease in the use of informal probation and a corresponding increase in petition filing.[139]

There is no reason why the same view should not be held by a judge who, aware of the diversion program, contemplates the cases of those who "make it" to court. He is likely to see these cases as meriting punishment rather than treatment. And the more he regards the delinquency adjudication business as punitive, the more he is likely to be fed serious cases warranting punishment.

There is another reason for regarding delinquency as essentially a criminal proceeding. Since *Gault*, the courts have begun to treat delinquency law as a branch of criminal law. The *Gault* majority expressed its desire to impose only minimal procedural safeguards and to prevent the delinquency adjudication from becoming equivalent to criminal conviction as a matter of law or as a matter of common understanding.[140] But the courts have, as indicated earlier, been testing delinquency law by the same constitutional standards as apply to criminal proceedings. Furthermore, they have begun to treat the delinquency adjudication as being tantamount to criminal conviction for a number of collateral

139. Cressey and McDermott, *Diversion From the Juvenile Justice System*, pp. 25–26.

140. 387 U.S. at 22–27.

purposes. For double jeopardy purposes, for instance, a delinquency adjudication may bar a subsequent trial as an adult for the same offense.[141] Similarly, the Supreme Court has recently held that a witness who has previously been adjudicated a delinquent and placed on probation may be cross-examined about the adjudication in order to show that his fear of further sanctions might bias his testimony. In enunciating this rule, overriding state laws guaranteeing the confidentiality of juvenile court proceedings, the Court explicitly drew an analogy between the delinquency adjudication and the criminal conviction: as the latter may be exposed on cross-examination, so may the former.[142] As a matter of substantive and procedural law, then, delinquency proceedings are coming to be regarded—not all at once, not everywhere, not for all purposes, but increasingly—as equivalent to criminal proceedings.

As all this happens, it seems virtually impossible to prevent the stigma of the delinquency adjudication from assuming an essentially criminal character. The *Gault* majority thought the delinquency stigma was already "only slightly less" than the stigma of criminal conviction. In part for this reason, it rejected the traditional view that the juvenile offender was not being treated as a criminal and that confinement in a so-called training school was not incarceration. And so the Court surrounded the process of adjudication with many of the same safeguards that apply to criminal proceedings, thereby further eroding the distinction between delinquency and crime.

There was thus an element of self-fulfilling prophecy about *Gault*. The Court's perception of the delinquency stigma may or may not have been accurate at the time. But by acting on that view, the Court helped set in motion forces very likely to make it so. The use of criminal standards and safeguards, and the growth of PINS jurisdiction and diversion programs to siphon off less serious cases—these developments portend a purification of the once-murky delinquency category. With a reduction in the heterogeneity of cases all classed as delinquent, the significance of such an adjudication should be very much what the Court thought it was already approaching in 1967.

Not, of course, that *Gault* accomplished all this by itself. There was much movement in these directions in the early 1960s. But there is no gainsaying the extent to which *Gault* was a watershed in all of these

---

141. *Breed v. Jones,* 421 U.S. 519 (1975).
142. *Davis v. Alaska,* 415 U.S. 308 (1974). Compare *Gault,* 387 U.S. at 25.

developments. The Supreme Court acts on the basis of "the facts" as it sees them; it also alters and creates "facts" for others to see. By treating delinquency as essentially a criminal matter, and by requiring others to do so, the Court helped to make it so.

Ironies of Judicial Reform

The *Gault* decision has been hailed (and reviled) as a "revolution" in juvenile justice. The decision purported to reverse the developments of more than half a century, during which a separate court system for juveniles had operated on its own distinctive assumptions. The "revolution" was said to consist in the transformation of that system by the imposition of constitutional requirements. Due process would bring the juvenile court system back into the legal mainstream, the mainstream based on the adversary model.

Looking back over the pattern of responses to *Gault* and what they reveal about the process of change through judicial decision, a number of ironies of the "*Gault* revolution" stand out. These have to do with the relation of: (1) the character of policy laid down in a decision to the character of the audience to which the policy is addressed, (2) formality to informality in judicial procedure, (3) procedural change to substantive change, and (4) change within the intended area of impact to change outside it.

Gault was addressed to an institution—the courts—that the Supreme Court presumably knew as well as it knew any institution in the society. The Court might reasonably have thought that the requirements it imposed would be implemented more or less as intended, albeit grudgingly in some courts. For juvenile courts "consisted of functionaries whose job was to administer law, who, collectively and individually, put a high value on 'compliance with law.' Likewise, the nature of their work made them more sensitive to the procedural basis of justice than, for example, lay persons."[143] Despite these advantages, the anticipated results did not follow, or at least were greatly diluted along the way. Although juvenile court judges and lawyers place a premium on compliance with law and the procedural basis of justice, they also entertain a number of other beliefs about the best way to handle juveniles in trouble, these

143. Lemert, *Social Action and Legal Change*, p. 159.

beliefs seriously qualifying their commitment to the adversary process for juveniles. The tenacity of these beliefs led them to seek ways of adapting *Gault*, rather than pursuing the decision to its ultimate implications.

For this among other reasons, the formality and adversary ethos the Court assumed it was imposing on a more or less controllable environment largely failed to materialize. Many juvenile courts found ways to minimize the frequency of counsel's appearance and managed to absorb the impact where counsel did appear by channeling his activities in an approved, even helpful direction. Lawyers more often played a mediating than an adversary role. Where there was more judicial receptivity to the decision, counsel found ways to represent juveniles that were not the ways that had been envisioned. The emphasis was on negotiation rather than confrontation, on coming to terms with the evidence rather than challenging it. Some of these techniques were imported from adult criminal courts. The Supreme Court's formal requirements fostered the growth of informal arrangements by putting lawyers in a position to negotiate and by providing them with the constitutional weapons to do so. The anticipated "revolution" did not happen.

But another one did. Ostensibly a procedural decision, *Gault* had substantive effects. It catalyzed a series of reforming impulses that are bringing about structural change in the work of the juvenile courts and in the handling of juvenile offenders. The theme of this change is decriminalization of much behavior that formerly was punished as delinquency. In this the influence of *Gault* coalesced with several other forces —including another Supreme Court decision, *Robinson* v. *California*— to effect a reform of juvenile law about which the *Gault* opinion purported to say nothing.

Gault's impact, of course, was supposed to occur in juvenile court. The Court thought it was acting on that institution alone, and indeed only on the trial process. Yet a convincing case can be made that *Gault's* greatest impact has been outside the juvenile court hearing it was intended to reform. It affected the work of intake officers and state legislators alike. There was, in short, no way to limit the impact to one discrete segment of the interconnected parts of the juvenile justice system, just as there was no way to confine the impact to the purely procedural realm.

The short of it is that formal requirements tend to give rise to informal arrangements that avoid the recurrent need to resort to the formal procedure, procedure spills over into substance, and change overflows boundaries dividing parts of a system. Nor does *Gault* show the courts to constitute a more controlled environment for reform than any other. This last point is important enough to warrant pursuing it further in the next chapter.

CHAPTER SIX

Mapp v. *Ohio*: Police Behavior and the Courts

The civil suit is not the only vehicle through which courts can attempt to influence the conduct of government officials. The criminal proceeding affords its own opportunities to affect the policies and behavior of bureaucracies that depend on the criminal sanction for the success of their mission. Most notably, of course, this applies to the police, but it may also be true of other agencies that define their responsibilities in terms of law enforcement.

There is some a priori reason to think that for controlling law enforcement organizations the criminal proceeding is a superior instrument to the civil suit. In a prosecution, the enforcement authorities are supplicants; they want something from the court—a conviction and a sentence —and it takes little imagination to think that they may be induced to pay a policy price to get it. Potentially, then, the threat of undoing the work of the police by denying them the convictions they seek is a formidable sanction to control their behavior. The power to convict or acquit is the trump card of the courts: every criminal must pass their way. If the police aim to invoke the legal process for punishment, the monopoly position of the courts means that their cooperation is required.

Over the past two decades or so, that cooperation has increasingly been conditioned on police observance of the Bill of Rights. Violation of a constitutionally guaranteed right of a suspect may result in the failure to convict him. The consequence of this is depicted in Cardozo's chiding epigram: "The criminal is to go free because the constable has blundered."[1] But the purpose of conditional enforcement is the obverse. If criminals go free when constables blunder, constables will blunder less. That, at least, is one of the behavioral premises of the various rules

---

1. *People* v. *Defore*, 242 N.Y. 13, 21, 150 N.E. 585, 587, *cert. denied*, 270 U.S. 657 (1926).

that exclude illegally obtained evidence from use in criminal proceedings. It is a premise well worth examining, for it raises the question of just how potent the sanction of judicial refusal to cooperate really is.

The premise, of course, contains within it still another assumption—that if the police fail to abide by the Constitution, criminals will indeed go free. It requires little elaboration, then, to see that the efficacy of a judicial policy of conditional cooperation in law enforcement depends upon just how that policy is enforced in court, whether it has an impact on police behavior, and what costs are associated with it.

One such policy of conditional cooperation that is ripe for analysis is the rule of *Mapp v. Ohio*,[2] which forbids state courts from using evidence obtained in violation of the Fourth Amendment's guarantee of freedom from "unreasonable searches and seizures."

Mapp applied to the states a rule of evidence long applied in federal courts.[3] It did so clearly, abruptly, and without qualification. Its effects can be and have been studied from several angles. And so many facets of *Mapp* have been before the Supreme Court in the last fifteen years that it is possible to get a clear view of what the Court seems to be thinking about the exclusionary rule. *Mapp* and the cases that have followed it thus provide some basis for comparing judicial assumptions with real-life behavior.

Mapp can be read two ways—as an expression of confidence or a counsel of despair. The majority opinion says that the exclusion of illegally obtained evidence will serve to encourage police observance of the Constitution. But it also says that so far nothing else has. Inasmuch as police behavior in the future is problematical, there is also a second ground of the decision. If the police violate the Constitution, the judiciary should not collaborate in the illegality by admitting the evidence, regardless of the impact on police behavior.[4] Depending on which of these two grounds is emphasized, *Mapp* may or may not be an opinion pregnant with great expectations. But it seems to have begotten them in some who saw it as a promise to bring the police to heel.

How the opinion is read makes a difference. If *Mapp* is merely a commitment to throw the Court's prestige and its control over evidence into the battle against official illegality, for whatever results those assets may bring, it is difficult to measure its effectiveness except perhaps in terms

2. 367 U.S. 643 (1961).
3. *Weeks v. United States*, 232 U.S. 383 (1914).
4. Compare *Shelley v. Kraemer*, 334 U.S. 1 (1948).

of judicial steadiness on the exclusionary course. But if something more is promised—an unflagging attempt to deter police invasion of privacy —*Mapp* has set for the courts a difficult task, and the extent of accomplishment can, in principle, be measured.[5] How the opinion is read, in other words, will determine how easily the reader will be disappointed by its results.

More often than not, *Mapp* has been read as an ambitious attempt to control police behavior.[6] It has especially been read that way by those members of the Court who are concerned about "the high price it extracts from society—the release of countless guilty criminals."[7] The common proclivity of those who see the costs imposed by the decision as being unduly high has been to regard the benefits as discouragingly few—a tendency not confined to views of the exclusionary rule or, for that matter, to the judiciary. The exclusionary "rule's prime purpose," these Justices have said, "is to deter future unlawful police conduct and thereby effectuate the guarantee of the Fourth Amendment against unreasonable search and seizures. . . ."[8] And, they have sometimes added (generally in dissent, when they were free to depart from a rationale still binding on the Court), "there is no empirical evidence to support the claim that the rule actually deters illegal conduct of law enforcement officials."[9] Read optimistically, *Mapp* in practice easily disappoints.

But read as adding only an imperfect weapon to the ongoing battle against official lawlessness—and equally as "enabling the judiciary to avoid the taint of partnership in official lawlessness"[10]—*Mapp's* presumed inability to deter police misconduct does not stamp it a failure.

5. Though, in practice, measuring the extent of unlawful police behavior is an exceedingly difficult job.

6. See, e.g., *Stone* v. *Powell,* 44 U.S.L.W. 5313 (U.S. Sup. Ct. 1976); *Linkletter* v. *Walker,* 381 U.S. 618 (1965).

7. *Bivens* v. *Six Unknown Named Agents,* 403 U.S. 388, 416 (1971) (dissenting opinion of Burger, C.J.). See also *Stone* v. *Powell,* 44 U.S.L.W. 5313, which drastically restricts enforcement of the exclusionary rule by means of federal habeas corpus for state prisoners. *Mapp,* the majority asserts, "often frees the guilty."

8. *United States* v. *Calandra,* 414 U.S. 338, 347 (1974).

9. *Bivens* v. *Six Unknown Named Agents,* 403 U.S. at 416 (dissenting opinion). In this dissent, Chief Justice Burger suggests the exclusionary rule be abandoned if Congress adopts an appropriate legislative alternative. But, in view of his empirical skepticism, it is only reasonable to ask whether there would be any assurance that a statute would have the effects *Mapp* is alleged not to have had.

10. *United States* v. *Calandra,* 414 U.S. at 357 (dissenting opinion).

This, indeed, is the way it has been read by those who consider the costs of freeing criminals a small price to pay for the vindication of the Constitution.

Some Justices are thus content to enforce the exclusionary rule even though it may not deter the police; others incline toward limiting or abandoning it as an experiment that failed. Significantly, though they evaluate its relevance differently, both sides now seem tacitly to agree on one "fact": if *Mapp* has deterred police misconduct, that secret has been very well kept.

Has the experiment failed? Must *Mapp* now stand, if at all, on the judges' desire to keep their hands clean?

The case against deterrence at the street level seems plausible enough. It rests on the apparent irrationality of connecting things that are not, by themselves, interconnected. Thomas Reed Powell once said, "If you can think about something which is attached to something else without thinking about what it is attached to, then you have what is called a legal mind."[11] *Mapp* imposes the opposite jurisprudential imperative on the police. They must now think about the criminal's responsibility for his crimes and his constitutional rights as if the two were inextricably connected. For the courts will make the former depend on respect for the latter. This being lawyers' reasoning, jailhouse lawyers have grasped the connection more surely than have stationhouse cops.

A more sophisticated case against police deterrence flowing from *Mapp* is based on conceptions of bureaucratic relationships. If it results in dismissal or acquittal, the exclusionary rule punishes the prosecutor. Yet he typically has little or no effective control over police activity. Even if the relationship of prosecutor to police does enable him to decline to prosecute cases in which evidence has been illegally obtained, large areas of police activity remain untouched by such a refusal, for much of the work of the police is not aimed at prosecution but at maintaining order and controlling anti-social behavior. Finally, even where prosecution follows arrest, the exclusionary rule assumes that the mission of the police is to see the case through to conviction, rather than to gather up the criminal and the evidence and let the prosecutor worry about the rest. The exclusionary rule, it is said, ignores the way in which

11. Quoted by Thurman Arnold, "Criminal Attempts—The Rise and Fall of an Abstraction," *Yale Law Journal*, vol. 40 (1930), pp. 53–80, at p. 58.

labor and accountability are divided up and the structure of incentives that follows from this division.[12] It is, in a word, naive.

Mapp, its detractors say, oversimplifies in another way. It assumes, not merely that policemen are motivated by the sanction of exclusion, but that they are willing and able to "read and grasp the nuances of the appellate opinions that ultimately define the standards of conduct they are to follow"—opinions often rendered several years after the illegal arrest or search has occurred. "Given a policeman's pressing responsibilities, it would be surprising if he ever becomes aware of the final result after such a delay."[13] By failing to take account of this dubious learning process, the *Mapp* rule overlooks the tenuousness of the links between law and practice.

Virtually all of this discussion of *Mapp*'s efficacy has taken courts and counsel for granted and has regarded the police as the unknown quantity. Both sides in the *Mapp* debate assume that, while the police may or may not be deterred by the exclusionary rule, the rule is enforced in criminal trials and its enforcement sets free "countless guilty criminals." They argue mainly over whether the benefits are worth the price. Yet experience with *Gault* should at least lead us to wonder about just how *Mapp* is enforced in court. As the impact of the exclusionary rule on police behavior in the field is an open question, so also is its impact in the courthouse. No benefit-cost calculation can be attempted without knowledge of both of these aspects of the exclusionary rule. Accordingly, they form the basis of the analysis that follows.

Deterrence: A Sometime, Some-Crime, Someplace Thing

Much of the empirical support for the proposition that *Mapp* does not deter the police from violating the Fourth Amendment has been quite crude. That illegal searches and seizures continue to be widespread despite the exclusionary rule is sometimes taken as evidence that the police are unaffected by the sanction of exclusion.[14] At the most basic

12. Some of these arguments have been made by Dallin H. Oaks, "Studying the Exclusionary Rule in Search and Seizure," *University of Chicago Law Review*, vol. 37 (Summer 1970), pp. 665–757; they have been espoused with great enthusiasm by Chief Justice Burger in his dissent in *Bivens* v. *Six Unknown Named Agents*, 403 U.S. at 416–18.

13. *Bivens* v. *Six Unknown Named Agents*, 403 U.S. at 417 (dissenting opinion).

14. Oaks, "Studying the Exclusionary Rule in Search and Seizure," pp. 683–86; James E. Spiotto, "Search and Seizure: An Empirical Study of the Exclusionary

level, such inferences take no account of whether there might not be many more illegal searches were it not for the exclusionary rule. At a more refined level, the fact that illegal searches are still conducted to obtain evidence of certain kinds of crimes does not mean that they are still conducted with the same frequency for evidence of other kinds of crimes.[15] That illegal searches are common in some cities does not mean that they are equally common in all cities. Deterrence cannot be viewed whole any more than law enforcement can be viewed as "a monolithic governmental enterprise."[16]

Gradually, the rudiments of a more discriminating approach have begun to emerge. What it suggests is that the extent to which police behavior is modified by *Mapp* depends on a complex set of local conditions, including, among other things, the extent to which the police are aware of the law of search and seizure and of the exclusionary rule, the type of offense involved, the particular police unit responsible for specific enforcement tasks, and the way in which local courts and lawyers handle search-and-seizure matters.

The role of police ignorance cannot be discounted. Ignorance of the law—even basic, long-standing rules of law, and even ignorance on the part of lawyers and judges—is apparently widespread:

the contents of legal rules very often do not get through to those whose actions they are supposed to shape. A vivid example of this turned up in a survey in New York City of minor personal injury accidents. When victims were asked why they had pressed claims against the other driver notwithstanding the fact that they conceded their own contributory fault, most of them showed they had no knowledge that the law declares that their own lack of care, however slight, bars recovery under the doctrine of contributory negligence. Indeed, they registered amazement amounting to disbelief that the law contained such a rule. The New Jersey pre-trial study showed that even judges are at times unaware of rules they are assumed to apply almost daily. Survey findings that certain rules of law are not getting home to those they are aimed

Rule and Its Alternatives," *Journal of Legal Studies*, vol. 2 (January 1973), pp. 243–78, at pp. 276–77.

15. Confession rates, for example, vary from crime to crime, and so did the impact of *Miranda* v. *Arizona*, 387 U.S. 436 (1966), on those confession rates, at least in one city. The impact of *Miranda* on confession rates was great in homicide and robbery cases, less significant in cases of burglary, receiving stolen goods, and larceny of an automobile, and negligible in forcible rape cases. Richard H. Seeburger and R. Stanton Wettick, Jr., "*Miranda* in Pittsburgh—A Statistical Study," *University of Pittsburgh Law Review*, vol. 29 (October 1967), pp. 1–26. *Mapp*, too, might have differential effects from crime to crime.

16. *Bivens* v. *Six Unknown Named Agents*, 403 U.S. at 416 (dissenting opinion).

at may help us put in better perspective the limits of at least some legal rules as instruments of social control.[17]

As opponents of the exclusionary rule have argued, the police often have only a crude and not necessarily accurate understanding of Supreme Court decisions. To the extent that they lack knowledge, they cannot be expected to comply.[18]

To grant, however, that ignorance may be widespread is not to say that it is evenly spread. Not all police officers are ignorant of what the courts expect of them. To be sure, police sources of information tend to be diverse and rather haphazardly organized. But some sources are more effective and reliable than others, and may be utilized more frequently by some officers and forces than by others. In a study of police reactions to *Miranda* v. *Arizona*,[19] a decision comparable to *Mapp* in its impact on police work, Neal A. Milner has examined the sources of information relied on by police and the content of information obtained from various sources.[20] Police officers in all four communities Milner studied obtained their information about *Miranda* and its requirements from an average of five or six different sources. The sources often held divergent views about the decision, and they imparted different kinds of information about it, with varying degrees of accuracy and subtlety. Not all officers or forces relied equally on the same mix of sources. Some police forces were more receptive than others to particular sources, such as the state attorney general's office (which stressed the positive contribution *Miranda* could make toward professionalizing the force) and the FBI (which explained the kinds of police behavior not prohibited by *Miranda*).

Without a doubt, Milner found that many policemen entertained fundamentally erroneous conceptions about what the decision did and did not forbid.[21] The nature and accuracy of the information received by officers were related to the identity of the sources from which it was

17. Maurice Rosenberg, "Court Congestion: Status, Causes, and Proposed Remedies," in Harry Jones, ed., *The Courts, the Public, and the Law Explosion* (Prentice-Hall, 1965), p. 56 (footnote omitted).

18. For a review of some of the major reasons the police fail to obtain legal information, see Stephen L. Wasby, "The Communication of the Supreme Court's Criminal Procedure Decisions: A Preliminary Mapping," *Villanova Law Review*, vol. 18 (June 1973), pp. 1086–1118.

19. 387 U.S. 436 (1966).

20. *The Court and Local Law Enforcement: The Impact of Miranda* (Sage Publications, 1971).

21. Ibid., p. 199.

obtained. There were abundant but not equal misunderstandings among police departments and officers about the scope of the decision and requirements for complying with it.[22] Some policemen knew much more about *Miranda* than did others, and thus were often those most favorably disposed toward complying with the decision.

What is true of *Miranda* is likely to be true of *Mapp*. In fact, the rules of search and seizure are far more complicated than *Miranda*'s confession rules, and they apply in spontaneous street encounters as well as in more controlled custodial situations. The rules lend themselves to misunderstanding, and indeed misunderstanding abounds. A survey of North Carolina criminal court judges, prosecutors, and defense lawyers showed that substantial minorities of each (18–34 percent) did not know that North Carolina adhered to the exclusionary rule before *Mapp* was decided.[23] Nearly one-third of the defense lawyers and judges (and 20 percent of the prosecutors) also thought general exploratory searches were permitted—reflecting ignorance of a cardinal principle of the Fourth Amendment. The responses indicate almost equal ignorance of other search-and-seizure matters.[24] If this is true of segments of the criminal bar and bench, it is only to be expected that police officers are often totally unaware of proper arrest and search procedures.[25] Again, however, what is known about the varying styles and performance of police departments provides strong indications that misconceptions about the Fourth Amendment are spread in a highly uneven fashion from city to city.

Not only is knowledge unevenly distributed; so is receptivity to the restraints of the Fourth Amendment. We have already seen that officers who knew more about *Miranda* tended more often to approve of the decision. James Q. Wilson has also shown that police departments differ greatly in the emphasis they accord to the maintenance of order, on the one hand, and the enforcement of criminal law, on the other.[26] The two are not the same thing. For some departments, arrest and prosecution

22. Ibid., pp. 199–204.

23. Michael Katz, "The Supreme Court and the States: An Inquiry into *Mapp* v. *Ohio* in North Carolina," *University of North Carolina Law Review*, vol. 45 (December 1966), pp. 119–51, at p. 132. Caution in interpreting the results of this study is dictated by the small size of the sample.

24. Ibid., pp. 135–36.

25. See Wayne R. LaFave, *Arrest: The Decision to Take a Suspect into Custody* (Little, Brown, 1965), pp. 504–06.

26. *Varieties of Police Behavior* (Harvard University Press, 1968).

are a central part of the policing function; for others, a very last resort. There is good reason to think that *Mapp* has a greater effect on the former than on the latter. Departments concerned with enforcing the law by arrest and prosecution tend to reward officers for abiding by rules.[27] They are likely to evince more concern for complying with court decisions affecting their work. But, more important, a department whose primary concerns run to matters other than arrest and conviction will generally accord the Fourth Amendment a back seat. What Wilson's analysis demonstrates is that there are systematic variations among departments in the extent to which they equate police work with vindication of the criminal law.

Variations from locality to locality are paralleled by variations from offense to offense and even from one stage of investigation to another:

At the beginning of a case, or in general patrolling activities, police are only slightly deterred by the prospect of loss of a conviction, because they are still exploring. . . . Similarly, they have little hesitancy about "frisking" a suspect against whom they have no reasonable cause to make an arrest. Once their explorations have borne fruit, however, they are apt to pay greater attention to the formalities of the rules of search and seizure. When these explorations indicate that a "big case" is in the making, then conditions have been provided under which court injunctions can be taken most seriously. The big case affords time to establish probable cause, to obtain a warrant, and most important, to use a police-informant rather than an addict-informant whose criminal status needs to be protected. Thus, the [exclusionary] rule seems to control police almost in direct relation to the gravity of the crime of the suspect.[28]

Related to the seriousness of the offense is the identity of the unit making the arrest and search. Here, too, there is some evidence that some units responsible for apprehending particular types of offenders have been affected by *Mapp* more than have others in the same police force. In New York City, total arrests by the Narcotics Bureau declined by 50 percent immediately after *Mapp*. In particular, the bureau's arrests on the street and in privately occupied rooms declined during this period.[29] These patterns tend to demonstrate responsiveness of the

27. Ibid., pp. 283–84.

28. Jerome H. Skolnick, *Justice Without Trial: Law Enforcement in a Democratic Society* (Wiley, 1966), pp. 224–25. See also Wayne R. LaFave, "Improving Police Performance Through the Exclusionary Rule: Current Police and Local Court Practices," *Missouri Law Review*, vol. 30 (Summer 1965), pp. 391–458, at pp. 421–26.

29. Note, "Effect of *Mapp* v. *Ohio* on Police Search-and-Seizure Practices in Narcotics Cases," *Columbia Journal of Law and Social Problems*, vol. 4 (March 1968), pp. 87–104, at pp. 92, 98.

Narcotics Bureau to *Mapp*. Inasmuch as privacy of the home is a core interest protected by the Fourth Amendment, warrantless searches and arrests in homes are frequently unlawful. Arrests made in street encounters, too, are likely to be based on mere police suspicion rather than probable cause, and hence often violative of the Fourth Amendment.[30] Consequently, reductions of rates of arrests made in these locations suggest efforts to tailor behavior to constitutional requirements.[31]

More, however, is involved. The mission of the Narcotics Bureau was to locate covert offenders; visible, open violations of the narcotics laws were left to uniform and plainclothes units. After *Mapp*, the Narcotics Bureau decided to concentrate on sales offenses, leaving arrests for mere possession, even covert possession, to uniform and plainclothes units. Apparently, it was this decision that resulted in the precipitous decline in the bureau's arrest rates.[32] Significantly, arrests by uniform officers for narcotics possession rose sharply after *Mapp*, but not enough to take up the slack left by the bureau's decision to abandon this field. Thus, *Mapp* seems to have had an effect on the proportionate emphasis given to various offenses in enforcement efforts. In this respect, moreover, it appears that *Mapp* resulted in a net gain in observance of the Fourth Amendment, though some offenders (as well as some innocent people) may have escaped apprehension for this reason. Here, then, is some evidence of both benefits and costs, conceived in the way the Supreme Court has debated the virtues of the exclusionary rule: deterrence at a price.

The decision of the New York City Narcotics Bureau to abandon its purview over possession offenses because of *Mapp* implies that it saw little point in pursuing a class of offenders whose conviction *Mapp* had made much more difficult. This casts doubt on the conventional wisdom in *Mapp* debates that the concern of the police for obtaining conviction is at best secondary to its concern to achieve other goals. Plainly, there are policemen and police units that do think primarily in terms of convicting offenders. The case of the Narcotics Bureau indicates that much depends on the unit's precise mission.

That is not the same as saying that specialized units conceive their mission in terms conducive to compliance with the Fourth Amendment

30. Cf. *Terry* v. *Ohio*, 392 U.S. 1 (1968); *Sibron* v. *New York*, 392 U.S. 40 (1968).

31. The figures may also suggest, however, a shift to tactics of harassment— about which I shall have more to say later.

32. Note, "Effect of *Mapp* v. *Ohio*," p. 93.

whereas all general patrol units do not. Specialized units, too, can be concerned with matters that accord conviction and the legality of arrests and searches a subordinate place in the scheme of things. In Chicago, for instance, the Vice Control Division made half of all the arrests and searches by police for narcotics violations in 1971. Yet fully 64 percent of all motions to suppress evidence were made in its cases, and 93 percent of these were granted. By contrast, the Task Force, a special unit working in high crime areas of Chicago, made 30 percent of the narcotics arrests and searches, but its searches accounted for only 11 percent of all the suppression motions (97 percent of which were granted).[33]

What accounts for the different rates of challenge? One explanation is the Vice Control Division's aggressive sense of its mission to ferret out narcotics violators. This seems to have led the division to emphasize crime control over conviction. One manifestation of this emphasis is the large number of searches it made in private residences: "All but one of the motions to suppress for searches within apartments involved the V.C.D."[34] Patrol and traffic officers and the Task Force, which did not focus single-mindedly on narcotics offenses, made few apartment searches, an important factor in their lower rates of searches challenged by motions to suppress.

It seems that the Chicago Vice Control Division entertained a broader conception of its mission than did the New York City Narcotics Bureau. There are no time-series data for Chicago, but the high rates of challenged searches suggest that the Vice Control Division was probably little affected by *Mapp*.

The evidence consists only of bits and pieces, but the fragments indicate it is a mistake to think that police behavior is never conditioned by the sanction of excluding evidence that might lead to conviction. As we have seen, in the case of serious crimes the policeman starts thinking fairly early of what is required to convict, and some of the things he thinks of are the restrictive rules of arrest and search. Even in less serious cases, there is some evidence of officers' disappointment with their inability to get Fourth Amendment requirements straight, when motions to suppress evidence have been granted.[35] The commonly reported willingness of some policemen to perjure themselves to prevent suppression motions from succeeding indicates that they care very much about conviction (though it may also imply that sanctions for perjury are un-

33. Spiotto, "Search and Seizure," p. 267.
34. Ibid.
35. Note, "Effect of *Mapp* v. *Ohio*," p. 97.

likely to be applied against them). Policemen often debate with prosecutors the appropriate charges to be lodged against suspects the police have apprehended, the officers typically arguing for more serious charges than the prosecutors think they can sustain.[36] Sample surveys of police attitudes toward the courts repeatedly show profound police disappointment with the courts for imposing little or no punishment on so many criminals.[37]

None of this evidence means that policemen are not sometimes equally or more interested in the maintenance of order, the confiscation of contraband, the harassment of deviants, or the reprimand of juveniles, than they are in securing convictions. But the evidence is hardly consistent with the rather too-sophisticated notion that the police have little or no concern with whether offenders are in fact convicted. On the contrary, what is known about police behavior suggests that, at some times and places, there is more than ample concern with obtaining convictions to cause police to pay attention to the requirements of the Fourth Amendment.

Deterrence that is partial, sporadic, not uniform: this is also the theme of the most ambitious quantitative study of *Mapp's* impact to appear so far, the research of Bradley C. Canon on arrest rates in twenty-six widely scattered jurisdictions.[38] Canon tested the comparative impact of *Mapp* on arrest rates in states that had and had not adopted the exclusionary rule before *Mapp*. The arrest data were drawn from twenty-three large cities and three state police organizations, about half of which were in pre-*Mapp* exclusionary states and half not. Arrest figures were compiled for about four years before and four years after *Mapp* was decided. The data pertained to the kinds of offenses for which arrests are often made as a result of searches likely to violate the Fourth Amendment: narcotics, stolen property, weapons, and gambling. If *Mapp* resulted in increased adherence to the requirements of the Fourth Amendment, this adherence would quite probably be reflected in declines in arrest rates for these particular offenses. Significant declines[39] did appear in half of the jurisdictions studied and in about 40

36. Skolnick, *Justice Without Trial*, pp. 199–201.

37. See Wilson, *Varieties of Police Behavior*, p. 50, n. 50. See also LaFave, *Arrest*, p. 429.

38. "Taking Advantage of a Quasi-Experiment Situation: The Impact of *Mapp v. Ohio*" (paper presented at 1974 annual meeting of the American Political Science Association; processed).

39. That is, rates below the predicted rates, based on projections from the pre-*Mapp* period.

percent of the total number of city-offenses.[40] Not only was the decline in arrest rates significant; it was also consistent from one type of offense to another, though not necessarily consistent within the same city. This, of course, is quite compatible with the earlier discussion of *Mapp*'s effect on particular offenses and on particular police units. The arrest rates of cities in both pre-*Mapp* exclusionary and non-exclusionary states were affected by *Mapp*.[41] In short, Canon's study shows that, even within a few years after *Mapp*, there were statistically significant changes in some cities in arrest rates for offenses particularly sensitive to the Fourth Amendment.

There are, of course, some things that Canon's study cannot explain. It cannot tell us whether the proportion of illegal arrests declined, since it focuses only on the rate of all arrests, legal and illegal. The clear implication, however, is that many of the arrests that were not made after *Mapp* were disproportionately of the illegal variety. Likewise, the Canon figures say nothing about those unlawful invasions of privacy that did not result in arrests because the invasion turned out to be mistaken. This, too, is an important omission, since protection of the innocent from unwarranted invasion of privacy is a central concern of the Fourth Amendment.

Canon's findings could also be consistent with a continuing pattern of unlawful searches accompanied by greater discrimination in the making of arrests. It is possible that some of the slackening of arrests following *Mapp* indicates that some police forces, units, or officers turned to harassing rather than arresting suspects against whom prosecutions could not be sustained after *Mapp*.

The point can be stated more generally. The parts of the criminal justice system are so interdependent that benefits gained by altering one aspect of the system can quickly produce costs in another. If, for instance, sentencing discretion is limited, prosecuting discretion will probably be enhanced. It is by no means clear that the latter is preferable to the former. Efforts to effect planned change in the criminal justice system often founder on just such displacement effects. In view of this, it would not be surprising if *Mapp* created incentives for the police to engage in

40. The city-offense figure is the number of offenses studied (four) multiplied by the number of jurisdictions studied.

41. From this, Canon argues that the prior state exclusionary rules had no impact in the states that had adopted them. Ibid., p. 24. But the data do not demonstrate that, since they contain no evidence on arrest rates before the state exclusionary rules were adopted.

new forms of unlawful behavior beyond the reach of the exclusionary rule.

Three such practices have been hypothesized. The first is the increase in police harassment of suspects referred to a moment ago. The second is an increase in police perjury about the circumstances surrounding challenged arrests and searches. The third is an increase in police corruption. This may take the form of intentionally conferring immunity from prosecution on paying criminals by making illegal searches and seizures, thereby spoiling the cases again them. There is evidence that in some locales *Mapp* fostered at least the first two of these practices.

Since *Mapp* does not constrain those aspects of police work that are not directed at prosecution, the decision constitutes an unintended inducement to emphasize those aspects of the job. In New York City, for example, *Mapp* was said to have been followed by an increase in what is called preventive patrol, a policy of aggressive stopping and searching in high-crime areas to create an atmosphere of police presence sufficient to discourage crime.[42] Stops and searches made pursuant to this policy generally do not lead to prosecution and conviction, and they generally do not conform to Fourth Amendment requirements.

In the first few years following *Mapp,* several state legislatures, fearing that the exclusionary rule might hamper police operations, also enacted so-called stop-and-frisk laws.[43] Typically, these statutes permit a policeman to stop for brief questioning anyone whom he "reasonably suspects" of criminal behavior and then to search him for weapons if the policeman fears for his safety. Some such practices may already have been customary among many police forces without express statutory authority, which may explain why more states did not adopt stop-and-frisk laws. However, such laws may have encouraged the police to engage in more street searches or pat-downs than previously: in New York City, 81.6 percent of street stops occurring in 1965, after passage of the law, were accompanied by frisks.[44] If the passage of stop-and-frisk legis-

42. Note, "Effect of *Mapp* v. *Ohio*," pp. 99–101.

43. See Comment, "Stop and Frisk," *Northwestern Law Review*, vol. 63 (January–February 1969), pp. 837–61, at pp. 854–58; Lawrence G. Stern, "Stop and Frisk: An Historical Answer," *Journal of Criminal Law, Criminology, and Police Science*, vol. 58 (December 1967), pp. 532–42. On the constitutional validity of stop-and-frisk practices, see *Terry* v. *Ohio*, 392 U.S. 1 (1968); *Sibron* v. *New York,* 392 U.S. 40 (1968).

44. President's Commission on Law Enforcement and Criminal Justice, Task Force on the Police, *Task Force Report: The Police* (Government Printing Office, 1967), p. 185.

lation or comparable administrative guidelines has in fact resulted in a greater incidence of such searches than previously (when their legal basis was cloudier), then a significant secondary consequence of *Mapp* has been to expand police authority on the street.

The New York practice of preventive patrol relates heavily to narcotics offenses. In the case of illegal liquor traffic and gambling, where *Mapp* and, in many cases, judicial hostility toward the law itself make conviction difficult, a common police reaction has also been to turn to a policy of harassment by making illegal arrests and confiscations.[45] In this way, the exclusionary rule not only fails to reach police activity directed at crime prevention through (often dubious) means other than prosecution; it may also encourage that activity.[46]

That *Mapp* has encouraged false testimony by police officers seeking to justify arrests and searches under the Fourth Amendment is virtually certain. In practice, police often act on the basis of suspicion that may be well grounded but not sufficient to constitute probable cause.[47] If their suspicion bears evidentiary fruit, they must then find a way to justify the action they took as of the time they took it. Sometimes this takes the form of embellishing the circumstances, sometimes fabricating them altogether. In New York City, immediately following *Mapp* there was a sharp decline in police allegations that narcotics were hidden on premises or on a suspect's person. There were also increases in allegations that narcotics were visibly held in the hand or arm, that money was seen passing, or that narcotics had been dropped or thrown to the ground.[48] Inasmuch as the sight of narcotics or of a narcotics sale is sufficient for probable cause, one response of police officers to *Mapp* was to alter their version of the events that gave rise to the search.[49]

So far, then, there is evidence of changing police behavior, but not all of it in the intended or anticipated direction. Along with compliance, there is increased emphasis on modes of illegal enforcement untouched by the exclusionary rule—in what proportions is not known. This prob-

45. Wilson, *Varieties of Police Behavior*, p. 106; LaFave, "Improving Police Performance Through the Exclusionary Rule," pp. 421–30; LaFave, *Arrest*, pp. 471–82.

46. LaFave, *Arrest*, p. 430.

47. For a good illustration, see Skolnick, *Justice Without Trial*, pp. 215–16.

48. Note, "Effect of *Mapp* v. *Ohio*," pp. 94–96.

49. See Skolnick, *Justice Without Trial*, p. 215; Comment, "Police Perjury in Narcotics 'Dropsy' Cases: A New Credibility Gap," *Georgetown Law Journal*, vol. 60 (November 1971), pp. 507–23.

lem of estimating magnitudes of deterrence versus displacement may be insurmountable. But some educated guesses are possible.

Perjury may be on the increase, but it is obviously either not so pervasive or not so successful as to preclude the granting of a significant number of suppression motions even in courts that are overtly hostile to the *Mapp* rule.[50] Put another way, perjury can dilute the application of *Mapp,* but it cannot begin to prevent it altogether.

Deflection of police energies to harassment is another matter. In theory, such a deflection might actually exceed the extent of newly induced conformity to the Fourth Amendment and render *Mapp* a net setback in the struggle for police observance of constitutional norms. The evidence currently available provides no way to prove conclusively whether the frequency of newly adopted harassment tactics does or does not exceed the frequency of newly induced compliance with the Fourth Amendment. Although virtually all harassment tactics involve some reliance on arrests, some do so less than others. This being true, diversion of energies to certain harassment tactics would not be fully reflected in arrest figures. There is, however, some reason to believe that whatever new emphasis was placed by some police forces on harassment fell short of changes in police behavior to conform to Fourth Amendment requirements.

A useful distinction can be made according to the purpose of the harassment. Some illegal tactics, such as those reported for New York City, are directed at crime prevention and detection. In the nature of this task, many illegal stops and searches are made that do not culminate in arrests, the process being nearly random. Other tactics, however, are directed at law enforcement and punishment of known criminals by the police. These generally do involve the making of arrests, even where prosecution and conviction are unlikely. Arrest then becomes a substitute for judicially imposed punishment, because it makes pursuance of illegal activity most inconvenient for those particularly susceptible to regular harassment—the prostitute, the gambler, the narcotics pusher.[51] It takes them out of circulation and sometimes results in confiscation of gambling apparatus, policy slips, or narcotics. It may also disrupt the daily operations of the organizations of which

50. See, e.g., the figures in Michael Ban, "Local Courts vs. the Supreme Court: The Impact of *Mapp.* v. *Ohio*" (paper presented at 1973 annual meeting of the American Political Science Association; processed).

51. See Note, "Effect of *Mapp* v. *Ohio,*" pp. 99–100; LaFave, *Arrest,* chaps. 21–25.

these functionaries are a part. Even in the case of casual offenders, there are incentives for the police to arrest suspects they know cannot be convicted. The mere fact of arrest (and prosecution, if it follows) is itself punishment for wrongdoing, attended by a variety of financial and other personal sanctions.[52]

Which type of harassment *Mapp* particularly fostered becomes the central question when inferences of police deterrence depend on arrest figures. If *Mapp* spurred police harassment for purposes of prevention and detection, this would not be fully reflected in the arrest figures. If, on the other hand, *Mapp* gave rise to increased harassment for enforcement and punishment, this would be reflected in the arrest figures. The decline in arrests shown by the Canon figures would mean that increases in police compliance with the Fourth Amendment probably exceeded increases in police harassment for enforcement and punishment.

On the present evidence, as I have said, it is not possible to tell. But comparing the two types of harassment with the nature of the *Mapp* sanction gives a clue to the probable answer. *Mapp* made it impossible to convict at least some defendants against whom evidence had been obtained illegally and, in many cases, against whom evidence could only be obtained illegally. It is true that the police tend to regard the exclusionary rule as lenient and contrary to good law enforcement practice. Even before *Mapp*, they sometimes used arrests to punish defendants whom they could not convict. As *Mapp* immunizes more such defendants from conviction, it seems quite probable that there will be more such punitive harassing arrests—but not necessarily a greater increase than the increase in grudging compliance with the Fourth Amendment.

Even so, the aggregate rate of gambling arrests—perhaps the arrest rate most likely to be affected by such harassment tactics—displayed trends no different from those of the other offenses Canon studied. On the basis of this datum, Canon speculates, "In some cities where the local culture more or less tolerates gambling the police may have used *Mapp* as an opportunity to decrease their enforcement efforts,"[53] while

52. For the argument that arrest and prosecution are often initiated when conviction is unlikely, in order to punish the "factually guilty" (i.e., not legally guilty) defendant, see Herbert Jacob and James Eisenstein, "Sentences and Other Sanctions Imposed on Felony Defendants in Baltimore, Chicago, and Detroit" (paper presented at the 1974 annual meeting of the American Political Science Association; processed), p. 10.

53. Canon, "Taking Advantage of a Quasi-Experiment Situation," p. 29.

in others they may have continued their practice of harassment by arrest.

That leaves harassment for purposes of prevention or detection, as opposed to harassment for punishment. In New York City, it was suggested that *Mapp* may have encouraged preventive patrol in the narcotics area. But in part this may have been the result of the Narcotics Bureau's contraction of responsibility, which left more enforcement to officers functioning on the street. In point of fact, New York City's narcotics enforcement strategy was being revamped continuously in the early 1960s, and other changes following *Mapp* may have become entangled in these reorganizations.[54] In terms of the structure of police incentives, it is difficult to see why *Mapp* would have encouraged increases in preventive patrol generally. In the first place, preventive patrol is an expensive enforcement strategy, which consumes inordinate manpower and material resources. Furthermore, it is a strategy the use of which tends to ebb and flow with community pressure for more intensive enforcement on the street. In its very nature, it is not usually productive in terms of convictions, and *Mapp* would have made it less so in these terms, because the arrests and searches that result from street stops based on suspicion are so often illegal. Unlike the strategy of arresting known offenders who cannot be convicted, preventive patrol is too random to be an effective harassment technique used in lieu of conviction. Whereas *Mapp* may have led the police to make more illegal arrests in order to punish or inconvenience some of the criminals whom *Mapp* made it impossible to convict, it seems unlikely that *Mapp* led the police to engage in widespread harassment for purposes of prevention and detection—at least beyond levels at which they were disposed to do so previously.

The point, it is worth reiterating, is important because conclusions based on studies of arrest figures would ignore a major cost of *Mapp* if they failed to estimate increases in illegal behavior not reflected in arrests. On the present state of the evidence, however, the Canon study of arrest data in twenty-six jurisdictions still supports the conclusions that *Mapp* had a deterrent effect on police behavior and that this effect probably exceeded the displacement (harassment) effect that *Mapp* also had. The deterrent effect was highly differential by city and by offense, but that is exactly what qualitative data have led us to expect. That is all the more reason to credit the findings.

54. I am indebted to James Q. Wilson for a helpful discussion of this and some of the other matters treated in this paragraph.

The Exclusionary Rule in Court

The exclusionary rule is a sanction mediated through the enforcement machinery of the lower criminal courts. If that machinery is in good repair and functioning efficiently, there is still reason, as I have said, to wonder whether it can alter police practice in the intended direction by excluding illegally obtained evidence from criminal proceedings. If, however, the machinery does not function as expected, the reasons for doubting the efficacy of *Mapp* will be multiplied. In particular, if illegally obtained evidence is not regularly excluded from criminal trials, the very sanction on which *Mapp* rests may be undermined.

Although the Supreme Court did not feel obliged to spell out assumptions so obvious, the *Mapp* decision implicitly posited that attempts would be made to introduce illegally obtained evidence at criminal trials, that there would be objections or motions to suppress the evidence, that these would be granted, and that many cases based on such evidence would then end in dismissal or acquittal. From this experience, the police would learn that invasion of privacy is futile and even counterproductive.

Most of the skepticism regarding *Mapp's* effectiveness has been directed at the last step, the learning curve the Court constructed for the police. Objections have been raised, as we have seen, about the extent to which the rules of search and seizure are communicated to the police, about the extent to which the police are moved by the desire to convict, and similar matters. Much less concern has been expressed about the accuracy of the Supreme Court's depiction of the role the lower criminal courts are to play in this process.

It has been noted in connection with *Gault* that the Supreme Court's assumptions about how its innovations will actually function at the trial court level can be somewhat wide of the mark. In *Gault*, the Court displayed what might be called an adversary bias, a confident belief that, with the presence of diligent counsel, the contested resolution of delinquency matters might become the norm. There was in *Gault* a considerable underestimate of the importance of informal procedures, such as negotiation, in the work of juvenile courts, even of those juvenile courts that were most receptive to the presence of counsel and to formal procedures in general. If this was true of *Gault*, it is true of *Mapp* many times over.

The point is best illustrated by the opinion in *United States* v. *Ca-landra*.[55] The question in *Calandra* was whether illegally obtained evidence must be excluded from grand jury proceedings, just as it is to be excluded from criminal trials. A divided Court held that the exclusionary rule does not apply to grand jury proceedings. The majority's reasoning is revealing. The prime purpose of the exclusionary rule is to deter. Excluding illegally obtained evidence from grand jury proceedings would, in the Court's view, hinder the work of grand juries without adding a significant increment to whatever deterrent effect the exclusionary rule already has on police behavior. Since illegally obtained evidence is inadmissible at the trial, it would be fruitless for the police to gather such evidence merely to obtain an indictment that would not result in conviction, the more so as prosecutors "would be unlikely to request an indictment where a conviction could not be obtained."[56] In other words, excluding evidence from the grand jury would yield few benefits that excluding it from the trial does not already yield, for what happens at the trial is determinative.

There was a vigorous dissent in *Calandra*. The dissenters argued that deterring the police misconduct was not the exclusive or prime purpose of the *Mapp* rule. Possibly this was because they, too, may have thought its success in those terms to be problematical; certainly they made no argument that it did deter. Instead, the dissent laid heavy stress on the need for courts to avoid condoning violations of the Constitution—the second ground of the *Mapp* opinion. In so doing, the dissenters abandoned the deterrence field. They did not take issue with the way in which the deterrence question had been framed by the majority. Despite the depth of their disagreement over the result in *Calandra*, all the Justices seemed agreed in thinking of the exclusionary rule as being enforced by objection to evidence at a criminal trial or by a motion to suppress made prior to the trial.

But the question needs to be asked: *What trial?* The vast majority of criminal defendants, state and federal, do not have a trial. Of the nearly 50,000 defendants whose cases are disposed of annually in the federal district courts, only about 7,300 (15 percent) go to trial. Between 20 and 25 percent of the cases are dismissed. The remaining 60 to 65 percent of the defendants plead guilty to some offense.[57] For state

55. 414 U.S. 338 (1974).
56. Ibid. at 351.
57. Administrative Office of the United States Courts, *1974 Annual Report of*

courts, the number of trials is typically lower. Guilty pleas are often entered in 70 to 80 percent of all cases, and trials generally account for 10 percent or less of all cases.[58] The disposition of criminal charges without trial is the norm; trial is the exception. This is even more the case for those convicted, nearly 90 percent of whom plead guilty.[59]

For the overwhelming majority of defendants who plead guilty to some offense and hence are punished without going to trial, indictment may be tantamount to conviction. There may be, therefore, a very strong incentive for the police to obtain evidence illegally which can be used in grand jury proceedings, even if that evidence would be inadmissible at a trial if one were ever held. Most of the time, indictment leads to a plea of guilty. Because the deterrence reasoning in *Calandra* is based on the criminal trial as the implicit norm, ignoring the way in which most criminal cases are actually disposed of, the opinion takes as given a structure of police and prosecution incentives that may prove to be purely fictitious.

The question is not whether excluding illegally obtained evidence at the trial is or is not a sufficient sanction to deter police misconduct. Rather, the question is twofold. First, how does the potential sanction of excluding illegally obtained evidence affect the cases of those who may never go to trial and who may never actually have occasion to invoke the exclusionary rule in court? Second, is the way in which the exclusionary sanction works in cases of non-trial disposition sufficient to preserve any deterrent effect it would have if all defendants went to trial and all illegally obtained evidence were excluded from such trials?

This abstract formulation can quickly be made more concrete. Con-

---

the Director, pp. A52–A53. The figures for earlier years are not dissimilar. The figures on dismissals probably include some cases that were dismissed at the trial, rather than before.

58. See Richard A. Brisbin, Jr., "The Pretrial Disposition of Criminal Cases by Rural Prosecutors: The Effects of Local Traditions and Political Power" (paper presented at 1975 annual meeting of the Midwest Political Science Association; processed), reporting data from widely scattered urban and rural jurisdictions.

59. See Donald J. Newman, *Conviction: The Determination of Guilt or Innocence Without Trial* (Little, Brown, 1966), pp. 3, 8; James Eisenstein, *Politics and the Legal Process* (Harper and Row, 1973), pp. 100–01; President's Commission on Law Enforcement and Criminal Justice, Task Force on the Administration of Justice, *Task Force Report: The Courts* (Government Printing Office, 1967), p. 9. Generally, there are more guilty pleas in misdemeanor cases, fewer in felony cases.

sider the case of the defendant who, after *Calandra,* has been indicted on
the basis of evidence he believes to have been obtained illegally. How
should he plead? Or, more precisely, should he accept the prosecutor's
offer to let him plead guilty to a lesser offense? His decision may turn
on his evaluation of how likely it is the evidence will be excluded if he
chooses to go to trial. Can he find out in advance? Certainly he can, if
the jurisdiction in which he has been indicted has a procedure for filing
a pre-trial motion to suppress illegally obtained evidence, as the federal
courts and some state courts do. Should he file such a motion? If he does
and the evidence is held inadmissible, his problems may be over. Since
there would then be no admissible evidence on which to convict, the
prosecutor himself may ask to have the indictment dismissed. But if
the defendant files the suppression motion and the evidence is held
admissible, his problems may just be beginning. The prosecutor's offer
of leniency may itself have been based on his uncertainty about the admissibility of the evidence. Once the uncertainty is cleared away, the
prosecutor may become much less disposed to negotiate. Perhaps filing
the motion is not such a good idea after all. Perhaps it is better to accept
the prosecutor's offer and plead guilty now. Uncertainty is the great
maker of bargains.

Note that if this defendant does plead guilty to some charge, *Calandra*
has indeed weakened whatever deterrent effect *Mapp* would otherwise
have. For this defendant, and for others like him, the fact that the disputed evidence was admissible before the grand jury is essentially dispositive of his case. If this is how the exclusionary rule works in practice,
there is good reason for police officers to gather evidence illegally, *even
when their purpose is prosecution and conviction,* for *Calandra* permits
convictions based on guilty pleas induced by evidence that may have
been illegally obtained. The conviction may not be for the serious
crime of which the defendant is believed guilty, and that may rankle the
police. But it is a conviction of some crime. Under the *Mapp* rule, that is
more than might have been obtained if the case had gone to trial. Given
the prevalence of guilty pleas, the only sure way to prevent illegally
obtained evidence from forming the basis of a conviction is to prevent
it from being used to secure an indictment.

This discussion should suffice to show that the lower criminal courts
are a vital link in the *Mapp* chain. How, then, does the exclusionary
sanction affect the cases of defendants who may never go to trial? Pre-

dictably, the data are not what we would want them to be, either in quality or quantity. But there is some evidence, and, as in the case of police behavior, it suggests divergent local patterns.

To begin with, a discount must be taken for ignorance on the part of lawyers and judges. I have previously noted the discouraging results of a survey conducted in North Carolina, which showed the existence of unfamiliarity with certain basic Fourth Amendment principles on the part of members of the criminal bench and bar.[60] A comparative study by Michael Ban of Boston and Cincinnati state criminal courts concludes that defense lawyers in both cities often did not know about *Mapp,* certainly not about all the ramifications that might affect the cases of their clients, and they were too busy to spend very much time doing the detailed legal research that might be required to support a persuasive motion to suppress.[61] The result of this and other factors was a small number of suppression motions filed in both cities. In the four and a half years immediately following *Mapp,* only 133 such motions were filed in Cincinnati, 421 in Boston; during those years, the number of search warrants issued totaled several times that number, not to mention the number of warrantless searches.[62] As in the case of police behavior, however, ignorance or reticence about filing motions to suppress does not appear to be evenly distributed. In New York City and Chicago, *Mapp* was followed by a considerable increase in the filing of suppression motions, at least in arrest and search areas such as narcotics that are heavily subject to Fourth Amendment challenge.[63] In Chicago, in one three-month period during 1971, more than 1,600 motions to suppress were filed.[64]

It may be, of course, that the Chicago police violate the Fourth Amendment more frequently or blatantly than do the Boston or Cincinnati police. Certainly, the frequency of suppression motions granted in the various cities—75 percent in Chicago, 40 percent in Cincinnati, 23 percent in Boston[65]—is consistent with that conclusion, and others have

60. Katz, "The Supreme Court and the States."

61. Ban, "Local Courts vs. the Supreme Court," pp. 12–15.

62. Ibid., p. 12.

63. Note, "Effect of *Mapp* v. *Ohio,*" p. 97; Spiotto, "Search and Seizure," p. 247.

64. Spiotto, "Search and Seizure," p. 250.

65. Computed from: ibid., p. 250 (1971 figures); Ban, "Local Courts vs. the Supreme Court," p. 13 (1961–65). In New York City narcotics cases in 1961–62, the rate of motions granted was 65 percent. Computed from Note, "Effect of *Mapp* v. *Ohio,*" pp. 92, 97.

suggested that the Chicago police use illegal arrest and search as a harassment technique.[66] The plausibility of this point is buttressed by the high frequency of motions granted in Chicago despite the large number of motions filed. Ordinarily, we would expect, all else being equal, that the more motions filed, the smaller would be the percentage granted. The reason for this is that, where such motions are filed routinely, a disproportionate number of unmeritorious motions find their way to court.

On the other hand, the figures may also reflect other factors. The first is that Chicago prosecutors exercise little or no screening function for Fourth Amendment violations, so that many cases are prosecuted that rest on illegally obtained evidence.[67] The judges may therefore feel obliged to perform the screening function neglected by prosecutors. Even so, the percentage of motions granted in Chicago is impressive. In this respect, the attitudes of Boston and Cincinnati judges toward the exclusionary rule become relevant. In both cities, *Mapp* generated hostility and resentment among most criminal court judges, many of whom questioned the expertise and authority of the Supreme Court in the field of police practice. As one Boston judge said, "we have an eyewitness seat and get splattered with the blood."[68] A few judges overcame their resistance and complied with *Mapp* to the letter. The decisions of the remainder, however, appear to have been colored by their hostility to the decision.[69] As in the case of *Gault's* implementation, judicial resistance to new requirements imposed by the Supreme Court can influence how and to what extent those requirements are effectuated. It may well be that the high percentage of motions granted in Chicago reflects a lesser degree of hostility to *Mapp* there or, more likely, a norm of subordinating that hostility to the need to screen cases. In Boston and Cincinnati, avoidance of *Mapp's* requirements constitutes the norm.

If ignorance of and hostility toward constitutional requirements are not uniformly distributed, neither is there any necessary uniformity in the way the potential exclusionary sanction affects the actual disposition of cases. In practice, motions to suppress may be handled under circumstances that either do or do not make the lawfulness of the search an

---

66. Oaks, "Studying the Exclusionary Rule in Search and Seizure," pp. 683–86.
67. Spiotto, "Search and Seizure," p. 249. Just how Boston and Cincinnati prosecutors function in this respect is unclear.
68. Quoted by Ban, "Local Courts vs. the Supreme Court," p. 6.
69. Ibid., pp. 5–12.

important part of the process of plea bargaining. Basically, this seems to depend on the procedural setting and on the inclination of local prosecutors.

Timing can be all-important. If suppression motions are litigated at a very early stage of the proceedings, they are unlikely to form part of the plea-bargaining process.[70] In Chicago, all but a few motions to suppress are heard in the preliminary-hearing court and are disposed of before indictment,[71] with dismissal of the charges virtually always following the granting of a suppression motion.[72] Under these circumstances, Fourth Amendment questions can scarcely play a role in plea bargaining, since they are disposed of before the process even begins.[73]

In Cincinnati, where relatively few motions are filed, court calendars are not particularly congested, mandatory felony sentences are in effect, and prosecutors are quite hostile to *Mapp*, motions to suppress rarely induce plea bargaining.[74] There are few occasions to cut a deal, little administrative advantage in doing so, not much sentencing flexibility around which to bargain, and—perhaps most important—little prosecutorial inclination to do so. Prosecutors contest the motions, rather than regard them as an invitation to discuss the charges.

Boston prosecutors take a different view. There, *Mapp* was easily integrated into an ongoing system of plea bargaining.[75] The suppression motion has become another of the defendant's weapons. This is possible because, contrary to Cincinnati's sterner system, the Boston courts dispense a rather lenient brand of justice. Quite often, the filing of a suppression motion is sufficient to obtain for the defendant who pleads guilty a reduction of an otherwise likely jail term, typically to probation. Thus, even where the exclusionary rule does not affect the likelihood of conviction, it can have a pronounced effect on the sentence.[76]

70. Albert W. Alschuler, "The Prosecutor's Role in Plea Bargaining," *University of Chicago Law Review*, vol. 36 (Fall 1968), pp. 50–112, at pp. 81–82, n. 73.

71. Of the few motions heard later, in the trial court, only 20 percent are granted, compared to 77 percent granted in the preliminary-hearing court. Spiotto, "Search and Seizure," p. 250.

72. Oaks, "Studying the Exclusionary Rule," pp. 684–87.

73. The New York City experience suggests a somewhat similar development. Following *Mapp*, guilty pleas in narcotics cases declined, while dismissals of charges increased. Note, "Effect of *Mapp* v. *Ohio*," p. 97.

74. Ban, "Local Courts vs. the Supreme Court," pp. 17–18.

75. Ibid., pp. 15–16.

76. This is also the conclusion of Albert W. Alschuler, "The Prosecutor's Role in Plea Bargaining," p. 82.

There is another possibility. Fourth Amendment issues may form part of the prosecutor's initial decision whether to bring charges. In the District of Columbia, for example, prosecutors review all cases before they reach court, and as many as 10 percent are dropped, because, among other reasons, evidence necessary to the case might otherwise be suppressed.[77] Significantly, relatively few suppression motions are filed or granted in the District of Columbia.

There are, then, three modes of dealing with Fourth Amendment issues. The issues may be litigated, they may be injected into the process of plea bargaining, or they may be handled by the exercise of prosecutorial discretion. There is no way of knowing how prevalent each of these modes of handling Fourth Amendment issues is. It is likely, however, that the problematic legality of a search often enters into plea bargaining and less often affects prosecutorial charging decisions. The hostility of judges toward *Mapp*, the ignorance of defense lawyers about the nuances of the Fourth Amendment, the general uncertainty about the outcome of suppression motions (few courts have Chicago's unusually early, pre-indictment motion practice)—all of these factors suggest that included among the large number of guilty pleas is a significant fraction of cases resting on evidence arguably obtained by methods that violate the Fourth Amendment. Likewise, the delicacy of prosecutor-police relations, the desire of prosecutors to leave hard and unpopular decisions to the courts, and the uncertain legality of many searches and seizures—these factors suggest that there are pronounced limits to the exercise of prosecutorial discretion not to bring charges.

The three modes, of course, are not mutually exclusive. Although, as I have said, the frequency of suppression motions varies widely, virtually every criminal court litigates some Fourth Amendment issues. For example, even in Boston, where plea bargaining often encompasses search-and-seizure issues, suppression motions are adjudicated in cases where bargained pleas are not arranged. (A common practice on the part of judges in such cases seems to be to deny meritorious motions, in order to exonerate the police officers, but then to enter a judgment of acquittal, in order to insulate the erroneous suppression ruling from appeal.[78]) Similarly, even in those jurisdictions where "only evidence which is admissible at the trial is considered in making the charging decision . . . there is some indication that the likelihood of a guilty plea may temper

77. Oaks, "Studying the Exclusionary Rule in Search and Seizure," pp. 688–89.
78. Ban, "Local Courts vs. the Supreme Court," p. 16.

this practice in some instances."[79] Considerations of plea bargaining may thus affect prosecutorial decisions to screen out cases that rest on illegally seized evidence.

Which of these modes of handling Fourth Amendment issues is most likely to deter police misconduct? There is no ready answer to this question, although it would seem fairly obvious that the occasional practice in Boston of denying suppression motions and then entering acquittals is least calculated to demonstrate to the police the cause-and-effect relation between the illegal search (held to be legal) and the acquittal (ostensibly entered on other grounds).

The assumption of *Mapp* was that suppression motions would be litigated and granted where evidence was illegally seized, thereby bringing home to the police the message that Fourth Amendment violations do not pay. But where litigation is the dominant mode of disposing of search-and-seizure issues, there is as yet no clear connection between those dispositions and observable police behavior. In New York City, suppression motions are most often granted in narcotics cases where plainclothesmen have gathered the evidence, much less often in Narcotics Bureau cases.[80] But, as we saw, it was the Narcotics Bureau that altered its policy in response to *Mapp*, and that decision was not traceable to judicial decisions on particular suppression motions. Chicago's courts are especially receptive to suppression motions, but the Chicago police have been accused of continuing to use illegal arrest and search as enforcement tools. The Cincinnati courts are less receptive, though litigation is the dominant mode of resolving Fourth Amendment issues in Cincinnati and some 40 percent of the suppression motions filed in those courts between 1961 and 1965 were granted. But detailed examination of arrests, convictions, seizures, and stolen property recoveries in Cincinnati before and after *Mapp* seems to indicate that *Mapp* had no discernible impact on police practices in that city[81]—not a surprising conclusion when one considers the hostility toward the exclusionary rule expressed by the judges, prosecutors, and even some defense lawyers charged with effectuating it.[82]

For purposes of maximizing deterrence, there is some reason for

79. Frank W. Miller, *Prosecution: The Decision to Charge a Suspect with a Crime* (Little, Brown, 1969), p. 37. See generally ibid., pp. 37–41.
80. Note, "Effect of *Mapp* v. *Ohio*," p. 97.
81. Oaks, "Studying the Exclusionary Rule in Search and Seizure," pp. 689–96.
82. Ban, "Local Courts vs. the Supreme Court," pp. 9–12, 17–18.

thinking that prosecutorial screening may be the most effective way of enforcing the *Mapp* rule. The causal connection between the illegal search and the decision not to prosecute is as clear as it is when dismissal of an indictment follows the granting of a motion to suppress evidence. Equally important, the exact grounds of the decision not to prosecute are likely to be explained to police officers by prosecutors somewhat more often, more fully, more informally, and in more understandable terms than they are by judges granting motions and dismissing indictments.[83] Furthermore, the prosecutor is perhaps a more influential force for compliance than the more distant judge, whose loyalty to the cause of "law and order" is often viewed by the police as equivocal.[84]

Jerome Skolnick describes prosecutor-police interactions in terms that suggest the utility of prosecutorial screening:

when the trial deputy [preparing his case] questions the police, he is not at all reluctant to criticize the policeman's action in the case. For instance, in one such interaction observed, the policeman was told that his failure to caution the defendant in a recorded statement might prejudice the jury unfavorably. According to several deputies questioned on this matter, it is indeed the policy of the office to "educate" policemen.

Furthermore, the police seem not to resent such "correction," and appear to enjoy their role as "assistants" to these higher-ranking law enforcement personnel. . . . At the Superior Court level, the policeman and the district attorney become part of the same team. Thus, although the prosecutor plays a magisterial role in the sense of assessing with a critical eye the validity of complaints and the strength of a case he ultimately represents law enforcement. In playing this role, however, he not only interprets criminal law to the policeman, but also, in the process of interpretation, *legitimizes its authority* and tempers police resentment toward criminal law.[85]

The key point, says Skolnick, is that the prosecutor is a "sympathetic ally." He

need not be successful in making the policeman approve of the strictures of due process of law, which he typically does not admire himself. By accepting their legitimacy, however, he demonstrates to the policeman that it is at once possible to disagree with the rules of the game as they are laid down, and at the same time to carry out the enforcement of substantive criminal law— if one learns skillfully how to interpret these rules into action.[86]

83. Cf. LaFave, *Arrest*, pp. 505–06, for the inefficacy of communications from the courts to the police, and pp. 514–17, for the unused potential of the prosecutor's office on this score.

84. See Wilson, *Varieties of Police Behavior*, p. 50.

85. *Justice Without Trial*, pp. 201–02 (emphasis in the original).

86. Ibid, p. 203.

Police-prosecutor relations do not always assume this character. But they are much more likely to do so when prosecutors undertake an active program of screening cases and refusing to charge in cases resting on illegally obtained evidence.

In cases where the lawfulness of a search and seizure forms part of the negotiations for a plea of guilty, the deterrent impact of *Mapp* is very much in doubt. The effect of the exclusionary rule is then generally to lower the sentence, rather than to make conviction impossible. Both police and prosecutor have still obtained a conviction. Light sentences are common enough so that this outcome is not likely to be viewed as a setback for the police. Nor does the outcome embody an official condemnation of police behavior. In addition, in most cases the plea bargain can probably be attributed to several factors, only one of which is the illegally obtained evidence. As a matter of fact, even unmeritorious suppression motions may be sufficiently burdensome for the prosecutor to handle as to constitute a defense weapon in the fight for a lenient, bargained sentence.[87] Thus, even where the bargain can be traced to a suppression motion, it is not necessarily traceable to an *illegal* search. Under these circumstances, it is understandably difficult for the police to believe that the bargain resulted from an application of the exclusionary rule.

It is not possible to be certain about how the various modes of disposition of search-and-seizure issues affect police behavior. What is more, it will be difficult to construct a properly controlled study of the impact of various modes of disposition. Too many other variables will be present. Nevertheless, it does seem that the ambiguity of the bargained-sentence disposition renders it the least likely of the three modes to deter police invasions of privacy. It is also the mode of disposition most likely to produce undesirable side effects, such as proliferation of charges by prosecutors, so that they have something to concede in negotiations in order to offset the defendant's Fourth Amendment weapon.[88]

The decision of the Supreme Court in *Calandra* encourages the resolution of search-and-seizure issues through the plea-bargaining process. By making indictments returnable on the basis of illegally obtained evidence, the decision makes it feasible and even tempting for a prose-

87. Alschuler, "The Prosecutor's Role in Plea Bargaining," p. 56; Ban, "Local Courts vs. the Supreme Court," p. 15.

88. For overcharging as a prosecution weapon in bargaining, see Eisenstein, *Politics and the Legal Process*, p. 113.

cutor to bring charges based on evidence that would have to be excluded from a trial, in order to see whether the defendant will plead guilty to the charges, either with or without negotiations.

In terms of bureaucratic relationships, *Calandra* makes it more difficult for a prosecutor to say "No" to the police. He can no longer blame his inability to predicate a prosecution on illegally seized evidence on the exclusionary rule, for that rule does not come into play unless and until there is a trial—an event the rarity of which the police may be presumed to understand, even if they do not understand all of the nuances of Fourth Amendment doctrine.

No doubt, before *Calandra* there were prosecutors who charged defendants on the basis of illegally obtained evidence in the hope of securing guilty pleas.[89] *Calandra*, however, makes it harder for a prosecutor who is disposed to screen cases for Fourth Amendment violations to do so, for he can no longer justify to himself and to the police his refusal to seek indictments on the ground that such attempts are foreclosed by the exclusionary rule. It is clear to him now, if it was not before, that such indictments can be obtained and can result in guilty pleas. These developments do not augur well for prospects of continuing or extending the deterrent effect of *Mapp* on police behavior.

Mapp's Effect and Its Assumptions

From its inception, the exclusionary rule has been appraised in terms of benefit-cost ratios. Implicitly, the Justices have been asking how many units of police deterrence can be achieved for how many units of unpunished guilt. Some have also added to the cost side the incentive *Mapp* provides for the police to resort to illegal enforcement that is not directed at prosecution and therefore not subject to the exclusionary rule.

Until recently, there has been little sustained effort to search for empirical evidence regarding the deterrent effect of the exclusionary rule. Consequently, it is not surprising to find, as detractors of the rule have said, that the empirical foundations of the deterrence argument are still shaky. In fact, the empirical foundations of both sides of the argument

89. Miller, *Prosecution*, p. 39, points out that, where a prosecutor is fairly certain of a guilty plea, he does not tend to concern himself much about a lack of legally admissible evidence.

are shaky. While it is not possible at this point to compute a precise benefit-cost ratio, enough is known to evaluate some of the major criticisms of the exclusionary rule.

The deterrence argument for excluding illegally obtained evidence contains many unstated assumptions. Some of these have been brought to the surface and subjected to extensive criticism. Much of the criticism so far, however, seems highly overdrawn or mistaken. The bureaucratic relations or division-of-labor critique that was identified earlier is particularly in need of qualification. Blanket assertions that the police generally are unconcerned about conviction fail to account for many aspects of police behavior. As I have suggested, concern with conviction is very much a function of locale, offense, stage of investigation, and sometimes police unit involved. Receptivity to the judicial sanction varies accordingly.

Similarly absolute assertions that prosecutors have little or no influence over police officers are also far too sweeping. The Milner study of attitudes toward *Miranda* demonstrated that some police forces are especially receptive to opinions and information emanating from state attorneys' offices. The Skolnick study of police behavior in the field showed that—at least where there was prosecutorial discretion not to charge where constitutional violations tainted the evidence—prosecutors often explained constitutional requirements to the police and chastised them for violations, and the police regarded criticism from this source as helpful and legitimate. Patterns of police-prosecutor relations vary, perhaps depending in part on extent of the prosecutor's exercise of discretion in the charging decision. At the very least, it is premature to conclude that prosecutorial influence is generally negligible.

The suggestion that rebuke from the courts, in the form of appellate opinions rendered years after the challenged search, comes too late and cannot realistically be expected to guide behavior also seems unfounded. In Chicago, where statistics on both first-instance and appellate determinations of suppression motions are available, it is quite clear that appeals are relatively rare: 215 appeals in a full seven-year period, compared to 1,539 motions in the preliminary hearing court in a mere three-month period and 69 motions in the trial court in a two-month period. Appeals are far less likely to result in exclusion of evidence than are determinations made in the court of first-instance: 9 percent compared to 75 percent.[90] The Chicago courts are, of course, exceptional in

90. Computed from Spiotto, "Search and Seizure," pp. 250–52.

that they handle an extraordinary number of pre-trial motions and grant them at an unusually high rate, thereby reducing the number of occasions for appellate correction. Still, it would require changes of many orders of magnitude in the lower-court and appellate figures to conclude that appellate determinations have a primary effect on the police. (Their effect on lower courts does not seem open to much doubt, but this is another matter.)

Furthermore, in both Chicago and New York, the granting of a suppression motion generally results in prompt dismissal of the charges, a sanction that policemen understand and dislike.[91] Thus, even where litigation is the primary mode of disposing of search-and-seizure issues, relatively prompt trial-court dispositions play the major role in the application of the exclusionary rule to Fourth Amendment violations. The part played by appeals is minor. A fortiori, appeals play an even lesser role where plea bargaining or prosecutorial screening is the usual way of resolving Fourth Amendment issues. There are many obstacles to communicating judicial norms to the police, but delay in deciding appeals is not one of them.

There is also great uncertainty about the cost side of the analysis. Quite apart from the difficulties of estimating the extent to which Mapp encourages resort to tactics of harassment, it is not at all clear that Mapp, as implemented thus far, has resulted in freeing large numbers of criminals. First of all, literally nothing is known about whether police forces attempting to comply with Mapp have responded by investing energies and resources in developing new, lawful techniques of investigation and enforcement that might substitute for illegal arrests and searches. Incentives certainly existed for them to turn to such strategies of substitution. If they did so, there would be an increase in compliance with the Fourth Amendment without an equivalent increase in the number of guilty persons going free. Depending on the compliance strategy adopted, Mapp's costs and benefits may or may not be in equilibrium.

Even without information on police innovation in investigatory techniques, there is reason to doubt that large numbers of the guilty go free, if by that we mean that they are not convicted. To the extent that arrest rates show declines attributable to Mapp and dismissal rates show increases,[92] some criminals may be going free, although the cost cannot

91. Note, "Effect of Mapp v. Ohio," p. 97.
92. As in New York City. See ibid.

be assessed on the basis of these data alone. More needs to be known about whether the police are simply being more discriminating in making arrests and whether the dismissal figures reflect dismissals of all charges against a defendant or merely of some of a cluster of related charges.

Most important in calculating the costs of *Mapp* is the effect of the exclusionary rule on plea bargaining. In jurisdictions where *Mapp* plays a role in the process of negotiation, reduction of sentence rather than acquittal is the common result. As I have argued, this hardly seems optimal for fostering police observance of the Fourth Amendment. By the same token, however, it is not quite the same social price as the outright dismissal of all charges pending against a guilty defendant. That the Court believes implicitly that dismissal or acquittal is the practical result of the exclusionary rule indicates again that the Justices think in terms of the trial model of criminal practice, despite the fact that the overwhelming majority of cases are resolved without trial.

There are, of course, powerful forces working against the efficacy of the exclusionary rule, forces that help explain its partial and variable effects on police behavior. I have reviewed a number of them: ignorance of Fourth Amendment rules on the part of police, bar, and bench; police use of enforcement techniques that do not culminate in prosecution; the hostility toward *Mapp* on the part of trial judges, who sometimes seem ready to find searches lawful whenever possible (together with police perjury, which sometimes provides a factual foundation for such favorable judicial decisions); and the fact that the legality of many searches is never determined authoritatively and decisively, either by judges or prosecutors, even in cases which result in prosecutions, because of the prevalence of guilty pleas.

Most of these conditions do not lend themselves readily to sweeping change. Concerted efforts might be made to reduce the level of ignorance about the Fourth Amendment, and particularly to utilize prosecutors to inform the police on such matters. Police perjury, too, might be controlled somewhat, although it would prove very difficult to eliminate it altogether. Widespread judicial hostility seems, for the most part, to inhere in the composition and situation of criminal trial courts. The injection of Fourth Amendment issues into the process of plea bargaining, which probably dilutes the deterrent effect of *Mapp*, might be limited. In enforcing the Fourth Amendment, the federal courts might well insist on the availability of some pre-trial suppression procedure and might even require a particular brand of suppression procedure, such as Chicago's early motion practice, that would tend to keep search-and-seizure issues out of the plea-bargaining process.[93] On this score, the reexamination of the *Calandra* grand-jury exception to the exclusionary rule is clearly in order. Not only does *Calandra* facilitate the resolution of Fourth Amendment issues by plea bargaining; it also adds a confusing element of inconsistency to the enforcement of the exclusionary rule. The inconsistency is likely to convey to police officers exactly what it reflects: judicial ambivalence about the exclusionary rule. Abandonment of *Calandra* would fortify the willpower of prosecutors already disposed not to charge in cases involving unlawful searches. Through all of these means, marginal improvements in the efficacy of the exclusionary rule might be achieved, but sweeping improvements seem doubtful.

If this assessment is correct, then, for the present, appraisal of *Mapp*'s success still depnds on varying interpretations of the purposes of the exclusionary rule. Viewed modestly, as an attempt to add judicial influence to the struggle for police legality, for whatever positive results that will bring, *Mapp* cannot be stamped a failure, for it does seem to have brought positive results. Viewed maximally, as a decisive intervention that will bring police behavior into conformity with the Constitution, *Mapp*, as I have said, disappoints. But that is mainly a reflection of the unrealistic character of the maximal view. The judicially fashioned rule of exclusion turns out to be only one of many influences and pressures on police behavior. Perhaps this is an unstartling conclusion, but it may not be altogether obvious. In view of the monopoly position of the courts in the processing of criminals, the view that judicial cooperation might be conditioned on police observance of the Constitution appears quite compelling in the abstract.

Yet, as a strategy to compel observance of judicially enunciated rules, denial of the criminal sanction to nonobservant police officers has a number of practical weaknesses. Knowledge of the rules cannot be taken for granted. Incentives to obey the rules once known are not invariably present; or, to turn it around, the courts' position in the processing of criminals is less than a monopoly when enforcement techniques other than prosecution are considered. To a considerable extent, the police *are* a dependent bureaucracy—that is, one that needs judicial cooperation—but the extent to which they are in this position is far less than complete.

93. Cf. *Jackson* v. *Denno,* 378 U.S. 368 (1964).

As *Gault* also showed, the collaboration of lower courts can be less than perfect. Nor is this merely a comment on outright resistance to particular decisions. Procedural differences in various court systems around the country and in the operations of prosecutors' offices affect just how *Mapp* is enforced, apart from whether attitudes are favorable toward *Mapp* or not. The Court in *Mapp* assumed it was announcing a uniform national rule. Much of the debate over whether the guarantees of the Bill of Rights, including the Fourth Amendment, should be applied against the states—and, if so, just how—has revolved around the appropriateness of imposing a single standard across the country. The evidence shows this in some ways to have been a highly academic debate. The uniform rule turns out to be enforced quite differently by the courts of various localities—a fact that may help to explain the finding that *Mapp*'s effects on the police have also been uneven from city to city. Diverse local conditions of several kinds have profoundly affected the implementation of the supposedly uniform national rule.

Mapp was also framed with only formal criminal-justice processes in mind. The Supreme Court has continually assumed the existence of a functioning institutional substructure of lower criminal courts disposing of cases by trial. In fact, however, a cogent case can be made that *Mapp*'s principal effect was not felt in the courtroom but in the corridors, where the exclusionary rule often altered the structure of informal relations between prosecutors and defense counsel.

There are, no doubt, times when courts formulating rules of law must pay heed only to formal, manifest, and legitimate processes, ignoring the informal practices that grow up around them. But in framing a rule calculated to affect behavior that is itself outside the realm of the formal, manifest, legitimate processes, it is hazardous to proceed without prior knowledge of at least the principal links between formal institutions and the behavior to be affected.

The *Mapp* experience can thus be summarized in terms of three dichotomous themes: the monopoly position of the courts in granting convictions versus the plurality of police objectives; the enunciation of uniform rules implemented in a non-uniform fashion; and the emphasis on formal institutions and procedures in a field rampant with informal arrangements. *Mapp* exemplifies the judicial propensity to see things whole and homogeneous, when in fact they are fragmented and heterogeneous.

CHAPTER SEVEN

Judicial Capacity Appraised

The problems of vision, the problems of information, the problems of management and control that emerge from the four case studies just reviewed are of considerable magnitude. No doubt the *Area-Wide Council* case is the most extreme instance of failure in judicial policymaking. Uninformed by an understanding of the relation of Model Cities to Community Action or of the place of the Philadelphia controversy in the nationwide Model Cities experience, unable to see the Philadelphia dispute in its social context, overtaken by events on the ground, uninfluential with decisionmakers elsewhere, the *Area-Wide Council* decisions were redeemed in the end only by the good intentions of the judges and their good sense in bowing at last to political forces they could not overcome. The other cases were somewhat less fluid and somewhat easier to fasten a hold on. Yet no problem turned out to be quite what it seemed, and no decision accomplished exactly what was intended. Amendment from the judgment seat may not always be confusion, but it does indeed seem to be heir to the perils of prophecy and to a number of other hazards as well.

Armed with illustrative material, we are now in a position to take a second look at some of the attributes of adjudication as they have manifested themselves in the case studies.

Summing Up: Limitations of Litigation

When we begin to look at the four case studies against the general picture of adjudication painted in chapter 2, what comes most prominently to mind is the contrast between the broad sweep of the decisions

255

and the narrow framework within which they were rendered. *Mapp*
quite self-consciously laid down new limits for the police. *Gault* installed
a new regime for juvenile courts. *Hobson* set new standards for measuring allocative decisions in education. The *Area-Wide Council* decisions
chose one conception of the Model Cities program over another. Yet,
in each case, the lawyer's customary search for "the controlling issue"
led the court to a view of the case, put in terms of the rights of the
parties, that was significantly narrower than the innovation the decision
actually imposed. In the *Area-Wide Council* case, it was whether there
was a "right to participate" in changes of "basic strategy." In *Gault*, it
was whether a juvenile charged with conduct that rendered him liable
to be committed to an institution was to be accorded counsel, notice of
the charges, the privilege against self-incrimination, and the right to
confront adverse witnesses. *Hobson II* dealt with the issues in the nar-
rowest framework of all, by leaving aside resources already equally
distributed and resources subject to economies of scale or otherwise
beyond the control of the school system, and zeroing in only on teachers' salaries per pupil. All of the opinions spoke exclusively of "rights."
Only *Mapp* adverted to alternatives, and these it dismissed as ineffective
to achieve police compliance with the Fourth Amendment.

These narrow formulations generally omitted any explicit consideration of costs. In *Hobson*, the anticipated costs in terms of annual disruption due to teacher transfers in the midst of the school year played
no part in the decision. In fact, the court had no data on the rate of
enrollment changes in schools across the District of Columbia, although,
after the first wave of transfers, enrollment changes were a prime determinant of the per-pupil allocation of teachers' salaries and therefore
of the extent of disruption.

Gault and *Mapp* did obliquely advert to the costs of the decision, in
interesting ways. *Gault* turned a potential cost of the adversary regime
it imposed into a benefit. The opinion took note of social science "findings" that adversary proceedings were conducive to rehabilitation and
on this basis concluded that some good might result from the decision.
The Court seemed eager to have this reassurance, but it seems safe to
say that contrary findings would not have changed the result.

In *Mapp*, the potential costs of the decision were viewed in the most
direct terms. The fear was that some criminals might go unpunished
because of the exclusionary rule, and the Supreme Court's response was
that this was an acceptable price to pay for insuring the integrity of the

judicial process, whatever the benefits in terms of altered police behavior might be. There was no consideration of costs measured in terms of the incentives *Mapp* created for police officers to engage in unlawful behavior beyond the reach of the exclusionary rule. Only much later did these potential secondary costs, especially harassment of suspects in lieu of prosecution, come to the Court's attention. (In general, they have reinforced the determination of those Justices who doubt the efficacy of *Mapp*'s deterrent impact to cut back on the scope of the exclusionary rule without abandoning it entirely.) The realization of the existence of these potential costs was delayed by about a decade. Equally important, no serious assessment has yet been made of the number of criminals who in fact go unpunished because of the exclusionary rule. As discussed in chapter 6, because of plea bargaining there is reason to believe that *Mapp* results in reduced sentences more often than in no punishment at all.

In all, these cases suggest that the judicial process is a poor format for the weighing of alternatives and the calculation of costs. This is very much what was anticipated in chapter 2.

I also advanced the proposition in chapter 2 that the courts' function of declaring rights and duties did not generally encompass exercises of the power to tax and spend. Yet judicial decisions that allocate governmental resources often affect the composition of the budget. The only such allocative decision in these cases is *Hobson II*, which required adjustments in per-pupil expenditures on teachers' salaries. These adjustments were made by the transfer of teachers from advantaged to disadvantaged schools, rather than by the hiring of new teachers for the disadvantaged schools.

What this means in practice is that *Hobson II* decreed a redivision of a constant pie or, to put it differently, a leveling down. Short of finding that absolute minimal standards were not being met at the disadvantaged schools, it is difficult to see how the decree could have required new spending on teacher services. Under the Equal Protection Clause, all that is required is a fair distribution of resources the system has chosen to distribute, not the creation of new resources. By themselves, the courts are generally confined to redistribution and are unable to effect an expansion of budgetary resources.

Had the issue of equalization arisen in the legislative rather than the judicial forum, there would have been no such constraint. Indeed, resistance to redistribution might have been quickly and effectively manifested, and the issue might have been resolved by a leveling up. At all events, the choice of the judicial forum restricted the range of possible outcomes. It is also true, however, that the judiciary tends to be far more sensitive to claims grounded in equal protection and therefore more willing to order leveling of any kind.

Of course, judicial decisions that are nominally redistributive can put pressure on the other branches to implement them by expansive exercises of the spending power. This is especially likely if a court finds a failure to meet minimum standards, not just an inequitable distribution above the minimum. This accounts for the considerable increase in state spending that followed the laying down of minimum standards of care prescribed for Alabama mental hospitals.[1]

From this standpoint, it takes no great imagination to sense the bureaucratic temptation to manipulate the courts into ordering changes that will have the effect of expanding bureaucratic budgets. Such temptations may have been present in one case that arose in the District of Columbia, and it is worth pursuing it here briefly for the light the case sheds on the relation between decision forum and decision outcome.

The case is *Mills* v. *Board of Education*,[2] in which a federal district court ordered officials of the District of Columbia government and school system to provide education geared to the needs of pupils theretofore excluded from the schools because they constituted severe behavior problems, or were emotionally disturbed, retarded, or hyperactive. The court declared that there was a right to education and that pupils who could profit from special instruction were entitled to it, whether that involved special education programs within the public schools or tuition grants for outside placement.

Needless to say, the foremost obstacle to implementing this decision proved to be budgetary. The court explicitly rejected shortage of funds as an excuse for total failure to educate handicapped or disturbed children, saying in effect that, if new funds could not be obtained, then existing funds would have to be redistributed.[3]

When the case was initially decided, the school system was prepared to enter into a consent decree with the plaintiffs, acknowledging the violations and providing a remedy. This agreement was thwarted by

1. See chapter 1, p. 6.
2. 348 F. Supp. 866 (D.D.C. 1972).
3. Ibid. at 876.

other city officials reluctant to assume financial responsibility. There is a hint that the willingness of the school officials to enter into a consent decree was based on their hope of obtaining additionally budgeted funds to meet the requirements of the decree.

As things turned out, this hope was dashed, largely by the attitude of the city government, which took essentially the position that, since school enrollments were declining, the schools could fund these special programs out of their existing budget. But while enrollments were declining, school programs were still expanding (moving, for example, from half- to full-day kindergartens), and so the budget had little slack. The Department of Human Resources, for its part, refused to acknowledge financial responsibility for the special education of any pupils except those few who had been declared wards of the court.

This left the school system in exactly the position envisaged by the court: it had to redistribute existing funds, and that is what it did.[4] It abolished certain other special programs in order to absorb the new burdens it had to assume. It also made a virtue of necessity, arguing that the best way to handle all but the most severe problem pupils was by what is called mainstreaming, that is, keeping them in regular classes wherever possible. In fact, there was little choice, for the funds did not exist to adopt alternative modes of placement on a large scale.[5]

The court thus forced the school system to restructure its budgetary priorities. Whatever the initial expectations were about using the decree to force additional budget allocations, those responsible for appropriation requests and action failed to cooperate. *Hobson* does not stand alone as an illustration of judicially ordered leveling down.[6]

I suggested in chapter 2 that, in defining rights, the judicial process is

4. It should be added, however, that a change of school administrations took place during this period, and the new administration proved less committed to and less adept at pushing for additional funds for special education than its predecessor had.

5. I have relied for these conclusions on three main sources: interviews with many of the leading participants, documents filed with the court, and additional documents and records provided by school officials and their lawyers.

6. Still another illustration is provided by the New Orleans jail litigation. In 1970, conditions at the jail were found unconstitutional, and in 1972 it was ordered closed, on the implicit assumption that a new jail would be built. Years later, the same jail was still being used, though some changes in food handling and hospital care had been made. See *Hamilton v. Schiro*, 338 F. Supp. 1016 (E.D. La. 1970), *further relief ordered sub nom. Hamilton v. Landrieu*, 351 F. Supp. 549 (1972).

prone to carve up related transactions and to treat as separate those events and relationships that are intertwined in social life.

Two of the cases illustrate this point rather graphically. In *Hobson*, as I have emphasized, the process of narrowing the issues led the court to frame a decree that affected only a few resources. It is interesting to contrast this with the Office of Education regulations under Title I, which required the equalization of each element in the total resource mix. The Supreme Court's handling of the exclusionary rule exemplifies this aspect of piecemeal decisionmaking more dramatically. *Mapp* held that illegally obtained evidence was inadmissible in state criminal trials. Well over a decade later, however, *Calandra* held illegally obtained evidence to be admissible in grand jury proceedings. In *Calandra*, the Court, majority and minority alike, treated the grand jury question as if it had no relationship to the trial question, as, indeed, formally it does not. In practice, however, as I have argued, both are part of an entire criminal prosecution process; conviction often occurs after guilty pleas are entered following indictment by grand jury. In the light of the prevalence of plea bargaining, it is artificial to regard trials and convictions as being one part of the criminal justice process and grand jury proceedings and indictment as being another, quite severable part. The deterrent objectives of the exclusionary rule are affected by both parts. But the case-by-case character of adjudication makes it difficult for the courts to see such interrelationships.

In chapter 2, in considering the way in which the piecemeal nature of adjudication fragments what is merged, I neglected to consider the opposite possibility—that adjudication might also merge what is fragmented. This it does, too, because of the limited capacity the courts have for sensing the relevance of social facts and for ascertaining them.

In each of the four cases, the courts assumed that they were dealing with homogeneous environments, or at least they had no inkling to the contrary. We saw in some detail that, unbeknownst to the court, the Philadelphia pattern of citizen participation was only one of several; that, in equalizing per-pupil expenditures on teachers' salaries, *Hobson* ignored the existence and differential status of two categories of teachers; that *Gault* took no note of the divergent styles of juvenile courts and of the lawyers who functioned in them; and, most prominent of all, that *Mapp* and *Calandra* assumed, not only the uniformity of police forces but of judicial modes of enforcing the exclusionary rule, when in fact there are three distinct ways in which such a rule might be enforced, each with its own likely consequences for police behavior. The courts recurrently assume—and are given no information that would lead them not to assume—that they are working with more or less uniform situations for which a single rule will suffice.[7] The problem is to frame the right rule. Repeatedly, however, the situations turn out to be diverse rather than uniform, and the single rule often operates perversely and disparately for just such reasons. This is perhaps the most striking of all the conclusions, and one of the most important since it relates the process of judicial decisions to their outcomes.

Courts make, interpret, and expound law. Given their position in the institutional system, it is neither surprising nor illegitimate that the courts have a built-in emphasis on formal, manifest relationships, on those specified, for instance, in the Model Cities Act and the guidelines issued by the Department of Housing and Urban Development, in juvenile codes and codes of criminal procedure. Inevitably, much of the material required for expounding law is itself legal material, such as statutes and regulations. Moreover, the divergent patterns of informal relations that spring up around formal structures are not adequately reflected in those legal materials. Though the informal ethos and networks of relationships that exist in, say, juvenile court vary widely from one such court to another, the specified, formal functions of juvenile courts vary very little. Consequently, the bias of the judicial process for formal, manifest relationships leads the courts systematically to neglect or underemphasize the diversity that exists just below the surface of formal relationships. The more congruent informal patterns of behavior are with formal structures, the more accurate will be the courts' view of the facts. Unfortunately, however, such congruence can never be taken for granted. In all four cases, a misleading uniformity of the target institutions was conveyed by the formal materials.

How far the courts should or can go beyond the formal materials of decision in the search for an accurate and whole view of the relevant social milieu admits of no easy answer. But it insistently demands an

7. I might go even further and suggest also that courts tend to prefer single-factor explanations for the behavior they must review. The *Hobson* court, for example, rejected all explanations for longevity pay except the presumed greater productivity of more experienced teachers. See chapter 4, n. 138 and accompanying text. The court's perspective on the recruitment and retention of teachers was significantly more narrow than the perspective of those who must manage school systems. It may well be that the adjudicative format fosters this kind of constriction of managerial considerations. It certainly encourages the simplification of heterogeneity.

attempt, which I shall make in the next section, at least by highlighting some of the difficulties of social science inquiry in a legal setting. This much is clear, even now: on the one hand, the piecemeal character of adjudication tends to distort social facts in the direction of isolating related phenomena; on the other hand, the emphasis on the individual litigants' case and the reliance on formal rather than behavioral materials both distort social facts in the direction of a usually fictitious uniformity. *Mapp* and *Calandra* show that both of these distortions can be present at the same time.

The lack of attention to consequential facts that we identified in chapter 2 as a characteristic of the judicial process is easily documented in these four cases. The courts tended to devote much more attention to the nature of the ailment they had diagnosed than to the workings of the cure they had prescribed. When they looked forward, they concentrated on ends rather than means, on benefits rather than costs, and on first-order consequences rather than second-order consequences. They were forward-looking only within a very restricted range.

When the issue before a court is framed narrowly in terms of rights, a subtle adjustment of the judicial lens takes place. To focus on rights is to highlight the proposed innovation and to blur into the background the character of the receptacle for that innovation. In *Gault*, the Court ignored the juvenile-court environment in which counsel was to function. In the *Area-Wide Council* case, the court defined the issue to be whether HUD had violated the Model Cities Act by eliciting and approving changes in Philadelphia's plans without citizen participation. This focus pushed aside the competitive dimension of the Philadelphia dispute, which determined whether the violation the court found could ultimately be corrected. Similarly, in *Hobson*, the court declared the existence of a right quite apart from the incentives the school system had to implement it in one way rather than another. Finally, in *Mapp*, the Court sensed the problematic character of police compliance, but took it completely for granted that lower courts would exclude illegally obtained evidence from criminal trials. All four courts ignored the milieux in which their decisions were destined to be put into action, and all four were therefore at the mercy of the forces that came into play following their decisions.

Only the court in *Hobson I* made a determined attempt to relate the requirements of the decision to the effects it sought. The court believed that per-pupil equalization of expenditures on teachers' salaries and benefits would occur as a secondary consequence of the faculty integration and pupil busing that was part of its order. As we saw, this calculation failed to take into account the school system's ability to achieve faculty integration without mass teacher transfers and the quite limited extent of busing that resulted from the first decision. In other words, a deliberate and straightforward calculation was upset by forces that, while not particularly complex, were beyond the reach and beyond the anticipation of the court. This miscalculation took four years to rectify. In *Hobson II*, the court moved from a strategy of indirect equalization to direct equalization. But again, its best estimate of likely consequences took no account of the differences between classroom and resource teachers, especially the lesser standing of the latter with school administrators, principals, the collective bargaining agreement, and the teachers' union. The decree also affected only regularly budgeted funds, and thus created incentives for principals eager to keep resource teachers to fund resource programs outside the regular budget, as well as to boost enrollments. Each calculation the court made was subject to deflection.

Further, the attention Judge Wright devoted to gauging probable effects was directed entirely to anticipated benefits. Compliance costs were never addressed once the court settled on its formulation of rights under the Equal Protection Clause. Costs, in terms of both disruption due to mid-year teacher transfers and the disregard of educational program criteria in favor of equalizing dollar values, later proved to be significant.

Finally, three of the four decisions had second-order consequences. For example, *Hobson II* increased the amount of the school system's data about and understanding of itself; it militated against local hiring in community schools; it exacerbated frictions between the school board and superintendent. *Mapp* had effects on the apportionment of work among certain police units; it seems to have helped routinize police perjury and harassment of suspects who cannot be convicted consistent with the exclusionary rule. *Gault* aided the movements toward persons-in-need-of-supervision laws and diversion, and may have altered the composition of the delinquency docket of juvenile courts. Only the *Area-Wide Council* decisions seem to have had no secondary effects, largely because they had few, if any, primary effects.

Some of these consequences might be regarded as beneficial, some as harmful. All of them would be difficult to foresee and control in any event. But, so far as can be judged, no court was sensitized to the probability that they would occur.

The record suggests that the courts are better equipped with machinery to discover the past than to forecast the future. Plainly, they spend more time apportioning responsibility for violations of law than planning for a new regime of conformity to the law they fashion.

That, at least, is the situation in prospect, when the decision is rendered. But what is it in retrospect, after the effects have been felt? Is there the possibility of corrective action to insure results that are wanted and filter out those that are not?

The four cases make plain the impotence of the courts to supervise the implementation of their decrees, their impatience with protracted litigation, and their limited ability to monitor the consequences of their action. Called upon increasingly to perform administrative functions because they are not burdened with administrative rigidities, the courts are also not blessed with administrative capabilities.

Virtually no supervision or policy review occurred after *Gault* was decided. The implementation of the decision was left to the juvenile courts, and the Supreme Court received no feedback about what the decision meant in practice. Follow-up litigation concentrated on new constitutional issues raised by juvenile court proceedings, rather than refinements on *Gault* that might have provided the Court with impact information.

The Court only slowly and dimly became aware of some of *Mapp's* consequences. As additional search-and-seizure cases found their way to the Supreme Court, the Justices' doubts grew about the ability of the exclusionary rule to deter police misconduct, as did their sensitivity to the possible side effects of the rule. But the information was fragmentary, it came late, and it did not extend to such matters as the role of the exclusionary rule in prosecutorial discretion or plea bargaining. What feedback was received was attributable to the recurrent character of Fourth Amendment issues, compared to the much less frequent appeals that characterize juvenile court proceedings.

Much more impact information found its way back to the lower courts that decided the *Hobson* and *Area-Wide Council* cases. These cases kept bouncing back to court, each time updating the courts on the consequences of their decisions. If generalized, this suggests, paradoxically, that the lower the court, the less authoritative the decision, and the narrower the impact, the greater will be the impact information received by the court to enable it to make corrective adjustments. But it must be added that in both of these instances the cases came back only because the victorious but dissatisfied litigants brought them back, and then not for general policy review but for review of the impact of the decisions solely on the parties to them.

The *Area-Wide Council* case, of course, was in the court of appeals three times, and on the final occasion the court backtracked in the light of events that had transpired on the ground. This change of direction was facilitated by the fact that three totally different panels of judges heard the three appeals. The panel that heard the third appeal was thus not emotionally committed to an earlier decision that did not work out. While the third panel pretended to consistency with the earlier decisions, it still tacitly admitted the existence of a fait accompli. The random assignment and rotation of judges does seem to make policy review easier.

The *Hobson* case returned to court for recalibration of the remedy in the light of the ineffectiveness of the remedy devised in the first instance. The revised remedy then passed through several organizational sieves on its way to the classroom, producing a result of which the litigants did not approve but which they tolerated rather than returning again to court.

In both cases, the return to court provided the courts with consequential facts that enabled them to conduct a limited policy review, but in neither was there anything like the continuing supervision that an administrative agency might provide. Four years passed between *Hobson I* and *Hobson II*, and the court knew precious little in the interim about the effects of its decree. The review that the court conducted in the *Area-Wide Council* case was, in fact, required because of its inability to monitor and supervise the implementation of its earlier decision. In its third decision, the court of appeals bowed to the consequences of its very failure to make its will effective. Intermittent intervention to review what *has* happened is not the same thing as continuing supervision to shape what *will* happen.

Furthermore, as the courts lack the manpower and the will to administer their decrees, so do they tire quickly of even the responsibilities that periodic review entails. It will be recalled that Judge Wright, for all of his energy and perseverance through *Hobson I*, was reluctant to sit in *Hobson II*. The court of appeals opened the third *Area-Wide Council* opinion with an expression of its weariness with a case whose end was "nowhere in sight." (In the *Mills* case, too, the court has often expressed its impatience with the drawn-out character of the proceedings.) Cases requiring repeated intervention quickly wear out their welcome in court.

This should not be surprising. Judges are not recruited for their managerial interest or aptitude, and they often have little tolerance for administrative detail. The broad scope of their dockets leads them to eschew excessive investment in learning more than they care to know (and more than they can use in later cases) about Model Cities or educational production functions or, for that matter, hospital administration or welfare payments.

Despite this, the recurrent character of the *Hobson* and *Area-Wide Council* cases is still encouraging for another reason. *Hobson* came back to court for recalibration of the remedy because the court's initial order required the school system to do something, rather than refrain from doing something. The same was true of the *Area-Wide Council* decisions. I have argued that it is in the area of requiring affirmative conduct that the courts' capacities for forecasting and monitoring are most severely taxed. Yet, in these two cases, the courts were at least eventually apprised of what followed their decisions, and in one of them (*Hobson*) the court was in a position to take at least some corrective action. The courts may be deficient in administrative machinery, but they may not be quite as impotent to readjust their previous decisions in the light of impact facts as we perhaps supposed. Much, of course, depends on the fluidity of the situation with which the court is dealing. On this score, *Hobson* was easier to grasp hold of than was the *Area-Wide Council* case.

One of the most difficult problems faced by the courts is judging how representative the cases before them are. All four cases appear to have been somewhat extreme in ways likely to induce judicial action. In *Hobson*, the questions of unintentional discrimination were resolved against a background of de jure segregation. The changes ordered by HUD in the Philadelphia Model Cities program were made without even a semblance of consultation with the Area-Wide Council. The warrantless search of Miss Mapp's premises was particularly needless and offensive, and the officers who made it pretended they had a warrant. Most egregious of all, Gerald Gault received a six-year maximum commitment for a lewd phone call that it is not wholly certain he made, that commitment ordered without any inquiry into alternatives to committing him. All of these cases had something special about them, but all were the vehicles for general lawmaking.

No doubt there is something to be said, in terms of building public support, for making law from egregious cases. Controversial, innovative decisions are more easily justified when they spring from extreme circumstances. On the other hand, general law made from exceptional cases is not likely to be accorded much legitimacy by the knowledgeable bureaucrats and specialists who sense that the court was misled by unrepresentative cases.

This was certainly true of *Gault*, which better-informed lower courts knew to be atypical of the run of juvenile cases. In Providence and Portland, most juvenile court judges and intake officers expressed "some misgivings about the scope of the [*Gault*] decision, particularly about what some see as the Supreme Court's 'overreaction' to a particularly sordid—and unrepresentative—juvenile case."[8]

The choice of an egregious case as a vehicle for innovation is dangerous, too, because it distorts the dimensions of the problem before the court. Occasionally, but not often, courts have sensed this. For more than a year before the Court decided *Miranda* v. *Arizona*, the Clerk of the Supreme Court

had been marking certain appeals with the initials "E.C.," to indicate that they were to be held until some future time. By November 22, 1965, approximately 140 appeals had been marked "E.C." and held—including *Miranda* v. *Arizona* and the three other petitions for certiorari that were granted that evening. The code "E.C." meant that they were "Escobedo Cases," and the Court's announcement that it would hear them meant that it would finally deal with the criminal justice problem that had haunted the Supreme Court for decades—confessions.[9]

The Court was about to lay down a "broad legislative code to cover future police conduct," and the four cases it settled on were "as representative of police interrogation situations as *Escobedo* had been unique."[10] Or, at least, so the Court intended.

Plainly, these were exceptional measures made possible because the

---

8. Richard J. Maiman, "Private Attorneys in Juvenile Court: The Impact of *In re Gault*" (paper prepared for delivery at the 1974 annual meeting of the American Political Science Association; processed), p. 3. See also Bradley C. Canon, "Organizational Contumacy and the Transmission of Judicial Policies: The *Mapp, Escobedo, Miranda* and *Gault* Cases," *Villanova Law Review*, vol. 20 (November 1974), pp. 50–79.

9. Fred P. Graham, *The Self-Inflicted Wound* (Macmillan, 1970), p. 154.

10. Ibid., pp. 155, 156.

Court had already decided to elaborate on *Escobedo* and the abundance of confession cases allowed it to pick and choose a spectrum of police behavior to work with. But it is an unusual, rarely replicable, and at bottom primitive way of attempting to gain a representative view of the problem. Most of the time, litigants rather than courts do the steering, and the judges have no way of knowing whether they have before them a balanced or a distorted view of the landscape.

Indeed, the question of representativeness rarely occurs to them, for the traditional function of courts, to make law out of concrete cases, rendered the question of representativeness far less important than it has become over the last twenty or so years. When they do sense an issue of representativeness, their epistemological framework leads them to repair to legal sources: does the law allow what has happened to happen? If it does, then a general legal corrective may be required.

This was the technique of verification employed by the Supreme Court in *Gault*. The Court saw that Gerald Gault had been harshly treated. But it did not ask: "How often does this happen?" Instead it asked: "Does Arizona's juvenile code permit this to happen?"

This is a misleading technique. That certain conduct may occur under a given law and that it has occurred constitute no assurance that such conduct is recurrent, not to mention typical. Furthermore, to infer behavioral facts from sources of law is, as I have suggested earlier, to bias the findings in favor of the uniformity that tends to characterize the statute books and to suppress the diversity that tends to characterize actual behavior.

One case at a time, then, is hardly an optimal mode of general decisionmaking. The facts of a "leading case" may lead nowhere, for the case may not even have a twin in the realm of behavior from which it emerges. In the end, knowing everything about the instant case is no substitute for knowing something about the run of cases. The dangers of egregious cases are the dangers of parochialism.

This generally discouraging picture—itself drawn from only four cases—leads us to inquire whether some policy areas, some kinds of issues, or some target institutions are more promising candidates for judicial intervention than others.

The *Area-Wide Council* case was an exceptional example of judicial inefficacy, but it contains some unexceptional lessons. Social programs like the Model Cities program are unusually poor candidates for judicial participation. They are likely to set in motion political forces that do not stand still long enough for courts to fasten a hold on them. The administrative and political contexts of the program are likely to be both complex and unfamiliar to the courts. Especially if the program constitutes a new or experimental approach to a social problem, prior case law and experience will furnish no guide.

The sources of law in social programs will be highly specific legislation, regulations, and local arrangements, all of which combine to give life to the programs. Courts are not good interpreters of such mixes. The fact that in the *Area-Wide Council* case the court of appeals was unaware of the "maximum feasible participation" provision of the Community Action program is a reflection of the secondary role that statutory law still plays at this late date in the development of the common law system. The starting point of legal reasoning—the place to look for analogies and standards—continues to be prior judicial decision. It is inconceivable that the court should have been unaware of a judicial opinion that had laid down a citizen participation standard so closely related to the standard at issue in the Model Cities program. But because the standard was in another statute, it was not called to the court's attention. This kind of omission is likely to recur in social program litigation.

If, in addition to the unfamiliarity of the program and the location of analogies and related standards, the program has a limited duration, as Model Cities did, it is especially unamenable to judicial participation in shaping it. It takes time for conflicts to crystallize into litigation and for lawsuits to be decided and appealed. By the time a final decision is rendered, the relevant actors may have "struck their deals," as they did in Model Cities programs across the country.

Gault suggests another negative conclusion. *Gault* purported to be a purely procedural decision, laying down the requirements of procedural due process for juvenile proceedings. Lawyers and judges, as I said in chapter 2, are masters of procedure. For that reason, procedural innovations might carry less risk for the courts than substantive innovations. Their expertise in tailoring a procedure to a problem and in limiting the impact of procedural requirements should give them greater ability to steer toward intended effects and away from unintended ones.

This proves a highly dubious proposition when the procedure the courts are revising is not their own but that of some other courts. *Gault's* procedural reforms spurred substantive effects, and even the purely procedural side of the decision did not work out according to plan.

One of the reasons this was so is that the Court in *Gault*, as in *Mapp*, entertained an idealized image of trial courts and trial lawyers. It acted as if juvenile and criminal cases are disposed of by adversary proceedings, by full-fledged trials. Trials of course occur, and the possibility of a trial affects other modes of disposing of cases. But it is not enough to make law for all cases as if all cases come to trial.

Because *Gault* and *Mapp* involved areas close to the experience of the courts, the Justices' familiarity might be presumed an asset. But it does not seem to have been helpful. Not only is the idealized adversary image of trial courts at odds with practice, but commitment to the adversary mode of resolution as an ideal seems to be far greater among appellate judges than among juvenile and state criminal trial judges. The enthusiastic collaboration of lower courts in efforts to make their proceedings more adversary or more regular in other ways cannot be taken for granted. *Gault* and *Mapp* together suggest that even well-traveled paths have their stones.

If social programs are poor candidates for judicial intervention, if purely procedural reforms are as apt as substantive changes to go astray, if familiar "legal" terrain can prove hazardous, then what can be said about redistributive and allocative judicial decisions? *Hobson*, of course, was such a decision, and it suggests three problems that may often attend such efforts.

The first I have already discussed. The allocation of resources puts the courts deep into budgeting decisions, with no assurance that additional expenditure will be forthcoming. There is reason to believe that judicial leveling will tend to be leveling down rather than up.

Second, a considerable investment of judicial resources is likely to be spent adjusting and readjusting, allocating and reallocating. This will be particularly likely if indeed the decision is not followed by an infusion of new money, for then the school authorities or the hospital authorities or whatever authorities are involved, still committed to the former distribution, seek to comply with the initial decree in ways that affect their program priorities only marginally. From the court's standpoint, this kind of implementation may not be adequate. Hence the need to recalibrate the decree periodically. At the end of a succession of time-consuming readjustments, the court and the parties may wonder whether the investment was justified by the return.

Third, their doubts on this score may be reinforced by the neglect of qualitative criteria of performance—in *Hobson*, considerations of educational program—in favor of quantitative criteria. The seemingly perverse way in which reallocation often takes place may also affect organizational morale adversely, as it surely did in *Hobson*.

Courts seem less able to cope flexibly with these problems by trading off quantitative against qualitative values than administrators are likely to be. And if *Hobson II* is any guide, the scope of the resources to be redistributed may make sense only when viewed in terms of the litigation process that brought it about.

Finally, a word about target populations. The proximity of a target population to the courts is no guarantee of faithful effectuation of court orders. The juvenile court officials subject to *Gault* were as proximate and as accustomed to living with legal requirements as any are likely to be. That did not prevent them from conceiving of their mission in rehabilitative terms and of seeing the relation of rehabilitation to courtroom procedure in a way diametrically opposed to the way the Supreme Court saw it. Much the same could be said regarding lower court reactions to *Mapp*.

The dependence of the target organization on the court for the success of its mission may be another matter. The Supreme Court in *Mapp* adopted the strategy of conditional cooperation on the assumption that the police were indeed dependent. The assumption proved only partially true. Some police forces and units emphasize law enforcement and securing convictions more than the maintenance of order, some less. But all place some emphasis on convictions, and to that extent tend to be amenable to the incentives of the conditional cooperation strategy. *Mapp* suggests that a court should not readily assume that a bureaucracy is as dependent on judicial cooperation as its formal mission seems to make it. But if a bureaucracy is dependent, or partially so, as the police are, it may respond to a change of the terms on which judicial cooperation will be forthcoming.

Mapp is also informative about the number of target populations to which court decrees apply. Although the Court did not sense this, *Mapp* involved not one but two sets of targets: the police and the lower state courts. This double filtration system, as it were, greatly complicated and refracted the effectuation of the decision. The attainment of the Court's goal was dependent on the relative emphasis the particular police force accorded to securing convictions, discounted by its continuing ability to secure them or to secure equivalent punishment without complying with Fourth Amendment requirements. But this depiction of police behavior was itself in part a function of prosecutorial and judicial enforcement of *Mapp*. Two otherwise similarly disposed police forces might be differently affected by *Mapp* if in one city the exclusionary rule were usually enforced through adjudication of suppression motions while in the other city the rule were enforced by the reduction of sentences during plea bargaining. In other words, the number of possible outcomes of *Mapp* was a complicated product of the interaction of "raw" police incentives with modes of judicial enforcement. Under these circumstances, the fragmented and partial quality of *Mapp's* effects can readily be understood.

The *Mills* case, which was discussed earlier, reinforces the conclusion that two target populations are likely to be far more difficult to manage than one. The plaintiffs in *Mills* obtained an order against officials of the school system and of the District of Columbia Department of Human Resources. The school system acknowledged responsibility for those pupils who could be placed in non-residential school programs. The DHR assumed its customary responsibility for those children who had been declared wards of the court. This left uncertain the status of children who were not wards of the court but who required residential care. Neither the DHR nor the school system believed it should pay for their expenses. Before the decree was rendered, these children were either in programs unsuited to their needs, or were placed in private facilities by their parents, or were receiving no education at all.

On this issue, the two bureaucracies reached stalemate. At one point, the school system even attempted, unsuccessfully, to bill the DHR for the costs of residential care. Supported by the mayor, the DHR asserted that compliance with the decree was primarily a matter for the school system and was not the citywide problem school officials had tried to make it. Caught on this bitter dispute, implementation of the decree lagged. The plaintiffs periodically brought the case back to court, and the court found itself in the position of umpire in an interdepartmental battle, a position it was unwilling to assume. Finally, the two bureaucracies came to terms after the defendants had been found in contempt of court. But the terms were in fact a victory for the DHR,[11] and what that meant was that school resources were not to be augmented from outside despite the new needs created by the decree.

The *Mills* decree actually activated a bureaucratic dispute by creating new rights. Split responsibility for effectuating court decisions

11. For an outline of the terms, see *Washington Post*, April 16, 1975.

will, all else being equal, compound the problems of translating judicial declarations of policy into intended consequences.

These conclusions tend to vindicate the skepticism about judicial capacity that was expressed in the opening chapters of this book. In a sense, the case studies do this all too well, because they do not readily yield any clearcut lines that separate cases in which the courts can proceed fairly confidently from those in which they should proceed only cautiously, if at all. All four cases give pause; in three of them the balance of goal attainment, on one hand, against costs and unintended consequences, on the other, remains very difficult to weigh.

The absence of clearcut standards by which to draw distinctions hints, of course, that the problem is something generic. The new burdens assumed by the courts seem to raise questions of capacity whatever the issue area or the target environment, or at least they raise these questions in ways that crosscut issue areas and target environments.

This leads me to emphasize a different set of distinctions about the appropriate scope of judicial action—distinctions that are at once more ad hoc and closer to the limitations that emerge from the cases. In contemplating action in the course of litigation, lawyers and judges should ask: whether the situation they propose to control is too fluid to grasp by means short of day-to-day management; whether the case is representative of some universe of cases onto which a rule can be fastened; whether the social milieu is too diverse for a single rule; whether there are sufficient incentives to induce those formally subject to the court's orders to adopt the court's goals and implement them in other than perverse ways; whether the interaction of several targets will combine "chemically" to transform the decree on the ground; and whether the court can find out what is happening to its decree after the decree has been rendered. These were questions not asked in the four cases discussed here—not asked because the judicial process channels the inquiry into other directions.

This may seem unduly exhortative in tone. But much of the problem of judicial overextension lies with insufficient attention to these threshold inquiries. In the enthusiasm for framing orders assumed to be more or less self-executing, Holmes' admonition—and others of similar simplicity—have been forgotten: "In determining whether a court of equity can take jurisdiction, one of the first questions is what it can do to enforce any order that it may make."[12]

12. *Giles* v. *Harris*, 189 U.S. 475, 487 (1903).

The hortatory quality of this advice can be diminished by translating it into action. It is an ironic fact that the courts have shown much more ingenuity in attempting to transform other institutions than in transforming themselves for that job. Certainly, insufficient attention has been given to enhancement of the judicial capacity to handle behavioral data and to foresee the consequence of their decisions. These are the subjects of the next sections.

Social Facts and Social Science

The justified concern with having the courts improve their capacity to absorb and process behavioral data raises a number of significant issues, ranging from the most basic to the most technical. It would be a mistake to assume that judicial incapacity in gathering and using behavioral data derives merely from problems of the admissibility and presentation of evidence. It does involve that, but the difficulties also entail some fundamental differences between legal inquiry and social science inquiry. These differences may lead us to wonder whether there are not certain occasions when courts might be better advised not to search for behavioral data. I shall therefore begin this discussion with an exploration of some of these differences, then turn to some of the contributions behavioral data might make to judicial decisionmaking. After that, I shall analyze the deficiences exposed by the handling of social facts in the four cases, and finally consider some ways of enhancing judicial capacity to take account of social facts.

There seems an inescapable tension between attending to the unique facts of the litigants' case and to the recurrent facts of a run of cases. Emphasizing recurrent patterns of behavior risks denigrating the significance of the individual case before the court. As I have said repeatedly, the facts of the individual case may not be typical of a pattern or of the predominant pattern. To the extent that the courts' widened responsibilities for social policymaking force greater attention to the latter, the quality of the individual justice they dispense may suffer.

A heavily behavioral jurisprudence also poses potential risks for judicial independence. How far afield should judges go in search of behavioral truth? Should they use information acquired outside of court, as Justice Murphy and Judge Clark did? Should they seek to inform themselves about the politics of the litigation before them, where that might be helpful to its resolution, as it might have been in the *Area-Wide Council* case? At the extremes, there are issues involving the integrity of the judicial process raised by the quest for a full view of the social milieu from which cases come. It is, however, important not to exaggerate this point: it is a matter of the extremes.

There is also a divergence between the legal and behavioral conceptions of matters of fact. The conventional legal conception of a "fact" is an event that has transpired or is likely to transpire, or a state of affairs in existence or likely to be in existence: "an actual occurrence," says *Black's Law Dictionary*. A legal fact, in other words, though not necessarily in the past, nevertheless has a static quality to it. Social facts, by contrast, involve patterns of behavior. They are therefore not necessarily immutable. Patterns can and sometimes do change, especially at the lower levels of analysis at which verifiable propositions are likely to be found. If law is to follow behavior, it must constantly monitor such changes—a most difficult undertaking.

If it is difficult for law to follow behavior, perhaps behavior should simply follow law. That alternative is not acceptable either. It would mean that courts would disregard social facts and make law solely on the basis of normative considerations. Such a course entails the risk that the law so made will be utterly out of touch with real life. The potentially ephemeral character of some findings is a danger to be aware of, but it is no excuse for avoiding data altogether. As in many dilemmas, a balance is required—in this case, between law that responds to behavior and law that tries to shape it. So far, there has been too little of the former.

A further problem relates to the availability of social science evidence. On important issues, it is probable that there will be few, if any, conclusive findings. Indeed, it is practically certain that there will be more negative findings than positive ones—that is, findings that two variables are not related in a way that they might be thought to be related. This puts the court back where it started. It must decide; it cannot wait.[13]

Moreover, there will almost surely be a mismatch of levels of analysis. The large questions that the courts confront may at best be decomposable into several empirical questions, with data available, perhaps, on only one or two of these.

13. See Paul L. Rosen, *The Supreme Court and Social Science* (University of Illinois Press, 1972), p. 202.

In *Gault*, for example, the issue of whether juvenile courts ought to continue to proceed on the therapeutic-parental model or be reconstituted along adversary-criminal lines contained within it several potential empirical questions. Suppose the relevant research showed—as it might have but did not—that the adversary mode of proceeding is more conducive to the rehabilitation of most offenders than the parental mode, but that those who go through an adversary proceeding and are not rehabilitated are more permanently stigmatized and more likely to recidivate than comparable offenders who go through a parental proceeding. This would be more complete empirical information than is available on most problems faced by courts—and more than was actually available in *Gault*. But, as it points in two directions, it would be far from answering the issue before the court, which would have to embrace (and trade off) both sets of findings.

In *Lemon* v. *Kurtzman*,[14] the Supreme Court invalidated state statutes providing for the payment of teachers' salaries in secular subjects in parochial schools. One reason was the Court's fear that the annual appropriations provided by the state legislatures would furnish occasions for divisive religious controversy of the kind the Establishment Clause was designed to prevent. The Court's assumption was that conflict over direct material benefits was likely to be more intensely divisive than other kinds of religious strife. There are, I believe, excellent reasons to doubt the validity of this assumption; symbolic values seem to me to provide at least equally good fuel for sectarian controversy.[15] But social science has no firm findings on an issue this broad and will not have any for quite some time. It would be an abuse of social science to ask the Court to forsake its intuition on empirical grounds. The facts that social science can offer lie at a much lower level of generality than the level at which judicial decisions must often operate.

These general problems indicate that the fit between law and social science is not a comfortable one and will not be for some time. Excessive reliance on behavioral data poses risks for adjudication, but often relevant behavioral materials do not even exist. Rarely does there seem to be a good mesh.

Yet in spite of these basic problems, courts pay too little attention to social facts and, when they do, they obtain and process their materials

14. 403 U.S. 602 (1971).
15. Cf. Joseph Gusfield, *Symbolic Crusade: Status Politics and the American Temperance Movement* (University of Illinois Press, 1963).

in a generally unsatisfactory way. Every so often, behavioral material is available or potentially available to inform a court's decision, but it is rarely used effectively.

An interesting example of the possibilities is provided by *Shapiro v. Thompson*,[16] in which the Supreme Court held it impermissible for states to impose durational residence requirements of up to one year as a condition of eligibility for welfare benefits. As of 1967, forty states had such durational residence requirements.[17] In striking them down, the Court proceeded on the highly debatable ground that states had no legitimate interest in protecting their treasuries against a swell of migrants seeking higher benefits. The majority did not pause to ask whether welfare recipients actually do tend to migrate calculatively in response to opportunities for high benefits in those states that provide them. Had the Court asked this question, it might have found the evidence for calculative migration to be scant and doubtful indeed.[18] Had it been able to defer decision on the question until good evidence was available, it would have found the calculative migration hypothesis largely discredited.[19] A decision that found the states to be protecting themselves against imaginary dangers while inflicting hardship on the newly resident poor would not have raised the same moral ambiguities that were raised by the decision as written.

While *Shapiro* missed—or came too soon to benefit from—some empirical aids to decision, *Miranda v. Arizona*[20] relied on the wrong kind, and the reliance may have undercut the efficacy of the decision. Police officers have criticized the *Miranda* opinion for the undue weight it gave to police manuals advocating somewhat draconic interrogation practices. Inferring the existence of widespread police practice from the advice the manuals offered the police, the Court provided a vulnerable

16. 394 U.S. 618 (1969).

17. Irene Lurie, "Legislative, Administrative, and Judicial Changes in the AFDC Program, 1967–71," in Subcommittee on Fiscal Policy of the Joint Economic Committee, *Studies in Public Welfare: Issues in Welfare Administration: Intergovernmental Relationships* (Government Printing Office, 1973), p. 105.

18. See Gilbert Y. Steiner, *The State of Welfare* (Brookings Institution, 1972), pp. 85–88.

19. See I. N. Fisher and S. W. Purnell, "The Connection Between Migration and Welfare Dependency in the Chicago Metropolitan Area" (Rand Corporation, 1973); Eugene G. Durman, "The Impact of the Elimination of Residency Laws on Public Assistance Rolls," *Journal of Legal Studies*, vol. 4 (January 1975), pp. 199–218.

20. 384 U.S. 436 (1966).

and uninformed treatment of that issue of behavioral fact.[21] The Court had taken great pains to select several cases that seemed representative of police practice across the country, but then it filled in the gaps with materials of dubious stationhouse impact.

What the *Miranda* criticism means is that the sources of judicial information can affect not only the soundness of a decision, but also its legitimacy and ultimately its impact. A decision out of touch with the reality familiar to the specialized functionaries affected by the decision may inspire resistance rather than respect. Even without a specialized audience for a decision, a dubious empirical foundation can provide a focal point for resistance. This, of course, has been clear ever since the Supreme Court's use of Kenneth Clark's memorandum in *Brown* v. *Board of Education*.[22] It becomes doubly important, then, that the courts be attuned to issues of social fact and have some ability to deal with them.

All four cases examined in this book suffered from deficiencies on this score. In *Mapp*, there was no inquiry into social facts at all. The opinions in the *Hobson* and *Area-Wide Council* cases are replete with strong sentiments about the origins of the litigation. In the former, a "power structure" was castigated. In the latter, the roots of the problem were said to lie in "powerlessness" and in the common proclivity of those who pay pipers to call tunes. These expressions are reminiscent of Robert Presthus' remark, cited in chapter 2, that generalist decisionmakers are prone to fill in gaps in their information with their own "generalized normative axioms."

Hobson and *Gault* paid explicit attention to social science findings on matters of social fact. The court in *Hobson* found as an empirical matter that teacher experience was positively related to pupil performance, while the *Gault* majority found that more formal judicial procedure would be conducive to the rehabilitation of juvenile offenders. Both of these findings proved to be unsupported by evidence, and in-

21. Neal A. Milner, *The Court and Local Law Enforcement: The Impact of Miranda* (Sage Publications, 1971), p. 230. There are, however, grounds to doubt that the police would have accorded the decision more legitimacy had it been better informed. Cf. Stephen L. Wasby, "The Communication of the Supreme Court's Criminal Procedure Decisions: A Preliminary Mapping," *Villanova Law Review*, vol. 18 (1973), pp. 1086–1118, at p. 1104. State supreme courts also attacked this aspect of *Miranda*. See Canon, "Organizational Contumacy and the Transmission of Judicial Policies."

22. Cf. Hadley Arkes, "The Problem of Kenneth Clark," *Commentary*, vol. 58 (November 1974), pp. 37–46.

deed there are bodies of evidence suggesting the absence of such relationships.

In both cases, as I have earlier contended, social science findings were not determinative but supportive. They put the veneer of science on law made by other means and are, for that reason, independently important. By shoring up a result reached on other grounds, social science can help insulate the decision from criticism. In short, just as behavioral material can sometimes weaken a decision (as in *Miranda*), so can it impart unwarranted legitimacy to a decision. The occurrence of either possibility impairs the quality of public debate about particular judicial decisions.

The courts' treatment of social science materials in *Hobson* and *Gault* has a common theme: the materials were received second hand, and much was lost in translation. Judge Wright accepted the plaintiffs' economists' summary of research findings on the significance of teacher experience. The *Gault* majority accepted the Crime Commission's statement of "evidence" on the relation of formal procedure to rehabilitation. Both courts relied on summaries, both to the detriment of accuracy and completeness. This experience suggests that one of the most formidable problems faced by courts in search of social facts is their vulnerability to the presentations of social science advocates and social science interpreters.

The advocates are part and parcel of the adversary system, which encourages the parties to engage their respective experts. The adversary process helps clarify many issues. It only seems to obfuscate behavioral issues.[23]

The interpreters do not purport to be partial to a point of view, though they often are. The Crime Commission, for example, was clearly committed to juvenile court reform. The reliance of courts on interpreters derives from their lack of social science expertise; their propensity to give undue weight to statements of official bodies (such as commissions and government departments) that they assume to be neutral; and their need to find shortcuts—concise, intelligible presentations that will obviate the inevitable delay in decision that accompanies detailed investigation of complex issues of social fact. Courts, it must again be remembered, are very short on machinery and staff. This is both their strength and their weakness. It means that judicial decisions really do emanate from judges and not their delegates (though opinions are often

23. For a good example, see ibid.

drafted by law clerks). But it also means that these few resources are easily strained by the presentation of complicated empirical data.

Against this background, one of the principal goals of proposals to improve judicial capacity to handle social science issues ought to be to free the judges from reliance on the advocates and interpreters and the behavioral hearsay they often impart. The rules of evidence, however, conspire to keep the judges dependent on filtered knowledge.

The courts are permitted, for example, to take judicial notice of matters of fact said to be notorious; that is, they may find them as facts without requiring formal proof. But judicial notice does not extend to disputed facts or facts not widely accepted as true.[24] Almost by definition, social facts are not in the obvious or notorious category. If behavioral patterns were in the category of what everyone knows, they would present no problem to begin with.

Expert testimony is a more conventional way of eliciting social facts, but its deficiencies are formidable. The new Federal Rules of Evidence permit the courts to appoint their own expert witnesses,[25] and this has long been advocated by writers on evidence.[26] As a practical matter, the appointment will usually be made on the agreement or nomination of the parties, as indeed the Rules contemplate. An alternative is for the court to appoint a social science consultant or even a special master to take testimony and render a report.

These attempts to find objective expertise risk a delegation of the judicial fact-finding function to the designated expert, since his findings are unlikely to be rejected by the judge who appointed him. They are also, of course, a departure from the adversary process—that is their raison d'être—and may mean that the participation of the parties in the development of material that may be determinative of their controversy is sharply limited, despite whatever special precautions may be taken to keep them informed of the consultant's work.[27]

The use of expert witnesses, whether they are the parties' witnesses or the courts', poses a more general problem. Since the studies on which the witnesses rely are themselves hearsay, reliance on the experts rein-

24. Note, "Social and Economic Facts—Appraisal of Suggested Techniques for Presenting Them to Courts," *Harvard Law Review*, vol. 61 (April 1948), pp. 692–702, at p. 696.

25. Federal Rules of Evidence, Rule 706.

26. See, e.g., Charles T. McCormick, *Evidence* (West Publishing, 1954), pp. 34–38. Cf. Rosen, *The Supreme Court and Social Science*, pp. 201–02.

27. Note, "Social and Economic Facts," pp. 700–02.

forces the tendency already fostered by the rules of evidence for the judge to avoid going right to the source, to the studies that inform or misinform the experts.

This tendency to filter the facts is also reinforced by the common exception to the hearsay rule for government reports.[28] The new Federal Rules carry forward this special treatment for government reports, while excluding scholarly studies unless literally read into evidence.[29] Indeed, learned treatises and articles are not admissible at all unless referred to by an expert witness on direct or cross-examination, and even then "may not be received as exhibits."[30] These deplorably antique provisions give government reports an undue advantage over other materials that is not justified by superior veracity of such reports. In fact, government reports are themselves quite often second-hand, inferior versions of the material that is excluded as hearsay. This anomaly encourages the judge to rely on only one of several versions of the facts. It restricts the diversity of his sources. It leaves him where it found him, at the mercy of advocates and interpreters.

It is true, of course, that the rules of evidence tend to be relaxed in non-jury cases, and social facts are most likely to be found by a judge rather than a jury. Nonetheless, the thrust of these rules and the way in which they are likely to be implemented perpetuate an already unsatisfactory situation. They carry forward the presumption that scientific studies are generally hearsay, and that judges cannot be trusted to read anything but summaries.

It would be far preferable to admit books and articles on matters of social fact directly into evidence as exhibits, not require as a precondition that an expert refer to them in his testimony, abolish the favored position of government reports, and permit counsel to attack the reliability of the studies directly. This is no panacea, but it would bring the judge one step closer to the original materials, permit him more easily to check the statements of advocates and interpreters, and—since the studies will be more readily accessible to the judge—perhaps encourage expert witnesses to gear their presentations more closely to what the studies do and do not in fact show. So far, expert witnesses have had too much latitude to parade their own preferences as science.

28. Leonard H. Goodman and others, "Sources and Uses of Social and Economic Data: A Manual for Lawyers" (Bureau of Social Science Research, 1973; processed), pp. I-2, I-3.

29. Federal Rules of Evidence, Rule 803.

30. Ibid.

There is another point here as well—one that transcends the importance of direct contact of the judge with the studies in any one case. If the courts are permitted and encouraged to go directly to the books and articles that support the parties' empirical positions, this procedure furnishes the best hope for building judicial expertise in the interpretation of social science materials, as well as greater sensitivity to the need to ask empirical questions and to the limits of social science findings. Lawyers who deal regularly in medical malpractice cases become accustomed to reading medical reports and often become quite proficient at evaluating them. More slowly perhaps, similar capabilities may be developed among judges once they make a habit of digging into the frequently inelegant prose of the social sciences.

In some jurisdictions, the judge is permitted to consult scholarly publications—not as *evidence* but as part of the legal *argument*.[31] Thus, studies may be referred to in briefs. This is logical as far as it goes, since social facts are facts that pertain to the formulation of an appropriate rule of law. But it means, practically, that the opportunity for the parties to contest the behavioral assertions in their opponents' briefs (or the conclusions of the judge's subsequent forays into the library) will be severely limited by briefing schedules that typically allow insufficient time to consult experts on matters raised for the first time in the briefs. Social science materials should be widely available to the courts, but they are factual materials and do not belong in briefs, from which alleged facts, once stated, are not easily dislodged.[32]

This leaves unspecified the role of the appellate courts in passing upon social facts developed in the trial courts. As we have seen in an earlier chapter, the federal rule is that the findings of fact made by the trial court are shielded from review on appeal unless they can be shown to be "clearly erroneous."[33] This rule rests on the trial judge's superior opportunity to judge credibility by observing the demeanor of the witnesses. There is, however, as we have seen, authority that the clearly erroneous rule extends even to findings of fact based on documentary evidence.[34]

Findings of social fact, however, whether based on testimony or docu-

31. Goodman, "Sources and Uses of Social and Economic Data," p. I-5.
32. See Paul A. Freund, *The Supreme Court: Its Business, Purposes, and Performance* (Meridian Books, 1961), pp. 150–54. Cf. McCormick, *Evidence*, p. 707.
33. Federal Rules of Civil Procedure, Rule 52(a).
34. Charles Alan Wright, *Federal Courts* (2d ed.; West Publishing, 1970), pp. 429–32.

mentation, should not be similarly insulated from review. The credibility of an expert witness is not really measured by his demeanor; it is measured by comparing his assertions with the scholarly literature and his own data that purport to support the assertions. An appellate court can do this every bit as well as a trial court, and the inexperience of judges in evaluating such material argues for the widest latitude for correcting errors.

As a matter of law, too, the application of the clearly erroneous standard to social facts seems misconceived. Social facts are relevant to the task of framing an appropriate rule of law. To make the trial judge the final arbiter of such facts may have the effect of making him the final arbiter of the law as well as the facts.[35]

If the judges are able to dip into social science materials more regularly and directly than they generally have until now, what will they find?

If the research contains positive findings, the courts will no doubt discover that the environments they must take account of contain a good deal more diversity than the law is accustomed to assume. Even if the research findings are negative, the failure to demonstrate a consistent relationship may also mean, as I have shown in earlier chapters, that local conditions combine in curious ways to produce divergent outcomes. This may make the courts more cautious about dealing with diversity by means of uniform rules.

If so, that is a useful function of social science: it should help the courts decide when to intervene and when not to intervene, as well as how to intervene. And general cautiousness about social facts is well warranted by judicial experience. Courts have been too slow to raise empirical questions and altogether too quick to answer them once raised. Social science material has most often been ignored because its relevance has not been perceived. Less often but equally unfortunately, it has been paid more heed than its reliability warranted. Too rarely has it been approached with the circumspection that is merited by the partial, tentative character of most findings and by the imperfect fit between them and the legal questions to which they may have some relevance. Available data usually cannot be simply plugged in to the case at the appropriate point.

Reliance on social science—honest, balanced reliance—is likely to be a "conservative" influence on the courts, or, more accurately, an influence

35. Note, "Social and Economic Facts," pp. 699–700.

tending to inhibit judicial action and to be permissive of action taken by others.[36] For, more often than not, social science does not have the answer that is sought, or it has a negative answer: that two conditions do not appear to be related to each other. At least that is the likelihood on the important questions of social policy that find their way to litigation. Then, too, social science is likely to introduce complexities that shake the judge's confidence in imposed solutions that he projects will be effective if only they gain "compliance." At its very best—and especially if behavioral material is resorted to with some regularity—social science can help shake loose the "generalized normative axioms" that sometimes move judges to action. Repeated exposure to specialized information sometimes has such iconoclastic effects. When, as often happens, social science dictates no answer either way, the courts will be forced back to what they do best: deciding cases on the basis of close reasoning derived from the ethical premises whose implications they are, above all, appointed to work out and articulate.

Attending to the Consequences of Decisions

I have made the point several times that judicial decisions have traditionally tended to be backward-looking, that the courts are well equipped to see the past and present fairly clearly, and ill equipped to gauge the future. Yet, in making social policy, the courts really sit as planners choosing among options, no matter how uncongenial such a description of their role might be to them.[37]

If that is one valid description of their role, it is worth remarking that the options, if presented at all, are presented by counsel. But for some of the reasons that courts find it difficult to think in terms of alternatives and consequences, lawyers have the same difficulties, and their participation therefore reinforces the structural characteristics of adjudication that are at odds with planning.

All of this makes it important to think more deeply about the ways in which courts might consider the probable consequences of their decisions. As before, I shall divide this issue into forecasting and monitoring, for where prediction proves difficult retrospective adjustment may

36. See, e.g., *San Antonio School Dist.* v. *Rodriguez*, 411 U.S. 1, 42–43 (1973).
37. See Sir Geoffrey Vickers, *The Art of Judgment* (Chapman and Hall, 1965), pp. 90–91.

still be possible. Accordingly, I shall begin by asking whether, using the four cases as starting points, it is possible to discern patterns of consequences of judicial decisions. Then I shall speculate on whether the ability of courts to anticipate and track consequences can be augmented.

The starting point is sheer compliance. In the four cases, compliance (in the narrow sense of those subject to a decision abiding by its terms) was not perfect.

The city defendants in the *Area-Wide Council* case did not act with alacrity to reintegrate the AWC into the Philadelphia Model Cities program. Instead, they carried on their competition for control of the community. This may not have been exactly noncompliance, but it was not exactly compliance either.

In *Hobson*, the school system generally adhered to the court's orders, but on both occasions did so in a manner that prevented the secondary effects desired by the court from occurring. Following *Hobson I*, busing and teacher transfers were kept to a minimum. Following *Hobson II*, implementation by transferring resource teachers (after the first year) met the strict arithmetical requirements of the decree, but was not exactly what the court had in mind when it spoke of equalization of teacher resources. In addition, local school administrators were sometimes able to evade the impact of *Hobson II* by soliciting funds outside the regular budget, by preventing transfers through devices to boost enrollments, and the like.

There was some outright defiance of *Mapp*, though often concealed in perverse findings of fact on motions to suppress.[38] *Gault*, too, encountered resistance among juvenile court judges and intake officers, some of whom failed to advise minors and their parents of their newfound constitutional rights or imparted the advice in a partial or discouraging way. The reason for this lack of compliance is, of course, the sweep of the decisions. Decided by the Supreme Court, *Gault* and *Mapp* applied nationwide. The *Area-Wide Council* and *Hobson* decisions applied only to the parties before the courts; others could ignore them without having to defy them. By and large, that was the fate of those decisions outside the two cities in which they were rendered.

But, even where they were welcomed, *Gault* and *Mapp* had consequences determined by the various environments into which they were

38. Cf. Walter F. Murphy, "Lower Court Checks on Supreme Court Power" *American Political Science Review*, vol. 53 (December 1959), pp. 1017–31.

received. The chemical metaphor is to me the most revealing one: the innovation could be turned into a different compound depending on its reception at the pre-innovation environment. In all four cases, evasion or defiance played some role in blunting the effects of the decisions, but the greater part was played by the integration of the decision into its environment. Not lack of compliance but mode of compliance is the prime determinant of consequences. And in all four cases, lack of over-sight and lack of hindsight combined with lack of foresight to make all sorts of combinations possible.

Mapp and *Gault*, both Supreme Court decisions, also had more con-spicuous second-order consequences (*Mapp* on the allocation of police tasks, *Gault* on the substantive work of juvenile courts), and both also had legislative consequences (stop-and-frisk laws in a few states, PINS laws in many). The wider applicability of Supreme Court de-cisions activates more interested parties to adapt their behavior to the new factor injected by the decision into the whole field of behavior or to deploy their forces to seize the initiative created by the decision, either to build on it or to reverse it.

Whether legislation results, however, seems to depend above all on a couple of easily ascertained factors: the extent to which the organiza-tions interested in the decision can handle its burdens or opportunities administratively and the extent to which there is an attentive, special-ized public receptive to messages from authoritative decisionmakers. The police could adapt to *Mapp*, for the most part, without legislative aid. The juvenile court professionals, a ready-made audience for *Gault*, could not seize its potential all by themselves.[39] To put it differently, if a single bureaucracy is the target of a decision, the chances are that it can produce second-order consequences all by itself. Non-bureaucratic groups (or fragmented bureaucratic groups) affected by a decree are more likely to turn to legislation, as anti-abortionists did after *Roe* v. *Wade* and Spanish-speaking organizations did after *Lau*.[40]

39. For the character of the juvenile justice reformers and their opponents in California, see Edwin M. Lemert, *Social Action and Legal Change: Revolution Within the Juvenile Court* (Aldine, 1970). For a general perspective, see Daniel P. Moynihan, "The Professionalization of Reform," *The Public Interest*, no. 1 (Fall 1965), pp. 6–16.

40. Marilyn Falik, "The Impact of the Supreme Court Decision on Abortion: Political and Legislative Resistance v. Court Reactions" (paper prepared for de-livery at the 1974 Annual Meeting of the American Political Science Association; processed); Dexter Waugh and Bruce Koon, "Breakthrough for Bilingual Educa-tion," *Civil Rights Digest*, vol. 6 (Summer 1974), pp. 18–26. See Nathan Hakman,

This leads to a reflection on the growing political science literature on the impact of court decisions—one that I think will help illuminate the character of the consequences of judicial decisions in general. Most of these studies have defined impact to mean compliance or its absence, and they have been concerned to identify the conditions fostering compliance or non-compliance. Impact also tends to be viewed as occurring or not occurring in the intended forum. That is, if the decision outlaws school prayers, the impact studies examine school board responses pro and con. If the decision requires counsel to be accorded to criminal suspects, the impact studies observe whether the police provide counsel. There has been little investigation of effects in a variety of sectors.[41] The impact studies, furthermore, take the cases one at a time—each is assumed to have its own impact, apart from the others. The cases examined here—and others—suggest, however, (1) that the significance of court decisions is not primarily measured in terms of compliance, (2) that it lies heavily in the consequences of compliance (often in second-order consequences), (3) in consequences registered in other forums besides the intended forums, and (4) sometimes in consequences produced as much by the interaction of several court decisions as by any one of them.[42]

At least some of the consequences in the four cases (but certainly not the legislative ones) were foreseeable, if only there had been a structure or setting in which questions of consequences could have been addressed. *Mapp* is revealing on this score. *Mapp* took its audience to be the police, ignoring lower courts, because it was not required to look ahead. (A change in police behavior was an end; lower court behavior

---

"The Impact of Judicial Opinions: Another Critical Analysis of Political Science Folklore" (paper prepared for delivery at the 1974 Annual Meeting of the American Political Science Association; processed), p. 12: "Only one instance was found in which administrators sought remedial action in legislative bodies or attempted to stimulate clientele pressure for reversal of judicial decisions."

41. See Raymond A. Bauer, *Second-Order Consequences: A Methodological Essay on the Impact of Technology* (M.I.T. Press, 1969), pp. 38–39.

42. In addition to *Gault's* interaction with *Robinson v. California*, discussed in chapter 5, *Hobson's* interaction with *Mills* provides an illustration of this point. In *Hobson I*, "ability tracking" of pupils was made rather difficult, and the school system abolished its tracks. In *Mills*, guidelines were established for procedures to be followed in the case of undisciplined students. This has made suspension of students extremely difficult. *Mills* also, as pointed out earlier, resulted in "mainstreaming"—that is, the integration of problem pupils in ordinary class situations. All these results, taken together, have created a considerable homogenization of pupils of diverse aptitudes and problems in the District of Columbia schools.

was simply a means. The means were taken for granted.) Had the prevalence and relevance of plea bargaining, for example, been called to the Court's attention in connection with *Mapp*, in a setting that made it legitimate and incumbent to think of plea bargaining and the exclusionary rule as related problems, little judicial imagination would have been required to see that the exclusionary rule might simply have reduced sentences in ways not likely to deter police misconduct. Likewise, in *Hobson*, had the court's attention been called, in a comparably conducive setting, to the unlikelihood of compliance through busing or changes in school boundaries, to the different status of resource and classroom teachers under the union contract, and to the rate and significance of enrollment changes, the probable direction of transfers over time might have been clarified. Then the court could have decided explicitly whether the probable mode of compliance comported with its conception of what was required of the school system.

But the appropriate setting was not present, for reasons already examined at length. Part of the problem of anticipation is to create a format for foresight. This will not be easy. Sometimes it may involve separate memoranda and hearings on the proposed remedy, after the legal questions have been decided. These are not all that unusual in complicated injunction cases. Sometimes the better way to proceed may be to deal with both rights and remedies at the same time, for if there is a possibility that no suitable course of action exists, that may affect the court's decision on the rights of the parties as well.

Either way, however, the structure of the inquiry should be somewhat different from the customary inquiry on remedies. In the past, the prevailing party has had the burden of putting forward the remedy he prefers, often in the form of a proposed decree, and arguing in support of it. The burden is on the losing party to attack it or (in practice, less frequently) to propose alternatives. If the courts are to think in terms of alternatives, this is not an appropriate way to go about it. The burden should be on the winning party to put forward every plausible alternative remedy that might be consistent with the court's decision on the legal issues, together with assessments of projected consequences and costs. Then the losing party's adversary presentation can assume a more useful form, and the court can be helped to weigh alternatives and probable costs against probable benefits.

The issue of remedy has come to be considered a legal question not generally warranting a factual presentation. The evidence usually closes before the court's decision on the rights of the parties, and usually does not reopen thereafter. This, too, is generally inadequate in social policy cases. Since the decision on the remedy entails a forecast of behavior, it presents factual as well as legal questions, though, to be sure, these are questions about the future rather than about the past. But that is all the more reason to regard the facts as problematical rather than settled.

Settling on the right format in each case will be a challenging responsibility. But in this the courts are aided by their undeniable expertise about their own procedure and their demonstrated willingness to innovate in procedural matters where there is a promise of a substantive payoff. In addition, we have seen graphically how judicial format can structure the result—*Hobson II* being the outstanding example of this.[43] This, too, suggests that there is unused potential in procedural devices.

If the courts are in the business of forecasting, what is their method of foresight to be? Where should they start their reasoning? What kinds of logic should they employ?

One common tool of judicial thought will not be very useful: analogy.[44] The prerequisite of analogy is experience. The courts are short on experience with consequential facts. Ultimately, if they make more use of impact feedback, they may build a bank of experience from which to draw analogies. But that is a long way off.

A more promising method of analysis is suggested by Daniel Bell's stimulating inventory, "Twelve Modes of Prediction."[45] Several of Bell's modes of prediction rely on "the principle of limited possibilities."[46] This principle concentrates attention on the constraints operating in a system of action. It postulates that often there are only several "ideal types" of action possible. Each type may be linked to a different motive for action or to a different functional requisite for action. Where this is the case, it becomes possible to work out most of the alternative combinations of possibilities. What remains thereafter is to assign probabilities to the various possibilities.

The method of beginning with the constraints operating on those charged with implementing alternative decrees and working through from this to likely consequences of each accords well with the results

43. See chapter 4, the section on "Narrowing the Issues."
44. Cf. Bauer, *Second-Order Consequences*, pp. 30–41.
45. "Twelve Modes of Prediction—A Preliminary Sorting of Approaches in the Social Sciences," *Daedalus*, vol. 93 (Summer 1964), pp. 845–80.
46. See especially number 6, "Structural Requisites," in ibid., pp. 857–59, and numbers 3 and 10, pp. 854–55, 863–65.

of the four case studies. That is, our "postdiction," especially of *Mapp* and *Hobson,* might have been prediction had the courts thought in terms of narrowing the range of possible modes of implementation, which is exactly what the relevant actors in lower courts and the school system, respectively, ended up doing. This approach has the additional virtue of emphasizing the potential diversity of patterns, usually diversity within a limited range. As I have indicated, courts have had special difficulty anticipating diversity.

I do not mean to hint for a moment that this solves the problem of forecasting for the courts. At best, it provides only a starting point, a way to enter the problem. Prediction in uncertain, often intractable, surroundings remains for the courts, as for all decisionmakers, the most hazardous of enterprises. Yet it forms an inescapable part of all decision, too long escaped by the courts, which have operated on the unfortunate assumption that how a party implements a court order is no part of judicial business. Chips cannot be left to fall where they may.

Happily, neither the courts nor other decisionmakers need rely solely on prediction. There is also correction, but this process, too, must be set up and structured. There are, as indicated previously, many reasons why decisions, once rendered, tend to be regarded as business concluded and many other reasons why this is not a satisfactory state of affairs. The difficulty of forecasting makes it doubly important "to become empirical, to act and depend upon an adequate system of feedback to report those consequences that are of sufficient importance to warrant an adjustment of course."[47]

If the parties themselves provide feedback, that is, of course, useful. But they are inconstant allies in this effort. They may not have "staying power."[48] Even when they do, and when the results displease them, there may be reasons why they do not choose to return to court, as was the case with both sides in the years after *Hobson II* was rendered.

Should the courts then rely on independent outside monitors appointed to follow the results of their decisions? Attractive though this may sound, there are reasons to doubt that it would generally work out in practice. Neutral third parties quickly develop their own interests in particular outcomes. The experience of certain of the regulatory com-

47. Bauer, *Second-Order Consequences,* p. 185.
48. Joel F. Handler, "Social Reform Groups and the Legal System: Enforcement Problems," University of Wisconsin–Madison, Institute for Research on Poverty, Discussion Paper 209-74 (June 1974; processed).

missions and of what passes for evaluation inside the federal government suggest some of the unfortunate possibilities that seem to inhere in appointments of this kind. On the whole, it seems to me better to confine the primary responsibility for generating and evaluating feedback to litigants, lawyers, and judges. But this leaves unanswered the question of how the courts will be informed of consequential facts.

To a small but increasing extent, as judicial impact is highlighted as a subject of scholarly concern, the law reviews and social science journals can begin to provide the judges with information on the consequences of their decisions and of others analogous to theirs. But this is far short of enough. Other devices are necessary and can be employed.

One such technique is revealed by *Hobson II*. A requirement that records be kept specially on compliance and its consequences, and that reports be rendered by those subject to decrees, might be useful if inserted in some decrees. It would facilitate later inquiry and, because of the public character of the records, create incentives for close adherence to the court's intentions. The tentative or experimental decree and the decree that expires on a date certain unless renewed on a showing of continuing need are also useful ways of providing automatic, timed feedback and countering the propensity to let unsatisfactory arrangements harden into accepted habits and routines.

The problem with such devices is the one last named. Because they prevent arrangements from being viewed as permanent, they may impede planning, where that is a significant part of the business of the court's target institution. This dilemma has been aptly spelled out by Sir Geoffrey Vickers:

In the unpredictable area of life where ". . . wisdom lies in masterful administration of the unforeseen . . ." rigidity is to be feared and flexibility is to be prized; and this is the source of the dilemma which faces would-be regulators, whether in the board room of a small enterprise or at the centre of government. Massive change demands massive commitments and hence no small element of rigidity. Unpredictable change demands flexibility. Change both massive and unpredictable makes inconsistent demands for rigidity on the one hand and flexibility on the other, and poses the most basic policy choice of all, the choice of what to regard as regulable. For the decision to retain liberty of action and hence flexibility by deferring commitment is in fact the decision to regard the situation as for the time being too uncertain to regulate, a decision which may be wise but which has its own costs.[49]

To this dilemma Sir Geoffrey proposes some possible resolutions,

49. *The Art of Judgment*, p. 81.

but for us the dilemma is not yet serious enough to warrant extrication by his methods. The decrees of the courts have so far been too permanent, too stable. What is required is more flexibility, more tentativeness, and more policy review to redress the balance.

The problem is more acute at the Supreme Court level than in the lower federal courts. First of all, Supreme Court decisions have ramifications far beyond the parties to the suit. Second, they are also far more likely to engender second-order consequences and other-forum consequences. Third, since the Supreme Court issues no decrees (only opinions and mandates given effect by lower courts), it has no ready format for making post facto adjustments. Reports on implementation and motions for modification will be addressed to the lower courts. The broad consequences of a Supreme Court decision may therefore outlive even a modification or vacation of the decree in that very same case by the federal district court. There is thus a mismatch between the scope of the decisions (broad) and the scope of potential corrections (narrow). Non-parties may be acting on the basis of a decision long after new facts have rendered it obsolete for the parties themselves.

The feedback mechanisms discussed so far do not address this problem and, to the extent that they do provide information and correction, they will actually make the disjunction between the policies governing the behavior of parties and non-parties worse. To some extent, the greater publicity accorded the effects of Supreme Court decisions can help redress this deficiency. To some extent, the Court can help itself by choosing clusters of cases for subsequent review, especially cases representative of diverse patterns, but that brings us back to the vexing question of how courts know they have representative cases before them. To some extent, finally, the Court can choose cases on a preferential basis for review that have been to the Court before and have been subject to later correction in the light of impact information.

When the courts receive impact information, it will generally be of two kinds. The first is illustrated by the results of *Hobson I*, the second by the results of *Hobson II*. In *Hobson I*, the court thought teacher transfers and pupil busing would produce expenditure equalization, but they did not. This is perhaps best denominated a factual error in forecasting. The court thought *Hobson II* would eventuate in more equal distribution of teacher services, as it did. But it also resulted in annual disruptions by teacher transfers, in greater inequality at the extremes, and in other such unanticipated costs. If we consider these costs to outweigh the equalization benefits of *Hobson II*, then they amount to an error in welfare terms, though not in factual terms.

These two types of error are not always equally detectable, but welfare errors are probably less detectable than factual errors in estimating consequences. Costs may show up only much later and in more far-flung forums than benefits. Put differently, costs may be more widely shared than benefits, and they are certainly less easily verifiable than at least the intended benefits are, since they are typically unintended and therefore not targeted for inclusion in reports and other monitoring efforts. The distinction, therefore, is a particularly important one for courts to keep in the forefront of their attention, lest they cast their net too narrowly.

Finally, a word about the limits of monitoring consequences. Whenever a court has a chance to track the effects of its decisions, of course it should. But if monitoring edges over into constant supervision, or if the latter is what is really required, the task is more appropriate for a bureaucracy than for a court, and it should be left there. Where episodic intervention would not be enough, that is a sign that there is no judicial question presented.

Judges and Others: Reflections on Relative Institutional Capacity

If this has been a skeptical book, it invites an equally skeptical rejoinder. For every judge who acts on imperfect information, students of Congress can produce three legislators. For every judge who assumes his orders to be effective, students of bureaucracy can adduce untold instances of lack of administrative follow-up. In a period in which the discovery is being made that effective policymaking and implementation are scarce, there is plenty of incapacity for officials to share.

This is an important point, but it is not the whole point and it risks being a misleading point. It brings to mind the common propensity to treat the judicial process as if, on a given issue, it were the whole governmental process, when in fact it interlocks with several others, each of which may contribute its share to the total result. I have tried to take account of that, but necessarily the focus here has been primarily on the courts. Even more important, however, the counter-skeptics implicitly raise the question of whether some institutions perform some tasks better than other institutions do. Merely to assert that all processes are not wholly apt for the problems they confront is not to conclude an inquiry; it is to begin one. That inquiry—into relative institutional capacity —has, of course, stalked this study from its inception. Are there, after all, distinctive patterns of judicial action, or are the difficulties I have identified really inherent in all policymaking processes?

Much has to be conceded to the counter-skeptical position. All institutions are flawed, and some flaws are shared among institutions. Yet, though they have more areas of overlap than at first appear, not all institutions are flawed in exactly the same way or degree. In each of the four cases, the courts saw or at least emphasized aspects of the situation before them that were different from the aspects that might have been recognized by other kinds of decisionmakers. For example, in *Gault* the Supreme Court saw instantly how aberrational juvenile court procedures had become in the total legal system. This observation might not have occurred as quickly or sharply to legislators or administrators. There are overlaps among processes, but they are not perfect congruences.

Consider the question of setting agendas. Courts are dependent on litigants for ignition. Formally, legislators and administrators have no such requirements. Yet they respond to different sets of constraints on the initiation of action. The freedom they seem to have, to act or not act, quickly becomes hedged in, so that it no longer becomes accurate to say that they possess a kind of control over their agenda that is denied to judges. As a matter of fact, no decisionmaker really sets his own agenda.[50] But that makes it more rather than less important to compare the ways in which issues do get placed before those who must act on them.

Similarly, the scope of decision has traditionally been thought to be more confined among judges than among legislators. Courts are prevented from deciding some things by canons of judicial restraint and by threshold doctrines that keep certain issues away from them. At the same time, judges are virtually required to decide some other issues. Formally, legislators do not have to decide anything, but they are also free to decide almost everything. Yet this formal freedom is misleading. Legislators often hesitate to innovate; they prefer to wait and see.[51] Cer-

50. See Samuel P. Huntington, *The Common Defense* (Columbia University Press, 1961), p. 189.

51. See C. Thomas Dienes, "Judges, Legislators, and Social Change," *American Behavioral Scientist,* vol. 13 (March–April 1970), pp. 511–21.

tainly the catalog of ways to prevent action on the part of Congress and state legislatures is longer, more diverse, and more impressive than the rules of jurisdiction and procedure that impede action in the courts.

Furthermore, although legislative outputs do not have to be justified by reference to evidence and reason, as court decisions do, they are not necessarily more flexible on that account. The legislative repertoire may be equally limited by electoral or cultural constraints that foreclose some solutions and mandate others.

Legislative surveillance of impact, when it occurs, through oversight and appropriation hearings and other devices, is distinctly more regularized than judicial follow-up is. Yet it does not always occur. Frequent elections, which produce new majorities, often prevent legislators from reviewing and trimming programs they have enacted. Just as litigants may lack staying power, so may reformers in the legislative process, whose activity may trail off noticeably after the enactment of legislation.[52] Here, again, the difference lies within a narrow compass, but it is a difference nonetheless. For policy review, judges require litigants to return to court. Legislators may rely on interest groups to rekindle their awareness, but they may also develop their own interest in tracing the implications of a policy; or a bureaucracy set up to administer the policy may unavoidably call its consequences to the attention of the legislators who enacted it.

Judges' decisions are actually made by judges. Congress is far more dependent on staff work. Still, despite growing staffs, congressmen seem generally able to insure that they do not lose control over significant decisions.[53] Personal and committee staffs are able to provide background information they have gathered, but its scope and depth are not necessarily always superior to the information developed in the course of litigation. Nevertheless, it seems plausible to assume that one thing a congressman will not take for granted is the homogeneity of his environment; unlike the judge, he thrives on knowledge of diversity.

It is sometimes said that legislators bargain while judges decide. On the other hand, it is also said that judges bargain over decisions just as legislators do. Neither assertion is quite on the mark. Enough is now known to lead to the conclusion that, on multimember appellate courts,

---

52. See Murray Edelman, *The Symbolic Uses of Politics* (University of Illinois Press, 1964).

53. Susan Webb Hammond, "The Changing Role of the Personal Professional Staff in Congressional Decision-Making" (paper prepared for delivery at the 1974 Annual Meeting of the American Political Science Association; processed).

bargaining and compromise do sometimes take place, and in some state courts there are strong norms in favor of compromise and against dissent.[54] But the bargaining that occurs is not usually the same kind that occurs in a legislature. For one thing, it rarely changes outcomes. It is generally directed at obtaining a shift in a majority opinion, a deletion of a sentence or paragraph, the strengthening of one ground of decision over another, or the stifling of a dissent. It is also less frequent among judges than among legislators, as well as being more marginal to their work, and it usually reflects concern about institutional integrity, rather than about policy substance. The heart of the judicial process cannot really be described in terms of negotiation.

I have talked a good deal about the potential unrepresentativeness of the parties before the courts. But somewhat the same argument can be made about the supplicants before legislatures and administrators. They are, in the main, those with the most intense preferences, and they, too, may convey a skewed picture of the problem they purport to represent. The difference, of course, is that, while legislators may accord access to such interested parties, they need not confine themselves to the information provided by those parties. The courts, for the most part, are more dependent on the parties that come before them for the view of the issues that they obtain.

A proper inventory of the characteristics of administrative organizations along similar lines would, I think, yield generally similar results. There would be more overlap with the courts than the formal separation of powers would lead us to believe, but still some significant differences, albeit sometimes differences merely in degree. A couple of examples will make the point.

Unlike the courts, many bureaucratic organizations aspire consciously

54. Walter F. Murphy and Joseph Tanenhaus, *The Study of Public Law* (Random House, 1972), pp. 155–58; Murphy, *Elements of Judicial Strategy* (University of Chicago Press, 1964), pp. 65–66, 68–73, 187–97; J. Woodford Howard, "On the Fluidity of Judicial Choice," *American Political Science Review*, vol. 62 (March 1968), pp. 43–56; Note, *Yale Law Journal*, vol. 83 (May 1974), at pp. 1202, 1212–19, 1225–26; Alpheus Thomas Mason, *Harlan Fiske Stone: Pillar of the Law* (Viking, 1968), pp. 360–65, 399–402; Alexander M. Bickel, *The Supreme Court and the Idea of Progress* (Harper and Row, 1966), pp. 46–47. On consensus in state supreme courts, see Robert J. Sickels, "The Illusion of Judicial Consensus: Zoning Decisions in the Maryland Court of Appeals," *American Political Science Review*, vol. 59 (March 1965), pp. 100–04; H. Stephen Whitaker, "The Florida Supreme Court: Internal Procedures," *Florida State University Governmental Research Bulletin*, vol. 4 (December 1967), pp. 1–6.

to plan. But, in practice, few do, as the many discussions of incrementalism and "satisficing" in organizations attest. It is true that the courts positively reject the idea of planning, but to what extent this difference in institutional mythology is paralleled by a difference in policymaking behavior no one has yet endeavored to learn.

The ability of bureaucracies to carry out policies more or less as intended has, of course, also been doubted. As Anthony Downs, among others, has argued, every bureaucracy "leaks"; orders passing from the top to the bottom of an organization are subject to distortion.[55] Wonderment is now beginning to be expressed that government policies are carried out at all, given the obstacles they confront.[56] Resistance, unintended consequences, and second-order consequences are not the distinctive fate of court orders, but of all orders. Yet it seems to me that Woodford Howard has a point when he argues that administrative enforcement is generally stronger and more effective than judicial enforcement, partly because it can be self-starting and self-perpetuating (it need not wait for litigants), and partly because, for some problems at least, administrative tools are sharper and more numerous.[57]

Where, in the end, does all this lead? Surely not to the conclusion that it makes no difference which forum is chosen to resolve a problem, for clearly it does (though it is well to bear in mind Samuel Huntington's admonition that in the United States nearly every decision "can be appealed to another body or another forum"[58]). It makes a difference, but the difference can be very subtle. What I have tried to do is to show what happens to problems that find their way to the judiciary, and why it happens. But as these notes toward an inventory of comparative capacities suggest, parallel research along some of the same dimensions of decision that we have explored would seem very much in order. The counter-skeptical position deserves no less.

But if there is more than a germ of validity in counter-skepticism, so I believe there is also validity in the skepticism about judicial capacity which has informed this study. For even on the present state of knowledge, there are problems the judiciary seems peculiarly short on re-

55. *Inside Bureaucracy* (Little, Brown, 1966), pp. 134–36.
56. See Jeffrey L. Pressman and Aaron B. Wildavsky, *Implementation* (University of California Press, 1973).
57. J. Woodford Howard, Jr., "Adjudication Considered as a Process of Conflict Resolution: A Variation on the Separation of Powers," *Journal of Public Law*, vol. 18 (Spring 1969), pp. 339–70, at pp. 365–66.
58. *The Common Defense*, p. 127.

sources to handle. Even now, Alexander Bickel and Harry Wellington's description of one such problem has the ring of authenticity to it:

The point is that the courts will draw from a body of experience not germane to the problem they will face. Given their limited means of informing themselves and the episodic nature of their efforts to do so, they will only dimly perceive the situations on which they impose their order. Even if they do perceive, they will necessarily come too late with a pound of "remedy" where the smaller measure of prevention was needed. Their rules, tailored to the last bit of trouble, will never catch up with the next and different dispute. They will allow or forbid and be wrong in either event, because continuous, pragmatic, and flexible regulation alone can help. They will on most occasions naturally shy away from basing their judgments on what they are accustomed to regard as "political" factors incompatible with their disinterestedness, although these may form the only sensible context of questions before them. And they will thus find themselves resting judgment on trivia or irrelevancies. All this will not only, by its sheer volume, divert the energies of the courts from their proper sphere but will also tend to bring the judicial process into disrepute by exposing it as inadequate to a task with which it should never have been entrusted.[59]

Such problems are easier to identify by illustration than by description. It may be the limited scope of consultation, or the inability of courts to see how their policies work out, or the difficulty of dealing with unusually fluid or broad problems in an episodic and narrow framework, that stamps the judicial process as more limited for some policy problems than other institutions are. But when the institutional comparisons are all in, it still seems certain that there will be some policy problems that are beyond the capabilities of even the most able judges to handle well.

The distinctiveness of the judicial process—its expenditure of social resources on individual complaints, one at a time—is what unfits the courts for much of the important work of government. Retooling the judicial process to cope with the new responsibilities of the courts means enhancing their capacity to function more systematically in terms of general categories that transcend individual cases. Some such innovations are required. And yet, it would seem, there is a limit to the changes of this kind that courts can absorb and still remain courts. Heightened attention to recurrent patterns of behavior risks inattention to individual cases. Over the long run, augmenting judicial capacity may erode the distinctive contribution the courts make to the social order. The danger is that courts, in developing a capacity to improve on the work of other institutions, may become altogether too much like them.

59. "Legislative Purpose and the Judicial Process: The Lincoln Mills Case," *Harvard Law Review*, vol. 71 (November 1957), pp. 1–39, at p. 25.

Index of Cases Cited

General Index

Adjudication. *See* Judicial process
Adjudicative facts. *See* Historical facts
Administrative-law doctrine, 69
Administrators. *See* Bureaucracy
Allard, Robert E., 28n
Alper, Benedict S., 212n
Alschuler, Albert W., 244n, 248n
American Bar Association, 26–27
Amicus curiae, 44n–45n
Ann Arbor, Michigan, relations between CDA and citizens' groups, 98–99
Antecedent facts, 51
Area-Wide Council case, 66, 85n; appeals court decision, 85–91, 93–94, 95–96; AWC suit, 83–84; consequential facts in, 262; court conception of "widespread" versus "maximum feasible" citizen participation, 88–89; district court decision, 85, 86, 94–95; effect on citizen participation, 97–105; effect on Model Cities program, 97–99; HUD progress on Model Cities program during litigation in, 91–92; outcome of, 94–97, 255; problems in implementing decision, 264, 265, 268; secondary effects of, 263; social facts in, 278
Area-Wide Council (AWC), North Philadelphia: conflict with Model Cities administration, 79, 80; disintegration of, 92–93; formation of, 77; litigation over citizens' participation in Model Cities program, 83–97; relations with city government, 78–79; replaced by Advisory Citizens' Committee, 92, 93, 95–96; staff of, 77–78
Arkes, Hadley, 278n
Arnold, Thurman, 223n
Arnstein, Sherry R., 78n

Arrests: in gambling cases, 236; *Mapp* decision's effect on, 227–28, 231–32; in narcotics cases, 228–30
Asher, Herbert B., 29n
Aubert, Vilhelm, 57n, 61, 62n
Austin, John, 2
Automotive safety standards, 4, 5
Averch, Harvey A., 141n, 142n
AWC. *See* Area-Wide Council

Ban, Michael, 235n, 242, 243n, 244n, 245n, 246n, 248n
Baratz, Joan C., 108n, 116n, 123n, 126n, 146n, 156n, 161n, 163n, 165n
Barker, Ernest, 88n
Barron, Roger, 210n
Bauer, Raymond A., 287n, 289n, 290n
Baum, Martha, 182, 183
Bazelon, David, 210n
Behavior: courts' use of data on, 50–51, 274–75; forecasting future, 49; importance in social policy litigation, 46–47; influence of courts on, 52, 58, 60, 106; normative versus instrumental, 57. *See also* Social facts
Bell, Charles G., 29n
Bell, Daniel, 289
Bentham, Jeremy, 1, 2, 20, 21
Bereano, Philip L., 33n, 39n
Berman, Harold J., 193n
Bickel, Alexander M., 9, 56n, 61n, 298
Binder, Leonard, 39n
Bishop, Joseph W., Jr., 1n
Black, Hugo L., 54n
Boston, Massachusetts: extent of compliance with *Mapp* decision, 243; status of suppression motions in, 242, 244, 245
Brennan, William J., Jr., 14n, 16n

reaction to *Area-Wide Council* case decision, 103–05; revised citizen participation policy, *1969*, 82–83, 86–87, 99–103; on role of CDAs, 71–72

Department of Human Resources, D.C., 259, 272

Derthick, Martha, 164n, 179n

Deterrence. *See* Exclusionary rule; Police

Dienes, C. Thomas, 294n

Dinitz, Simon, 181n

Di Nunzio, Michael A., 98n, 102n

Discrimination in employment, 14, 15, 42, 43–44, 57

District of Columbia schools: administrative problems in integrating, 116; busing in, 117; capacity utilization rates, 129–30, 132; Clark Plan for, 163–64; community versus centralized control of, 162–63, 165; economies of scale, 122–24, 128–32, 133; effect of *Hobson I* decision on, 116–18; effect of Supreme Court *1954* desegregation decision on, 107; enrollment, 116, 150, 154, 155–57; expenditure inequality, 114–15, 117, 118, 119–20, 127, 128–29, 131–32; homogenization of students in, 187n; neighborhood school policy, 112, 113; optional zones, 108, 110, 115; racial segregation of, 108, 110–13; resource inequalities in, 113–14, 121, 125; tracking system, 108–09, 110, 115

District of Columbia, status of suppression motions in, 245

Douglas, William O., 16n, 54n

Downs, Anthony, 31n, 45n, 297

Dror, Yehezkel, 57n

Duffee, David, 186n, 192n

Durman, Eugene G., 277n

Economic Opportunity Act of *1964*, Green Amendment, 72

Economies of scale, effect on school expenditure disparities, 122–24, 128–32, 133

Edelman, Murray, 295n

Education cases, 4–5; relating to language deficiencies, 16–17, 41. *See also Hobson I; Hobson II*

Eisenstein, James, 236n, 240n

Elementary and Secondary Education Act of *1965*, 118; equalization as condition for eligibility under Title I, 136, 162–63

Emerson, Robert M., 189n, 190n, 201n

Employment policy, courts and, 4, 14–

15. *See also* Discrimination in employment

Enforcement. *See* Compliance with judicial decisions

Environmental cases, 10

Equal Protection Clause, 111, 134, 136, 169, 257

Evidence: admissibility of illegally obtained, 49–50, 241; to secure an indictment, 241; for verification of social facts, 48

Exclusionary rule: attitude of judges toward, 243; benefit-cost evaluation of, 249–52; effect on crime prevention, 234; effect on police conduct, 221, 223–24, 238, 252; effect on sentencing, 248; grand jury proceedings and, 239; interpretations of purpose of, 253; in non-trial dispositions, 240–41; purpose of, 222, 239; relation to plea bargaining, 288

Falik, Marilyn, 286n

Federal Rules of Evidence, 280, 281

Feeney, Floyd, 210n

Ferster, E., 186n

Fisher, I. N., 277n

Flag Salute Case, 54–55

Fortas, Abe, 172

Foster, Jack Donald, 181n

Fourth Amendment, 221; exclusionary rule to guarantee, 222; judiciary's unfamiliarity with principles of, 242; litigation of issues relating to, 245–46; *Mapp* decision and, 229, 231; plea bargaining to deal with issues relating to, 245–46, 251, 252; police compliance with, 229–30, 235; police violation of, 242–43; prosecutorial discretion in dealing with issues of, 245, 247–48, 251

Fox, Sanford J., 188n, 210n, 211n

Frankfurter, Felix, 88n

Freund, Paul A., 8n, 40n, 282n

Friedman, Lawrence M., 2n

Friedman, Ruth, 188n, 198n, 201n

Fuller, Lon L., 33n, 38n, 59, 193n

Gault, In re, 66; on alternatives to juvenile courts, 176, 209–12, 213; categories of juvenile offenders resulting from, 205–09; consequential facts in, 262; costs of decision, 256; Court's assumptions on compliance with decision, 238; Court's treatment of behavioral findings in, 184–85; effect on decrim-